# THE GREAT FAÇADE

## Vatican II and the Regime of Novelty in the Roman Catholic Church

Christopher A. Ferrara

Thomas E. Woods, Jr.

**THE REMNANT PRESS * Minnesota**

# THE GREAT FACADE

**Library of Congress Cataloging-in-Publication Data**
Ferrara, C. A. and Woods, T.E.
The Great Façade: Vatican II and the Regime of Novelty in
the Roman Catholic Church

Includes index.

ISBN: **1-890740-10-1**

PRINTED AND PUBLISHED
IN THE UNITED STATES OF AMERICA

**First Edition**
**Second Printing**

Remnant Press
21170 W. Linwood Drive NE
Wyoming, Minnesota 55092

Visit us online at www.RemnantNewspaper.com

Cover illustration by Thomas Brannon

To the Holy Catholic Church,
*Mater et Magistra*

Peter has no need of our lies or flattery. Those who blindly and indiscriminately defend every decision of the supreme Pontiff are the very ones who do most to undermine the authority of the Holy See— they destroy instead of strengthening its foundations.

— MELCHIOR CANO, theologian of the Council of Trent

# CONTENTS

## SECTION III
### Toward a Solution

# Acknowledgments

We have accumulated several considerable personal debts over the course of writing this book, and wish to express our gratitude to those who helped make its publication possible.

We wish to thank Msgr. Charles T. Moss, Fr. James McLucas, S.T.D., John O'Malley, and *Catholic Family News* editor John Vennari for their review of the manuscript and their invaluable suggestions. Thanks to also to Michael J. Matt, editor of *The Remnant*, where the articles that gave birth to the idea for this book first appeared. Mike has been a constant source of encouragement and we consider ourselves fortunate to call him a friend.

Chris Ferrara extends special thanks to his wife and children for their patience over the course of this project.

Tom Woods would like to thank Miss Heather Robinson (soon to be Mrs. Thomas Woods) for her unflagging encouragement from this book's beginnings to its completion.

The responsibility for the book's content is, of course, solely our own. We offer it well aware of the magnitude of the task we have undertaken, but hopeful that it will help Catholics to understand what has happened to their Church over the past several decades and how, with the help of God, she may return to the stature and health she enjoyed not to long ago.

*Christopher A. Ferrara*
*Thomas E. Woods, Jr.*
April 2002

# THE GREAT
# FAÇADE

# Introduction

That the period following the Second Vatican Council has been a debacle for the Catholic Church is now beyond serious dispute. The widespread infiltration of the Catholic clergy by homosexuals over the past forty years, and the systematic attempt by bishops to conceal thousands of criminal acts by sexually deviant priests (not to mention the once-unthinkable emergence of a "gay culture" in the Catholic priesthood), are but further symptoms of an ecclesial disease that is raging out of control after being left untreated for decades.

Predictably enough, the Church's liberal critics have seized upon the recent scandals to call for the abandonment of clerical celibacy, and even the popular election and recall of bishops and local pastors—as if such measures could solve the problem of homosexual corruption in the clergy. While the liberal prescriptions are as dishonest as they are illogical, they provide an insight into the origin of the current crisis in the Church, for liberals are always ready to prescribe cures for the diseases liberalism itself causes in the institutions it infects. The liberals are now prescribing cures for yet another institution infected by liberalism: the Roman Catholic Church. The invasion of the human element of the Church by liberalism—and only this—is what has triggered the current ecclesial crisis.

As we will endeavor to demonstrate in this book, the post-conciliar infection of the Catholic Church by liberalism was self-induced. Through a series of decisions without parallel in Church history, the Church's own leaders, including the conciliar popes, have imposed what can only be called a *regime of novelty* upon the Church since Vatican II. The effect of that regime (whether or not intended) has been largely to strip the Church of her natural defenses against infiltration and corruption. The Council's much-vaunted "opening to the world" was, in truth, a suppression of the Church's immune system, resulting almost immediately in the many-faceted disease that now afflicts her. In reaction to this regime of novelty, there has emerged in the postconciliar epoch a movement known as Roman Catholic traditionalism, which seeks a restoration of the elements of traditional Catholic teaching and *praxis* that have been suppressed under the new regime. This book is both a defense of that movement and a call for Catholics to join it.

This book began as a series of essays written in the summer of 2000 for *The Remnant*, a biweekly traditional Catholic newspaper published in St. Paul, Minnesota. We were so gratified by reader response, and so convinced of the importance of the subject matter, that we decided to make them available in a single volume.   At least that was our first intention.

In the process, however, we edited, revised, completely rearranged and greatly expanded what we had written, more than doubling our original text. The essays grew into a book written around a theme. While the finished product retains some of the feel of a collection of essays, this is not altogether regrettable. At the same time, there is an identifiable continuity throughout the pages that follow.  What we are attempting here is a brief overview of the past forty years, as well as a series of reflections on how faithful Catholics can make sense of the present confusion.

In order to understand some of what follows, however, it is helpful to recount the events that led us to write the essays in the first place. Earlier in 2000, *The Wanderer*, a weekly Catholic newspaper, had begun to serialize a pamphlet (by a former *Remnant* columnist) entitled *Traditionalists, Tradition and Private Judgment*.[1] Although presented as a reliable guide to the "errors" of Roman Catholic traditionalism, it seemed to us to contain nothing more than the same tired, illogical accusations that have been hurled at Catholic traditionalists since the close of the Second Vatican Council.

---

[1] *The Wanderer*, June 22, 2000, and six subsequent weekly issues.

In addition to the author of *Traditionalists, Tradition and Private Judgment* (henceforth "the Pamphlet"), there are other players in the drama that led to this collection of essays. *The Wanderer* was apparently induced to publish the Pamphlet by the appearance of a tract entitled *We Resist You to the Face*, written by Michael Matt (editor of *The Remnant*), John Vennari (editor of the traditionalist newspaper *Catholic Family News*), Atila Guimarães, and Dr. Marian Horvat. *We Resist You to the Face* takes its title from St. Paul's famous rebuke of St. Peter at Antioch because of Peter's scandalous refusal to sit at table with the Gentiles he was charged by Our Lord Himself to convert: "I withstood him to the face, because he was to be blamed" (Galatians 2:11). This episode is cited by St. Thomas Aquinas as an example of how the faithful may, in certain cases, have the right and even the duty to rebuke their prelates, not excluding the Supreme Pontiff himself.

Unfortunately, the title of the tract was exploited by demagogues in the "conservative" Catholic camp, who cried "schism" and endlessly recited the title without ever addressing the merits of the authors' contentions. (We will refer to *We Resist You* henceforth as "the Statement.") The result was a classic case of judging a book by its cover. While we do not subscribe to every formulation of the Statement, a considerable part of our work was a defense of its basic thesis: that Catholic teaching itself demonstrates that Catholics have the right and even the duty to oppose certain papally approved innovations of the postconciliar period, because these innovations—all without precedent in Church history—have manifestly caused confusion among the faithful and grave harm to the common good of the Church.

Personal relations between the *dramatis personae* must also be noted. One of the Statement's authors, Michael Matt, is the cousin of *The Wanderer*'s current editor, Alphonse Matt, who has made *The Wanderer* into the flagship of "conservative" opposition to the traditionalist position and the defense of "conservative" accommodation to the postconciliar reforms. Their respective fathers, Walter Matt and Alphonse Matt, Sr., had a parting of the ways at *The Wanderer* back in 1967, when Walter left to found *The Remnant*. Their parting resulted from the controversy that persists in the Church to this day: Alphonse Matt, Sr., maintained that Vatican II and the reforms it engendered could not be criticized, whereas Walter Matt perceived a duty, for the good of the Church, to express loyal opposition to the conciliar and postconciliar novelties, especially the liturgical reforms imposed by Paul VI. We make no secret of which position we believe has been wholly vindicated in the ensuing quarter-century of doctrinal confusion, clerical scandal and general deconstruction in the Catholic Church.

We split the reply to the Pamphlet between us, with each of us writing something of a rebuttal to each installment of the Pamphlet as it appeared in *The Wanderer*. We cannot emphasize enough, however, that what motivated us then, and what motivates us to publish this book now, was not any sense of an urgent necessity to refute the Pamphlet in its actual content. The Pamphlet, we found, was not especially insightful, to say the least; it was, in fact, diffuse, meandering, reckless in its accusations and in many parts simply inane.

But what the Pamphlet did accomplish by finding its way into *The Wanderer* was that it provided a public provocation in the form of two principal accusations: First, it claimed that there was an equivalence between traditionalists, to whom it applied the label "integrists" (a term the Pamphlet's author never got around to defining), and modernists, in that both "integrists" and modernists "thrive on opposition to the living Magisterium" of the Church. Second, it accused certain traditionalists/integrists—by obvious implication the authors of the Statement—of the canonical crime of "schism," of breaking communion with the See of Peter and thus ceasing to be Catholics. But the Pamphlet failed to substantiate these grave accusations with any systematic argument or presentation of evidence. Not only did the Pamphlet fail to identify any doctrines of the "living Magisterium" from which traditionalists supposedly dissent, but it also failed to provide so much as one quotation from the statements of any traditionalist to support its charges of heterodoxy and schism. The Pamphlet was, in fact, little more than a collection of epithets.

Indeed, in reviewing the Pamphlet's exceedingly slim presentation, we were reminded of Cardinal Newman's *Apologia Pro Vita Sua*, in which he gave this assessment of the infamous pamphlet written against him by his justly forgotten accuser, Charles Kingsley: "[T]he Pamphlet...is as slovenly and random and futile in its definite charges, as it is iniquitous in its method of argument." In our own use of the term "the Pamphlet" throughout this book, we mean to recall the plight of Cardinal Newman in having to confront baseless accusations against him only because an incompetent and dishonest accuser had managed to circulate them widely. We do not mean to suggest any grandiose comparison of this little book with Newman's work of genius in the *Apologia*.

Thus it was not any merit of the Pamphlet that prompted our essays, but rather the prominent exposure given its provocative, if completely unproven, charges by *The Wanderer*, a widely respected Catholic newspaper with a large readership. Such a provocation could not, we thought, be allowed to pass without comment in the historical record.

Because there was so little one could say about the meager content of the Pamphlet itself, however, our reply quickly developed into something far more substantial than a mere rebuttal. It became, rather, a restatement and defense of the main lines of the entire traditionalist position, written from the perspective of two reasonably well-informed lay Catholics, whose principal qualifications are that they know the Faith and that they are eyewitnesses to the results of what can only be called the postconciliar debacle in the Catholic Church.

As we have already noted, the controversy has usually been described as a split between "conservative" and "traditionalist" Catholics. Robert Lewis Dabney, one of the most influential Southern theologians at the time of the War Between the States, once observed wryly that Northern conservatives had never managed to conserve anything. The same verdict applies to those who until now have been generally described as "conservative" Catholics. Since they have not in fact *conserved* anything, but rather have defended every one of the abrupt changes in the life and activity of the Church imposed upon Catholics with Vatican approval in the wake of the Second Vatican Council, we believe that the term "conservative" invites confusion among casual readers, for whom it carries a positive connotation, while attaching a venerable designation to people whose actions—or inaction, as the case may be—merit no such honor.

Publisher Neil McCaffrey introduced the term "right-wing liberal" to describe the figure we have in mind. The "right-wing liberal" is orthodox on doctrine: he believes in the seven sacraments, the four last things, the Commandments, the absolute and binding nature of traditional Catholic morality. Following the experimental trail blazed by Vatican II, however, he considers all else to be negotiable. Anything that does not touch directly upon the Deposit of Faith is subject to change. The only real *essentials* of the Catholic faith, according to him, are moral and doctrinal propositions.

This position is superficially plausible. It is accurate in the sense that, from the perspective of traditional Catholic theology, while a Catholic who pertinaciously denied a central dogma of the Church—original sin or the Virgin Birth, for example— would be liable to condemnation as a heretic, a man of good will who believed that contingent circumstances called for adaptation of the Church in its external manifestations, though perhaps naïve, unwise, or even grossly mistaken, would not call down upon himself the same condemnation. It is the difference between opposing the *depositum fidei* and making an error, however catastrophic, in prudential judgment.

However, too great a deprecation of so-called "nonessentials" fails to reckon with the role played by practices which, as the Popes themselves have taught, are hallowed by tradition and popular piety and are in fact necessary to the transmission, preservation and common understanding of what is "essential" to Catholicism—in short, the ecclesiastical traditions, as opposed to those which are strictly Apostolic (descended from the Apostles themselves). These "nonessentials" are, in fact, the very things that mediate the *depositum fidei* into the living reality of the Faith as something that is lived and experienced by members of the Church. The

Rosary and a multitude of other devotions, for example, are crucial to the spiritual lives of the faithful, even if they are not, strictly speaking, "essential" to Roman Catholicism. It was precisely by suppressing such alleged "nonessentials" that the Protestant Reformation in England was able gradually to diminish the Catholic faith that those devotions had nourished among the population.[2]

Likewise, while the form of the liturgy is not, strictly speaking, an article of faith, it is the principal means by which the Faith has been taught to generation after generation of Catholics at Sunday Mass. To treat the form of the liturgy carelessly is to invite disaster. It was no less than Pope Pius XII (when he was still Msgr. Pacelli) who confided to Msgr. George Roche his fears about the rise of liturgical innovators in the Church and the "suicide of altering the faith in her liturgy."[3] Cardinal Alfons Stickler, who served on Vatican II's Liturgy Commission, has argued that the Greek Orthodox, lacking the visible center of unity that the Catholic Church possesses in the person of the Pope, nevertheless maintained the dogmatic aspects of the Christian faith in their integrity precisely because of their reverence for their traditional liturgy, the sacred purveyor of that faith.[4] Moreover, there is a certain piety that animated the saints, and that ought to inform the Catholic conscience today, that positively forbids us to treat even the so-called "changeable" aspects of the Faith as dispensable. With good reason, then, did Pope Pius IV prescribe a profession of faith that included the following: "The apostolic and *ecclesiastical* traditions, and all other *observances* and institutions of that same

---

[2]Eamon Duffy, *The Stripping of the Altars: Traditional Religion in England, c.1400-c.1580* (New Haven, CT: Yale University Press, 1992).

[3]Msgr. Georges Roche, *Pie XII, Devant L'Histoire* (Paris: Editions Robert Laffont, 1972), p. 52. The same book recounts Pius XII's astonishing prediction of the postconciliar revolution in light of the Message of Fatima. This is discussed in Chapter 3.

[4]Alfons Maria Cardinal Stickler, "Erinnerungen und Erfahrungen eines Konzilsperitus der Liturgiekommission," in Franz Breid, ed., *Die heilige Liturgie* (Steyr, Austria: Ennsthaler Verlag, 1997), p. 166.

Church I most firmly admit and embrace.... I also receive and admit the received and approved *ceremonies* of the Catholic Church used in the solemn administration of all the aforesaid sacraments." We can learn a great deal in this regard from St. Teresa of Avila, who once said that she would die a hundred deaths for the smallest ritual of the Catholic Church.

The so-called "conservative" Catholic is, therefore, rather too easily acclimated to the radical changes in the texture of Catholic life that have followed the Council. He is unlikely to raise much of an objection to postconciliar practices perennially considered unthinkable in the Church, such as Holy Communion being received in the hand or distributed by the unconsecrated hands of female "extraordinary ministers of the Eucharist." As long as the teaching on the Real Presence of Christ in the Eucharist is officially retained, the "conservatives" say, such innovations are of no great moment.

Again, however, the matter is not so simple. When the German Protestant Martin Bucer suggested that English Protestants introduce the practice of Communion in the hand, he did so because, as he said at the time, this novel practice would undermine two Catholic teachings at once: the priesthood and the Real Presence. Allowing the faithful to receive the Eucharist in their hands would tend to establish the belief that the Host was nothing more than ordinary bread (so indeed why shouldn't the faithful be able to touch it?) and that there was nothing special or unique about the priest that should entitle him alone to handle the sacred species. Bucer knew full well what he was doing.

We can also indict the "conservative" position for having utterly failed to stem the revolutionary tide of the past thirty-five years. Its approach simply has not worked. The Left has proceeded with determination and severity in its forcible introduction of novel practices throughout the life of the postconciliar Church, including but not limited to the liturgy. The so-called conservatives, on the other hand, made concession after concession to these vandals, claiming that since these changes were not to dogma *per se*, they were not worth fighting over. The Left was sure of itself; the Right hedged. The result should have surprised no one.

Thus the "conservative" position has several major failings, all of which we will explore in these pages. The one on which we will focus the most attention is the conservative's dogged insistence on ignoring or explaining away glaring differences between preconciliar and postconciliar practice and ecclesial attitudes, and even common teachings below the level of Catholic dogma. Novelties that were condemned as intolerable threats to the Faith are suddenly recommended as the work of the Holy Ghost. (As we will discuss, while these new practices — ecumenism, for instance — are not in themselves strictly matters of Catholic doctrine, in the traditionalist view they tend materially to undermine doctrines to which the Catholic is absolutely bound.) That there is absolutely no parallel for this in all of Church history should go without saying. The conservative position, however, has generally been to accept the novelties without question, regardless of the warnings of previous Popes and of the terrible trials these novelties have visited upon the Church. The conservatives have been positively hostile toward those of us who have demanded to know how the novelties can be reconciled with the condemnation of those very novelties before the Council. For example, "conservatives" see no contradiction of Church tradition in a "simplified" Mass said entirely out loud in the vernacular, when Pope Pius VI condemned the Synod of Pistoia's demand for precisely such a Mass as "rash, offensive to pious ears, insulting to the Church, favorable to the charges of heretics against it [the traditional Latin Mass]."[5] The current Will of the Legislator, rather than the coherence and faithfulness to ecclesiastical tradition one has the right to expect from the Vatican, has suddenly became the supreme norm. Given the Church's emphasis over the centuries on the importance of human reason, the legal positivism of the "conservatives" seems to us ludicrous and impossible to accept. As we will demonstrate from the teaching of Church fathers and doctors, this attitude of blind obedience to every single act of

---

[5]Pius VI, *Auctorem Fidei* (1794), in Henry Denzinger, *The Sources of Catholic Dogma* (St. Louis, MO: B. Herder, 1955), section 1533. (Hereafter DZ, followed by section number.)

ecclesial authority without exception is not Catholic; it makes of the Church exactly what the Protestants falsely claim it to be: an absolute dictatorship governed by an absolute monarch.

For these reasons, we have employed the term "neo-Catholic" to refer to Catholic personalities in the mold of the Pamphlet's author.[6] This term eliminates the confusion that the complimentary term "conservative" might cause, and better evokes the willingness of this group to accept the introduction of novelties affecting virtually every aspect of the Faith as it is lived and practiced by Catholics in the pews, even if those novelties patently lack any continuity with ecclesiastical tradition and are palpably offensive to the *sensus catholicus*.

As for the controversy over the Pamphlet itself, in the end there is little one can say about the affair except that it was a sad and tiresome thing. It demonstrated yet again the neo-Catholic's perverse inclination to complain merely about the effects of the postconciliar crisis (including the rise of militant traditionalism), without ever acknowledging the ultimate cause. Surveying the devastated vineyard, the neo-Catholic will not even entertain the possibility that the state of the kingdom has something to do with the acts and omissions of the king.

So, for example, in typical neo-Catholic fashion, the Pamphlet's introduction suggests that the liturgical revolution that drove the author himself from his own parish was entirely the fault of nameless "liturgical experts." But here are the facts:

- Those same "experts" were summoned to their task by Vatican Council II in *Sacrosanctum Concilium*, which called precisely for the use of "experts" to revise the liturgy from top to bottom.

---

[6]This term was first suggested by the renowned Presbyterian convert Gerald Christian Matatics, who is now a Catholic traditionalist. Mr. Matatics, while still a Protestant, was a careful observer of the phenomenon of "neo-evangelicalism," by which the more traditional Protestants underwent a process of liberalization that he was aghast to see in the Catholic Church after his conversion.

- These "experts" were unleashed upon every diocese of the world by the will of Paul VI, who approved their destruction of the traditional Latin liturgy.

- Pope John Paul II surveyed the same destruction during his many travels and pronounced it a great "renewal" on the twenty-fifth anniversary of *Sacrosanctum Concilium*, later adding altar girls to the mix.

It is not as if the Roman rite was dismantled while the conciliar Popes were momentarily distracted. Yet as the neo-Catholics would have it, the one man on earth divinely appointed to guard the sacred liturgy throughout the Church is the only one who is *not* responsible for its present condition.

We have every reason to hope that good will come from this exploration of the controversy between Roman Catholic traditionalists and those we call neo-Catholics. As we have already indicated, the publication of the Pamphlet, empty provocation though it was, served as an occasion to restate and refine the entire case for the restoration of Roman Catholic Tradition in all its integrity — not merely the return of a few bits and pieces of what was taken from the faithful overnight some thirty-five years ago, but the integral whole in its original condition.

And perhaps more than a few readers of this book will be prodded to confront, if they have not done so already, the cause that lies behind the innumerable symptoms of the raging disease whose progress *The Wanderer* itself has chronicled in such minute detail for so many years. We will have accomplished a great deal if we persuade even a few of those Catholics who are not yet traditionalists that, in their own efforts to understand the postconciliar crisis, the time has come for them to turn their attention, at long last, to Rome.

# Section I

# The Scope of the Problem

# Chapter 1

# Defining Terms

There is nothing more useless than a debate in which the parties fail to define their terms and the exact nature of the controversy between them. This book presents the controversy between Roman Catholic traditionalists and those we call neo-Catholics. Following up on the Introduction, we will endeavor to define these terms more amply.

First of all, what do we mean by the term "traditionalist"?[7] As suggested by the Introduction, a traditionalist is nothing more or less than a Catholic who continues to worship as Catholics had always worshipped and to believe as Catholics

---

[7]It is essential that we make clear at the outset that this book is not intended to lend any support to the claim that the See of Peter is currently vacant due to the "heresy" of the Pope ("sedevacantism"), or that Paul VI promulgated an invalid rite of Mass. Those who attack traditionalists on the basis of these views are, so far as we are concerned, jousting with straw men. We do not deny that the former hypothesis is an accepted theological opinion in the Church, recognized as such by doctors of the Church, commentaries on canon law and so forth. We do deny, however, that present-day sedevacantists have proven their claim that the conciliar Popes lost their offices due to heresy, which involves the obstinate post-baptismal denial or doubt of an article of divine and Catholic faith (for example, the Assumption), not just any teaching of the Magisterium (for example, the undoubtedly vindicated preconciliar papal condemnation of the ecumenical movement). Cf. Canon 751.

had always believed until approximately 1965, when, in the name of Vatican II, the Church began to undergo a series of unprecedented "reforms" that altered virtually every aspect of ecclesial life.

Regarding the liturgy, traditionalists continue to believe what the Popes had constantly taught for more than nineteen centuries, up to and including Pope John XXIII in *Veterum Sapientia* (1962): that the traditional Latin liturgy of the Roman Rite, a work of the Holy Ghost down the ages, was not subject to radical revision.

As for Christian unity, traditionalists continue to regard the Church as Catholics had always been taught to regard her before 1965: that is, the one true Church to which the separated brethren must *return*, not merely the most perfect of many "Christian churches and ecclesial communities" moving toward "full communion" at some unknown terminus of the "ecumenical movement." Only thirty-five years before the bronze doors opened on Vatican II, Pope Pius XI forcefully restated the traditional teaching on true Christian unity in his encyclical *Mortalium Animos*, which condemned the developing "ecumenical movement" as a threat to the very foundations of the Christian faith, and forbade any Catholic participation in it:

> So, Venerable Brethren, it is clear why this Apostolic See has *never* allowed its subjects to take part in the assemblies of non-Catholics; for the union of Christians can *only* be promoted by promoting *the return to the one true Church* of those who are separated from it.... Let them therefore return to their common Father, who, forgetting the insults heaped upon the Apostolic See, will receive them in most loving fashion. For if, as they continually state, they long to be united with Us and ours, why do they not hasten to enter the Church, the Mother and mistress of all Christ's faithful? Let them hear Lactantius crying out: "The Catholic Church is alone in keeping the true worship. This is the fount of truth, this the house of Faith, this the temple of God: if any man enter not here, or if any man go forth from it, he is a stranger to the hope of life and salvation." Let none delude himself with obstinate wrangling. For life and

salvation are here concerned, which will be lost and entirely destroyed, unless their interests are carefully and assiduously kept in mind.[8]

The traditionalist maintains that in point of fact no Catholic is obliged to embrace a single one of the novelties imposed upon the Church over the past thirty-five years. For example, there is no actual papal command that Catholics participate in interreligious prayer meetings with Hindus, Muslims and rabbis, or joint liturgical services with pro-abortion Protestant "bishops," even though Pope John Paul II engages in these activities himself and commends them as realizations of Vatican II. Indeed, no Catholic is even obliged to attend the new rite of Mass devised by Pope Paul VI, since throughout the liturgical revolution other rites of Mass untouched by the Pauline innovations (principally the Eastern rites) have always remained available. Nor, for that matter, has any papal decree of the past thirty-five years actually banned the traditional Latin Mass in the first place, as John Paul II's own cardinalate commission informed him in 1986.[9]

Finally, a traditionalist is someone who believes that the postconciliar novelties — especially the new liturgy and the new ecumenism — ought to be abandoned because they have caused grave harm to the Church, as shown by overwhelming empirical evidence of drastic ecclesial decline in nearly every area immediately following the appearance of the novelties. This is not simply (as neo-Catholics constantly argue) the fallacy of *post hoc ergo propter hoc*,[10] but rather an inference of cause and effect virtually compelled by the available evidence.

For example, the imposition of the new Mass was followed immediately by drastic declines in Mass attendance; the reform

---

[8]Pius XI, *Mortalium Animos*, nn. 10, 11. Emphasis ours here and throughout, unless otherwise indicated.

[9]This question is discussed at length in Chapter 7.

[10]Literally, "after this, therefore because of this." Such reasoning is at work anytime someone claims a causal connection between events A and B simply because B followed A in temporal sequence.

of the seminaries by the immediate emptying of the seminaries; the abandonment of attempts to convert Protestants in favor of "ecumenical dialogue" by a drastic decline in conversions. To attribute all of these developments to "coincidence" is ridiculous.[11]

What, then, do we mean by the term "neo-Catholic"? Before answering, we must first anticipate the banal objection that we are "generalizing" about neo-Catholics and neo-Catholicism. Of course we are. The focus of this book is the *idea* of neo-Catholicism as a system of novel practices and attitudes that first emerged in the Church during the 1960s. While the neo-Catholic idea can be illustrated with the objective statements and actions of particular individuals who are part of this new constituency of the Church (many of whom will be quoted here), it is not for us to make any judgment about the Catholic fidelity and personal piety of these people — even though (as we shall also show) the leading lights of neo-Catholicism are all too ready to denounce their traditionalist brethren as "schismatics" and cast them into outer darkness, without benefit of any canonical declaration by competent Church authorities.

In fact, we are quite prepared to admit that the lively faith of many who would fit the description "neo-Catholic," as we define the term, puts to shame many of those who call

---

[11]It is an empirical fact, demonstrated by every available statistic, that the postconciliar liturgical reform and the commencement of programmatic "ecumenism" and "dialogue" were followed immediately by precipitous declines in the number of priests, the number of new ordinations, the number of seminarians, the number of conversions and baptisms, and the percentage of Catholics attending Mass. In the immediate aftermath of the Council, an astounding 50,000 priests defected, and today there remain approximately 50,000 fewer Catholic priests than there were *thirty-one years ago.* In 1997 there were fewer baptisms in the United States than there were in 1970! See, e.g., statistical analysis of the priesthood in *L'Osservatore Romano*, 13/20 August 1997, and "The Index of Leading Catholic Indicators," *The Latin Mass*, Winter 2000, presenting extensive data from the Vatican's *Statistical Yearbook of the Church* and other standard reference works.

themselves traditionalists.[12] (And, naturally, in many cases the converse is just as true.) That individual neo-Catholics are pious, however, is beside the point. The point of this book is to demonstrate that in both theory and practice the neo-Catholic *idea* has caused enormous damage to the life of the Church as a whole, as seen by the sudden postconciliar decline in baptisms, conversions, vocations, Mass attendance and general adherence to Catholic doctrine on the part of those who still call themselves Catholic.

So, based on the objective words and deeds of some of the more prominent neo-Catholics, we can safely generalize about the neo-Catholic idea. Particular applications aside, it is the idea that with the advent of the Second Vatican Council a new sort of orthodoxy suddenly arose in the Church—an orthodoxy stripped of any link to ecclesiastical traditions once considered an untouchable sacred trust. It is the idea that by virtue of Vatican II the Church has, in some manner never clearly explained, progressed beyond what she was before the Council to a new mode of existence, and that this progression requires an assent on the part of the faithful that is somehow different from the assent required to the constant teaching of all the previous councils and Popes. When neo-Catholics say—as they do with depressing regularity—that traditionalists are "anti-Vatican II," they are saying more than they seem to realize. They are saying that in large measure our Faith has come to be defined, not by the entire teaching of a Magisterium that can never change, but by a single Council and the revolutionary reforms and new attitudes it engendered—all of them outside the realm of Catholic doctrine as such. This is why, when

---

[12]Traditionalist writer Michael Matt made this point in an article entitled "The Ugly Traditionalist," which appeared in *The Remnant* of February 15, 2000. That article demonstrates that the leaders of the traditionalist movement are capable of recognizing problems within the traditionalist current, unlike neo-Catholic leaders, who admit to no excesses within their own ranks, even including the bizarre charismaticism promoted by such neo-Catholic organs as the Franciscan University of Steubenville.

pressed to do so, neo-Catholic critics of traditionalism are unable to identify any *doctrines* of the Magisterium to which traditionalists have failed to assent in their alleged "rejection of Vatican II."

What this means is that the neo-Catholic idea is nothing less than a form of progressive or liberal Catholicism—whether a given neo-Catholic knows it or not, or is, subjectively speaking, a liberal by intention. For, as we will demonstrate, the distinctive legacy of Vatican II that the neo-Catholic celebrates and demands that we all embrace does not consist in doctrine, but in *a defense of ecclesial novelties,* many of which were explicitly reproved before the Council.

If this assessment seems harsh and uncharitable, let it be confirmed by a leading neo-Catholic himself. In a recent article in *Crisis* magazine entitled "Sensibly Center-Right," neo-Catholic luminary George Sim Johnston lauds the book *Being Right: Conservative Catholics in America,* a compendium of the views of a host of Johnston's fellow neo-Catholic leaders, lumped together with pieces written by doctrinaire liberals. In the process of praising the book, Johnston lays bare the whole truth about the neo-Catholic idea:

> The featured players [James Hitchcock, Helen Hull Hitchcock, George Weigel and James Sullivan, formerly of Catholics United for the Faith] do not locate themselves on the theological "right." They embrace Vatican II, don't pine for the Tridentine liturgy, and support the *historically radical ecumenism* of John Paul II.... By any historical measure, the "conservatives" in this volume *are progressive Catholics.* Until recently, their views on the role of the laity *would not have played well with the Roman curia.* Nor would their choice of philosophical mentors: von Balthasar, de Lubac, Congar, Danielou—not to mention John Courtney Murray.... Unlike the Sadducees on the Catholic left and the Pharisees on the truly Catholic right, the "conservatives" in this volume understand the pontificate of John Paul II because they understand the Second Vatican Council. They understand that Christ founded a teaching Church whose doctrines are not

subject to whim and manipulation. But they also realize that the Church, being human and organic, *has to change. Vatican II was the antidote to the triumphalism, legalism, clericalism, and, yes, Jansenism, that plagued the Church forty years ago.*[13]

This passage contains the neo-Catholic idea in a nutshell: the devastated Roman rite is a mere Tridentine artifact not worth "pining" over. Liberals are Sadducees, traditionalists are Pharisees, while the progressive "conservatives" are "sensibly center-right." The preconciliar Church is casually denigrated as legalistic, clericalistic and even Jansenistic, while Vatican II is presented as a font of divine illumination that revived a moribund Church. Johnston goes on to note that *"neo-conservative* Catholics like...[George Weigel] are not looking for a 'nostalgia-driven restoration in which modernity is rejected root and branch'" — as if Catholic ecclesiastical traditions that stood for centuries were nothing but a collection of memorabilia to be discarded like the detritus of popular culture. "Rather," says Johnston, "they [the neo-conservative Catholics] would like to see the deepest dynamics of Vatican II finally come into play."

What is meant by the "deepest dynamics of Vatican II" is anyone's guess, but this kind of talk is typical of the neo-Catholic idea. According to Johnston, the "neo-conservative Catholics" and the "historically radical" ecumenist, John Paul II, understand each other, because they all understand "the deepest dynamics of Vatican II." The Council has become a kind of semi-gnostic key to the practice of the Faith — its ineffable teachings understood by few, but without possession of which one is no longer fully Catholic. Johnston even claims that the Pope is serving as the "guide and inspiration [for] a genuine Catholic renewal" which he describes as "a populist phenomenon...unfolding outside the official Catholic apparatus." (This "populist phenomenon" does not include any traditionalists or Tridentine Masses.) This gnostic-progressivist vision of the Church is the neo-Catholic idea in full swing, cut

---

[13]*Crisis*, May 1996, p. 6.

loose from all the ecclesiastical traditions, customs and practices that were abandoned in the postconciliar reforms.

A neo-Catholic, then, is someone who more or less lives according to the neo-Catholic idea. The neo-Catholic will maintain that every single one of the postconciliar novelties—including such things as altar girls—must be accepted and defended as legitimate "developments" of Catholic Tradition, even though they are utterly without precedent in the history of the Church. The one and only test that neo-Catholics recognize for the legitimacy of these "developments" is that they were approved by the conciliar Popes. As we will show from neo-Catholic writings, the axiom that papal approval renders something traditional is fundamental to neo-Catholic thought. Thus, in *The Pope, the Council and the Mass*, a lay treatise that has become the bible of neo-Catholicism, we find the following: "If the Church officially approved of a practice...it follows that what the Church approves is, *by definition*, compatible with Catholic Tradition; for the Church, especially the Holy See, is, again, the arbiter and judge of tradition."[14] The neo-Catholic, therefore, recognizes no real qualitative distinction between the Pope's doctrinal teaching and his legislation, commands, administration or public ecclesiastical policy. In essence, whatever the Pope says or does in the exercise of his office is *ipso facto* "traditional" and incontestable by the Pope's subjects.

Under this principle, of course, tradition is robbed of all objective content, becoming essentially whatever the Pope says it is. Thus, altar girls would have to be accepted as a "traditional" practice, and the new Mass of Paul VI, which he himself called "this novelty,"[15] as a "traditional" rite of Mass. In fact, *The Pope, the Council and the Mass* seriously proposes that what Paul VI explicitly called novel was *not* novel: "The Novus Ordo and the other postconciliar liturgical reforms were thus

---

[14]James Likoudis and Kenneth D. Whitehead, *The Pope, the Council and the Mass* (rev. ed., W. Hanover: The Christopher Publishing House, 1981), pp. 71-72. (Hereafter PCM.)

[15]Cf. Audience address of November 26, 1969.

hardly novel and unheard-of when they came about."[16] And yet in the same book it is admitted that after Vatican II "the Catholic Church embarked on a series of reforms and changes which have scarcely left a single Catholic unaffected; and which, in many respects, have *changed the external image of the Church.*"[17] When the neo-Catholic remarks this fact, he remarks it blandly, as if it were not a calamity beyond words that for the first time in Church history those entrusted with preserving her common good would dare to alter the very image of the Bride of Christ by stripping away her immemorial liturgy, her immemorial customs and a host of other precious ecclesiastical traditions almost overnight, causing grave confusion and scandal among the faithful. Surveying the vast effects of this incalculable disaster some thirty-five years later, the neo-Catholic (Johnston being a perfect example) professes to wonder what all those "nostalgic" traditionalists are fussing about.

In sum, neo-Catholics gladly defend and practice a form of Catholicism that would have horrified any Pope before 1960. To appreciate this, one need only imagine Pope St. Pius X attending what today's neo-Catholic would consider a "reverent Novus Ordo Mass," with women, their heads uncovered, serving as "lectors," altar girls assisting the priest and handling the sacred vessels, the priest facing the people over a table, horrendous and doctrinally suspect vernacular translations proclaimed entirely in a loud voice, ecumenically oriented "Eucharistic prayers" that omit every reference to the Mass as propitiatory sacrifice, banal hymns and even pop music, the handshake (or hug) of peace, Communion in the hand, and lay men and women distributing the Sacred Host and Precious Blood to standing communicants. How would St. Pius X react to this spectacle? Obviously, he would react as traditionalists do; and, as Pope, he would order it to cease immediately. But for the neo-Catholic, the same spectacle poses no problem whatever, and in his view of the

---

[16]PCM, p. 75.
[17]Ibid., p. 11.

situation calls only for "obedience" to the ruinous innovations that produced it.

Whether he knows it or not, therefore, the neo-Catholic has broken with Tradition. This is not just a question of the appearance of the Church as a visible commonwealth in her worship and other *praxis*, but also of novel orientations, attitudes and liberal tendencies never been before seen in Catholics who considered themselves faithful.

A prime example is the "Catholic charismatic renewal," an "ecclesial movement" of babbling, "Spirit-filled," interdenominational congregations, who gather in sports arenas and other large venues to be thrilled by raucous music and the exhortations of "anointed" preachers, many of them Protestant ministers.[18] The movement is founded on a clearly heterodox pneumatological conception of the Church, which regards the institution of the Catholic Church as but a visible manifestation, however admirable, of a preexistent pan-denominational "union in the Holy Spirit" with objective heretics. This grotesquerie has penetrated nearly every diocese in North America, and is vigorously promoted by the decidedly neo-Catholic Franciscan University of Steubenville and Mother Angelica's Eternal Word Television Network (EWTN), the media flagship of neo-Catholicism. (That EWTN's strange brew of traditional devotions and appalling novelties is considered rock-solid Catholicism today only indicates the depth of the current crisis.)

Another example is the "neo-Catechumenal Way," a movement whose very name would suggest it is the perfect embodiment of neo-Catholicism. Active in dioceses throughout the world, this Judaized, semi-gnostic, intra-ecclesial sect

---

[18]John Vennari, "A Catholic Charismatic Jubilee," a five-part series that appeared in the August, September, October, and November 2001 and January 2002 issues of *Catholic Family News*. Vennari has been the primary chronicler of the charismatic movement, and has documented its behavior via videotape, audiotape, and studies of their own literature. He has also written at length on EWTN's promotion of charismaticism.

conducts private, closed-door Saturday night "liturgies" which have been dispensed from all compliance with even the radically liberalized liturgical laws of the Novus Ordo. The neo-liturgy of this sect has no Offertory, and the congregation dances the *horah* around the altar-table before consuming a Host the size and consistency of a personal pan pizza, which tends to crumble and leave fragments all over the floor. The sect's lay founders, Kiko Arguello and Carmen Hernandez, who exhibit a shocking familiarity with the Pope, have concocted a neo-catechism in which the movement's adherents are trained to varying levels of gnostic initiation into the thinking of Kiko and Carmen. This "catechism" is rife with heterodoxy, including the proposition that the Church went astray after the eighth century and became obscured by an accretion of unnecessary customs and structures — precisely what the Protestants say — until its essence was freed again by Vatican II. The sect is armed with a letter of commendation from the Pope himself — which, sad to say, is quite authentic.[19] (The Pope has repeatedly praised this "ecclesial movement" as one of the "fruits of Vatican II."[20])

---

[19]Fr. Enrico Zoffoli has written an extensive exposé of the movement entitled *La Via Neo-Catecumenale*, a compendium of testimonies documenting the heterodoxy and gross liturgical abuses of the movement in Italy, where (as in the United States) it is systematically undermining the parish structure and the integrity of the family by dividing spouses from each other. The movement's neo-catechism and gnostic characteristics have been exposed by former "neo-catechumenate" Mark Alessio in a series of articles in *Catholic Family News*.

[20]"The catechumens of the first centuries were a very important reality in the Church: I believe that what they did for the faith in those days, *the Neocatechumenal Communities are doing today*." (Papal visit to the parish of St. Timothy, Rome, 10 February 1980.) John Paul II's many tributes to the movement are collected at members.aol.com/_ht_a /fatherpius /neo3.html. A letter from John Paul II to Msgr. Cordes of the Pontifical Council for the Laity, dated August 30, 1999, specifically approving the movement's activities, appears to be genuine. See, members.lycos.co.uk/jloughnan/append7.htm

One could multiply the examples of neo-Catholic movements that have sprouted like weeds in the devastated vineyard of the postconciliar Church. (The pan-denominational Focolare and Communion and Liberation movements are two others.) But even if these movements do not claim a majority of neo-Catholics as formal members, they are all compatible with the neo-Catholic mentality, which defends them because it has learned to accept the most outrageous and destructive ecclesial innovations as a matter of course, and even as a sign of health and "ferment" in the Church. What is common to all these movements is a rejection of the Church's supposedly "triumphal" and hidebound past, her immemorial Latin liturgy and her divinely conferred status as the one true Church outside of which there is neither Church nor salvation.

Moreover, as we will demonstrate, whether or not they have actually joined one of the more overtly pathological, anti-traditional "ecclesial movements," the generality of neo-Catholics has yielded ground in a number of areas implicating Catholic doctrine: on *extra ecclesiam nulla salus* (the dogma that there is no salvation outside the Church); on the liturgy; on sacred music; on the anti-modernism of the preconciliar Popes; on the preconciliar papal warnings regarding Masonic conspiracies against the Church (which many neo-Catholics find amusing); on the constant condemnation of worship in common with non-Catholics; on the duty of every man and every *nation* to profess the Catholic faith; on the necessity of the Social Kingship of Christ as embodied in the Catholic confessional state; on the right and duty of the Catholic state to restrain the public manifestations of false religions; on the condemnation of the errors of modern liberalism in the *Syllabus* of Pius IX, including "freedom of religion," "freedom of speech" and "freedom of conscience"; on the literal truth of the Bible as history, especially the first three Chapters of Genesis; on evolution; on classroom sex education (neo-Catholics generally approve "chastity education" curricula, which involve children in classroom discussion of sex); on mixed marriages, and so on.

If one considers as an ensemble all the postconciliar novelties the neo-Catholics have either embraced or defended in the short span of thirty-five years, one sees a mode of religion that is all but unrecognizable as Catholic from the preconciliar standpoint. We know this not by our own lights, as if we were the Magisterium, but by a simple empirical comparison of what was always practiced and believed before the Council with what we see today. Speaking of the new liturgy alone, Msgr. Klaus Gamber has rightly observed:

> A Catholic who ceased to be an active member of the Church for the past generation and who, having decided to return to the Church, wants to become religiously active again, probably would not recognize today's Church as the one he had left. Simply by entering a Catholic church, particularly if it happens to be one of ultra-modern design, he would feel as if he had entered a strange, foreign place. He will think that he must have come to the wrong address and that he accidentally ended up in some other Christian religious community.[21]

In addition to the liturgy, one can also make a comparison between the classic precision and kingly majesty of preconciliar Church teaching (seen in the above-quoted passage from *Mortalium Animos*, issued only thirty-seven years before Vatican II) and the current muddle of ambiguous "pastoral" and ecumenical formulations. Every objective sign of the vigor of the Church tells us that the conciliar changes comprising neo-Catholicism have eroded adherence to the infallibly defined dogmas, especially *extra ecclesiam nulla salus*. The general result has been a *de facto* detachment of the greater part of Catholics from the Church's own precisely crafted dogmatic framework, leaving them to drift in a kind of quasi-Catholicism that may not contain any explicit heresy, but that the preconciliar Popes

---

[21]Klaus Gamber, *The Reform of the Roman Liturgy: Its Problems and Background* (Harrison, NY: Foundation for Catholic Reform, 1993), p. 107.

simply would not regard as authentically and integrally Catholic. Anyone who honestly considers the absolutely unparalleled postconciliar transformation of the vocabulary and *praxis* of the Church would have to admit this.

Neo-Catholicism claims to be motivated by "true" fidelity to Tradition and "true" obedience to the Magisterium, even if that fidelity and obedience have required a series of humiliating about-faces that have undermined the very credibility of the Church. As Joseph Cardinal Ratzinger, Prefect of the Congregation of the Doctrine of the Faith, has admitted regarding the suppression of the traditional Mass by Paul VI: "A community is calling its very being into question when it suddenly declares that what until now was its holiest and highest possession is strictly forbidden, and when it makes the longing for it seem downright indecent."[22] Yet the neo-Catholic is not disturbed by this threat to the Church's credibility, nor by any of the other self-inflicted blows to her image that have followed in rapid succession, with Vatican approval, since the Council. The neo-Catholic "follows" the Pope, no matter what: "I would rather be wrong with the Pope than right without him" is one of the more risible neo-Catholic bromides.

It needs to be stressed again that we have no intention of suggesting an *en bloc* condemnation of neo-Catholics as a counterweight to the *en bloc* condemnation of traditionalists as "integrists" and "schismatics" by certain neo-Catholic luminaries—charges we discuss in the second Section of this book. That the neo-Catholics have accommodated themselves to the postconciliar revolution does not entitle us to question their orthodoxy or personal piety—any more than neo-Catholics are entitled to question (as they so often do) the Catholic *bona fides* of traditionalists who do not share their quiescent attitude in the face of disaster.

The very emergence of neo-Catholicism reflects an unparalleled situation in the Church, giving rise to a crisis of

---

[22]Joseph Cardinal Ratzinger, *Salt of the Earth,* trans. Adrian Walker (San Francisco: Ignatius Press, 1997), p. 176.

conscience concerning what our duty as Catholics requires. For while there have always been would-be innovators in the Church, and traditional Catholics to oppose them, *never in the history of the Church have the innovators been the Popes themselves.* As Msgr. Klaus Gamber observed in *The Reform of the Roman Liturgy*: "It is most certainly *not* the function of the Holy See to introduce Church reforms. The first duty of the Pope is to act as primary bishop, *to watch over the traditions of the Church*—her dogmatic, moral and liturgical traditions."[23] But what happens when the Popes, for the first time ever, venture novelties that effectively abolish a number of those traditions? Neo-Catholicism is one attempt at an answer to that question—an answer we presume has, in most cases, been arrived at in good faith, even if history is already demonstrating that this answer is profoundly wrong.

In sum, traditionalists are convinced that the correct answer to the current ecclesial crisis is a total restoration of the ecclesiastical and apostolic traditions that were abandoned or suppressed an historical moment ago for the sake of the unprecedented postconciliar experiment in reform, and a return as well to the uncompromising Scholastic clarity and vigor of the preconciliar Magisterium. The neo-Catholics, on the other hand, see no fundamental problem with the approved postconciliar novelties (all of which they defend as consistent with Catholic Tradition), and tend to question the Catholicity of traditionalists for believing otherwise.

These, then, are the parties—traditionalist and neo-Catholic—and this is the controversy between them. The final outcome of the controversy may well determine the direction of the Roman Catholic Church in the Third Millennium.

---

[23]Gamber, *The Reform of the Roman Liturgy*, p. 97.

# Chapter 2

# The Problem of Novelty

*"Pass not beyond the ancient bounds
which thy fathers have set." Proverbs 22:28*

As the Introduction and previous chapter suggest, our debate with the neo-Catholics centers around one word: *novelty*. We have noted that the neo-Catholic tends to condemn the traditionalist Catholic for the latter's instinctive opposition to novelty. What the neo-Catholic fails to recognize is that this instinct is as important to the health of the Church as the instinct of self-preservation is to the health of living creatures.

The Church's perennial counsel against the embrace of substantial ecclesial novelties of *any* kind, not just doctrinal ones, was recapitulated by Pope St. Pius X in his monumental encyclical *Pascendi*:

> But for Catholics nothing will remove the authority of the second Council of Nicea, where it condemns those "who dare, after the impious fashion of heretics, to deride the *ecclesiastical traditions*, to invent novelties of some kind...or endeavor by malice or craft to overthrow *any one of the legitimate traditions* of the Catholic Church".... Wherefore the Roman Pontiffs, Pius IV and Pius IX, ordered the insertion in the profession of faith of the following declaration: "I most firmly admit and embrace the apostolic *and ecclesiastical* traditions and *other observances* and constitutions of the Church."

Elsewhere in the encyclical the Pope exclaimed, "Far, far from our priests be the love of novelty!"

The Magisterium's constant abhorrence of ecclesial novelty is nowhere more apparent than in the anathemas of the Second Council of Nicea, cited and reaffirmed by Saint Pius X in *Pascendi*. Convened by Pope Hadrian I in 787 to deal with the iconoclast heretics and the bishops who had supported them with illicit decrees, Nicea II issued these anathemas:

> If anyone does not *confess* that Christ our God can be represented in his humanity, let him be anathema.

> If anyone does not *accept* representation in art of evangelical scenes, let him be anathema.

> If anyone does not *salute* such representations as standing for the Lord and his saints, let him be anathema.

And, lest there be any doubt that all of the received and approved ecclesiastical traditions of the Church are to be regarded as part of the Church's untouchable patrimony:

> If anyone rejects *any* written or *unwritten* tradition of the church, let him be anathema.

Does this mean, as the neo-Catholics charge, that traditionalists are "immobilists" who hold that *nothing* in the Church may ever change and that the Church must remain frozen in time? This is a caricature of the traditionalist position. Traditionalists, being Catholics, recognize and embrace legitimate change in the Church through *gradual growth in the content* of ecclesiastical tradition. The Rosary is the perfect example of a gradually developed devotion that is now an integral part of the Church's spiritual patrimony. What Pope would dare to abolish or rewrite the prayers of the Rosary? And yet the neo-Catholics tell us there was nothing terribly amiss in Paul's VI's *de facto* abolition of the received and approved traditional rite of Mass and his revision of the entire liturgy by committee! Never, before Paul VI, had there been ecclesial change in the sense of a sudden *amputation* of something the Church had received and approved over the centuries as one of her traditions. (Which is not to mention that the traditional Mass combines both Apostolic and ecclesiastical tradition, as we discuss elsewhere.) Nor had the Church ever seen, before Vatican II, the abrupt introduction of innumerable ecclesiastical novelties in virtually every area of the Church's life.

Neo-Catholics have no answer to the claim that St. Pius X would be even more horrified than today's traditionalist by the postconciliar novelties, especially the new liturgy and the new "ecumenical" activity of the Church. They have no answer because they know it is true. The *sensus catholicus* abhors innovation; and not just innovation in what neo-Catholics misleadingly call the "substance" of the Faith—as if everything else could be changed with safety. The teaching of St. Pius X, echoed by all his predecessors, is that not only apostolic Tradition, but *all* the ecclesiastical traditions and customs that have been woven into the life of the Church over the centuries must be defended against unnecessary and dramatic change, lest the Church's commonwealth be so disrupted that the faithful are thrown into a state of confusion and alienation that endangers the Faith itself.

That is precisely what has happened in the postconciliar epoch. Since 1960 the Church has been overtaken by a swarm of novelties without precedent: a new rite of Mass, a new liturgical calendar, new sacramental rituals, a new ecumenism, a new rapprochement with non-Christian religions, a new "dialogue with the world," a new rule of life in seminaries, priestly orders and convents, a "new evangelization," and even a "new theology," whose new vocabulary has largely replaced what the Pamphlet (in typical neo-Catholic fashion) belittles as "high metaphysical abstractions" in the Church's preconciliar teaching.

As John Henry Cardinal Newman showed in his *Essay on the Development of Christian Doctrine*, the sudden emergence of some novelty in the Church that is not the natural and almost imperceptible outgrowth of everything that came before it would be a sign, not of life and growth, but of corruption—just as the sudden emergence of a tumor is a sign of corruption in the human body. As Newman put it, a proposition "is likely to be a true development, not a corruption, in proportion as it seems to be the *logical issue* of its original teaching" (emphasis in original). Likewise, as "developments which are preceded by definite indications have a fair presumption in their favor, so those which do but contradict and reverse the course of doctrine which has been developed before them, and out of which they spring, is certainly corrupt."[24] It is manifest that every one of the suddenly emergent postconciliar novelties has produced a corresponding corruption in the Church:

- The new liturgy has produced a loss of Eucharistic faith and respect for the Blessed Sacrament and a decline in Mass attendance.

- The new liturgical calendar and cycle of readings have produced (as Msgr. Klaus Gamber noted) a loss of the sense of place and a diminished inculcation of scriptural lessons, especially the "hard sayings" of Scripture, which have been largely eliminated or neutralized by tendentious translations that are really dishonest paraphrases.

- The new ecumenism has produced a relative protestantization of the Catholic liturgy and faithful, accompanied by the confirmation of Protestants in their errors and the accelerated moral and doctrinal decomposition of Protestant sects over the course of the "ecumenical dialogues." (Ironically enough, the evangelical sects that have shunned the ecumenical venture, such as the Missouri Synod Lutherans and

---

[24]John Henry Newman, *An Essay on the Development of Christian Doctrine* (1878; repr., Notre Dame, IN: University of Notre Dame Press, 1989), pp. 195, 199.

the Southern Baptists, are those that remain closest to Catholic moral teaching.)

• The new rapprochement with non-Christian religions has produced the near-extinction of the Church's traditional missionary activity which aimed at saving souls whose false religions imprisoned them in darkness (as Pius XI described Islam, for example); and this development has been accompanied by the perception that good hope is to be entertained for the salvation of all non-Christians — the very proposition condemned in Pius IX's *Syllabus of Errors*.[25]

• The new sacramental rituals have produced a loss of the understanding of what the sacraments mean,

---

[25]"We must have a least good hope concerning the eternal salvation of all those who in no wise are in the true Church of Christ." Syllabus, n. 17. It should be noted that the doctrines of baptism of desire and invincible ignorance cannot allow one to say that there is "good hope" for the salvation of those who belong to non-Catholic religions, since Pius IX himself forbade any speculation to that effect in his allocution *Singulari quadem*:

Not without sorrow we have learned that another error, no less destructive, has taken up its abode in the souls of many Catholics, who think that one should have good hope of the eternal salvation of all those who have never lived in the true Church of Christ. Therefore, they are wont to ask very often what will be the lot and condition after death of those who have not submitted in any way to the Catholic faith.... Far be it from Us, Venerable Brethren, to presume the limits of divine mercy, which is infinite [His Holiness then expounds the doctrine of invincible ignorance], but as long as we are on earth, weighed down by this mortal mass which blunts the soul, let us hold most firmly that, in accordance with Catholic teaching, there is 'one God, one faith, one baptism' [Eph. 4:5]; it is unlawful to proceed further in inquiry (DZ 1646-1648).

baptism in particular having become in practice a mere initiation rite, with the subject of original sin barely mentioned, if at all.

- As Paul VI admitted, "the opening to the world has produced a veritable invasion of the Church by worldly thinking"[26] the world, on the other hand, has only hastened to descend toward utter barbarity, while Church authorities continue to insist upon "dialogue" rather than teaching with the authority of God, condemning error and warning the world that its sins merit eternal damnation.

- The reform of the seminaries, the priestly orders and the convents has produced an emptying of all three, and a deeply neo-modernist formation in the few men and women who still enter. (Only a return to the traditional rule and formation in some places has produced new vocations in any great numbers.)

- The "new evangelization" (in conjunction with the new ecumenism and the new liturgy) has produced a profound decline in conversions and vocations compared with the immediate preconciliar period, but also a great number of semi-autonomous "ecclesial movements" of bizarre character. These include a frenzied, pan-denominational, charismatic gnosticism, horrifying to behold, which replaces the sound piety and inward composure exemplified by the saints of the Church.

On the matter of the Church's new vocabulary, the search for a new way of "speaking to the world" has produced a bewildering collection of neologisms lacking any of the classical precision of Catholic doctrine: "collegiality," "dialogue," "dialogue with the world," "interreligious dialogue,"

---

[26]Speech of November 23, 1973.

"ecumenism," "ecumenical venture," "ecumenical dialogue," "partial communion," "imperfect communion," "reconciled diversity," "the Church of the new Advent,"   "the new springtime of Vatican II," "the new Pentecost," "the new Evangelization," "the civilization of love," "the purification of memory," "responsible parenthood," "solidarity," "the globalization of solidarity," "the Spirit of Assisi," "what unites us is greater than what divides us," and so on. Although these words and phrases evade any precise definition, they have become the watchwords of postconciliar thinking.

*Never before in Church history has the activity of the Church come to be governed by slogans and buzzwords that appear nowhere in the perennial Magisterium.* In consequence, never has the Church's message been so uncertain, as even the 1999 Synod of European bishops was forced to admit.[27]

In sum, the historical record of the postconciliar novelties is indisputably a record of corruption, failure and confusion in every area those novelties have touched. As Cardinal Ratzinger has candidly admitted:

> The results of the Council seem cruelly to have contradicted the expectations everybody had, beginning with John XXIII and Paul VI.... [W]e have been confronted instead with *a continuing process of decay* that has gone on largely on the basis of appeals to the Council, and thus has discredited the Council in the eyes of many people.[28]

---

[27]Archbishop Varela, for one, admitted that "The mammoth evangelising and educational task of religious orders...has altogether disappeared in some areas or sectors. There can be no doubt that the reasons for this alarming situation are numerous and complex. Nonetheless, it is certain that its deepest roots are to be found in *secularisation within the Church*, that is, in the diminishing or *abandonment* of the Truth of faith in our own lives and pastoral commitments." See "European Synod: Bishops Begin to Admit Postconciliar Crisis," UnaVoce.org.

[28]*L'Osservatore Romano*, November 9, 1984, later to be known as *The Ratzinger Report*.

Cardinal Ratzinger went on to say: "It is my *opinion* that the misfortunes the Church has met with in the last twenty years are not due to the true Council itself, but to an unleashing *within the Council* of latent, aggressive, polemical and centrifugal forces." Some seventeen years after the Cardinal's remarks, however, the evidence of an even deeper "process of decay" permits us to advance beyond the Cardinal's opinion—and he was careful to say it was only that—to express an opinion of our own: that the "true Council" is indeed part of the problem. And the problem is novelty.

Part 4 of the Pamphlet, in accord with neo-Catholic thinking, claims that John Paul II has decreed definitively that the Council and all the innovations it engendered are perfectly in line with Tradition, and that no one may suggest or even think otherwise. To support this extravagant claim, the Pamphlet quotes, not an encyclical, a *motu proprio* or some other formal papal teaching addressed to the universal Church, but a single sentence from a speech by John Paul II to a symposium on the implementation of Vatican II: "To read the Council assuming it supposes a rupture with the past, when in reality it is aligned with the everlasting faith, is clearly erroneous."[29]

In the first place, the Pamphlet exhibits typical neo-Catholic confusion about the scope of the Magisterium when it asserts that a papal speech to a symposium means that "Rome has spoken" and that "the question is closed for any Catholic." If papal speeches to particular groups could bind the universal Church, then it would be inevitable that the Pope would bind the Church to error. For example, every Catholic would now be required to believe, as the Pope declared in a sermon on the death penalty, that "the dignity of human life must *never* be taken away, even in the case of someone who has done great evil" and that the death penalty should be abolished as "cruel and unnecessary."[30] Clearly, no Catholic is obliged to believe that the death penalty may *never* be imposed or that it should be

---

[29]Zenit news report, February 27, 2000.

[30]*L'Osservatore Romano,* weekly English edition, N. 5-3, February 1999, p. 8.

abolished as a moral evil. Such a teaching is undeniably contrary
to all Tradition, as was (to give a remote historical example) the
repeated sermonizing of Pope John XXII on the particular
judgment, wherein that fourteenth-century Pope denied that the
blessed departed enter immediately into eternal beatitude after
purgatory, and the condemned immediately into hell after
judgment.[31] In neither case was the Pope speaking with any
intention to bind the universal Church to a matter of doctrine.
(John XXII retracted his erroneous view on his deathbed.)

Moreover, to say that the Council is "aligned with the
everlasting Faith" or that the Council as a whole does not
"suppose a rupture with the past" (it is remarkable that a Pope
would even have to make such protestations about an
ecumenical council) is not quite the same thing as saying that
every novel formulation in the conciliar texts is perfectly in line
with Tradition. We recall that in the *nota praevia* (preliminary
note) to *Lumen Gentium* the council expressly disclaimed any
intention to formulate binding doctrine unless it openly
declared such intention.[32] The Council wished to have the
freedom to indulge in non-traditional "pastoral" formulations,
whose very novelty alarmed a number of the Council fathers,
leading to the *nota praevia*. On this point we have the
posthumously revealed testimony of Bishop Thomas Morris, a
Council father: "I was relieved when we were told that this
Council *was not aiming at defining or giving final statements on*

---

[31]"John XXII," *Catholic Encyclopedia,* 1913; Philip Hughes, *A History
of the Church,* vol. 3: *The Revolt Against the Church: Aquinas to Luther*
(1947; repr., London: Sheed and Ward, 1979), pp. 153-55.

[32]"In view of the conciliar practice and *pastoral purpose* of the
present Council, the sacred Synod defines matters of faith and morals
as binding on the Church only when the Synod itself openly declares
so." Addenda to *Lumen Gentium,* Explanatory Note of the Theological
Commission, in Walter M. Abbott, S.J., ed., *The Documents of Vatican II*
(New York: America Press, 1966), pp. 97-98. In disobedience to the
command of Paul VI, the Preliminary Note was demoted to the status
of an addendum to *Lumen Gentium* in published editions of Council
documents.

*doctrine*, because a statement of doctrine has to be very carefully formulated and I would have regarded the Council documents as *tentative and liable to be reformed*."[33] Once the Council was over, however, we were suddenly told that it had been a veritable Vesuvius of Catholic doctrine. This hardly seems fair to the Council fathers, who were assured otherwise by the Council's theological commission.[34]

Considering the Pope's symposium statement further, it does not seem to us that the Holy Father was saying exactly what the Pamphlet's author claims he said. Here we find that the author has carefully cropped a quotation to avoid certain words he evidently viewed as inconvenient. In the immediately preceding sentence in the Zenit news account from which the Pamphlet quotes, the following appears: "[I]t is necessary not to lose the genuine intention of the Council Fathers; on the contrary, it must be recovered, overcoming cautious and partial interpretations that impeded expressing to the maximum the *novelty* of the Council Magisterium."

In other words, the Pope said that the Church has been *too cautious* in expressing "to the maximum" the *novelties* of Vatican II. Here John Paul II echoes the sentiment of Paul VI, who declared: "The important words of the Council are *newness* and

---

[33]*Catholic World News*, January 22, 1997. This testimony was confided to Catholic journalist Kieron Wood with the understanding that it would not be published until after Bishop Morris' death, which occurred recently.

[34]In *The Pope, the Council and the Mass*, the authors assert: "The term 'pastoral council' as applied to Vatican II is merely a popular description and does not refer to any specific type of council recognized by the authority of the Catholic Church (the teachings and decisions of which would not necessarily be as binding upon members of the Church as a 'dogmatic' council)" (p. 33). The authors ignore the *Nota Praevia*. Further, as Cardinal Ratzinger observed in 1988: "The truth is that this particular Council defined no dogma at all, and deliberately chose to remain on a modest level, *as a merely pastoral council...*" (Address to the Chilean Bishops, July 13, 1988). The claim that Vatican II was not a pastoral council is part of neo-Catholic mythology.

updating...; the word *newness* has been given to us as an *order*, as a program."[35]  What this statement could possibly mean is among the innumerable mysteries of postconciliar thinking.

And when one consults the original text of the Pope's symposium remarks, one finds the following sentence immediately *after* the one selected for the Pamphlet: "What has been believed by 'everyone, always and everywhere' is the authentic *newness* that enables every era to perceive the light that comes from the word of God's Revelation in Jesus Christ."

The Pamphlet's misuse of the papal address is shameful, but it serves as a good example of how neo-Catholics strive to conceal the full import of what the Pope says so often about Vatican II, in order to maintain the fiction that it fits seamlessly into the line of all the other councils.  It cannot be denied, however, that Vatican II is the first council in the history of the Church whose strict continuity with Tradition *is not self-evident*.[36] If it were self-evident, Cardinal Ratzinger would not have been motivated to publish comments like the following:

> The Second Vatican Council has not been treated as part of the entire living Tradition of the Church, but as an end of Tradition, a new start from zero.... That which was previously considered most holy—the form in which the liturgy was handed down—suddenly appears as the most forbidden of all things, the one thing that can safely be prohibited. It is intolerable to criticize decisions which have been taken since the Council; on the other hand, if men make question of ancient rules, or even of the great truths of the faith...nobody complains or only does so with great moderation.... *All of this leads a great number of people to ask themselves if the Church of today is really the same as the Church of yesterday, or if they have changed it for something else without telling people.* The one way in which Vatican II can be made plausible is to present it as it

---

[35] *L'Osservatore Romano*, July 3, 1974, quoted in Romano Amerio, *Iota Unum* (Kansas City, MO: Sarto House, 1996), p. 112.

[36] The only possible exception to this statement is the Second Council of Constantinople, which we discuss in Chapter 12.

is; one part of the unbroken, the unique tradition of the Church and of her faith.[37]

But why should the Council have to be *"made* plausible" if, as the neo-Catholics would have it, the Council's plausibility — that is, its complete harmony with Tradition — is already perfectly clear?

That the Council and the conciliar Popes have given us *something* utterly novel is admitted in Pope John Paul II's inaugural encyclical, *Redemptor Hominis.* Referring in part to "the new ecumenical orientation" of the Church introduced by the Council and the conciliar Popes, His Holiness declared:

> Entrusting myself fully to the Spirit of truth, therefore, I am entering into the rich inheritance of the recent pontificates. This inheritance has struck deep roots in the awareness of the Church in an *utterly new way, quite unknown previously, thanks to the Second Vatican Council,* which John XXIII convened and opened and which was later successfully concluded and perseveringly put into effect by Paul VI....[38]

Before Vatican II, when has a Pope ever proclaimed a whole "new orientation" of the Church, ecumenical or otherwise? And what other council in Church history disclosed anything *"utterly* new" and *"quite* unknown previously" in the realm of doctrine? How can a *doctrine* of the Church, if it *is* a doctrine, be something "quite unknown" before 1965? Are we now to understand that the Holy Spirit could have left the Church unaware of some important truth of the Faith for nearly 2,000 years?

Unlike the author of the Pamphlet, some neo-Catholic commentators are honest enough to admit that the Council and the conciliar Popes have introduced true novelties into the Church. Taking the bull by the horns, they openly declare that John Paul II is an innovator, who sees in Vatican II (as did Paul VI) a mandate for previously unheard-of progressivist

---

[37]Statement to the Bishops of Chile, 1988.
[38]*Redemptor Hominis*, n. 6.

undertakings. A striking example of candor in this regard is found in John Beaumont's review of neo-Catholic George Weigel's biography of the Pope: "One possible cause for concern in relation to the phenomenon of Pope John Paul II is the sometimes *breathtaking nature of his innovative teaching. It is natural* for Catholics to be wary *and wonder whether all of this can fit in with the tradition.*"[39] It certainly would be only natural to wonder whether "breathtaking" innovations are traditional! Beaumont lets this bomb drop without seeming to notice the explosion. He contents himself with the later observation that, since we have a "guaranteed Church," we should assume that breathtaking innovations are merely "developments" of settled doctrine.

But such explanations are unsatisfactory. They offer no answer to the sedevacantists, who pounce upon such lame arguments and pronounce victory: "See," they exclaim, "a change in Church teaching is admitted! But since the Church cannot change her teaching, those who have changed it, including the Pope, cannot be members of the Church!" In rebutting the sedevacantists, we must offer a more sensible explanation for the "phenomenon of John Paul II" and the postconciliar developments as a whole than: "Fear not, all these breathtaking innovations are traditional."

Let us propose an explanation here.

When the Holy Father used the phrase "everyone, always and everywhere" in the address to the symposium on Vatican II, he was referring to the criterion by which the Church knows that a doctrine is Catholic: that everyone, everywhere in the Church, has *always* believed it. To use the classic formula of St. Vincent Lerins: *quod ubique, quod semper, quod ab omnibus creditum est* (what has been believed everywhere, always and by everyone). Even papal pronouncements respect this criterion, and cases of the infallible definition of doctrine are aimed precisely at declaring what has been believed *quod ubique, quod semper, quod ab omnibus*. John Paul II here proposes a resolution

---

[39]"A Life for These Times," *Culture Wars*, May 2000, pp. 46-47.

of the apparent oxymoron of novel tradition by suggesting that the Church has always believed in "authentic newness." But if the Church has always believed in authentic newness, whatever that means, then why has the Church not always said so? And in what, exactly, does this authentic newness consist *in terms of Catholic doctrine?*   Is there any real *doctrinal* content to the conciliar "program" of "newness" remarked by Paul VI and carried out by his successor?

Or is John Paul II referring to Catholic doctrine at all when he uses such phrases as "utterly new," "quite unknown previously" and "the new ecumenical orientation"? What is the import of such phrases if they do not refer to *doctrines* a Catholic must believe?

As the First Vatican Council solemnly declared, not even the Pope can give us new doctrines of the Faith. "For the Holy Spirit was not promised to the Successors of Peter that by His revelation they might disclose new doctrine, but that by His help they might *guard* the revelation transmitted through the apostles and the deposit of faith, and might faithfully set it forth."[40] The Pope is divinely appointed to guard, explicate and pass on the content of Revelation descended from the apostles, but he is incapable of discovering therein any new doctrines, because *they have not been revealed to us by God.* No one denies that there has been legitimate development of doctrine over the centuries in the sense of more explicit and binding statements of what has *always* been believed. But as the First Vatican Council also solemnly declared: "Hence, also, that understanding of its sacred dogmas must be perpetually maintained, which Holy Mother Church has once declared; and there must never be a recession from that meaning *under the pretext of a deeper understanding.*"[41] Thus, so far as Catholic *doctrine* is concerned, "breathtaking" innovations in the space of a single pontificate, or "developments" that are "utterly new" and "quite unknown previously" are, as the Church herself infallibly teaches, beyond the power of the Magisterium.

---

[40]Denzinger, 1836.

[41]Denzinger, 1800, citing Vatican Council I, can. 3.

Therefore, it would appear to us to be impossible that the postconciliar novelties in teaching (we are not here considering disciplinary measures or canon law that are subject to change) could be Catholic doctrines in the proper sense. Yet we have before us today a multitude of seemingly novel teachings, especially in the previously non-existent fields of "ecumenism" and "dialogue." What precisely is this unparalleled profusion of ecclesial novelties? Are we dealing with Catholic doctrine that we must embrace? Has the Church discovered in the past thirty-five years theological truths that had been hidden for nearly twenty centuries? Has the impossible happened?

We invite the reader to consider whether any of the postconciliar novelties we have already outlined are reducible to a concrete statement of Catholic doctrine that would bind the universal Church to adhere with either a religious assent or the assent of faith to a *proposition* Catholics had not always believed before Vatican II. We are convinced that no such discrete doctrinal propositions can be found anywhere in the teaching of the Council or the conciliar Popes, nor anywhere in the entire vast program of postconciliar innovation. Rather, it seems to us that the postconciliar novelties all operate below the level of the authentic Magisterium and are to be found entirely in the realm of the pastoral in various forms: activities, "orientations," undertakings, initiatives, dialogues, exhortations, opinions, observations, predictions and statements of fact, and ambiguous new expressions—all of which lack the character of binding Catholic doctrine.

As a matter of fact, the failure of the postconciliar novelties to rise to the level of formal, binding doctrine, even though they are "teachings" of a kind, is the reason the sedevacantists are wrong to accuse the Council and the conciliar Popes of heresy and to declare the papal throne vacant. As already noted, there can be no heresy without the obstinate denial of some article of divine and Catholic faith, and this cannot be found in any of the pronouncements of the conciliar Popes; nor can their conduct, as such, constitute a formal heresy, for heresy is a *propositional* offense, not a form of physical misconduct, even if that misconduct gives scandal.

This is not to say that one cannot find, at a level *below* the universal Magisterium, numerous apparent propositional contradictions between pre- and postconciliar teaching concerning a number of lesser matters, and neo-Catholics are at their most unreasonable when they deny this.[42] But none of these apparent contradictions involves the formal repudiation of any article of divine and Catholic faith, even if it can be shown that the new teachings tend *materially* to oppose Catholic tradition. It is no use ignoring such things as the following:

- A line of preconciliar Popes condemned any collaboration with Communists or participation in Communist movements because of danger to the faith of Catholics from any close cooperation with atheists, but in *Pacem in Terris* Pope John XXIII taught the novel distinction that the supposedly positive aims of Communist movements could be supported apart from the immoral founding principles of Communism—the very distinction rejected as a trap for the faithful by Pius XI in *Divini Redemptoris*.[43]

---

[42]We say *apparent*, because only the Church herself can finally resolve these matters, and this is one reason the authors of the Statement call upon the Holy Father to open a "respectful discussion with Church authorities" about how these apparent contradictions, which have never before been seen in the Church, can be resolved.

[43]See John XXIII, *Pacem in Terris*. "It should be remembered that false philosophical doctrines on the nature, origin, and destiny of the universe, and of man, cannot be identified with historical movements that have economic, social, cultural, and political goals...." Having thus severed Communist movements from Communist doctrine, Pope John commended the "positive elements" of Communist movements which "conform to the dictates of right reason and are the spokesmen of the just aspirations of the human person."

Compare: Pius XI: "In the beginning, Communism showed itself for what it was in all its perversity, but very soon it realized that it was thus alienating people. It has therefore, changed its tactics [by] hiding

- The preconciliar Popes uniformly condemned the contention that the received and approved rite of Mass had fallen into obscurity and ought to be "simplified,"[44] but Paul VI approved an entirely new and simplified rite which Cardinals Bacci and Ottaviani were constrained to protest as "a striking departure from the Catholic theology of the Mass as it was formulated in Session XXII of the Council of Trent."

- The preconciliar Popes taught that the Latin liturgy must be preserved as a barrier against heresy and a bond of unity in the Church, but Paul VI taught that it must be abandoned because "understanding of prayer is more important than the silken garments in which it is royally dressed"[45] — thus contradicting

its real designs behind ideas that are in themselves good and attractive.... Under various names that do not suggest Communism...[t]hey try perfidiously to worm their way even into professedly Catholic and religious organizations..., [t]hey invite Catholics to collaborate with them in the realm of so-called humanitarianism and charity; and at times make proposals that are in perfect harmony with the Christian spirit and the doctrine of the Church.... See to it, faithful brethren, that the Faithful do not allow themselves to be deceived." *Divini Redemptoris*, n. 57.

[44]See, e.g., the apostolic constitution *Auctorem Fidei* (1794), wherein Pius VI condemned the Synod of Pistoia when it proposed "'recalling it [the liturgy] to a greater simplicity of rites, by expressing it in the vernacular language, by uttering it in a loud voice'; as if the present order of the liturgy, received and approved by the Church, had emanated in some part from the forgetfulness of the principles by which it should be regulated — rash, offensive to pious ears, insulting to the Church, favorable to the charges of the heretics against it."

[45]General Audience, November 26, 1969. Compare, *Mediator Dei*, 59-60, wherein Pius XII condemned liturgical innovators "who make use of the vernacular in the celebration of the august eucharistic sacrifice" and reminded the faithful that the use of Latin in the Roman

even the teaching of his own immediate predecessor, Pope John XXIII.[46]

- The preconciliar Popes and Councils condemned the idea of an all-vernacular Mass in which the Roman Canon was said aloud, but Paul VI approved it and pronounced it good, as does his successor. [47]

- After forbidding women altar servers in *Inestimabile Donum* 18, in line with an unbroken 2,000-year-old tradition, John Paul II suddenly reversed himself and now teaches that altar girls are an enrichment of the liturgy.[48]

---

liturgy "is a manifest and beautiful sign of unity, as well as an effective antidote for any corruption of doctrinal truth...."

[46]See *Veterum Sapientia* by John XXIII: "In the exercise of their paternal care they [the bishops] shall be on their guard lest anyone under their jurisdiction, *eager for revolutionary changes*, writes against the use of Latin in the teaching of the higher sacred studies or *in the liturgy*, or through prejudice makes light of the Holy See's will in this regard or interprets it falsely." *Veterum Sapientia*, February 22, 1962. It can hardly be a sign of the working of the Holy Ghost that this Apostolic Constitution was discarded within months of the close of Vatican II.

[47]Cf. *Auctorem Fidei*, Pius VI, nn. 33, 66.; Council of Trent, Can. 9 on the Holy Sacrifice of the Mass: "If anyone says that that the rite of the Roman Church, according to which a part of the canon and the words of the consecration are pronounced in a low tone, is to be condemned, or that the Mass ought to be celebrated in the vernacular only...let him be anathema."

[48]Angelus Address, September 3, 1995: "To a large extent, it is a question of making full use of the ample room for a lay and feminine presence recognized by the Church's law. I am thinking, for example, of theological teaching, *the forms of liturgical ministry permitted, including service at the altar....* Who can imagine the great advantages to pastoral care and the new beauty that the Church's face will assume, when the feminine genius is fully involved in the various areas of her life?" The suggestion that the Church has neglected the "feminine genius" for 2,000 years is rather a harsh implicit judgment on all the

- The preconciliar Popes condemned any common worship with Protestants as a danger to the Faith, but the Council opened the door to it and John Paul II (expressly and by example) teaches that common prayer and even joint liturgies with Protestant ministers (who condone abortion, contraception and divorce) is essential to the "search" for "Christian unity."[49]

- The preconciliar Popes taught that the schismatic Orthodox must return to the Catholic Church, but the Balamand Statement, whose teaching is commended by the Pope in *Ut Unum Sint* 60, states that thanks to "radically altered perspectives and thus attitudes" engendered by Vatican II, the Catholic Church will train new priests "to pave the way for future relations between the two Churches, passing beyond *the outdated ecclesiology of return to the Catholic Church*."[50]

---

Pope's predecessors, to say nothing of the entire assembly of saints. We are unaware of any among the Church's many female saints who would have been anything but horrified and appalled at the suggestion that their presence at the altar would have been an enrichment of the liturgy rather than a profanation.

[49]Cf. the 1917 Code of Canon Law, cc. 1258 and 2316, forbidding any active participation by Catholics in worship with Protestants; *Mortalium Animos* by Pius IX, and the 1949 Instruction of the Holy Office on the "ecumenical movement," which forbade any form of common worship at discussion groups authorized by the local bishop, and required that the "Catholic truth" on "the return of the dissidents to the one true Church" be presented.

[50]Balamand Statement, nn. 13 and 30. The Balamand Statement (1993) was cited approvingly by Pope John Paul II in *Ut Unum Sint*, n. 59.

- The constant teaching of the Church is that the New Covenant supersedes the Old, but Cardinal Walter Kasper, speaking as the papally appointed President of the Pontifical Council for Religious Relations with the Jews, declared that *"the old theory of substitution is gone since the Second Vatican Council. For us Christians today, the covenant with the Jewish people is a living heritage, a living reality....   Therefore, the Church believes that Judaism, i.e., the faithful response of the Jewish people to God's irrevocable covenant, is salvific for them, because God is faithful to his promises."*[51]

- The preconciliar Popes taught that the Catholic Church and the Mystical Body of Christ were one and the same thing and that the Catholic Church was the one true Church, but the Balamand Statement on relations between the Catholic Church and the Orthodox declares that "the Catholic Churches and the Orthodox Churches recognize each other as sister Churches, responsible together for maintaining the *Church of God* in fidelity to the divine purpose...."[52]

- The act of consecration of the world to the Sacred Heart, promulgated by Pius XI only thirty-five years before Vatican II, prays for the deliverance of souls from "the darkness of idolatry or of Islamism," and their entry "into the light and kingdom of God," but Vatican II teaches in *Lumen Gentium* 16 that Muslims *"together with us* adore the one merciful God."

---

[51]Address at the 17th meeting of the International Catholic-Jewish Liaison Committee, New York, May 1, 2001.

[52]Balamand Statement. What exactly is this "Church of God," and how can it be faithful to "the divine purpose" if it is jointly maintained by the Catholic Church and churches that reject the papal primacy and are not in communion with the Holy See?

- Although the Church has condemned and opposed the diabolical religion of Islam since it was first invented by the man called Muhammad, John Paul II (citing *Lumen Gentium* 16) recently declared that "the two religions [Catholicism and Islam] can be signs of hope, making the world more aware of the wisdom and mercy of God," and he further declared in March 2000, "May St. John the Baptist protect Islam...."[53]

- *Mortalium Animos* by Pius XI condemned as error the belief that all religions are more or less good and praiseworthy, whereas John Paul II has taught that God has bestowed spiritual treasures on *every* people in the form of their various religions; and in keeping with this view the Pope has repeatedly invited "representatives" of all religions—monotheistic, polytheistic and even *non*-theistic—to Assisi to offer prayers for world peace (which prayers he evidently regards as pleasing to God), even allowing the use of rooms in the Sacred Convent of St. Francis to conduct pagan rituals in honor of various gods and spirits during the Assisi event in 2002.[54]

---

[53]General Audience Address, May 5, 1999; Prayer and Exhortation on March 21, 2000, in Wadi Al-Kharrar: "May St. John the Baptist protect Islam...."

[54]In *Mortalium Animos*, Pius XI taught that pan-denominational congresses "can nowise be approved by Catholics, founded as they are on *that false opinion which considers all religions to be more or less good and praiseworthy,* since they all in different ways manifest and signify that sense which is inborn in us all, and by which we are led to God and to the obedient acknowledgment of His rule. Not only are those who hold this opinion *in error and deceived,* but also in distorting the idea of true religion they reject it, and little by little turn aside to naturalism and atheism, as it is called; from which it clearly follows that *one who supports those who hold these theories and attempt to realize them, is altogether abandoning the divinely revealed religion.*"

- In *Quanta Cura* and the appended *Syllabus of Errors*,
  Bl. Pius IX condemned the errors of liberalism on
  which modern political societies are based, including
  the principle that "liberty of conscience and of
  worship is the proper right of every man, and should
  be proclaimed and asserted by law in every correctly
  established society," but in *Dignitatis Humanae*
  Vatican II taught that "religious freedom must be
  given such recognition in the constitutional order of
  society as will make it a civil right." Cardinal
  Ratzinger openly admits that *Dignitatis Humanae*
  (together with *Gaudium et Spes*) is "a countersyllabus,
  a revision of the Syllabus of Pius IX" which corrects

---

Compare John Paul II in *Redemptoris Missio*, 55: "He [Christ] does
not fail to make himself present in many ways, not only to individuals
but also to entire peoples through their *spiritual riches*, of which *their
religions* are the main and essential expression, even when they contain
'gaps, insufficiencies and errors.'" And compare also n. 6: "In the
process of discovering and appreciating the manifold gifts — especially
the *spiritual treasures* — that *God has bestowed on every people*, we cannot
separate those gifts from Jesus Christ, who is at the center of God's
plan of salvation." Likewise, *Redemptor Hominis*, 11 speaks of the
Church's "deep esteem for the great spiritual values, indeed for the
primacy of the spiritual, which in the life of mankind finds expression
in religion... The Fathers of the Church rightly saw in the various
religions as it were so many reflections of the one truth, 'seeds of the
Word,' attesting that, *though the routes taken may be different, there is but a
single goal* to which is directed the deepest aspiration of the human
spirit as expressed in its quest for God..." No distinction is made
between revealed and natural religion.

It must be noted that when the early Fathers spoke of "seeds of the
Word," they were referring to Greek philosophy, not the pagan
religions, which they considered diabolical. In his *First Apology*, St.
Justin Martyr, for example, refers to the execution of Socrates on
account of his efforts to persuade the pagan polytheists of the existence
of one God: "Socrates attempted to make these things known and *to
deliver men from demons*...he was put to death through the agency of
men who delight in evil."

"the one-sidedness [!] of the position adopted by the Church under Pius IX and Pius X."[55]

• The preconciliar teaching (repeated even in the 1992 version of the Catechism, but deleted in the 1997 version) affirmed the right and *duty* of the state to impose the death penalty for sufficiently grave offenses, but John Paul II has recently taught that the death penalty is "cruel and unnecessary" and should never be imposed "even in the case of someone who has done a great evil" — thus contradicting not only the 1992 version of the Catechism, but even the 1997 version, which at least allows for the death penalty in certain unspecified though "practically non-existent" cases.[56]

---

[55]Cardinal Josef Ratzinger, *Principles of Catholic Theology* (San Francisco: Ignatius Press, 1982), p. 381.

[56]Sermon at World Trans Dome, January 27, 1999, published in *L'Osservatore Romano*, Weekly English Edition, N. 5-3, p. 8. Section 2266 of the 1992 version of the Catechism of the Catholic Church provides that "*the traditional teaching of the Church* has acknowledged as well founded *the right and duty* of legitimate public authority to punish malefactors by means of penalties commensurate with the gravity of the crime, not excluding, in cases of extreme gravity, the death penalty." The 1997 definitive Latin version of the Catechism, however, changes "the traditional teaching" to: "The traditional teaching of the Church does not exclude recourse to the death penalty, *if this is the only possible way of effectively defending human lives against the unjust aggressor*...." The 1997 Catechism then goes on to state that such cases are [according to Pope John Paul II in *Evangelium Vitae*] "rare if not practically non-existent" because "of the possibilities which the state has for effectively preventing crime, by rendering one who has committed an offense incapable of doing harm...."

It is self-evidently false that the state can now render aggressors "incapable of doing harm," since imprisoned murderers often kill other prisoners or prison guards, or kill again among the general population if paroled. Thus, the alleged "development" of Catholic teaching in the space of *five years* between the 1992 and the 1997

- While Pius XII, in *Humani Generis*, forbade the presentation of the theory of evolution as if it were a proven fact,[57] John Paul II has given numerous statements which do precisely that, including his famous 1996 declaration that evolution is "more than a mere hypothesis."[58]

---

versions of the Catechism is based entirely on an error of fact concerning the capabilities of modern penal systems. Further, the 1997 Catechism fails to explain why the supposed "possibilities" of preventing *future* violence by convicted killers would eliminate the need of capital punishment as just retribution for *past offenses*. There appears to be a confusion here between punishment and protection of society.

[57]N. 16: "Some, however, rashly transgress this liberty of discussion, when they act as if the origin of the human body from pre-existing and living matter were already completely certain and proved by the facts which have been discovered up to now...." The liberty of discussion to which Pius XII referred was to be restricted to those with expertise in *both* theology and the natural sciences. DZ, 2327. Pius XII's prudent caution in this area rightly followed from the solemn teaching of Vatican I (which in turn cited the Fourth Lateran Council) that God "*immediately* from the beginning of time fashioned *each creature out of nothing*, spiritual and corporeal, namely angelic and mundane; and then the human creation, common as it were, composed of both spirit and body." DZ, 1783. Neo-Catholic proponents of "theistic evolution" have never demonstrated how their views can be reconciled with the Catholic teaching that Eve was (in some manner) created *from* Adam in the literal sense, as the Pontifical Biblical Commission of Saint Pius X bound Catholics to believe. DZ, 2123.

[58]In typical neo-Catholic fashion, leading neo-Catholics attempted once again to distance the Pope from his own words and actions, claiming that his statement to the Pontifical Academy of Sciences on October 22, 1996, that the theory of evolution is "more than a mere hypothesis" should have been translated from the French (*plus qu'une hypothèse*) as "more than one hypothesis" when it clearly denotes "more than *a* hypothesis." The proposed translation was nonsensical in context, as the English edition of *L'Osservatore Romano* later noted in a correction providing the proper translation. (See *Catholic World Report*, February 1997, p. 4.) The official Italian language translation in

- While the constant teaching of the Church, reflected in the Apostles' Creed and even the new Catechism (§ 631, et seq.), is that after the Crucifixion and before the Resurrection, the Soul of Christ descended into Hell (*sheol*, or the Limbo of the Fathers) to deliver the souls there into Heaven, John Paul II asserted in his audience address of January 1, 1989, that this teaching means only that Christ's Body experienced death and was placed in the earth (i.e., the Tomb), while His soul was glorified in Heaven.[59]

---

*L'Osservatore Romano* was correct from the beginning: The Pope said "more than a mere hypothesis" (piu che una mera ipotesi). In any case, the Pope has frequently stated his belief that the theory of evolution is a proven fact. As just one of many examples, on April 26, 1985, the Pope addressed a symposium entitled "Christian Faith and the Theory of Evolution," praising the assembled evolutionists for their work, and declaring: "[B]elief in evolution and the properly understood teaching of creation do not stand in one another's way. Creation represents itself in the light of evolution as an event extending through time.... Therefore I welcome this symposium...." *L'Osservatore Romano*, April 27, 1985, p. 4.

[59]Cf. Ludwig Ott, *Fundamentals of Catholic Dogma* (1955; repr., Rockford, IL: TAN, 1974), ch. 3. § 12. As John Paul stated on that occasion: "His soul, separated from the body, was glorified in God, but his body lay in the tomb as a 'corpse.'... Jesus experienced the state of death, that is 'the separation of body and soul,' as in the case of all people. This is the primary meaning of the words 'he descended into hell'.... Obscure as it is [!], the Petrine text confirms the others concerning the concept of the 'descent into hell.'... It is Christ—laid in the tomb, but glorified in his soul admitted to the fullness of the beatific vision of God—who communicates his state of beatitude to all the just, whose state of death he shared with regard to the body." Thus, the descent of Christ into hell, according to this address, means merely Christ's bodily descent into death and His entombment in the ground, not any literal descent into the region of Hell (sheol) where the souls of the just were waiting for the Redemption. This novel opinion was in no way imposed upon the Church.

- While the *de fide* teaching of the Church, revealed by Christ himself, is that the souls of the damned are in hell, John Paul II has suggested that it has not been revealed to us that any human beings at all are in hell.[60] Here the Pope appears to flirt with the thesis of von Balthasar that one can "hope" that *not a single malefactor in all of human history* has gone into eternal punishment.[61] (The Pope wished to bestow the cardinal's red hat on von Balthasar, who dropped dead only hours before receiving it.)

- The preconciliar Popes, following the teaching of St. Paul, taught that the wife was subject to the authority of the husband and must obey him as the Church obeys Christ (assuming the husband's commands are just and moral), but John Paul II has taught that St. Paul meant that this subjection was *mutual* and that he was merely speaking in a way suited to the culture of his time.[62]

The Pope's teaching on wifely subjection to the husband, just noted, bears particular examination as an example of apparent contradictions between the teaching of the pre- and postconciliar

---

[60]Audience Address and catechesis of July 28, 1999: "Damnation remains a real possibility, but without a special revelation it has not been given to us to know *if* and which human beings are definitely involved." (La dannazione rimane una reale possibilità, ma non ci è dato di conoscere, senza speciale rivelazione divina, se e quali esseri umani vi siano effettivamente coinvolti.) While we do not know *which* human beings are in hell, we certainly know *if* human beings are there. Otherwise, one would have to hold that Our Lord's parable of the sheep and the goats and His admonition that "few there are" that find the narrow way of salvation are only bluffs.

[61]Hans Urs von Balthasar, *Dare We Hope 'That All Men Be Saved'?* (San Francisco: Ignatius, 1988).

[62]Compare *Arcanum* by Leo XIII and *Casti Connubii* by Pius XI with *Mulieris Dignitatem* by John Paul II on this point.

Popes. In his encyclical *Arcanum*, on Christian Marriage, Leo XIII forcefully and clearly restated the traditional teaching:

> The husband is *the chief of the family and the head of the wife*. The woman, because she is flesh of his flesh, and bone of his bone, *must be subject to her husband and obey him;* not, indeed, as a servant, but as a companion, so that her *obedience* shall be wanting in neither honor nor dignity. *Since the husband represents Christ, and since the wife represents the Church,* let there always be, both *in him who commands and in her who obeys,* a heaven-born love guiding both in their respective duties. For "the husband is the head of the wife; as Christ is the head of the Church.... *Therefore, as the Church is subject to Christ, so also let wives be to their husbands in all things.*"

In *Mulieris Dignitatem*, however, John Paul II states:

> The author of the Letter to the Ephesians [i.e., St. Paul] sees no contradiction between an exhortation formulated in this way and the words: "Wives, be subject to your husbands, as to the Lord. For the husband is the head of the wife" (5:22-23). The author knows that this way of speaking, so profoundly rooted *in the customs and religious tradition of the time,* is to be understood and carried out in a new way: as a "mutual subjection out of reverence for Christ" (cf. Eph 5:21).... Whereas in the relationship between Christ and the Church, the subjection *is only on the part of the Church,* in the relationship between husband and wife, the "subjection" *is not one-sided but mutual.*

It must be noted, first of all, that John Paul II presents his teaching in *Mulieris Dignitatem* as a personal "meditation" written in the first person.[63] This is typical of the manner in which, during the postconciliar era, the faithful have been presented with a profusion of papal pronouncements whose level of authority and binding nature are far from apparent, but

---

[63]"And it seems to me that the best thing is to *give this text the style and character of a meditation*" (the Pope's own emphasis).

which neo-Catholics portray as definitive teaching that no one may question.

To all appearances, this meditation on St. Paul's Epistle to the Ephesians flatly contradicts the teaching of Leo XIII, who emphasized precisely the point that Ephesians 5:22-23 — which is to say, God Himself — teaches that subjection is required not "*only* on the part of the Church" to Christ, as John Paul II asserts, but *also* on the part of the wife to her husband, because in the order of familial authority the husband represents Christ and the wife represents the Church, as Pope Leo taught explicitly in the above-quoted passage. It is significant that John Paul II quotes only the beginning of the key sentence from Ephesians — "For the husband is the head of the wife" — while omitting the conclusion: "*as Christ is the head of the Church.*"

John Paul II also apparently contradicts Pius XI on the same point. In *Casti Connubii*, Pius XI, referring explicitly to the teaching of Leo XIII, affirmed that the order of the family ordained by divine law "includes...the *primacy of the husband* with regard to the wife and children, *the ready subjection of the wife and her willing obedience*, which the Apostle commands in these words: 'Let women be subject to their husbands as to the Lord, *because the husband is the head of the wife, and Christ is the head of the Church.*'" Pius XI further taught that "this subjection of wife to husband in its degree and manner may vary according to the different conditions of persons, place and time. In fact, if the husband neglects his duty, it falls to the wife to take *his place* in directing the family. But the structure of the family *and its fundamental law, established and confirmed by God,* must always and everywhere be maintained intact." That is, wifely submission to the husband's authority to direct the family is part of divine law itself.

Indeed, it is impossible to see how authority could exist any more in the family than in the Church if there were a "mutual subjection" and no ruler-subject relation between the spouses. The whole notion of "mutual subjection" is a conundrum, since there cannot be a subject without a ruler, nor a ruler without a subject, and neither the Church nor the family can have two heads.[64]

Also troubling is the Pope's suggestion that St. Paul's teaching is but "a way of speaking" arising from "the customs and religious tradition of the time." In the first place, the "religious tradition of the time" was Christianity. Furthermore, does not St. Paul mean exactly what his words signify, and what Pope Leo XIII and Pope Pius XI both affirmed they signify—that the wife is subject to the husband as the Church is subject to Christ? Is not God Himself the author of those words, which were written "wholly and entirely, with all their parts, *at the dictation of the Holy Ghost*," to recall the teaching of Pope Leo in *Providentissimus Deus*? Are the Catholic faithful to conclude, then, that God dictated His revelation of the divinely ordained constitution of the family in language that was culturally determined and needed to be "unpacked" by historico-critical exegesis, and that Pope Leo, Pope Pius and all their predecessors misinterpreted Ephesians by reading it too literally? What then of St. Paul's teaching on homosexuality, and all the other "hard sayings" of the New Testament? Were these, too, "ways of speaking" that are now to be understood in some different sense? That is surely not what Pope John Paul II intends, but that is what his apparent revision of the "hard saying" on wifely subjection would suggest to some.

This example alone suffices to demonstrate that it will not do to insist, as the neo-Catholics do, that one is not even allowed to think that there could be a contradiction between the teaching of the conciliar Popes and their predecessors on any point, because every papal utterance is *ipso facto* consistent with Tradition. To assert that one Pope may never contradict another in anything

---

[64]There is certainly a sense in which husband and wife, unlike Christ and the Church, are subject to each other—in the order of charity. But the precise teaching of St. Paul in Ephesians relates to the order of authority, as Leo XIII and Pius XI made clear. In the order of authority there cannot be "mutual subjection" without authority being destroyed.

he proposes as Catholic teaching is to expand the charism of papal infallibility to include every single papal utterance touching on Catholic doctrine, contrary to the strict limits on papal infallibility in the definition of Vatican I, which we discuss further on. Given that the published statements of John Paul II (according to his neo-Catholic biographer, George Weigel) occupy ten linear feet of shelf space, the neo-Catholic notion of the utterly inerrant papacy is an invitation to disaster. Words have their objective meanings, and if two statements appear impossible to reconcile then a problem exists, whether or not the neo-Catholics choose to see it.

One could multiply the examples of apparent contradictions between pre- and postconciliar teaching on matters that—we emphasize—are not strictly *de fide*. But an exhaustive treatment of this problem is beyond our scope here. Added to these apparent contradictions are the many unprecedented and often scandalous papal actions in line with the new teachings, especially in the previously unknown realms of ecumenism and "interreligious dialogue"—actions the mere sight of which would have reduced the preconciliar Popes to a state of apoplexy. It requires very little imagination to envision how Pope St. Pius X would have reacted to such spectacles as John Paul II's interreligious prayer meetings at Assisi.

No one has more succinctly summarized the net result of the conciliar and postconciliar novelties than the recently deceased Bishop James W. Malone, of Youngstown, Ohio, who was an episcopal press liaison at Vatican II: "Like everyone else who internalized the Council, it changed everything that I was taught to believe."[65] As with all such statements of neo-Catholic sentiment, there was no explanation of what this could possibly mean. But in view of the statements of neo-Catholic commentators to which we have alluded, and the statements of John Paul II himself, Bishop Malone's remark is not nearly so extravagant as it might seem at first blush. The situation of the Church today readily lends itself to such assessments. And it is hardly "extreme traditionalism" to object that the ecclesial sea

---

[65]*The Latin Mass*, vol. 9, no. 3, Summer 2000, p. 9.

change remarked by so many neo-Catholics—even as they contradict themselves by insisting there has been no departure from Tradition—has produced confusion and real damage to the Church.

Now, for someone who is willing to overlook crucial distinctions and leap to unwarranted conclusions about the present crisis, it would be easy to say, with the sedevacantists, that all of these novelties and apparent contradictions of past teaching are "heresy," and that in consequence we have had no Pope since John XXIII or even Pius XII. The neo-Catholic's very insistence that no one may doubt that everything a Pope teaches is free from error plays right into the sedevacantist argument; for they need only demonstrate some error somewhere in the Pope's voluminous writings or speeches in order to "prove" that, according to the neo-Catholic's own principle of papal inerrancy, John Paul II cannot be the Pope.

But a careful examination of these novelties and apparent contradictions, one by one, shows that none of them involves the formal denial of an article of divine and Catholic faith, or an attempt to impose upon the Church, as a matter of *doctrine* to be held by the faithful, any explicit theological error. Not even John Paul II's recent statement "May St. John the Baptist protect Islam" is heresy, properly speaking, since the Pope's public expression of a wish that a false religion receive divine protection, while certainly scandalous and even stupefying, does not translate into a direct denial of any article of divine and Catholic faith.

The sedevacantists can point to innumerable facts that support the conclusion that we are living through the worst crisis in Church history, but they cannot show that the conciliar Popes have lost their offices through heresy—a judgment only the Church herself could make in any case. Yet in view of the mountain of empirical evidence of precipitous ecclesial decline immediately following the Council, can it be denied any longer that the swarm of novelties the Council engendered, the program and order of "newness" remarked by Paul VI, have tended *materially* to oppose the preconciliar teaching of the

Church? What else can account for the "process of decay" admitted by Cardinal Ratzinger?

As Paul VI himself rightly observed (without yet admitting the cause of it all): "It is almost as if the Church were attacking herself."[66] On another occasion he admitted that "the opening to the world has become a veritable invasion of worldly thinking. We have perhaps been too weak and imprudent."[67]

Whatever can go wrong will go wrong, even in the Catholic Church. Our Lord's promise of divine assistance to His Church does not mean that her human members are unable to inflict upon her the gravest possible wounds, short of the fatal wound of a formal defection from the Faith. That everything that can go wrong seems to have gone wrong within one generation is no excuse for abandoning the Holy Father to the unproven theological theory of the vacant papal chair, nor for leaving him to the tender mercies of the neo-Catholics, who think that mindless applause for every papal word and deed is the way to show true loyalty to the Pope.

The sedevacantists and the neo-Catholics are animated, then, by the same error: that the Magisterium embraces whatever the Pope says or does in the exercise of his office. Proceeding from this error, they reach different but equally untenable conclusions: the latter claim that we must embrace the oxymoron of novel tradition or a "Magisterium" that appears to contradict itself, while the former claim that we have had no Pope since John XXIII.

On the other hand, the traditionalists we would defend have been in just the right place all along: the postconciliar novelties are neither Magisterial nor formally heretical; they do not actually bind the Church to *an act of belief* in what is wrong. The Pope is still the Pope, and yet this is the worst crisis the Church has ever endured, in part because the conciliar Popes, helped along by the blind "obedience" of the neo-Catholics, have

---

[66]Speech of Dec. 8, 1968, to the Lombard College, quoted in Amerio, *Iota Unum*, p. 6.
[67]Speech of November 23, 1973.

refused to acknowledge that there is a crisis, but instead persist in the very novelties that have engendered it.

What are Catholics to do in the face of this terrible and mysterious situation, which has no parallel in the history of our beloved Church? Shall we do nothing? Shall we applaud what even Paul VI lamented as the "self-demolition" of the Church?[68] Or shall we do what the authors of the Statement have done and declare our loyal opposition to what is happening?

---

[68]"The Church is in a disturbed period of self-criticism, or what could better be called self-demolition." Speech to the Lombard College, December 7, 1968.

# Chapter 3

# Viruses in the Body of Christ

"A day will come when the civilized world will deny its God,
when the Church will doubt as Peter doubted."
–Msgr. Eugenio Pacelli (before he became Pius XII)

During a conversation when he was still Msgr. Pacelli, serving as Vatican Secretary of State, Pius XII made an astonishing prophecy about the coming upheaval in the Church:

> I am worried by the Blessed Virgin's messages to Lucy of Fatima. This persistence of Mary about the dangers which menace the Church is a divine warning against *the suicide that would be represented by the alteration of the faith, in her liturgy, her theology and her soul*.... I hear all around me innovators who wish to dismantle the Sacred Chapel, destroy the universal flame of the Church, reject her ornaments and make her feel remorse for her historical past.[69]

Pius XII's biographer, Msgr. Roche, noted that at this moment in the conversation, according to a Count Galeazzi, "the gaze of the Pope, seen through the lenses of his glasses, became supernatural, and there emanated from his tall and slender body an irresistible mystical force." Pius XII then said (in answer to an objection from a curial cardinal):

---

[69]Roche, *Pie XII Devant L'Histoire*, p. 52.

A day will come when the civilized world will deny its God, *when the Church will doubt as Peter doubted.* She will be tempted to believe that man has become God. In our churches, Christians *will search in vain for the red lamp* where God awaits them. Like Mary Magdalene, weeping before the empty tomb, they will ask, "Where have they taken Him?"[70]

Pius XII had his own plans for an ecumenical council—a council to combat the neo-modernist insurgency described in his own prophecy and which he himself would condemn in his encyclical *Humani Generis.* Pius XII was never able to summon his council before he died, but Blessed John XXIII summoned his. Pope John claimed that his council was "completely unexpected, like a flash of heavenly light."[71] In the short span of years following this "completely unexpected" council, all of Pius XII's fears about the Virgin's messages to Sister Lucia have come to pass. Which of our neo-Catholic accusers has not himself "searched in vain for the red lamp" in some denuded sanctuary of the postconciliar "liturgical renewal"?

The neo-Catholics will generally deny that Vatican II had anything to do with the current state of the Church, but eyewitnesses without an agenda can offer more objective testimony. No eyewitness is more compelling than Msgr. Rudolf G. Bandas, himself a conciliar *peritus.* Only two years after the Council had ended, Msgr. Bandas was constrained to ask: "How could our Church be so profoundly blighted in so short a time?" Answering his own question, Msgr. Bandas cited progressivist Bishop Helder Camara's praise of Pope John for his "courage on the eve of the Council in naming as conciliar experts many of the greatest theologians of our day. Among those whom he appointed were many who emerged from the black lists of

---

[70]Ibid., p. 53.

[71]*Council Daybook,* National Catholic Welfare Conference, Washington, D.C., vol. 1, p. 26.

suspicion"—that is, from the censures and condemnations of Pius XII and his Holy Office.[72]

Two of the many who emerged from the "black lists of suspicion" to take key roles at the Council were Edward Schillebeeckx and Hans Küng. It was Schillebeeckx who wrote the crucial 480-page critique employed by the "Rhine group" bishops to coordinate their public relations campaign against the traditionally formulated preparatory schemas for the Council, which led to abandonment of the Council's entire meticulous preparation. The ultimate result was the ambiguity-laden conciliar texts that afflict the Church today.[73] Schillebeeckx was later placed under Vatican investigation (but never disciplined) for his outrageously heterodox views on the historicity of the Virgin Birth, the institution of the Eucharist, the Resurrection, and the founding of the Church. He even dared to argue that the words "This is My Body...This is My Blood" were never actually spoken by Our Lord, and that Our Lord never planned to found a Church.[74] Küng, as is widely known, was finally stripped of his license to teach Catholic theology, after an eleven-year investigation culminating in the 1979 decree of the Congregation for the Doctrine of the Faith (formerly the Holy Office). Yet Küng remains to this day a priest in good standing,

---

[72]*The Wanderer*, August 31, 1967, p. 7. The year 1967 was the very year in which Walter Matt left *The Wanderer* to found *The Remnant* because of his dispute with Alphonse Matt, Sr., over *The Wanderer's* editorial blindness toward the Council as the origin of much of the current crisis. Walter Matt has confirmed to us that the publication of Bandas' eyewitness testimony in *The Wanderer* was a precipitating cause of the rift between the two brothers, as Alphonse Matt would not hear any criticism of the Council. Msgr. Bandas was, in fact, Walter Matt's pastor at St. Agnes Church in St. Paul, Minnesota, during the 1960s. Mr. Matt reports that Bandas went to the Council "full of hope, and returned a broken man."

[73]Ralph M. Wiltgen, *The Rhine Flows into the Tiber* (1967; Devon, England: Augustine Publishing Company, 1978), p. 23.

[74]Carl Bernstein and Marco Politi, *His Holiness* (New York: Doubleday, 1996), p. 417.

who still teaches theology at a secular institute at the University of Tübingen, to which Küng's heterodox activities were transferred by the College of Catholic Theology at Tübingen in an obvious ploy to circumvent even the limited sanction imposed upon him.[75]

Looking back on the Council, Msgr. Bandas was forced to conclude that the amnesty Pope John had naively extended to "great theologians" like Schillebeeckx and Küng had been a catastrophic mistake:

> No doubt good Pope John thought that these suspect theologians would rectify their ideas and perform a genuine service to the Church. But exactly the opposite happened. Supported by certain Rhine Council Fathers, and often acting in a manner positively boorish, they turned around and exclaimed: "Behold, we are named experts, our ideas stand approved."... When I entered my tribunal at the Council, on the first day of the fourth session, the first announcement, emanating from the Secretary of State, was the following: "No more periti will be appointed." But it was too late. The great confusion was underway. It was already apparent that *neither Trent nor Vatican I nor any encyclical would be permitted to impede its advance.*[76]

We have been careful to make clear that none of the postconciliar novelties consists of binding Catholic doctrine as such. The Magisterium cannot have given us any new Catholic doctrines in the postconciliar era, for this is impossible. That is why our neo-Catholic accusers are never able to formulate their accusation of traditionalist infidelity to "the Council" or the conciliar Popes in terms of any explicit doctrinal proposition; traditionalists are accused of "dissenting"...dissenting from *what*? From novel programs and novel attitudes, perhaps, but

---

[75]R. Wining, *La Theologie contemporaine* (Paris: Centurion, 1983), p. 451; cited in Atila Sinke Guimarães, *Animus Delendi – I* (Los Angeles: Tradition In Action, Inc. 2000), p. 158.

[76]*The Wanderer*, August 31, 1967, p. 7.

not from anything Catholics are actually commanded to embrace as a matter of faith and morals.

If, as we endeavored to show in the previous chapter, the postconciliar novelties are not discrete and identifiable doctrines of the Faith, then what are they? There is, first of all, the new liturgy devised by Paul VI, which Msgr. Klaus Gamber justly describes as "the destruction of the Roman rite."[77] There is also a welter of non-Magisterial pronouncements by the Pope and high-ranking prelates, some of them presented in the preceding chapter, which seem to repudiate prior teaching on lesser matters, not at all *de fide*, such as the Pope's opinion that in "modern society" the death penalty must never be imposed. Having separated out these elements of novelty, it seems to us that we are left only with certain *notions* operating below the level of Catholic doctrine. These notions literally cannot be put into words in any doctrinal sense.

For our present purposes we focus on two of these notions: "ecumenism" and "dialogue," both of which were introduced into the Church at Vatican II. These two notions, together with the new liturgy, are the three basic elements of the unparalleled postconciliar innovation of the Church. We propose an analogy as a means of understanding these notions and their effect upon the Mystical Body in the postconciliar epoch — the analogy of the virus.

*Stedman's Medical Dictionary* defines the word "virus" as "an infectious agent which lacks an independent metabolism and is incapable of growth or reproduction apart from living cells." That is, a virus is not itself a living thing, but rather a mere particle of RNA or DNA. This particle cannot reproduce unless it finds a living cell whose machinery it can employ to make copies of itself. A virus contains just enough information to reproduce itself by finding cells to infect and turn to its purpose. In fact the *only purpose* of a virus is self-replication.

By analogy, then, we maintain that certain verbal "viruses" have infected the Mystical Body of Christ. These viruses are

---

[77]Gamber, *The Reform of the Roman Liturgy*, p. 97.

*pseudo-concepts,* which, like actual viruses, have minimal informational content. Just as a virus hovers between life and non-life, these pseudo-concepts hover between meaning and non-meaning. They *seem* to mean something, but upon close examination we find no real meaning. As viruses are particles of RNA or DNA rather than complete living cells, so these pseudo-concepts are *particles of an idea* which do not amount to an intelligible abstract concept. These viral pseudo-concepts in the Mystical Body of Christ, like actual viruses, exist only to reproduce themselves, which they do by infecting the understanding of *genuine* concepts with precise meanings — namely, the perennial teachings of the Magisterium.

We contend that by introducing "ecumenism," "dialogue" and various other "viral" pseudo-concepts into the Mystical Body, Satan has found a means to confuse, divide and wreak havoc upon the human element of the Church, *without the Church ever having taught an actual error of doctrine,* which is impossible. Quite the contrary: the pseudo-concepts in question cannot be called doctrinal errors as such, because they are not reducible to a proposition whose words would signify the formal contradiction of an existing Catholic doctrine. Indeed, the terms "ecumenism" and "dialogue" contain nothing in themselves that contradicts prior Church teaching; like actual viruses, these terms remain inert until they come into contact with something they can infect. That is why when neo-Catholics say that traditionalists "dissent" from "ecumenism," for example, they are unable to articulate precisely what it is about this notion that requires our assent. That is because *this notion does not involve any intelligible Catholic doctrine.*

This is easily demonstrated. Any Catholic doctrine will fit nicely into the template phrase "X means that...," where X is the Catholic doctrine in question. Thus, the Immaculate Conception *means that* from the first moment of her conception the Blessed Virgin Mary was preserved free from all stain of original sin. Likewise, transubstantiation *means that* at the moment of the Consecration the substance of the bread and wine are miraculously changed entirely into the substance of Christ—

Body, Blood, Soul and Divinity—so that nothing of the bread and wine remains, but only the appearances of these.

Applying our template phrase to "ecumenism," however, we immediately encounter an intellectual dead end. The phrase "ecumenism means that" cannot be completed, just as the phrase "an elephant means that" cannot be completed. Ecumenism, like an elephant, cannot be defined as an abstract concept, but only *described or indicated,* as in: that is an elephant. Ecumenism, like an elephant, is a *thing,* or rather a collection of things known as "ecumenical activities." Ecumenism certainly *is* something, just as an elephant *is* something. Ecumenism *is,* so they say, "a movement for Christian unity." But movements are by their nature contingent and ever-changing things, and no Catholic can be obliged to believe in a "movement" as if it were a definable Catholic doctrine.

The same is true of "dialogue." Dialogue is not a Catholic doctrine, but rather the name given to a collection of activities: a series of endless conversations with various non-Catholics that have thus far led nowhere and produced nothing of value.

Satan understands better than any other creature that the Magisterium can never officially teach error. But what if the human members of the Church could be induced to embrace *non*-doctrines and *non*-teachings that cause confusion and division over the meaning of the actual doctrines of the Magisterium? We are convinced that this is what has happened in the postconciliar Church: Verbal "viruses" have invaded the Mystical Body, disguising themselves as Catholic doctrines to which we are expected to adhere. And yet we find that we cannot adhere to them, because they do not have any doctrinal content; they are not definite teachings that oblige our assent to some definite proposition. While these viruses have been able to infect many individual cells of the Mystical Body, they have not actually altered the Deposit of the Faith, because we have the divine assurance that the Church can never *officially* teach error.

Exploring the analogy further, we note that a virus has certain characteristics that are analogous to the pseudo-concepts with which we seem to be dealing in the postconciliar Church.

First, the virus appears suddenly, from outside the body; that is, it is foreign to the body. Second, it can enter the body successfully only if there is some opening to it in the immune system. Third, once the virus enters, it adds nothing to the life of the body, but rather causes only disorder and weakness, rendering the body unable to engage in normal, vigorous activity. We believe all three of these elements are present with the verbal viruses "ecumenism" and "dialogue."

We first consider "ecumenism." There is no question that this verbal virus entered the Church from outside her, as Pope John Paul II has frankly admitted. In his enyclical *Ut Unum Sint,* His Holiness noted that "the ecumenical movement really began within the Churches and Ecclesial Communities of the Reform" around 1920.[78] That is, "ecumenism" originated with Protestant sects, not the Catholic Church; and being a "movement," as opposed to a doctrine, it obviously has no roots in the perennial Magisterium. Quite the contrary, in 1928 Pius XI promulgated *Mortalium Animos* in order to declare the Church's opposition to any involvement in this new movement of Protestant origin. Pope Pius issued his condemnation after duly noting (with evident contempt) the pretense of a "longing for unity" on which the new movement sought to engage Catholics:

> This undertaking is so actively promoted as in many places to win for itself the adhesion of a number of citizens, and it even takes possession of the minds of very many Catholics and allures them with the hope of bringing about such a union as would be agreeable to the desires of Holy Mother Church, who has indeed nothing more at heart than to recall her erring sons and to lead them back to her bosom. *But in reality beneath these enticing words and blandishments lies hid a most grave error, by which the foundations of the Catholic faith are completely destroyed....* And here it seems opportune to expound and to refute a certain *false opinion,* on which this whole question, as well as *that complex movement by which non-Catholics seek to bring about the union of the Christian churches depends.* For

---

[78]*Ut Unum Sint,* n. 65.

authors who favor this view are accustomed, times almost without number, to bring forward these words of Christ: "That they all may be one.... And there shall be one fold and one shepherd," with this signification however: *that Christ Jesus merely expressed a desire and prayer, which still lacks its fulfillment....* [A]lthough many non-Catholics may be found who loudly preach fraternal communion in Christ, yet you will find none at all to whom it ever occurs to submit to and obey the Vicar of Jesus Christ.... For if, as they continually state, they long to be united with Us and ours, why do they not hasten to enter the Church, the Mother and mistress of all Christ's faithful?[79]

Pius XI recognized that the Protestant proto-ecumenists were cynically exploiting the prayer of Our Lord (which was in fact fulfilled 2,000 years ago with the founding of His Church) in order to induce the Church to open itself to a non-Catholic movement whose effects could only be harmful to the faithful. Activating the Church's immune system, Pius XI repelled the virus of ecumenism by forcefully restating the Church's constant teaching on the only acceptable means of achieving true Christian unity: "And so, venerable brethren, it is clear why this Apostolic See has never allowed its subjects to take part in the assemblies of non-Catholics; for the union of Christians can *only* be promoted by promoting the *return to the one true Church* of those who are separated from it, for in the past they have unhappily left it.... Let them therefore return to their common Father, who, forgetting the insults heaped upon the Apostolic See, will receive them in most loving fashion...."[80]

This teaching was repeated emphatically in the 1949 admonition of the Holy Office of Pius XII concerning the "ecumenical movement." The admonition instructed the bishops that in any "ecumenical" discussions they might authorize, the Protestant interlocutors must be presented with "the Catholic truth" and "the teaching of the Encyclicals of the Roman Pontiffs

[79]*Mortalium Animos,* nn. 4, 5 and 7.
[80]Ibid., nn. 7, 10 and 11.

on the return of the dissidents to the Church."[81] The Catholic doctrine of the return of the dissidents was stressed again by Pius XII himself on December 20, 1949, a scant thirteen years before the opening of Vatican II: "The Catholic doctrine will have to be proposed and exposed totally and integrally: what the Catholic Church teaches about the true nature and means of justification, about the constitution of the Church, about the primacy of the jurisdiction of the Roman Pontiff, about the only true union which is accomplished with *the return of the dissidents* to the only true Church of Christ will not at all be obliged to be passed over in silence or covered over in ambiguous words."[82] (As we discuss in Chapter 8, the ecumenical virus has induced an open repudiation of this teaching at the highest levels of the Church, including Presidents of Pontifical Councils.)

A remarkable historical note is that in keeping with this constant teaching, the bishops of the Netherlands issued a pastoral letter in 1948, a scant fourteen years before Vatican II, explaining that Catholics could not attend an ecumenical congress in Amsterdam because "the division among Christians can be ended *in only one way*, by the return to the Church, by the return to that unity which in her has remained intact...." The Dutch bishops noted that such congresses could not produce anything of value because "the *dissidents* are so far away from and so foreign to the Church that they no longer understand her language," and that if the Church participated in congresses with the dissidents "she would by that very fact concede that the unity which Christ has willed has not endured in her, and that strictly speaking the Church of Christ does not exist" — a direct reference to the teaching of *Mortalium Animos*.[83] Instead of ecumenical congresses and common prayer with the dissidents, the Dutch bishops prescribed a "votive Mass for the removal of schism."

---

[81] AAS 42-142.

[82] "On the Ecumenical Movement," December 20, 1949.

[83] Pastoral letter of Netherlands Bishops, July 31, 1948.

Today, less than sixty years later, the Dutch hierarchy is the most liberal in the world, and Catholicism is all but dead in the Netherlands. It is inconceivable that the Dutch hierarchy, or any other national hierarchy, would affirm today the teaching on the return of the dissidents as the only way to Christian unity. What happened? We maintain that what happened was the injection of a verbal virus—the virus of ecumenism—into the Church.

Continuing with our analogy, the virus of ecumenism can be seen entering the Church through an opening in her immune system—namely, the Second Vatican Council. One can even pinpoint the precise historical moment when the Council presented such an opening and it was instantly exploited. On October 13, 1962—the third day of the Council and the anniversary of the Miracle of the Sun at Fatima—the Council Fathers met to vote on the composition of the conciliar commissions for review of the Council's preparatory schemas. In a typical exercise of the Church's immune system, some three years had been devoted to the preparatory schemas after Pope John's sudden announcement of the Council. The result had been a collection of documents written in a traditionally precise, scholastic manner (the schema on the liturgy being the lone exception, as we shall see). Under the Council's rules of procedure, the October 13 meeting was to be limited to a vote on the candidates the curia had proposed for the conciliar commissions, although each Father was free to write in his own choices. In violation of the procedural rules, Cardinal Achille Liénart seized the microphone and began reading a declaration demanding consultations among the electors and national bishops conferences before any vote. The vote was postponed and Pope John was cowed into allowing entirely new slates of candidates to be proposed, after a suitable period for politicking by the conciliar liberals. The liberal bishops of the Rhine countries ultimately succeeded in packing the commissions with their candidates, achieving majorities or near-majorities on all the key commissions once the election was held. As Fr. Ralph Wiltgen observed: "After this election, it was not hard to see which group was well organized enough to take over leadership at the Second Vatican Council. The Rhine had begun to flow into the Tiber."[84]

As reported in the French journal *Figaro*, Liénart's seizure of the microphone "had deflected the course of the Council and made history."[85] Moments later a Dutch bishop shouted out to a priest friend, as he left the Council hall: "That was our first victory."[86] Amerio notes that it was "one of those points at which history is concentrated for a moment, and whence great consequences flow."[87] That this could not have been a happy moment for the Church is demonstrated by the exultation of the modernists over the consequences of Liénart's action. For example, Hans Küng declared that "what had once been the dream of an *avant garde* group in the Church had 'spread and permeated the entire atmosphere of the Church, due to the Council.'" Even Cardinal Ratzinger lauded "the strong reaction against the spirit behind the preparatory work," and "the truly epoch-making character of the Council's first session." He pronounced the resulting absence of a single approved text during the first session a "great, astonishing and genuinely positive result."[88]

Almost immediately the Council's preparatory schemas were discarded, the one exception being the highly ambiguous

---

[84]Wiltgen, *The Rhine Flows into the Tiber*, p. 19.

[85]December 9, 1976, quoted in Amerio, *Iota Unum*, p. 85.

[86]Wiltgen, *The Rhine Flows into the Tiber*, p. 17.

[87]Amerio, *Iota Unum*, p. 85.

[88]Wiltgen, *The Rhine Flows into the Tiber*, p. 59. Words like "astonishing" and "surprising" are routinely ascribed to the Council, even by those considered to be theologically conservative. Cardinal Ratzinger, for example, has written of the Council: "After all the *surprises* that had emerged in the realm of theology proper, there reigned a feeling at once of euphoria and of frustration. Euphoria, because it seemed that nothing was impossible for this Council, which had the strength *to break with attitudes that had been deeply rooted for centuries....*" *Principles of Catholic Theology*, pp. 380-81. That theological "surprises" are alien to the perennial Catholic Magisterium poses no difficulty for the neo-Catholic mentality.

schema on the liturgy, which the ultra-modernist Fr. Schillebeeckx had pronounced "an admirable piece of work."[89] That schema ultimately became the Council's liturgy constitution, *Sacrosanctum Concilium*, whose disastrous loopholes merit a chapter of their own in this book (see Chapter 12). Incredibly enough, Liénart's seemingly impulsive—but actually carefully planned[90]—maneuver resulted in leaving the Second Vatican Council with no written preparation. As we know, the preparatory schemas were entirely replaced with more "pastoral" formulations, drafted in large part by the same people who had been (to recall the words of Msgr. Bandas) on "the black lists of suspicion" during the reign of Pius XII, including Schillebeeckx, Rahner, Congar and Murray. The ambiguities in these documents—the verbal viruses they contain—continue to bedevil the Church to this day. As Msgr. George A. Kelly observed: "The documents of the Council contain enough *basic ambiguities* to make the postconciliar difficulties understandable."[91] Ecumenism is certainly one of those basic ambiguities.

Thus, the "sterile" preparatory schemas were thrown into the wastebasket and replaced by documents laced with verbal viruses, chief among which was "ecumenism." The conciliar document *Unitatis Redintegratio* (UR) is replete with references to the term, which it never defines but only describes as a "movement, fostered by the grace of the Holy Spirit, for the restoration of unity among all Christians." The immediate question that arises is this: Given that before Vatican II the Church constantly taught that the only way to Christian unity was the return of the dissidents to the one true Church, what precisely does the "ecumenical movement" add to the picture? UR gives no clear answer to this question, but simply announces

---

[89]Wiltgen, *The Rhine Flows into the Tiber*, p. 23.

[90]Fr. Wiltgen's book reveals how Cardinal Liénart and Cardinal Frings of Germany planned a strategy to interrupt the business meeting and prevent any vote on the curial candidates. Ibid., p. 16.

[91]Msgr. George A. Kelly, *The Battle for the American Church* (Garden City, NY: Image Books, 1981), p. 20.

that Catholics are now to embrace this ill-defined "movement,"
even though it had been condemned by Pius XI only thirty-four
years earlier as a threat to "the foundations of the Catholic
faith."

Article 4 of *Unitatis Redintegratio* states that "The Sacred
Council exhorts, therefore, all the Catholic faithful to recognize
the signs of the times and to take an active and intelligent part in
the work of ecumenism." What are the signs of the times that
one is exhorted to recognize? UR does not say. And what is "the
*work* of ecumenism," given that ecumenism itself is not defined?
Again, no answer is given.

To this day Catholics have been given no clear idea of what
"the work of ecumenism" is. In Article 6 of UR we are told that
"the participation of Catholics in ecumenical work is distinct
from preparation and reception into the Church [of those who]
desire full communion." That is, ecumenism is something other
than evangelization or catechesis, but UR does not explain
precisely *what* that something is. We are told only that Catholics
must now engage in the ill-defined "ecumenical movement"
which involves ill-defined "ecumenical work." Such nebulous
directives have no parallel in any prior conciliar or papal
document at any time in Church history.

UR further states: "The change of heart and holiness of life,
along with public and private prayer for the unity of Christians,
merits the name, 'spiritual ecumenism.'" In the absence of any
definition of ecumenism, it is impossible to determine precisely
what is meant by *spiritual* ecumenism. What *kind* of public and
private prayer is called for? More specifically, what is to be the
prayer intention? Is it the return of the dissidents to the one true
Church? If the answer is yes, then why must we embrace an
"ecumenical movement" as opposed to praying for the return of
the dissidents and offering votive Masses for their return, as
even the Dutch bishops had done a few years earlier? If the
answer is no, where is the Council's explanation of exactly what
kind of "unity" Catholics are to pray for, if it is not the unity that
would be achieved by the conversion of the dissidents to
Catholicism?

Having failed to define ecumenism, UR nevertheless employs the term repeatedly, as if it had always had definite meaning: "Sacred theology must be taught with due regard for an ecumenical point of view." What is an ecumenical point of view? "Catholics engaged in missionary work in the same territories as other Christians ought to know, particularly in these times, the problems and the benefits which affect their apostolate because of the ecumenical movement." What problems, and what benefits? UR specifies none. Yet suddenly Catholics are informed that the very movement Pius XI condemned now offers missionaries benefits and problems – at one and the same time.

Though ecumenism received absolutely no satisfactory theological definition in the conciliar decree on ecumenism, it spread virus-like throughout the entire Church with phenomenal rapidity. The hitherto unheard-of notion literally erupted into the documents of the postconciliar Church. One of these earlier documents is the 1970 Directory on Ecumenism. The document's headings alone suffice to demonstrate how this verbal virus – which, as we can see, means almost nothing – has thoroughly infected the thinking of the Church:

*"General principles and aids to ecumenical education."*

Although Catholics at large had never heard of ecumenism before the Council, they are now informed that there must be "ecumenical education" only a few years after the Council.

*"The ecumenical dimension of religious and theological education."*

What is an "ecumenical dimension," given that there is no definition of ecumenism itself? No effort is made to explain the term.

*"The ecumenical aspect in all theological teaching."*

All theological teaching must suddenly acquire an "ecumenical aspect." But what is an "ecumenical aspect," given that "ecumenical" is not defined?

*"Conditions of a genuine ecumenical mind in theology."*

What is a "genuine ecumenical mind"? The Directory gives no indication.

*"Ecumenism as a special branch of study."*

*"Particular guidelines for ecumenical education."*

*"Those who have special ecumenical tasks."*

And so on, and so forth, all the way down to the present day. Although the term ecumenism has found innumerable applications since it first emerged in UR, it has yet to receive an intelligible definition in any Vatican document.

The virus of ecumenism spread so rapidly throughout the Body of Christ that by 1995 Pope John Paul II could say in his encyclical *Ut Unum Sint* that ecumenism "is not just some sort of appendix which is added to the Church's *traditional activity.* Rather, ecumenism is an organic part of her life and work, and consequently *must pervade all that she is and does....*" Although *Ut Unum Sint* is devoted entirely to "ecumenism," nowhere in its 110 pages is the term defined. One will search 2,000 years of Church history in vain for another example of an undefined neologism pervading all that the Church "is and does."

Perhaps the best evidence that no one knows exactly what ecumenism means, or exactly where it is leading us, is the Pope's own declaration to some Protestant ministers on October 5, 1991, during an "ecumenical prayer service" in front of St. Peter's tomb: "Ecumenism is a journey which is made together, *but we are not able to chart its course* or its duration beforehand."[92]

---

[92]*L'Osservatore Romano,* May 21, 1997.

That is, ecumenism requires the Church to embark on a "journey" with Protestants along an uncharted course! Before the Council, the course toward Christian unity was well marked out by repeated papal teaching: the dissidents must return to the one true Church. Catholics, on the other hand, were not expected to make a "journey" anywhere, as they were already residing in the ark of salvation, which others had left or failed to enter.

That no one can provide a sensible definition of ecumenism has not prevented the Pontifical Council for Christian Unity from producing an entirely new "directory" on how the Church is to implement "ecumenism." In paragraph 16 of *Ut Unum Sint*, the Pope notes that he specifically approved issuance of the 1993 *Directory for the Application of Principles and Norms on Ecumenism.* This document calls for nothing less than the "ecumenical formation" of every man, woman and child in the Catholic Church—from the highest prelates to the smallest child in catechism class. This is to be accomplished by, among other means, "workshops and seminars for the ecumenical formation of both clergy and laity, for the appropriate realization of *an ecumenical dimension to all aspects of life....*"[93] It should come as no surprise that neither the term "ecumenical formation" nor the term "ecumenical dimension" is defined. How there can be "an ecumenical dimension" to all aspects of life is left to one's imagination. But, amazingly enough, a notion unknown to Catholics at large before 1964 is now presented as something integral to their very existence. In physics, the search is on for a Theory of Everything. In the postconciliar Church, ecumenism has become a kind of ecclesial Theory of Everything, even if no one can explain the theory with any clarity.

Over and over again the *Directory* speaks of "the search for Christian unity," as if unity were something Catholics had to search for. The *Directory* informs us that there must be "flexibility of methods in this *search* for unity."[94] Flexible is

---

[93]*Directory,* n. 44(d).
[94]Ibid., n. 56.

putting it mildly. The *Directory* calls for joint "non-sacramental liturgical services" at Protestant churches, in which Catholics "are *encouraged* to take part in the psalms, responses, hymns *and common actions* of the Church in which they are guests."[95] What would St. Pius X have thought of this recommendation? Further, if these joint liturgical services are held in a Catholic parish, the visiting Protestant ministers "may have the place and *liturgical honors proper to their rank*...." What "rank" would that be, exactly, given that they lack holy orders and are thus mere laymen? And what "liturgical honors" should Catholic parishes bestow upon non-Catholic "ministers" whose doctrines stand condemned by the entire Magisterium, and whose moral teachings, after forty years of fruitless "ecumenical dialogue," are a sty of corruption?

The *Directory* provides (in accordance with postconciliar changes in canon law) that "the funeral rites of the Catholic Church may be granted to the members of a non-Catholic Church or ecclesial community," provided the local bishop deems it appropriate, *and the departed Protestant would not have objected!*[96] Yes, members of Protestant sects who rejected Catholic doctrines and dogmas may now receive a Catholic burial as if they had been loyal members of the Church.

In provisions that would be impossible to believe if they were not written for all to see, the *Directory* decrees that the bishops' conferences are free to establish norms for *joint ownership of church properties with Protestant congregations*— provided the local bishop thinks there is a good reason, and there is "a good ecumenical relationship between the communities."[97] What constitutes a "good ecumenical relationship" is, like everything else about ecumenism, left undefined. The *Directory* recommends that "Before making plans for *a shared building*, the authorities of the communities concerned should first reach an agreement as to how their

---

[95]Ibid., n. 118.
[96]Ibid., n. 119.
[97]Ibid., nn. 137-138.

various disciplines shall be observed, particularly in regard to the sacraments."[98] In other words, a Pontifical Council, in a document explicitly approved by the Pope, recommends that Catholic priests work out guidelines with Protestant ministers for celebration of the Holy Sacrifice of the Mass — in their jointly owned churches!

And what is to be done with the Blessed Sacrament in the contemplated Catholic-Protestant edifices? The *Directory* provides that "when authorization for such ownership *is given* by the diocesan bishop" — meaning that the Vatican really expects this sort of thing to go forward — "judicious consideration should be given to the reservation of the Blessed Sacrament…taking account of the sensitivities of those who will use the building, e.g., by constructing a separate room or chapel."[99] That is, when Catholics and Protestants acquire their joint worship facility, the Catholics ought to make sure that the Blessed Sacrament is kept out of it in order to accommodate Protestant "sensitivities." We recall here the prediction of Msgr. Pacelli before he became Pius XII: "In our churches, Christians will search in vain for the red lamp where God awaits them. Like Mary Magdalene, weeping before the empty tomb, they will ask, 'Where have they taken Him?'"

This, then, is what the virus of ecumenism has produced in the Church within a few short years. Anyone who is honest about our situation would have to admit that the preconciliar Popes would view the results with utter horror. But the "ecumenical venture" goes on, despite the lack of any clear notion of where it is leading us. The Pope's recent address on ecumenism is a remarkable, though surely unintended, admission that ecumenism is an ever-receding, inexpressible mirage. Speaking to the plenary assembly of the Pontifical Council for Promoting Christian Unity on November 13, 2001, the Pope urged that "words like crisis, delays, slowness, immobility and compromises be eliminated" in ecumenical

---

[98]Ibid., n. 140.
[99]Ibid., n. 119.

dialogue, and that instead "key words such as 'confidence,' 'patience,' 'constancy,' 'dialogue' and 'hope' be adopted." That is, one must resolutely avoid describing the *true state* of ecumenical activity.

The Pope went on to proclaim: "Prayer and constant listening to the Lord are indispensable, as he is the one who, with the force of the Spirit, converts hearts and makes possible all progress in the way of ecumenism." But what is it that the Lord is supposed to be telling us about "progress in the way of ecumenism"? And what *is* "the way of ecumenism" in the first place? In what sense is ecumenism a *way*? In what does this way consist, and where does it lead? What exactly will we find at the end of this way? How is the "way of ecumenism" different from the return of the dissidents to the one true Church? After some forty years of ecumenical activity, there are still no answers to such questions, for the questions are unanswerable. They are unanswerable, we believe, because the word ecumenism has no real meaning. It is a virus in the Body of Christ.

Even more troubling is the Pope's remark that "With rigorous and serene theological research, with constant imploring for the light of the spirit, we will be able to address even the most difficult and seemingly insurmountable questions in so many of our ecumenical dialogues, as, for example, that of the Bishop of Rome...." When did the authority of the Vicar of Christ (now called "the Bishop of Rome") become a "seemingly insurmountable question" in "many ecumenical dialogues," as opposed to *a divinely revealed truth* that Protestants must accept as a matter of faith in order to be united with us? And what is it that we are imploring the Lord to tell us about such "insurmountable questions," if it is not what the Magisterium has already taught as Catholic doctrine for centuries? Here again, there are no answers, for none can be given.

We next consider the course of the virus of "dialogue" in the postconciliar Church; and it is no less disturbing to Catholics with any sense of the Church's constant teaching and practice before 1965. No one can improve on Romano Amerio's description of the sudden appearance and rapid spread of this utter novelty throughout the Church:

> The word was *completely unknown and unused in the Church's teaching before the Council.* It does not occur *once* in any previous Council, or in papal encyclicals, or in sermons, or in pastoral practice. In the Vatican II documents, it occurs 28 times, twelve of them in the decree *Unitatis Redintegratio.* Nonetheless, through *its lightning spread* and an *enormous broadening in meaning,* this word, which is very new in the Catholic Church, became *the master-word determining postconciliar thinking,* and a catch-all category in the newfangled mentality. People not only talk about ecumenical dialogue, dialogue between the Church and the world, ecclesial dialogue, but by an enormous catechesis, a dialogical structure is attributed to theology, pedagogy, catechesis, the Trinity, the history of salvation, schools, families, priesthood, sacraments, redemption—and to everything else that has existed in the Church for centuries *without the concept being in anybody's mind or the word occurring in the language.*[100]

What Amerio describes is the spread of a verbal virus in the Mystical Body, which, like ecumenism, was injected into the Church via the documents of Vatican II—that is, the documents that replaced the Council's hastily discarded and virus-free preparatory schemas. The most striking admission of the virus's spread may be a statement by the Archbishop of Avignon, published in *L'Osservatore Romano* some eleven years after the Council: "At the Council the Church began again to love *this* world [emphasis in original], to open itself to it, *to become*

---

[100]Amerio's view carries considerable weight, since he was a *peritus* at Vatican II, who advised the Bishop of Lugano, a member of the Council's Central Preparatory Commission. He was thus intimately familiar with the process by which the Council's documents were created.

*dialogue*...."[101] The Church opens herself to this world; the virus of dialogue enters the Church; the Church then *becomes* dialogue. We are reminded here of Pope Paul's famous lament that "the opening to the world became a veritable invasion of the Church by worldly thinking."[102] And this development was lauded by an archbishop in the Pope's own newspaper.

Now, unlike "ecumenism," which is a pure neologism, the word "dialogue" is a classical word with a definite meaning; it means a conversation, usually around a theme. But what exactly does dialogue mean in the context of the postconciliar Church? As Amerio's remarks would suggest, it has evolved into a pseudo-concept that worms its way into everything. Like "ecumenism," the term "dialogue" has achieved an extension so broad as to lose to all real meaning.

This is demonstrated by a key Vatican document on "dialogue" entitled "Dialogue and Proclamation" (DP), issued by the Pontifical Council on Interreligious Dialogue in 1991. In DP we see that the notion of "interreligious dialogue" acts as a kind of co-virus with "dialogue," and that, like "dialogue," eludes precise definition. Hence DP frankly declares that "Interreligious dialogue between Christians and followers of other religions as envisaged by the Second Vatican Council is *only gradually coming to be understood.*"[103] That is, since Vatican II the Catholic Church has been busily engaged in an activity *she does not yet understand!* The Pontifical Council thus admits that the term "interreligious dialogue" is largely incomprehensible.

While the document makes no attempt to define either "dialogue" or "interreligious dialogue," it does inform us that there are different *forms* of dialogue: "the dialogue of life," "the dialogue of action," "the dialogue of theological exchange," "the

---

[101]*L'Osservatore Romano*, Italian Edition, September 3, 1976: "La Chiesa, al Concilio, ha ricominciato ad amare *questo* mondo, aprisi ad esso, e farsi 'dialogo'..." (emphasis in original).

[102]Speech of November 23, 1973.

[103]*Dialogue and Proclamation* (1991), n. 4b.

dialogue of religious experience."[104] In other words, as we have said, "dialogue," like "ecumenism," is not a doctrine but a *thing* — a collection of activities — which, like ecumenism, is now said to permeate not just the entire life of the Church but *all of human existence.*

Accordingly, the document announces that "All Christians are called to be personally involved in these *two ways* of carrying out the one mission of the Church, namely proclamation and dialogue."[105] After 1,961 years of Church history, we are informed for the first time that Our Lord did not commission the Church simply to proclaim the Gospel, but also to "dialogue" with other religions — an activity which "is only gradually coming to be understood"!

Since "dialogue" has suddenly become part of the divine commission, DP recommends that there be "special courses and study sessions to train people for *both* dialogue and proclamation." But how does one train for dialogue if the Church herself is only gradually coming to understand it? No answer is even suggested. DP further informs us that the Catholic Church "is invited by the Spirit to encourage all religious institutions to meet, enter into collaboration, and to purify themselves in order to promote truth and life, *holiness*, justice, love and peace...." There is not slightest suggestion here that the mission of the Church is to make converts to the true religion in order to save souls. Rather, the Church is presented as a collaborator with other religions so that other religions can become holier and promote peace and justice through "interreligious dialogue," which the Church is only gradually coming to understand.

DP does allow that despite the Church's newfound obligation to engage in interreligious dialogue, "it is useful to point out once again that to proclaim the name of Jesus and to invite people to become his [sic] disciples is a sacred and major duty which the Church cannot neglect. Evangelization would be

---

[104]Ibid. n. 42.
[105]Ibid., n. 82.

*incomplete* without it...."[106] That evangelization would be "incomplete" without an "invitation" to become a disciple of Christ is a rather curious way of putting it, given that the very purpose of evangelization is to make Christians of those who are evangelized. Also curious is that the document does not even suggest that the "invitation" to become a disciple of Christ involves becoming a formal member of the Roman Catholic Church. One of the symptoms of the viruses of ecumenism and dialogue is that the words "Catholic Church" have all but disappeared from postconciliar Vatican pronouncements. In keeping with this startling development, DP fails to mention the *Catholic* Church even once. A non-Catholic reader of DP would have no idea that proclamation of the Gospel has anything to do with people becoming Catholics.

Indeed, the very point of "dialogue" and "interreligious" dialogue" is to avoid any suggestion to the non-Catholic interlocutor that the Catholic Church alone speaks with the authority of its divine founder and is in possession of the totality of His revelation to man. For example, when introducing the Vatican *Instruction* on "dialogue" in 1968, Cardinal König told the press: "Dialogue puts the partners on an equal footing. *The Catholic is not considered as possessing all the truth*, but as someone who has faith and is *looking for that truth with others*, both believers and non-believers."[107]

No doubt the height of the fever engendered by the virus of dialogue was the World Day of Prayer for Peace at Assisi in October 1986. In the plaza outside the Basilica of St. Francis of Assisi, the "representatives of the world's great religions" stepped forward one by one to offer their prayers for peace. These "prayers" included the chanting of American Indian shamans. The Pope was photographed standing in a line of "religious leaders," including rabbis, muftis, Buddhist monks and assorted Protestant ministers, all of them holding potted

---

[106] Ibid., n. 76.

[107] Amerio, *Iota Unum*, p. 355, quoting I.C.I., No. 322, October 15, 1968, p. 20.

olive plants. The official Vatican publication on the World Day of Prayer for Peace at Assisi, entitled "World Day of Prayer for Peace," pays tribute to the "world's great religions" by setting forth their prayers, including an Animist prayer to the Great Thumb. The "world's great religions" are honored by the Vatican in alphabetical order: the Buddhist prayer for peace; the Hindu prayer for peace; the Jainist prayer for peace; the Muslim prayer for peace; the Shinto prayer for peace; the Sikh prayer for peace; the Traditionalist African prayer for peace (to "The Great Thumb"); the Traditionalist Amerindian prayer for peace; the Zoroastrian prayer for peace. In a glaring symptom of the end result of ecumenism and dialogue in the Church, the only prayer not included in the official book is a *Catholic* prayer for peace. There is only a Christian prayer for peace, which appears after the prayers of the "world's great religions" — and after the Jewish prayer. Catholicism has been subsumed into a generic Christianity.

At the beginning of this list of prayers of the world religions, there is an amazing statement by Cardinal Roger Etchegaray, president of the Pontifical Council on Interreligious Dialogue. According to Etchegaray, "Each of the religions we profess has inner peace, and peace among individuals and nations, as one of its aims. Each one pursues this aim in its own distinctive and *irreplaceable* way." The notion that there is anything "irreplaceable" about the false religions of the world seems difficult to square with the *de fide* Catholic teaching that God's revelation to His Church is complete and all-sufficient for the spiritual needs of men. Our Lord came among us — so Catholics were always taught — precisely to *replace* false religions with His religion, with even the Old Covenant undergoing this divinely appointed substitution. Yet the members of all the "the world's great religions" were invited to Assisi and asked for their "irreplaceable" prayers for world peace — the "irreplaceable" prayers of false shepherds who preach abortion, contraception, divorce, polygamy, the treatment of women like dogs, reincarnation of human beings as animals, a holy war against infidel Christians and countless other lies, superstitions and abominations in the sight of God.

Ten years after the "World Day of Prayer for Peace," Cardinal Etchegaray said something we would not have believed if it had not appeared on the Vatican's own website: "The spirit of Assisi is gliding over the bubbling waters of the religions and is already creating marvels of fraternal *dialogue*.... Spirit of Assisi, come upon us all!" What precisely is "the Spirit of Assisi"? What has the "spirit of Assisi" produced in the world that Catholics should call it down upon themselves? When a cardinal at the Holy See publicly enthuses about a novel spirit gliding over the bubbling waters of false religions, calls this novel spirit down upon the faithful, and praises false religions as "irreplaceable," Catholics with any sense of Tradition are instinctively aroused to opposition.

The "Spirit of Assisi," like ecumenism and dialogue, has produced nothing but more of itself—in the manner of a virus. The events of September 11, 2001, which make a mockery of "the Spirit of Assisi," need not be discussed here; they are already burned into the memory of the world. Suffice it to say that, in the years following the World Day of Prayer for Peace in 1986 (and reprises of the event in 1993, 1999, and 2002), Muslim militants have been shooting Christians on sight in various nations. In India, Hindu fundamentalists have been torturing and killing priests and nuns routinely since the "representatives of the world's great religions" held their potted plants for photographers. After the Hindu nationalist government of India set off three atomic bombs underground in 1998, people in New Delhi were dancing in the streets, shouting praise to their Hindu gods[108]—including Shiva, the Destroyer. Or perhaps the Hindu praise was directed to Shiva's wife, Kali, the goddess of death and destruction. Shiva is a very popular idol in some parts of India, where the people sacrifice goats to him. Irreplaceable? We do not think so.

---

[108] *New York Times,* May 17, 1998.

The Assisi event was repeated on January 24, 2002, when members of the various religions were assigned rooms in the monastery attached to the Basilica of St. Francis to perform various pagan rituals. Thus at a profoundly sacred Catholic site, where for centuries holy monks had prayed for the conversion of such souls, a (polytheistic) Jainist minister burned wood chips in his sacred urn, and practitioners of the other religions, including voodoo, observed their own "traditions."[109] They came to Assisi from the Vatican in what Church authorities called a "peace train," consisting of seven cars: one for the Pope, one for the cardinals and bishops, one for the Orthodox, one for the Jews and Muslims, one for the Protestant "ecclesial communities," one for the Buddhists, the Tenrikyoists, the Shintoists, the Confucianists and the Jainists, and, bringing up the rear, a caboose filled with Hindus, Zoroastrians and Sikhs.

The whole spectacle was carried out in the name of world peace. On the following day, India tested a nuclear missile and Israel bombed the Palestinian territories. Within a few weeks of Assisi 2002, Hindu and Muslim fundamentalists in India were slaughtering each other by the hundreds in a new wave of religious conflict, while the Arab-Israeli conflict escalated to the verge of all-out war, as the Israeli army conducted a massive invasion of the unofficial Palestinian capital of Ramallah, drawing protests even from members of the Israeli cabinet.[110]

This is how our warring world responded to the "Spirit of Assisi" and "interreligious dialogue." Yet the "dialogue" goes on and on, and the Vatican no longer says to the world that it

---

[109]EWTN and the other neo-Catholic organs did not show images of the sacrileges which then took place in those rooms, even though the images were broadcast, uncensored, on Italian television—as the Vatican wished them to be. One who followed EWTN's coverage of the event would have had no idea of what the Vatican apparatus itself was proud to have everyone see. Why are the neo-Catholics so intent on hiding this information?

[110]"Terrified Muslims Fill Refugee Camps in India," CNN.com, March 12, 2002; "Israel's Tactics Prompt a Fiery Disagreement in the Cabinet and Censure Abroad," New York Times, March 14, 2002, p. A15.

must become Catholic, that it must submit to the Social Kingship of Christ, in order to find true peace and eternal salvation. Instead, we have the Assisi events and statements from the Pontifical Council for Interreligious Dialogue, such as the one which declares that Catholics and Muslims should "share their faith," and that the "call to Islam" and "Christian mission" should be conducted "in a spirit of *collaboration*, and as a *service to mankind*."[111] Not even the events of "9/11" could persuade the practitioners of dialogue that there can be no "collaboration" and "sharing" between the true religion established by God and the religion invented by Muhammad.

In 1571, Pope St. Pius V, who gave us our Roman Missal, prayed for the defeat of the Islamic forces at Lepanto. Before he had even received news of the victory of the Christian fleet, he suddenly stood up, went to the window, and declared: "This is not the moment for business; make haste to thank God, because our fleet this moment has won a victory over the Turks."[112] Even the neo-Catholic historian Warren H. Carroll declares that "In more ways than one, he [St. Pius V] had saved Christendom."[113] But today, with Christendom in ruins, the neo-Catholics have nothing to say as the Vatican sends a delegation to the first mosque ever to be built in Rome, while a pontifical council tells us that the Catholic Church will now *collaborate* with Islam, which provides a "service to mankind."

What do our "neo-Catholic" friends say when confronted by astonishing reversals like these? They say nothing. For how can they admit the evidence of a catastrophe they have refused all along to recognize?

To recall, then, the three points of our analogy:

First, a virus appears suddenly, from outside the body; that is, it is foreign to the body.

---

[111] *L'Osservatore Romano*, May 28, 1997, p. 11.

[112] Warren H. Carroll, *The Cleaving of Christendom*, Vol. IV (Front Royal, Virginia: Christendom Press, 2000), p. 355.

[113] Ibid., p. 356.

Second, it can enter the body successfully only if there is some opening to it in the immune system.

As to the first and second points, the analogy clearly holds true. Ecumenism and dialogue suddenly appeared at an ecumenical council, whose entire preparation Pope John allowed to be tossed into the wastebasket, leaving the Church's immune system open to the ambiguities that found their way into the final documents approved by Pope Paul. Granted, none of the conciliar documents contains any explicit doctrinal error; and Paul VI did act decisively in several instances to prevent outright errors from being promulgated as Catholic doctrine.[114] But that is the point of this chapter: to explain how the Church could have fallen into its current state of confusion and weakness *without* a systematic failure of the Magisterium, which is impossible. It happened because of the introduction into the Church of verbal viruses, operating below the level of Catholic doctrine.

---

[114]The most famous example is Pope Paul's intervention forcing the Council to include the *Nota Praevia* to *Lumen Gentium*, which corrects LG's erroneous suggestion that when the Pope exercises his supreme authority he does so only as head of the apostolic college, wherein the supreme authority resides. Paul was alerted to this problem by a group of conservative Council Fathers, who finally persuaded him of LG's destructive potential: "Pope Paul, realizing finally that he had been deceived, broke down and wept." Wiltgen, *The Rhine Flows into the Tiber*, p. 232. In this instance, conciliar conservatives acted as "antibodies" against another verbal virus in the conciliar documents. But, as Amerio notes, "[I]n the whole history of the Church there is no other example of a gloss of this sort being added and organically joined to a dogmatic constitution such as *Lumen Gentium*.... It seems inexplicable...that the Council should issue a doctrinal document so imperfect as to require an explanatory note at the very moment of its promulgation." Amerio, *Iota Unum*, p. 91. It is only typical of the maneuvering at the Council that the *Nota Praevia*, which was supposed to introduce *Lumen Gentium*, was somehow demoted to the status of an appendix and "printed after it." Ibid.

Third, once the virus enters, it adds nothing to the life of the body, but rather causes only disorder and weakness, rendering the body unable to engage in normal, vigorous activity.

Can there be any doubt that the viruses of ecumenism and dialogue have nearly paralyzed the missionary activity of the Church, while tending to leave those outside her confirmed in their errors? The divine commission to make disciples of all nations necessarily exists in tension with these novel notions, which cannot but inhibit the Church's traditionally forthright proclamation that she alone is the ark of salvation—a dogma reaffirmed in Pius XI's rejection of the "ecumenical movement" a mere thirty-seven years before Vatican II.[115]

Are we not witnessing, then, what the third element of our analogy to the virus suggests: a drastically weakened Church, unable to engage in its normal vigorous activity of gathering souls to itself? What else but these verbal viruses could have induced such weakness in the Church—a weakness that developed suddenly after the Council, and in precisely those areas impacted by the new notions?

And yet, we must stress again, in the process of being infected by these viruses, the Church has never actually taught any doctrinal error at the level of the Magisterium, as opposed to having adopted ill-defined *ecclesiastical policies* to which neither a religious assent (i.e., the assent of prudence) nor an assent of faith can be required, policies not being proper objects of Catholic faith.

---

[115]"The Catholic Church is alone in keeping the true worship. This is the fount of truth, this the house of Faith, this the temple of God: if any man enter not here, or if any man go forth from it, he is a stranger to the hope of life and salvation. *Let none delude himself with obstinate wrangling.* For life and salvation are here concerned, which will be lost and entirely destroyed, unless their interests are carefully and assiduously kept in mind." *Mortalium Animos,* n. 11, quoting Lactantius.

If, then, our thesis is correct, in the postconciliar epoch the Adversary has unleashed his most brilliant stratagem—perhaps the final stratagem—in his long war against the Church: the use of non-doctrine to erode adherence to doctrine; the harnessing of good intentions and the dissipation of ecclesial energy in an almost feverish pursuit of illusory concepts, incapable of being realized or even adequately explained. Here we hasten to emphasize that in no way do we mean to imply any judgment on the subjective disposition of the churchmen who bid us to adhere to ecumenism and dialogue. Much less would we wish to give any impression of a judgment on the person of the Holy Father, whom no one on earth may judge.

Yet we cannot fail to note that papal policies and practical decisions, such as the decision to embark on an "ecumenical venture" with Protestants, do not enjoy the divine protection from error that attends a Pope's doctrinal teaching. As Dietrich von Hildebrand observed, a loyalty to the Pope by which "practical decisions of the Pope are accepted in the same way as *ex cathedra* definitions or encyclicals dealing with questions of faith or morals...is really false and unfounded. It places insoluble problems before the faithful in regard to the history of the Church. In the end this false loyalty *can only endanger the true Catholic faith.*"[116] (Just how problematical such blind loyalty can be is illustrated by the historical example of Pope Stephen VI, who had the corpse of his predecessor, Formosus, exhumed and thrown into the Tiber, declaring all his papal acts annulled, including ordinations. Stephen VI was reversed by Pope Theodore II, who was in turn reversed by Pope Sergius III, who declared once again that the ordinations of Formosus were invalid.[117] Had there been any neo-Catholics around in those days, they would have twisted themselves into pretzels denouncing as "schismatic" those who objected to any of the

[116]*Satan at Work*, p. 45; cited in Michael Davies, *Pope John's Council* (Kansas City, MO: Angelus Press, 1977), p. 174.

[117]Michael Davies, *Pope John's Council*, p. 175.

conflicting decisions of this line of Popes—decisions that had serious consequences for the Church.)

What is more, even lay people have eyes to see, and they can recognize an illness when they see it. Many, and not just traditionalists, have observed that the Mystical Body of Christ is now suffering from an illness unlike any she has ever suffered before. Not even the Arian crisis can compare with the multifarious ecclesial disorder and debility we are witnessing at this moment in history.

Aside from the widely acknowledged destruction of the liturgy, what else can account for the Church's current unexampled condition, if not these novel notions we have described as viruses in the Body of Christ? What other cause could have produced that seemingly impossible state of affairs foretold by Pius XII in the prophetic warning with which we began this chapter? If there is another answer to these questions, postconciliar history has yet to reveal it.

# Section II

# Accusation and Defense

# Chapter 4

# Liturgical Minimalism

*"[S]ee what things the enemy hath done*
*wickedly in the sanctuary..." Psalm 73:3*

One of the great bromides of neo-Catholicism is its claim that despite the recent profusion of liturgical and other novelties in the Church since Vatican II, "nothing of substance" has been changed. As the neo-Catholics would have it, we traditionalists are merely carping about non-essential "externals," whereas beneath the surface of the postconciliar changes the "substance" of the Faith remains intact.

The question, of course, is what is meant by "substance." If the substance of the Faith is narrowly defined as a set of doctrinal propositions that one can find in a book somewhere, and the bare essentials of the sacramental forms, one could easily demonstrate that this "substance" has not been changed by the postconciliar revolution in respect of any formal contradiction or explicit repudiation by some authoritative pronouncement of the Magisterium. For example, one can find classical restatements of Catholic teaching in the new Catechism, bobbing there like life buoys in a sea of excess verbiage and ambiguous Vatican II-speak, the likes of which have never been seen in any previous Roman catechism. Likewise, the new liturgy has not ended the valid confection of the Holy Eucharist—as if one could leave it at that and ignore the effects of the new liturgy upon Eucharistic faith and the life of the Church as a whole.

Thus, the Church has not failed in the sense that she has suffered the *total* loss of any of her *essential* elements, for this would be impossible, given the promises of Our Lord. But Our Lord never promised that the Church would be immune to the self-inflicted disruption, obscurantism and loss of institutional memory that afflict her today. The Arian crisis and the current crisis show us the alarming extent to which, as we have said, whatever can go wrong will go wrong, even in the Catholic Church. It is entirely possible that, just as in the time of Arius, the "substance" of the Faith can suffer dramatic loss, even to the point of the apparent near-death and near-disappearance of the Church itself. The divine assistance is no guarantee of the Church's size or vigor in any given epoch.

After some forty years of innovations that would have been considered unthinkable by the preconciliar Popes, only the willfully blind will still deny that the postconciliar era has been witness to what St. Pius X condemned in *Pascendi*: the ascendancy of those who "deride the *ecclesiastical traditions*...invent novelties of some kind...or endeavor by malice or craft to overthrow *any one of the legitimate traditions* of the Catholic Church." That this disaster could indeed befall the Church is the very reason Pius IV and Blessed Pius IX sought to prevent it by requiring a profession of faith — the "substance" of the Faith — that refers to *both* apostolic and ecclesiastical tradition. For the one cannot survive without the other, any more than the brain and the body can survive if separated. That the visible body of the Church has not died during the current crisis means only that the severance between apostolic and ecclesiastical traditions is not so complete as to be fatal. Here again the promises of Our Lord are at work. The Church clings to life despite her gaping wounds, just as she clung to life during the Arian crisis.

The claim that the "substance" of the Faith has not been changed by the onslaught of conciliar and postconciliar changes in the Church is, we submit, nothing but pretense that is impossible to maintain consistently in the face of reality. Every now and then a Vatican prelate, and even the Pope himself, will issue a statement that implicitly admits the stunning magnitude of the change. We have noted some of these statements in earlier chapters.

Perhaps the most dramatic example of this is to be found in a passage from John Paul II's 1988 *motu proprio, Ecclesia Dei,* which declares the excommunication and putative "schism" of Archbishop Lefebvre and the four bishops he consecrated for his Society of St. Pius X (SSPX), and also announces the establishment of the Ecclesia Dei Commission. The Holy Father's statement of the Commission's purpose is most revealing: "facilitating full ecclesial communion of priests, seminarians, religious communities, or individuals until now linked in various ways to the Fraternity founded by Mons. Lefebvre, who may wish to remain united to the Successor of Peter in the Catholic Church while preserving *their spiritual and liturgical traditions....*"

Now it is obvious that as of 1988 the members of the SSPX had not invented their own peculiar spiritual and liturgical traditions, nor have they invented any spiritual or liturgical traditions in the ensuing fourteen years. What, then, is meant by "*their* spiritual and liturgical traditions"? There can be only one answer: "their" spiritual and liturgical traditions are none other than those of the Roman Rite— which is to say, *our* spiritual and liturgical traditions before Vatican II. Since those traditions have been abandoned, from the Pope's perspective a special Vatican commission is now required to determine how those who continue to adhere to the former traditions of the Roman Rite may be "facilitated" in remaining united to "the successor of Peter."

The very suggestion in *Ecclesia Dei* that there now exists a kind of tension between the preservation of Catholic spiritual and liturgical traditions and communion with the Pope is itself utterly astonishing. But there it is for all to see. When our traditions suddenly became "their" traditions, adherence to those traditions just as suddenly became a *problem* with respect to ecclesial "communion." Since the Pope and nearly all the hierarchy have moved away from those traditions, Catholics who declined to move with them are perceived as having ruptured their "communion" with the Pope. At the same time, legions of liberal clerics, including bishops, are considered as being in full "communion" with the Pope, even though they undermine or openly dissent from settled Catholic doctrine and brazenly disobey papal disciplinary measures, many of which are repealed as a reward for their disobedience. Again, the only "schism" that alarms the Vatican is the "schism" of traditional clergy. The *de facto* schism of much of the hierarchy (noted by Cardinal Gagnon as to North America) is completely ignored.

Here we are confronted with empirical confirmation of the most profound crisis in Church history: a papal document has noted an apparent antinomy, which the Vatican thinks must be resolved, between adherence to the spiritual and liturgical traditions of the Roman Rite and adherence to the Vicar of Christ. And yet we are expected to believe that this situation does not represent any "substantial" change in the Church. No, the traditionalists in the SSPX — all traditionalists — are hallucinating; we are all worried about a mere illusion of change.

But even in denying a real change in the Church, the Vatican prelates who preside over the postconciliar revolution cannot help but admit the truth. In a recent magazine interview, for example, Cardinal Dario Castrillón Hoyos, head of the Ecclesia Dei Commission, declared that "one of the pastoral *emergencies* of our time and which everyone is having to address is to show that the Church today *is the same Church it has always been....*"[118] But why should it be a "pastoral emergency" to show that the Church has not changed, unless there were very good grounds to think otherwise? Since when has the Vatican had to "show" the faithful that their Church is still the same as always?

According to the neo-Catholics, however, nothing "of substance" has been changed. Having been deprived of the great feast of the Church's patrimony, especially in the liturgy,

---

[118]*30 Days*, N.11-2000, p. 17.

the neo-Catholics profess to wonder why anyone would think the faithful need more than the remaining crumbs. And even those few neo-Catholics who are willing to admit that the Mass of Paul VI is "inferior" to the rite of Mass that came down to us from Pope St. Gregory the Great (who in turn received it from his predecessors, adding only collects and prefaces), seem untroubled by their own admission of a liturgical catastrophe.

But if even some neo-Catholics can see the inferiority of the new rite, what possible excuse can there be for the Supreme Pontiff of the Catholic Church not to see that a huge mistake has been made? The problems of the new rite extend well beyond aesthetics, or the hubris of its architects in discarding beautiful prayers hallowed by tradition in favor of manufactured substitutes. The new rite is also markedly inferior in its presentation of Catholic doctrine. Anyone even minimally versed in Catholic Eucharistic teaching can see that the three new Eucharistic prayers are clearly deficient in their presentation of doctrine; the traditional teaching on the Catholic priesthood and its uniqueness vis-à-vis the priesthood of the faithful is likewise obscured. And yet if even a moderately educated Catholic can see this, how can the Pope fail to see it?

Predictably, the Pamphlet trots out the old "bad advisers" line, claiming that Paul VI was talked into promulgating the new missal by Annibale Bugnini. First of all, even had the combined rhetorical abilities of Socrates and Cicero been brought to bear on the matter, it is impossible to imagine Pope St. Pius X, or indeed *any* preconciliar Pope, allowing himself to be persuaded that the new Mass was in any way acceptable, let alone a positive good. Moreover, what was Paul VI doing talking to Bugnini in the first place? Advisers are not a mysterious given, like the sea and the stars. The Pope does not one day suddenly find himself surrounded by them. He chooses them himself. Paul *chose* Bugnini. And as Cardinal Alfons Stickler recalls, since Bugnini's work as secretary of the Council's Preparatory Commission for the Liturgy had not been considered satisfactory, he had not been named secretary of the

Conciliar Commission itself. It was Pope Paul himself who rehabilitated Bugnini by naming him secretary of the new Consilium responsible for the implementation of the reform.

Moreover, even in the absence of Bugnini's counsel it is obvious that Paul VI strongly favored the new rite over the old—not just as a way, supposedly, of attracting Protestants, but as a great thing in itself. Thus in his General Audience of November 26, 1969, Pope Paul noted with evident satisfaction that the new rite would draw the faithful "out of their customary personal devotions or their usual torpor." This cruel and unwarranted insult to the piety of many centuries of Catholic faithful—their *usual torpor?*—is a classic example of the contempt in which the postconciliar establishment holds the preconciliar Church, and we here see that even a Pope is not immune. Speaking of the importance of "participation," by which the Pope seems to have been referring to participation in its merely exterior manifestation, Paul VI noted that the new rite would be especially welcome to "modern people, so fond of plain language which is easily understood and converted into everyday speech." Here is yet another example of the spirit of Vatican II at work, and out of the lips of a Pope, no less: the perennial traditions of the Church, he says, are to give way in the face of modern sensibilities. In practice, the "plain language" of which "modern people" are so fond turned out to be banalities that read like instructions for operating a microwave oven. These same modern people, in turn, in whose name the liturgy was deformed and its language made "plain," no longer finding in the Mass the mysterious and supernatural, stopped attending Mass altogether. For this and many other reasons, neo-Catholic efforts to deny any connection between the Council, the "spirit of Vatican II," and the devastation in the Church cannot be taken seriously.

Anxious to persuade us of the new rite's validity, which we accept, the Pamphlet assures us: "Its General Instruction, together with a subsequent Foreword in 1970, stated explicitly that the Novus Ordo Missae was intended to express the traditional faith." Stop right there. Here we have a typical example of the fundamental dishonesty of the neo-Catholic position. Again, we do not disagree with the basic point the author is making here—namely, that the new Mass is valid as a rite. But the author conveniently neglects to tell us exactly *why* the General Instruction of the Roman Missal (GIRM), published in 1969, had to be supplemented by "a subsequent Foreword in 1970." The author surely remembers the answer from his days as a traditionalist, but his "monograph" mysteriously fails to account for this frantic shuffling of Vatican documents. The short answer is that the GIRM was so scandalously remiss in its minimalist delineation of the Mass as "the Lord's Supper" that by overwhelming demand the Vatican was forced to revise it. This episode alone suffices to reveal the absurdity of the neo-Catholic position: in 1969 they would have denounced anyone who dared to question the doctrinal rectitude of the GIRM; in 1970 they would have attacked anyone who *didn't* question it.

To claim that the new Mass represents a striking departure from tradition, which it obviously does, is not necessarily to say that it is invalid *per se*. We certainly do not think so, and neither do the overwhelming majority of traditionalists. Archbishop Lefebvre himself never held such a position. Having said this, however, surely we have a right to insist on more than *the bare minimum of mere validity*. No one hosting an elegant dinner party announces with pride that nothing at the table is fatally poisonous.

But for the neo-Catholic the bare minimum seems quite enough, and everything else is dispensable "externals." Thus, in *The Pope, the Council and the Mass*, we find the following defense of liturgical minimalism: "But Christ must always remain the proper object of our faith, and *never the externals of liturgical practice which admittedly have been confusing* over the past few years...."[119] It does not seem to have occurred to the authors that the "externals" of Catholic worship are what mediate faith in Christ and the Blessed Eucharist to the members of His Church,

---

[119]PCM, p. 25.

and that when the externals become "confusing" (as the authors admit), the faithful themselves become confused, and no longer believe as they once did. *Lex orandi, lex credendi.* The way one worships determines the way one believes.

Moreover, if so-called "externals" are dispensable, why even have a Mass liturgy at all? If the "essentials" of the Mass are just the bread, the wine and the words of the Consecration, why not have the priest simply confect the Sacrament, administer it, and send everyone home? Perhaps even this contains too much of the "external"; why not simply have laymen distribute previously consecrated Hosts to the faithful? (Come to think of it, this is one of the "legitimate options" the neo-Catholics defend.) And if indeed the neo-Catholic, faced with the logical conclusion of his thinking, grudgingly concedes that externals do count for something after all, how can he justify radical departures from "externals" that nourished the Catholic faith of nearly two millennia of worshipers? Why would anyone even want to?

As for the authors' false antithesis between Christ and "externals," this is something one would expect to encounter in Protestant theology, with its rejection of the incarnational aspect of divine worship. For the Catholic, the Incarnation of Our Lord has clear implications for divine worship. Although we must be careful not to be seduced by the false pleasures of this world, it is not a fundamentally evil world. God Himself lived in it, interacted with it, and used it to convey His Word. We, too, ought to use the created things of this world for the glory of God, to sanctify the created order in every area of endeavor—from philosophy to the arts, from literature to liturgy. For that reason, we wish to adorn our churches with beautiful things: statues, stained-glass windows, an impressive high altar, stunning vestments, and the sounds of Gregorian chant. For the same reason, we treat with great reverence the earthly vessels through which the things of God are transmitted to us.

The Protestant world, on the other hand, more or less ignores these implications of the Incarnation, and in general (there are indeed exceptions) holds in contempt the liturgical and incarnational aspects of Catholic life and worship. Luther reduced the sacraments to two, Baptism and the Eucharist, and denied the need for a sacramental priesthood to administer them. Other Protestants dispensed with the sacramental system altogether. The believer needed nothing other than his own, lonely faith. None of the things that he can encounter in this world are of any avail to him—not sacraments, not priests, not the Mass, and certainly not art, architecture, or sacred music. Where the Catholic wished to dignify these natural things by consecrating them to the service and worship of God, the Protestant rejects them as diabolical distractions from the worshipper's purely spiritual and individualistic path toward God.

As an incarnational religion, Catholicism should be the last to suffer gladly the dismantling of its traditional forms of worship. And yet that is what the new rite has done, as a whole and in its parts. We all know what a new-rite Mass looks like, with its denuded sanctuaries, embarrassing "hymns," and barren architecture. The Last Gospel, which was St. John's own meditation on the Incarnation, was removed. The wonderful texture of the liturgical year, with its various seasons, the Ember Days, and its countless traditions, has been flattened out into what the new rite refers to as "ordinary time," a designation we believe speaks for itself. One could go on and on. The neo-Catholic insistence that all that matters are the so-called "essentials"—e.g., the words of Consecration—reflects a profoundly sterile and anti-incarnational attitude that would have filled churchmen with contempt in every other generation but our own. It is, truly, a Protestant approach to worship, emphasizing the purely spiritual nature of worship and neglecting our created nature as human beings. The view that the sacred traditions of Catholic worship can safely be viewed as matters of indifference has absolutely no pedigree within the Catholic tradition.

Even when certain neo-Catholics admit that there is a liturgical crisis, they refuse to concede that anything dramatic should be done about it by Rome; their counsel, instead, is little more than to grin and bear it. One of the more preposterous neo-Catholic arguments is that we must accept the current condition of the liturgy as a penance, rather than as an outrage to be rectified in vindication of the infinite dignity of God. In *The Pope, the Council and the Mass,* after a discussion of the ruined state of the liturgy—for which the authors naturally blame everyone but Rome—we are offered this spiritual advice: "But in the face of all this, as in the face of other problems that will always confront us in this life, Christ still asks us for faith and still asks us *to take up His cross with regard to the liturgy too* if that is what is involved.... As a practical matter, this means following the Pope and the Council *even if it means suffering for us.*"[120] We have reached the very depths of the neo-Catholic idea when we find ourselves being asked to view the sacred liturgy as a cross to be borne, and the prescriptions of the Council and the conciliar Popes as good occasions for penitential suffering.

Referring to traditionalist organizations that do not view the wreck of the liturgy as a great opportunity for spiritual advancement, the author of the Pamphlet notes that "ironically, it is these very groups which turn out to be the most serious obstacle to true liturgical reform today, since many bishops, who would otherwise be open to more of the orthodox liturgical diversity which has always characterized the Church, are afraid of opening what they perceive to be a Pandora's Box."

We are to understand, then, that there are prelates out there who are sympathetic to a wider availability of the traditional Mass, but who balk at taking any major steps in this direction because a few small traditionalist publications are critical of the Vatican? In an article on his website, the author went further, arguing that if we traditionalists would only cease our polemics and approach the bishops "lovingly," then they would respond to the needs of their flock.

There is no point in reviewing the countless cases of good people humbly petitioning their bishops for a traditional Latin

---

[120]PCM, p. 159.

Mass under the terms of the papal indult, only to be ignored or actually scolded. Suffice it to say that the overwhelming majority of bishops are at best indifferent and at worst actively hostile to the kind of Catholic restoration of which the traditional Mass is so crucial a part. They will feel this way no matter what *The Remnant* or any other traditionalist newspaper says. Our own opinion is that there is room in the traditionalist movement for a number of different strategies—including both principled confrontation and gentle persuasion. At this stage our motto is: *whatever works.*

What we must not do, however, is deceive ourselves into thinking that all we need in order to win the bishops' favor is a fair hearing. Take the Most Rev. Thomas O'Brien, Bishop of Phoenix, Arizona. Not long ago O'Brien conferred the Sacrament of Confirmation at Phoenix's professional baseball stadium, where during the Mass people ate popcorn and hot dogs and sang hymns to the tune of "Take Me Out to the Ball Game." Nothing of "substance" has changed in the Diocese of Phoenix, eh?

Or perhaps we could approach the Most Rev. J. Kendrick Williams, Bishop of Lexington, Kentucky. A friend of ours met him once at her campus Mass, where each Sunday a different parishioner bakes the bread for Holy Communion. At the reception after Mass, His Excellency was clad in a polo shirt and khakis. But here, too, nothing "of substance" has changed. His Excellency is doubtless so concerned about his solemn duty of maintaining the traditions of the Church undefiled, surely all we need do is approach him lovingly and with sincerity, and he will grant us the spiritual nourishment we need. After all, he already allows the traditional Mass twice a month, at 5:00 p.m., and although the church bulletin contains no mention of its existence at the parish, surely we can understand His Excellency's circumspection when dealing with so subversive a thing as the traditional Roman rite.

We are living through the consequences of one of the most catastrophic decisions in the history of the Church. Popes and churchmen of centuries past had looked at the liturgy with a sense of awe, aware of how the Holy Ghost had guided its development over the centuries. They could scarcely have imagined laying their hands on it. Today, our shepherds have been infected by the hubris of modern man, which tells them that there is absolutely nothing, no matter how sacred, that is not subject to human modification. More than that, they have taken a theologically perfect and aesthetically stunning rite that even a civilized pagan could see was something extraordinary and stupendous, dumbed it down so that a second-grader would be insulted by the finished product, and actually called it an improvement.

Meanwhile, our neo-Catholic brethren either deny the problem altogether, or claim that nothing is wrong, because, after all, the formula of consecration is still present, so the "essentials" are untouched. "The Mass is the Mass!" they proclaim with smug certitude. Other neo-Catholics, being a bit more ambitious, long for the chance to have *their* committee revise the traditional rite, thus buying into the modernist premise that the product of over 1,500 years of tradition may rightly be subject to human manipulation—and by a committee, no less.[121]

It is true that some neo-Catholics will admit a "preference" for the traditional rite, but without admitting that this preference relates to anything "substantial." Nor do the neo-Catholics have any intention of laying the blame for this appalling act of vandalism where it obviously belongs. But it is only by facing the truth squarely that we can possibly hope to reverse the situation and begin the process of restoration. The liturgical minimalism of the neo-Catholics will get us nowhere.

---

[121]The neo-Catholic call for an "authentic" reform of the Mass, led by the *Adoremus* organization, is discussed in Chapter 12.

# Chapter 5

# Making a Virtue out of Doing Nothing

*"Not to oppose error is to approve it;*
*and not to defend truth is to suppress it."*
–Pope St. Felix III

Despite the fact that Rome itself cannot disclaim responsibility for the postconciliar debacle, it is also true that some of the most extreme devastation that has been visited upon the Church has taken place against the declared will of the Vatican, at the hands of people and organizations on the far left. That Rome has itself embraced a stunning series of novelties since the Council has been established. At the same time, the Pope and other top Vatican officials have spoken out in official statements about difficulties presented by, among other things, moral relativism, liberation theology, homosexual activism, and the secularization of Catholic universities. These are but a few areas in which our neo-Catholic brethren agree that the Church is undergoing serious trials at the hands of neo-modernists, clerical sexual predators and other subversives within her visible ranks.

Even here, however, it is difficult to come to agreement with them regarding the source of these problems or their possible solution. One reason for this is that the neo-Catholics cling to the most strained and contrived explanations for Rome's mystifying failure to defend the Church in a manner at all appropriate to present circumstances. Among other things, they argue that this failure to act against the Church's enemies—without and within—is not only not a sign of weakness, but is actually an act of genius.

Thus, when traditionalists raise objections to the Vatican's inaction, they are accused of lack of "trust in the Church" by their neo-Catholic critics. The basic neo-Catholic position is that Rome's ecclesial governance is a kind of zero-sum game in which it does not matter what Rome does or fails to do concerning threats to the Church's commonwealth, since it will all come out the same if we just sit back and let God handle it through His trusted ministers in the Vatican. "God is in charge of the Church," they solemnly assure us, as if God Himself wishes the Church to suffer gravely from a Pope's entirely preventable prudential errors. In the neo-Catholic view, the Pope cannot be blamed if he fails to do something—really *do* something—about the current crisis. For if Rome fails to act for decades, well, there was nothing Rome could have done anyway. But if Rome finally does act—say, by issuing some toothless document lamenting the crimes of homosexual predators in the clergy and stating that thousands of homosexuals really should not have been ordained to the priesthood over the past forty years—the neo-Catholic commentators will hail Rome's bold response. Then again, if no document is issued, Rome must have a reason for remaining mute. Under this peculiar standard of governance, one wonders how neo-Catholics could call any Pope, including the present Pope, great. Are they not all equally great, since (as the neo-Catholics would have it) the sum of all papal acts and omissions will always turn out to be zero in terms of relative harm or benefit to the Church, since "God is in charge"?

Yet when it comes to bishops other than the Bishop of Rome, the neo-Catholic has no difficulty recognizing that while "God is in charge of the Church" misgovernment by the Church's human element can cause grave harm that could have been prevented or rectified by good governance, and that the faithful have the right to be governed well. Thus, *The Wanderer*, for example, complains often and loudly about the malfeasance and nonfeasance of the world's bishops (and even cardinals outside the Vatican), while turning a blind eye toward Rome's general failure to rein in the heresy, scandal and subversion of the Church that *The Wanderer* itself has chronicled weekly for decades.

Let us first consider the matter of Freemasonry. In keeping with the unanimous testimony both of the preconciliar Popes and of the Masons themselves, traditionalists consider Freemasonry a serious threat to the welfare of the Church, and not a matter to be taken lightly. But for some reason it became fashionable in neo-Catholic circles in the decades following Vatican II to mock and to laugh at such concern. No such threat exists, they assure us. Thus Likoudis and Whitehead, in *The Pope, the Council and the Mass*, blithely dismiss the suggestion that any serious organized threat to the Church and the Mass could come from Masonic quarters. Their argument, advanced apparently in all seriousness, is that "[t]he Rock-man Peter is not at the mercy of conspirators of whatever persuasion."[122]

Evidently, the "Rock-man," in the person of Blessed Pius IX, lacked this neo-Catholic confidence in the Pope's magical power of immunity from conspiracies. Having failed to appease the Masonic forces of revolution in Italy by granting an ill-advised amnesty to political exiles and prisoners, the Pope fled for his life from the besieged Quirinal palace, disguised as a simple priest, after the Masons had stabbed his prime minister to death and fired into his anteroom, killing his secretary, Bishop Palma.[123] What followed was the temporary occupation of Rome, and St. Peter's itself, by Masonic militia, the destruction of the papal states, the total loss of the pope's temporal power, the erection of "democracy" in a "unified" Italy, and the ascendancy throughout Christendom of the very errors of liberalism that Bl. Pius IX—no longer a "political liberalist"— would later condemn in his *Syllabus*. The claim that the "Rock-man is not at the mercy of conspirators of whatever persuasion" rests upon nothing but ignorance (or willful disregard) of Church history.

[122]PCM, p. 146.
[123]Michael Ott, "Pope Pius IX," *Catholic Encyclopedia* (1908).

It is far from clear why any sensible Catholic would airily dismiss a concern that has inspired more papal documents than any other since the birth of Freemasonry in the eighteenth century.[124] Although enforcement has obviously been lax since the Council, a prohibition of Catholic membership in Masonic organizations is understood to form part of the 1983 Code of Canon Law (even if for some reason explicit reference to Masonry has been removed). Thus in 1983 the Congregation for the Doctrine of the Faith instructed the faithful as follows:

> Therefore, the Church's negative judgment in regard to Masonic associations remains unchanged, since their principles have always been considered irreconcilable with the doctrine of the Church, and, therefore, membership in them remains forbidden. The faithful who enroll in Masonic associations are in a state of grave sin and may not receive Holy Communion. It is not within the competence of local ecclesiastical authorities to give a judgment on the nature of Masonic associations which would imply a derogation from what has been decided above, and this in line with the declaration of this sacred congregation issued Feb. 17, 1981.

It is scarcely necessary to descend to the fever swamps of conspiracy theory to be concerned about an organization that over the years has repeatedly stated both its objectives and the means it intends to employ in order to meet them. Given the obstacle the Church poses to radicalism of all sorts, as well as her refusal to ratify all the demands of human ambition and desire, it would be amazing if there *weren't* an organized effort

---

[124]Freemasonry has been condemned in encyclicals and other papal pronouncements by Benedict XIV, Clement XIII, Pius VI, Pius VII, Leo XII, Gregory XVI, Leo XIII, St. Pius X, Pius XI, and Pius XII. The pertinent papal condemnations are catalogued and discussed in Paul A. Fisher's excellent study, *Their God Is the Devil* (American Research Foundation, 1991). Worthy of particular study is Pope Leo XIII's *Humanum Genus* (1884), in which His Holiness warned that the Freemasons "especially desire to assail the Church with irreconcilable hostility, and…they will never rest until they have destroyed whatever the Supreme Pontiffs have established for the sake of religion."

to harm and undermine Catholicism. Many Communists, remember, devoted their lives to what they considered the sacred cause of infiltrating secular organizations, even national governments, in order to weaken and destroy sources of resistance to the spread of the workers' paradise. (They also made some success of efforts to infiltrate the seminaries with their men—after all, the Church was a rather considerable obstacle to their plans.) Why is it so difficult for neo-Catholics to believe that the Freemasons, who have pledged themselves to destroy the Church—the institution they perceive as thwarting human desire through her commandments and inhibiting worldwide brotherhood by her exclusivist claims—might attempt to do the same to her?

According to the *Permanent Instruction of the Alta Vendita*, a Masonic document that both Blessed Pius IX and Leo XIII desired to be published, this was precisely how they aimed to proceed:

> Our final end is that of Voltaire and the French Revolution, the destruction forever of Catholicism and even of the Christian idea which, if left standing on the ruins of Rome, would be the resuscitation of Christianity later on.... The work which we have undertaken is not the work of a day, nor of a month, nor of a year. It may last many years.... Let the clergy march under your banner in the belief always that they march under the banner of the Apostolic Keys. You wish to cause the last vestige of tyranny and oppression to disappear? Lay your nets like Simon Bar-jona. Lay them in the depth of sacristies, seminaries, and convents.... You will bring yourselves as friends around the Apostolic Chair. You will have fished up a revolution in Tiara and Cope, marching with Cross and banner....

But since the admonitions and condemnations issued by an unbroken line of preconciliar Popes seem to hold so little weight with our interlocutors (see Chapter 11), let us consider a neglected postconciliar source: Bishop Rudolf Graber. Bishop Graber was an eminently respected and mainstream figure. Ordained in 1926, he served as a professor of Church history, theology, and mysticism at the Academy for Philosophy and Theology at Eichstatt, and was ordained Bishop of Regensburg by Pope John XXIII in 1962. Following Vatican II, he published a book in 1974 entitled *Athanasius and the Church of Our Times*, in which he compared the postconciliar crisis to the time of the Arian heresy in the fourth century. He also devoted considerable space to warning that we were seeing the realization of a long-standing Masonic program.

After quoting several enemies of the Church, including the Italian Communist party, as having observed a parallel between the French Revolution and Vatican II, Bishop Graber quotes one Pierre Virion as saying: "The great revolutions—and we are in the middle of one—do not come about spontaneously, but have their precursors, often only clandestinely, their prophets, sowing around themselves the seeds of revolt, and finally, their leaders and executors. They are preceded by the subterranean phase, which is followed by a second, that of incubation, before the eruption then takes place."[125] Discussing the Masonic vision of society and the world, Graber introduces the concept of *synarchy*: "What we are faced with here is the sum-total of the secret forces of all the 'orders' and schools which have joined together to set up an invisible world government. In the political sense, synarchy aims at the integration of all the financial and social forces which the world government, under socialist leadership naturally, has to support and promote. Catholicism, like all religions, would consequently be absorbed into a universal syncretism. Far from being suppressed, it would be integrated, a course which is already being steered in the principle of fellowship between clerics." We can only imagine what Bishop Graber would have thought had he lived to see such spectacles not simply between various Christian denominations, but among Buddhists, Sikhs, animists, and countless other "great religions," a development he could scarcely have imagined.[126]

---

[125]Bishop Rudolf Graber, *Athanasius and the Church of Our Times* (Hawthorne, CA: Christian Book Club of America, 1974), p. 32.
    [126]Ibid., p. 33.

Bishop Graber also cites ex-canon Roca, who had been made an honorary canon of the Church in 1869. Later excommunicated, canon Roca continued to preach revolution and "the coming of the divine synarchy under a Pope converted to scientific Christianity." Graber describes what Roca predicted: "The new church, which might not be able to retain anything of the Scholastic doctrine in the original form of the former church, will nevertheless receive consecration and canon jurisdiction from Rome.... [T]he divine cult, in the form directed by the liturgy, ceremonial, ritual and regulations of the Roman Church, will shortly undergo a transformation at an ecumenical council (!), which will restore it to the venerable simplicity of the golden age of the apostles in accordance with the dictates of conscience and modern civilization."[127] That scenario sounded a little familiar to Bishop Graber.

"The papacy will fall, it will die under the hallowed knife which the fathers of the last council will forge," Roca went on to say. "The papal Caesar is a Host crowned for the sacrifice" — by which he meant that the Pope, though not himself a Mason, would do their bidding. "Thus you will be proclaiming a revolution against the tiara and by the cope...a revolution which needs only a little spurring on to light the blaze of the four corners of the world."[128]

Such testimonies abound, says Graber. He quotes the Rosicrucian Dr. Rudolf Steiner on the revolution that he and his associates sought within the Church: "We need a council and a Pope to proclaim it." Paraphrasing a French heresiarch, Abbé Melinge (who used the pseudonym Dr. Alta), Graber points to the revolutionary program of "the replacement of the Roman faith by a 'pluri-confessional' pontificate, able to adapt to a polyvalent ecumenism, such as we are seeing established today in the intercelebration of priests and Protestant pastors." Melinge here refers to the actions of certain renegade priests, done without Vatican approval; today the Pope himself

---

[127]Marquis de Franquerie, L'infallibilité pontificale: Le syllabus et la crise actuelle de l'Eglise, undated manuscript, p. 48; cited in ibid., p. 35.

[128]Franquerie, L'infallibilité pontificale, p. 45; cited in ibid.

conducts joint services, including Vespers, with Protestant "bishops" — another development that would have shocked Graber.[129]

After quoting yet another Masonic admission, Bishop Graber concludes: "If in the face of these unambiguous admissions anyone still holds to the opinion that the events in the Church are marginal phenomena or transitional difficulties which will die down of their own accord in time, *he is simply beyond hope.* But all the greater is the responsibility of the leading men in the Church if they do not occupy themselves with these questions and imagine — cf. what was said above — that everything can be repaired by patching it up here and there."[130] Thus what we have on our hands, according to this widely respected churchman, is not a few reforms gone wrong, or the "unintended consequences" of a program instituted by men of good will (even if some men of good will may have consented to the new orientation through a catastrophic error in judgment), but a systematic, internally consistent attempt to evacuate the Church of her vigor and zeal, and indeed her very reason for existence. Once again, Graber was an eminent theologian and a respected and admired bishop — and here he warns about the machinations of a group the neo-Catholic sourcebook assures us is powerless to do the Church and the "Rock-man" any harm.[131]

---

[129]Graber, *Athanasius and the Church of Our Time*, p. 37.

[130]Ibid., pp. 70-71.

[131]The eminent Catholic laywoman Dr. Alice von Hildebrand recently wrote in *The Latin Mass* (Summer 2001) about the extensive documentation of both Communist and Masonic infiltration of the Church by Fr. Luigi Villa, of the Diocese of Brescia, Italy, who produced two books on the subject at the request of Padre Pio. She noted that every Italian bishop was given a copy of Fr. Villa's book *Paulo Sesto Beato?*, and that none has challenged any of his claims. Among other things, Villa claimed that Bishop Montini of Milan, the future Paul VI, had engaged in unauthorized secret correspondence with the Soviets while serving Pius XII as Undersecretary of State, and that a Vatican mole, Alghiero Tondi, S.J., a close advisor to Montini, identified to the Soviets the clandestine priests Pius XII had sent into Russia, after which the priests were arrested, tortured, executed or sent

Let us now proceed to the central contention of this chapter: namely, that the neo-Catholics have developed a systematic apologetic in favor of postconciliar papal inaction and timidity. It is well known that Blessed Pope John XXIII began the Second Vatican Council on a note of almost surreal optimism, happily proclaiming a suspension of the Church's condemnation of error: "Nowadays...the spouse of Christ prefers to make use of the medicine of mercy rather than the arms of severity. She considers that she meets the needs of the present day by demonstrating the validity of her teaching rather than by issuing condemnations.... We feel we must disagree with those prophets of gloom, who are always forecasting disaster, as though the end of the world was at hand."[132] Those sentiments became a kind of template for the next forty years, and we have seen the results of the new attitude.

The Pamphlet gamely defends Pope John's unfounded optimism, even today: "Yes, it is true that Pope John XXIII openly rebuked the joyless 'prophets of doom' who were too often unbalanced in their apocalyptic tractarian approach to the faith and modern world, but this was in the interests [sic] of the balance of the Church's kerygma." A balance of the Church's kerygma? What does this mean? Is there a kerygma-meter the Pope must consult to ensure that the Church's teaching contains equal measures of optimism and pessimism, regardless of how bad the condition of the world may be in a given era? Must the Church say (to borrow Jeremiah's lament) peace, peace, when there is no peace?[133]

This is by no means the position only of the Pamphlet's author, but is fairly standard fare within neo-Catholic circles.

---

to the gulag. In typical neo-Catholic fashion, historian Warren Carroll immediately attacked Mrs. von Hildebrand's veracity on the EWTN website, while providing no evidence that Mrs. von Hildebrand (or Fr. Villa) was unworthy of belief. Only after a protest by Mrs. von Hildebrand were Carroll's baseless remarks removed from the website.

[132]*Council Daybook*, National Catholic Welfare Conference, Washington, D.C., vol. 1, pp. 25, 27.

[133]Jeremiah 6:14.

Optimism about the compatibility of the values of modernity with those of the Church is routinely accepted as if it were dogmatic teaching—yet another reflection of the neo-Catholic inability (or refusal) to distinguish the opinions of particular churchmen from universally binding teaching.

Yet even the neo-Catholics cannot be completely unaware that the foremost "prophets of doom" in the twentieth century were *the preconciliar Popes*. Any reasonably diligent student of their teaching can easily find such statements as these:

**St. Pius X:**

We felt a sort of terror considering the disastrous conditions of humanity at the present hour. Can we ignore such a profound and grave evil, which at this moment much more than in the past is working away at its very marrow and leading it to its ruin?... Truly whoever ponders these things *must necessarily and firmly fear* whether such a perversion of minds is not the sign of announcing, and the beginning of the last times...*[E Supremi]*.

**Pius XI:**

With God and Jesus Christ excluded from political life, with authority derived not from God but from man,...the chief reason of the distinction between ruler and subject has been eliminated.  The result is that society is *tottering to its ruin* because it no longer has a secure and solid foundation *[Quas Primas]*.

**Pius XII** (*after* the end of WWII):

We are overwhelmed with sadness and anguish, seeing that the wickedness of perverse men has reached a degree of impiety that is *unbelievable and absolutely unknown in other times* [Letter of February 11, 1949].

Venerable brethren, you are well aware that almost the whole human race is today allowing itself to be driven into two opposing camps, for Christ or against Christ. *The human race is involved today in a supreme crisis,* which will issue in its salvation by Christ, or in its destruction [*Evangeli Praecones*, 1950].

In view of the repeated admonitions of his own immediate predecessors, what can be said about Pope John's optimism—especially when one considers that these Petrine "prophets of doom" issued their warnings about the incomparably bad state of the world *before* the worldwide legalization of abortion? The most succinct assessment belongs to Romano Amerio: "On this point, papal foresight indisputably failed."[134]

But not according to the Pamphlet. Not only does its author doggedly defend Pope John's optimism, but he also lauds it as "a stroke of psychological genius—the genius of the Holy Spirit to the eyes of faith." As the Pamphlet explains, the Pope's apparent folly was really a clever gambit of *reverse psychology*:

> Few expected such talk in such an hour...to pronounce on such optimistic things at just such a time, when the Soviet Union was exporting its atheistic opiate all over the globe.... The Communists would have preferred good old-fashioned anathemas, which would be easy enough for them to mock!

Here at least the Pamphlet delivers a somewhat novel observation. Unfortunately, it lacks any connection with reality. Did the author read any books or primary source material that lends support to this unheard-of contention? Or is this just another application of the neo-Catholic principle that since the Pope is the Vicar of Christ, his acts and omissions receive *a priori* confirmation as strokes of genius, regardless of what common sense may say to the contrary?

Common sense tells us that the Communists certainly would not have preferred to be anathematized by the Second Vatican Council, and history bears this out. Only weeks before the Council, the Vatican-Moscow agreement was negotiated in Metz, France, between Cardinal Tisserant and Orthodox Metropolitan Nikodim (head of the KGB-controlled Russian

---

[134]Amerio, *Iota Unum*, p. 82.

Orthodox Church). The very object of the agreement, whose existence is an historical fact confirmed by Msgr. Roche, Tisserant's personal secretary, was to bind the Council *not* to issue anathemas or condemnations against Communism.[135] In exchange, Pope John would be granted his fond wish that two Orthodox observers—which is to say, KGB agents in black robes—would come to attend the Council. The bargain was made, the observers came, and any Council Father who stood up to denounce Communism was told politely by Tisserant to sit down and shut up. Meanwhile, the written intervention by Archbishop Lefebvre and 450 other Council Fathers, calling for a conciliar treatment of Communism in line with the solemn condemnations of Pius XI and Pius XII, was deliberately withheld and left in the desk drawer of the Secretary for the Joint Commission that was drafting the Constitution on the Church in "the Modern World," *Gaudium et Spes*.[136]

The Pamphlet's "stroke of genius" theory thus encounters a major problem: Why would Nikodim have negotiated with the Vatican to *prevent* any condemnation of Communism by the Council if the Russians would have *preferred* condemnations to the Council's warm invitation to dialogue?

So the Council that met to discuss the problems of "the modern world" preposterously failed to mention the biggest problem of all: Communism, the worst form of systematized evil in human history, which was devouring Catholics by the millions at the very moment the Council began. The word "Communism" does not appear even once in the *Acta* of the Council.

---

[135]*Itinéraires*, no. 285, p. 152; cited in ibid., p. 76 n. 6.

[136]The entire intrigue is detailed by Wiltgen, *The Rhine Flows into the Tiber*, pp. 274-77. Wiltgen was an eyewitness to the furor over the "disappearance" of the written intervention of the 450 Council Fathers against Communism, hand-delivered to the Council's General Secretariat by Archbishop Lefebvre. Reception of the document was at first denied but then admitted. In any event, it was never allowed to reach the Council floor.

As the Pamphlet assures us, however, everything surrounding the Council was divinely inspired — not only the refusal to condemn Communism, but also Pope John's decision to toss its classically formulated, orthodox preparatory schemas into the garbage after the Council began, leaving the Council with no written agenda. Another stroke of genius, presumably, which anyone with the "eyes of faith" can see.

Now let us return to serious history. The Communists were delighted with the Council, thanks to the Vatican-Moscow Agreement. For them the Council was a dream come true. As the Italian Communist Party declared at its 11th Party Congress in 1964: "The extraordinary 'awakening' of the Council, which is rightly compared with the Estates General of 1789, has shown the whole world that the old politico-religious Bastille is shaken to its foundations."[137] And who could forget the unsolicited advice to Paul VI in *L'Unita*, the official publication of the Italian Communist Party, regarding Archbishop Marcel Lefebvre, a leader of traditionalist opposition to the conciliar liberals: "Be conscious of the danger that Lefebvre represents. And continue the magnificent movement of approach begun with the ecumenism of Vatican II."[138]

Extending the argument for his novel theory to the present day, the Pamphlet's author asserts that this "stroke of genius" on the part of John XXIII "could not be fully appreciated, perhaps, until Pope John Paul II and the fall of Communism which he helped to bring about, and which left the Church still standing and proclaiming her saving message to the nations!" But wasn't it supposed to be John Paul II's return to the Church's *condemnation* of Communism (within the rhetorical limits dictated by Cardinal Casaroli's pernicious *Ostpolitik*) that brought about the alleged fall of Communism, first in Poland and then in the rest of the former Soviet Union? Then there was

---

[137]Graber, *Athanasius and the Church of Our Time*, p. 64.

[138]Archbishop Marcel Lefebvre, *They Have Uncrowned Him* (Kansas City, MO: Angelus Press, 1988), p. 229. Here Lefebvre also notes that the Communist newspaper *Izvestia* demanded that Paul VI condemn him and his seminary at Ecône.

Reagan's famous "evil empire" and "Mr. Gorbachev, tear down this wall!" Not much in the way of "dialogue" there.

In any event, the Pamphlet's suggestion that the Church is "still standing" and proclaiming her message today simply because John XXIII agreed that the Council would *say nothing* and *do nothing* about Communism is — how shall we put this? — a bit extravagant. What is more, it should be no surprise to anyone that the "fall of Communism" is looking more and more like a very clever reorganization: The former Soviet Union continues to be governed by a collection of "ex-Communists" and recycled KGB agents. Since the "fall of Communism," the abortion rate has skyrocketed throughout Eastern Europe, where there are now more than two abortions for every live birth in Russia and one abortion per live birth in the rest of the region.[139] The Russian population is decreasing at the rate of 2,500 people per day, life expectancy is down, and pornography, the Russian mob and alcoholism are ravaging what is left of Russian society, causing many to clamor for the return of full-blown Communism. Vladimir Putin has systematically shut down the independent mass media[140] and is re-centralizing Moscow's authority over the former Soviet Union, which apparently is emerging from the political equivalent of Chapter 11: the same entity with a new name. No less a figure than Solzhenitsyn himself has declared that "Russian democracy is a myth," and that Russia's demographic trends are "frightening."[141] Even the Russian Orthodox Patriarch, Alexy II, has decried the spiritual degeneration of Russian society into occultism, satanism and assorted non-Christian sects since Communism's "fall."[142]

---

[139]Zenit, September 24, 1999.

[140]As reported by the London Times online edition of January 12, 2002: "Russia's last independent television station was closed yesterday, leaving the country's entire broadcast media under Kremlin control."

[141]NewsMax.com, March 21, 2000.

[142]CWNews.com, December 12, 1998.

As for the position of the Catholic Church in Russia, in 1997 the Communist-dominated Russian parliament enacted, and Boris Yeltsin signed into law, a bill on "freedom of conscience" that severely restricts the right of the Church even to exist in Russia without official permission, and the law prohibits any effort to proselytize the Orthodox. Besides which, as we have noted, the Vatican's representative, Cardinal Cassidy, agreed in the 1993 Balamand Statement that the return of the Orthodox to the Catholic Church was "outdated ecclesiology."[143] So much for Pius XII, all of his predecessors since the Greek Schism, and Our Lady of Fatima. Not surprisingly, despite the "fall" of Communism there are very few conversions to the Faith in the "former Soviet Union," where Muslims outnumber Catholics by at least 10 to 1.

In short, there is no sign of the conversion of Russia promised by Our Lady of Fatima if Russia were consecrated to her Immaculate Heart. There is no sign that Russia will even rise to the level of a morally decadent consumerist-democracy like the United States, the home of partial-birth abortion. As the neo-Catholics almost unanimously insist, however, we can be certain that Russia is converting because the Vatican informed us on June 26, 2000, that everything predicted in the Third Secret had already come to pass, and that (per Msgr. Bertone) the Consecration of Russia to the Immaculate Heart of Mary must no longer be requested—by anyone. As for the triumph of the Immaculate Heart prophesied at Fatima, Cardinal Ratzinger tells us in his commentary on the Message of Fatima that this triumph occurred when Mary agreed to be the Mother of God. That is, the triumph of the Immaculate Heart took place 2,000 years ago.[144] (In which case, why did Our Lady of Fatima say in 1917: "*In the end*, my Immaculate Heart *will* triumph?")

---

[143]Balamand Statement (1993), nn. 22, 30.

[144]As Ratzinger wrote in the Commentary: "I would like finally to mention another key expression of the 'secret' which has become justly famous: 'my Immaculate Heart will triumph.' What does this mean? The Heart open to God, purified by contemplation of God, is stronger than guns and weapons of every kind. The *fiat* of Mary, the word of

In the neo-Catholic scheme of things, we're not really supposed to discuss any of this—not even after the events of "9/11," which should make anyone uncomfortable with the Vatican's claim that the Message of Fatima is over and done with. The unparalleled evil observed by the preconciliar popes has only intensified. There is no peace, and the holocaust of abortion burns ever higher in the sight of God. Meanwhile, overt Communism still enslaves one-third of the world's population, while in Red China the Catholic Church endures persecution worthy of the Stalinist era, as the American bishops (claiming *sub rosa* Vatican approval) provide seminary training for future priests of the schismatic Catholic Patriotic Association, the pro-abortion "Catholic" church of the Chinese Communist regime.[145]

But just wait, the Pamphlet's author would say. Pope John's stroke of genius has not yet been manifested in all its plenitude. Any decade now we will understand completely how the Council's silence on Communism and its abandonment of condemnations saved the Church and the world.

But what do the neo-Catholics have to say about the Vatican's present failure to take any truly decisive action against the *internal* enemies of the Church? No one is being disciplined today, they tell us, because the Vatican is deftly avoiding the emergence of a schism, which an excessive application of discipline would surely bring about. In response to this claim

---

her heart, has changed the history of the world, because it brought the Savior into the world—because, thanks to her *Yes*, God could become man in our world and remain so for all time." Notice that the Cardinal removed the key words *"In the end"* from Our Lady's prophesy, thus eliminating any need to discuss the four future events she predicted: the triumph of her Immaculate Heart, the consecration of Russia, Russia's consequent conversion, and a period of peace for mankind. By judicious editing of Our Lady's words, four future events were transformed into one event 2,000 years ago, thus making the Fatima prophecy utterly pointless.

[145]See www.cardinalkungfoundation.org for the many details of the Vatican's inaction toward the Red Chinese regime's persecution of the Catholic Church.

(which is always advanced with no real evidence to support it), we ask the following: If the Pope is really so afraid of a schism that he will not impose strict discipline on anyone, then why did he immediately impose strict discipline and *personally declare* a schism as to Archbishop Marcel Lefebvre and the bishops he consecrated in 1988? Apparently, the alleged fear of schism extends only to disobedient *liberals*. (It has to be said, however, that the declaration of the Lefebvre "schism" is clearly a decision the Pope regrets, as witnessed by his recent insistence on reconciling the Society of St. Pius X by every means possible.)

While the neo-Catholics ponder this gaping hole in their theory, let us pose a related question: If the Pope is serious about reforming the Church, why does he appoint so many liberals to the highest positions of authority? Why, for example, did he elevate to the rank of cardinal Bishop Walter Kasper, who (as we show in Chapter 8) openly declares that Vatican II "abandoned" the teaching of the preconciliar Magisterium that Christian unity requires the conversion of Protestants and their return to the Catholic Church? Why did he appoint this man as head of the very Pontifical Council that is supposed to deal with the matter of Christian unity? Or, as another example, why did His Holiness create as a cardinal Bishop Karl Lehmann, who dissented from the ban on administering the sacraments to divorced and remarried "couples," and led the German hierarchy in its longstanding resistance to the Pope's rather timid effort to order the German bishops to cease issuing counseling certificates that women were using to obtain abortions under German law?[146]

---

[146]According to *The Tablet* (April 28, 2001), the Vatican Secretary of State, Angelo Sodano, "had originally supported Lehmann's position.... The question was whether the Church was colluding in abortion by issuing certificates confirming that pregnant women in distress had been given counselling, if these were then used to secure a termination. It had been Sodano's opinion that such matters could be decided by the local bishops' conferences, but eventually he was forced to sign a decree together with Ratzinger which compelled the German Catholic bishops to pull out...."

At the very moment in history when the Church desperately needs strong-willed and fiercely Catholic prelates, the neo-Catholics are inexplicably *lowering* their expectations of churchmen. In a recent mailing, *Crisis* magazine, apparently in all seriousness, advertised an upcoming symposium on the late John Cardinal O'Connor with these words: "Catholic leaders from around the country share their favorite stories and reminiscences about this wonderful man who is *easily* one of the greatest leaders in 2,000 years of Church history!" (emphasis theirs). This is the problem. Certainly, O'Connor was better than, say, Mahony or Gumbleton; yet he was still a liberal by any historical measure of the Church militant. For example, the same Cardinal O'Connor gave his *blessing* on national television to a young man who left the Catholic Church and converted to Judaism.[147] Cardinal O'Connor also co-authored a book (*His Eminence and Hizzoner*) with New York's former mayor, Edward Koch, one of the nation's leading proponents of abortion on demand and "gay rights." The Cardinal's public hobnobbing with pro-abortion politicians such as Koch and Mario Cuomo was notorious. At one point even *The Wanderer* ran a half-page ad publicly calling the Cardinal to account for giving scandal to the Church. The very fact that today certain neo-Catholics will heap praise upon a prince of the Church whose behavior would have caused international outrage forty years ago is a sobering indication of the depths to which we have sunk.

To this the neo-Catholics will reply that in recent years the tide has been turning with more "conservative" papal appointments. They cite the appointment of the likes of Cardinal Francis George, an excellent example of a churchman who, by the neo-Catholics' absurdly low standards, is now considered downright heroic. The "ultra-conservative" Cardinal George was recently seen in a Chicago-area mosque, attending the Muslim celebration of the end of Ramadan, together with a group of priests and nuns from his Archdiocese. The news

---

[147]John Vennari, "Cardinal O'Connor Blesses Apostasy," *Catholic Family News*, May 1999, pp. 3, 22. The Cardinal's verbatim statement on the television show *Nightline* is quoted at footnote 246.

account noted that George was "the first Chicago archbishop to attend such an event," and that "as the last verses of the Imam Senad Agic's melodious prayer resonated under the white and gold dome...clerics and lay people of both faiths bowed their heads."[148] On another occasion, this "ultra-conservative" was photographed for the *Chicago Tribune* as he held hands with a Muslim cleric and a Baptist minister during an "interfaith service" at "the Progressive Baptist Church"[149] — the sort of conduct expressly forbidden as gravely sinful under the preconciliar code of canon law.[150]

Then there is that other "ultra-conservative" elevated by the Pope: New York's Cardinal Edward Egan. During a "Mass of Supplication" in St. Patrick's Cathedral following the terrorist attacks of September 11, 2001, traditional Catholics were horrified to watch Egan leave the sanctuary and administer hugs to the Mayor of New York City, Rudolph Giuliani, and

---

[148]"George Breaks Fast with Muslims," *Chicago Tribune,* January 21, 1998, Section 2, p. 3.

[149]*Chicago Tribune,* March 12, 1998, Metro Chicago Section, p. 1.

[150]Canon 1258: "It is forbidden to actively participate in the worship of non-Catholics" *(communicatio in sacris)* ; see also Canon 2316: "One who cooperates *communicatio in sacris* contrary to the provision of Canon 1258 is suspected of heresy." It should be noted that the 1949 Instruction of the Holy Office on "the ecumenical movement" strictly forbade "any communication whatsoever in worship" with Protestants at mixed theological congresses permitted under strict conditions (including the requirement that Protestants be presented with "the teaching of the Encyclicals of the Roman Pontiffs on the return of the dissidents to the Church"). AAS 42-142. The Instruction did allow such congresses to begin and end with an Our Father or "some prayer approved by the Catholic Church" — a far cry from "interfaith prayer services" in Baptist temples, or the joint Vespers services and other liturgies the Pope himself has conducted with Protestant ministers in St. Peter's Basilica.

We do not intend to suggest that the cited canons are *de fide* teachings of the Church. Nevertheless, because of the obvious dangers to the faith of Catholics, the Church constantly forbade any form of *communicatio in sacris* with non-Catholics until 1983. The results of abandoning that prohibition speak for themselves.

New York State's Governor, George Pataki, both of them militantly pro-abortion politicians who are directly complicit in the mass murder of children in the womb, not to mention the advancement of "gay rights" in New York. The "Mass of Supplication" — which contained no reference to making reparation for sin — was interrupted repeatedly for standing ovations by the interfaith congregation.[151] This thoroughly Americanized and neutralized prelate is what passes for a rock of orthodoxy in the current ecclesial climate.

It is safe to say, using Cardinal Ottaviani as a benchmark, that in the current college of cardinals, appointed almost entirely by John Paul II, *there is not a single true conservative.* Cardinal Alfons Stickler is the lone exception, though he lost his right to vote in the conclave when he turned 80 — the casualty of yet another senseless postconciliar innovation.[152]

Sometimes, though, neo-Catholics will argue that the Pope doesn't really have much influence over the appointment of bishops. Here we see how the neo-Catholic, when pressed to confront the reality of Rome's complicity in the debacle, will retreat into an impenetrable shell of non-falsifiable excuses for papal acts and omissions. Everyone and everything is blamed for the condition of the Church except the one man ordained by God to serve as the Church's very center of unity and discipline.

---

[151]The entire spectacle was broadcast live on Fox News network.

[152]The "80 and out" rule was imposed by Paul VI in an obvious effort to keep cardinals with a "preconciliar" outlook from voting in the next conclave. In 1999, John Paul II reaffirmed the new rule with the curious explanation that "the reason for this provision is the desire not to add to the weight of such a venerable age the further burden of choosing the one who has to lead Christ's flock" (Reuters, May 15, 1999). Since a cardinal can *be* the Pope at age 80, it is absurd to argue that he is too old to *vote* for the Pope — all the more absurd in view of John Paul II's constant defense of "human rights." Why should a cardinal's *age* deprive him of the right to cast a vote in a papal conclave, especially given the wisdom that comes with age? Here again we see the tacit principle of the postconciliar revolution at work: all innovations must be defended, whether or not the defense is just or logical.

At any rate, surely the Pope has consciously and deliberately chosen at least *some* of the prelates who have given us the postconciliar debacle.

If Catholics at large become complacent about the papacy because its present occupant upholds Catholic moral teaching and the natural law—which, really, constitutes just about the least one should expect from the Supreme Pontiff of the Roman Catholic Church—it becomes very easy to conclude that the problems in the Church must be beyond Rome's control. But if we are to evaluate our present situation accurately and dispassionately, we need always keep in mind the greatness of the Popes with which the Church was blessed in the nineteenth and twentieth centuries, through Pius XII, and we need also to be realistic and honest in our assessment of the current Pontiff. John Paul, for one thing, really believes that we are witnessing a "new springtime" of Christianity. Doubtless our critics can dig up an old quotation from 1980 or 1981 in which the Pope deplores the confusion reigning within the Church, but such isolated statements are swamped by his almost infinitely more numerous rhapsodies about the fruits of the Council. He has traveled the world ceaselessly and has nary a criticism of the virtually institutionalized profanations of the liturgy to be found everywhere, in many of which he participates himself. The bulldozing of beautiful sanctuaries has caused him no visible anguish.

Meanwhile, however, the Pope's Ecclesia Dei Commission, against the will of the overwhelming majority of the priests of the traditionalist Fraternity of St. Peter, recently suspended the Fraternity's election of its own superior, imposed Fr. Arnaud Devillers as superior general in place of the deposed Fr. Josef Bisig, and ordered the removal of two perfectly orthodox rectors at the Fraternity's two seminaries, for no other reason than "to avoid and combat a certain spirit of rebellion against the present-day Church"—meaning insufficient docility toward the postconciliar novelties.[153] Cardinal Castrillón, who heads the Commission, told the Fraternity: "I promise that the papal

---

[153]Letter to the Priestly Fraternity of St. Peter, June 29, 2000.

Commission will be more present, from now on, in the seminaries and the other houses of the Fraternity, and will watch attentively for their good behavior. It may also happen that the Ecclesia Dei Commission will intervene again, should it become necessary."[154]

Did the Vatican "watch attentively" over the past forty years for "good behavior" at all the Novus Ordo seminaries that were becoming infested with homosexuals, whose criminal acts are, as we write, currently bringing ruin and disgrace to diocese after diocese throughout the world? Will the Jesuits and the Dominicans, whose orders have become sewers of heresy and scandal bearing absolutely no resemblance to their past or indeed anything related to Catholic tradition at all, also be subject to this kind of close Vatican supervision during John Paul's pontificate? To ask these questions is to answer them.

While we have no wish to delve into the details of the exploding homosexual priest scandal that Catholic dioceses have been attempting to hide for decades, we would like to hear the neo-Catholic excuse for why the same Vatican apparatus that "watches attentively" over traditionalist orders and seminaries to suppress "a certain spirit of rebellion" against various recent novelties in the Church, has done virtually nothing about the mountain of complaints and reports it has received from the faithful about sexual predators in the Novus Ordo. After forty years of the Vatican's total failure to enforce its own 1961 instruction that homosexuals should not be ordained or admitted to the seminary,[155] the homosexual infiltration of the hierarchy is now international in scope, with criminal convictions, lawsuits and payouts not only in the United States and America, but also in Austria, France, England, Ireland,

---

[154]Ibid.

[155]As reported by Catholic News Service, March 6, 2002, the Vatican instruction provided that "Those affected by the perverse inclination to homosexuality or pederasty should be excluded from religious vows and ordination."

Spain and even Poland.[156] With at least 80 priests having been handed over to the police in the Archdiocese of Boston alone in 2002, we have surely seen only the tip of a massive iceberg.[157] As even *The Wanderer* has reported, homosexual infiltration of the Catholic clergy has become so widespread that "straight" priests who honor their vows are being subjected to harassment and retaliation for speaking out against the "gay subculture" in the Church.[158] The same *Wanderer* piece notes that papal spokesman Joaquin Navarro-Valls has publicly questioned the validity of the ordinations of homosexuals—a statement with profound implications for the entire Church.   The problem of homosexuality in the priesthood has been something of an open secret in the years since Vatican II, and if its practitioners' ordinations may actually be invalid, one can scarcely contemplate the number of invalid Masses that have been offered through the decades as a result.  The procedural norms of "collegiality"—a term which all too often serves as sophisticated nomenclature for a simple refusal to discipline errant bishops—appear to have trumped any concern about this institutionalized sacrilege.

Then, too, there is the commonplace sexual abuse of women in Africa by priests who seem to regard their vows of celibacy as optional. Concerning this scandal, Reuters reported: "The Vatican is monitoring the situation...but *no direct action has been taken.*"[159] Vatican spokesmen Fr. Bernardo Cervellera (director of Fides, the Vatican's missionary news service) offered the astounding excuse that "the problem was limited to sub-Saharan

---

[156]Archbishop Juliusz Paetz of Poznan, Poland is under investigation by the Vatican after numerous priests complained for years that he was sexually exploiting them. See report by *Associated Press*, March 8, 2002.

[157]Newsday.com, March 7, 2002. A series of American dioceses has followed suit, disgorging lists of credibly accused sexual predators after hiding the names for decades. See, e.g., "Church Scandals Turn Into Avalanche," *Sun Sentinel*, March 10, 2002.

[158]Paul Likoudis, "Debates Rage Over Homosexuals in the Priesthood," *The Wanderer*, March 14, 2002.

[159]Reuters, March 20, 2001.

Africa and related to negative cultural views there of women and of the value of celibacy...." The *value* of celibacy? What about the priestly *vow* of celibacy before God? Fr. Cervellera added: "These are not cases of 'psychopathic' violence against women, but instead a 'cultural way of living' that is common throughout the region...."[160] We shall let that answer speak for itself.

We recall the neo-Catholic argument that there must be some brilliant strategy behind Rome's inaction in the face of the worldwide collapse of the Faith and the spread of heresy and scandal throughout the seminaries and the religious orders. Well, the neo-Catholics are going to have to think up some new explanation for all the disorder, because we have now seen that Rome *is* prepared to intervene and use its authority quite immediately — but only against Roman Catholic traditionalists. And this is the regime Catholics are supposed to applaud?

It is not as if we were without numerous historical examples of brave Popes who used all the force at their disposal to vindicate traditional Catholicism. Consider the position of Pope St. Gregory VII (1073-85): The Church was in desperate need of reform in his day. Simony was rampant and clerical celibacy had been all but abandoned. When Gregory moved to reinstate Church tradition, he was met with demonstrations of priests across Europe threatening to resist the Pope forever rather than relinquish their wives. The overwhelming majority of German bishops opposed him. But he did not back down. In fact, he became more aggressive still, going so far as to excommunicate Henry IV. It occurred to him that the reason he was having such difficulty implementing his reform program was that so much of the practical authority of naming and investing bishops had passed into the hands of the state. If he were to have any hope of achieving real reform, he had to reclaim the Holy See's critical prerogative of naming bishops. For centuries, the bishops' literacy and administrative talent had been tapped by kings and the emperor to perform temporal duties around the realm. Sympathetic bishops were considered essential to the lay

---

[160]CNN, March 21, 2001.

monarch, not only for what they could do in the area of administration, but also for serving to check upstart nobles who were always seeking to undermine the king's position. The suggestion that the power to invest such bishops ought to be taken from him struck Henry IV as the height of insanity. Gregory knew he faced opposition of a kind that modern Popes can scarcely imagine. Yet he did what was right, and although he did not live to see ultimate victory, which came a generation later, his fearlessness vastly increased the prestige of the papacy and set the Church on the road to the independence she needed to carry out her supernatural mission.

The Pamphlet devotes considerable space to a quite illegitimate appeal to the precedent of the Great Western Schism of the fourteenth and fifteenth centuries. As the argument goes, the Western Schism is an example of the unintended damage that can be done when a Pope is too vigorous in pressing the cause of reform. This is supposed to make us feel impertinent for so much as suggesting that papal vigor might be the recipe for the current crisis. But even a passing examination of the Western Schism reveals nothing of the kind.

For a variety of reasons, during the period from 1305-1377, the papacy resided not in Rome but in Avignon. Shortly after returning the papacy to Rome, Pope Gregory XI died. During the Avignon papacy, naturally, the French presence within the sacred college had grown enormously, consisting now of ninety Frenchmen, fourteen Italians, five Spaniards, and one Englishman. When the conclave to elect a successor to Gregory XI was summoned, the assembled cardinals deliberated amid the sounds of uproar and tumult outside. The local population wanted some kind of assurance that the papacy would not once again move to Avignon; what they wanted, therefore, was a Roman Pope, or at the very least an Italian. At one point, part of the mob managed to break into the conclave itself and demand that a Roman be elected. The conclave was also interrupted more than once by rocks being thrown through the windows and the sound of axes striking the doors.

At last Bartholomew Prignani (an Italian, though not a Roman) was elected, taking the name Urban VI. He moved vigorously against corruption and worldliness among churchmen—*as had other Popes in the past, without incident.* Urban, however, upon assuming the papal office, began acting in an extremely peculiar and belligerent way, quite uncharacteristic of the temperate Prignani the cardinals had known. We have testimony to the effect that he began publicly insulting his cardinals, even striking one. Cardinals appearing before him on standard Church business were violently denounced. Significantly, he told the French cardinals that he intended to add so many Italians to the sacred college that French influence would dwindle to nothingness—doubtless alarming to a French cardinalate that had grown accustomed to its newfound dominance. But he so alienated his cardinals through his abusive behavior that *every single one of them,* Frenchman and non-Frenchman alike, assembled in a second conclave to elect a new Pope. In fact, it was seriously suggested not only by cardinals at the time, but even today by quite a broad range of historians, that his unexpected elevation to the papacy had rendered Prignani mentally unbalanced, even insane.

It was in this context that we must understand the cardinals' decision to declare the original election—which had taken place under duress—nullified and to elect a new Pope, Clement VII. As historian Msgr. Philip Hughes notes: "Had Urban shown ordinary tact and prudence, there would never—it seems certain—have been the second conclave and the election of 1378."[161] If the Western Schism had really been a simple case of a vigorous pro-reform party leading to the walkout of a party of corruption, then why didn't all the saints favor the Roman (that is, pro-reform, anti-corruption) line of Popes? Are we going to suggest that some saints favored worldliness and corruption, the accusation Urban VI hurled at the cardinals? St. Catherine of Siena, St. Catherine of Sweden, Blessed Peter of Aragon, and Blessed Ursulina of Parma sided with Urban, it is true, but St. Vincent Ferrer, Blessed Peter of Luxemburg, and St. Colette all sided with Clement. The Western Schism was an

---

[161]Hughes, *A History of the Church,* vol. 3, p. 234.

extraordinarily complex event in which a variety of factors unique to that episode played a part—of which French-Italian rivalry within the episcopate, the apparent mental imbalance of Urban VI, and the unusual circumstances of the first conclave are but a few.  It obviously cannot be used to support a sweeping generalization about the alleged dangers of papal vigor—especially since papal vigor was quite successful when pursued by the non-insane St. Gregory VII and St. Pius X, to name but two.

Indeed the example of Pope St. Pius X has prompted two mutually exclusive neo-Catholic responses (sometimes, as in the case of the Pamphlet, offered by the same person): either that ecclesiastical discipline wasn't really so tough in the old days, after all, or that the strict discipline of the old days would be inappropriate to present circumstances.

Let us now consider the first of these arguments: the Pamphlet's repeated claim that even St. Pius X, after all, did not excommunicate wave upon wave of Modernists. As the Pamphlet's author was advised by one of us even before he advanced this argument, there were, naturally, disciplinary measures short of excommunication to which the Pope could and did have recourse. A recent history notes that, contrary to the Pamphlet's suggestion, "[t]he disciplinary regime laid down in the final section of *Pascendi*—nearly 20 percent of the whole text—was extremely detailed and rigorous."[162] Thus, in *Pascendi Dominici Gregis*, St. Pius X's encyclical against Modernism, the Pope commands that *vigilance committees* be established in every diocese to guard against the spread of Modernism, and that in the year following the issuance of the encyclical, and every three years thereafter, every bishop report to Rome on the progress of his efforts to eliminate this heresy. Pius X's instructions to the bishops in *Pascendi* deserve to be quoted at unusual length:

> But of what avail, Venerable Brethren, will be all Our commands and prescriptions if they be not dutifully and

---

[162]Marvin R. O'Connell, *John Ireland and the American Catholic Church* (St. Paul, MN: Minnesota Historical Society Press, 1988), p. 347.

firmly carried out? In order that this may be done it has seemed expedient to us to extend to all dioceses the regulations which the Bishops of Umbria, with great wisdom, laid down for theirs many years ago. "In order," they say, "to extirpate the errors already propagated and to prevent their further diffusion, and to remove those teachers of impiety through whom the pernicious effects of such diffusion are being perpetuated, this sacred Assembly, following the example of St. Charles Borromeo, has decided to establish in each of the dioceses a Council consisting of approved members of both branches of the clergy, which shall be charged with the task of noting the existence of errors and the devices by which new ones are introduced and propagated, and to inform the Bishop of the whole, so that he may take counsel with them as to the best means for suppressing the evil at the outset and preventing it spreading for the ruin of souls or, worse still, gaining strength and growth." We decree, therefore, that in every diocese a council of this kind, which We are pleased to name the "Council of Vigilance," be instituted without delay. The priests called to form part in it shall be chosen somewhat after the manner above prescribed for the censors, and they shall meet every two months on an appointed day in the presence of the Bishop. They shall be bound to secrecy as to their deliberations and decisions, and in their functions shall be included the following: they shall watch most carefully for every trace and sign of Modernism both in publications and in teaching, and to preserve the clergy and the young from it they shall take all prudent, prompt, and efficacious measures. Let them combat novelties of words, remembering the admonitions of Leo XIII: "It is impossible to approve in Catholic publications a style inspired by unsound novelty which seems to deride the piety of the faithful and dwells on the introduction of a new order of Christian life, on new directions of the Church, on new aspirations of the modern soul, on a new social vocation of the clergy, on a new Christian civilization, and many other things of the same kind." Language of the kind here indicated is not to be tolerated either in books or in lectures.

We order that you do everything in your power to drive out of your dioceses, even by solemn interdict, any pernicious books that may be in circulation there. The Holy See neglects no means to remove writings of this kind, but their number has now grown to such an extent that it is hardly possible to subject them all to censure. Hence it happens sometimes that the remedy arrives too late, for the disease has taken root during the delay. We will, therefore, that the Bishops, putting aside all fear and the prudence of the flesh, despising the clamor of evil men, shall, gently, by all means, but firmly, do each his own part in this work, remembering the injunctions of Leo XIII in the Apostolic Constitution *Officiorum:* "Let the Ordinaries, acting in this also as Delegates of the Apostolic See, exert themselves to proscribe and to put out of reach of the faithful injurious books or other writings printed or circulated in their dioceses." In this passage the Bishops, it is true, receive an authorization, but they have also a charge laid upon them. Let no Bishop think that he fulfills his duty by denouncing to Us one or two books, while a great many others of the same kind are being published and circulated. Nor are you to be deterred by the fact that a book has obtained elsewhere the permission which is commonly called the Imprimatur, both because this may be merely simulated, and because it may have been granted through carelessness or too much indulgence or excessive trust placed in the author, which last has perhaps sometimes happened in the religious orders. Besides, just as the same food does not agree with everyone, it may happen that a book, harmless in one place, may, on account of the different circumstances, be hurtful in another. Should a Bishop, therefore, after having taken the advice of prudent persons, deem it right to condemn any of such books in his diocese, We give him ample faculty for the purpose and We lay upon him the obligation of doing so. Let all this be done in a fitting manner, and in certain cases it will suffice to restrict the prohibition to the clergy; but in all cases it will be obligatory on Catholic booksellers not to put on sale books condemned by the Bishop. And while We are treating of this subject, We wish the Bishops to see to it that booksellers do not, through desire for gain, engage in evil trade. It is certain that in the catalogs of some of them the books of the Modernists are not infrequently announced with no small praise. If they refuse obedience, let the Bishops, after due admonition, have no hesitation in depriving them of the title of Catholic booksellers. This applies, and with still more reason, to those who have the title of Episcopal booksellers. If they have that of Pontifical booksellers, let them be denounced to the Apostolic See.

St. Pius X made it clear that these measures, however comprehensive, were inadequate in themselves: "It is not enough to hinder the reading and the sale of bad books—it is also necessary to prevent them from being published. Hence, let the Bishops use the utmost strictness in granting permission to print." There was also the matter of periodicals:

> With regard to priests who are correspondents or collaborators of periodicals, as it happens not infrequently that they contribute matter infected with Modernism to their papers or periodicals, let the Bishops see to it that they do not offend in this manner; and if they do, let them warn the offenders and prevent them from writing. We solemnly charge in like manner the superiors of religious orders that they fulfill the same duty, and should they fail in it, let the Bishops make due provision with authority from the Supreme Pontiff. Let there be, as far as this is possible, a special censor for newspapers and periodicals written by Catholics. It shall be his office to read in due time each number after it has been published, and if he find anything dangerous in it let him order that it be corrected as soon as possible. The Bishop shall have the same right even when the censor has seen nothing objectionable in a publication.

St. Pius X did not simply issue documents with no effort at enforcing compliance, as is the current practice. On September 1, 1910, three years after the promulgation of *Pascendi*, the Pope issued his *motu proprio Sacrorum Antistitum*, promulgating the Oath Against Modernism and commanding that it be administered to "all clergy, pastors, confessors, preachers, religious superiors, and professors in philosophical-theological seminaries," even including men being ordained to the subdiaconate. All but a handful of dissident theologians in Europe took the Oath. Thus, *every bishop and other Catholic cleric at the Second Vatican Council* had sworn the Oath Against Modernism. As Michael Davies notes:

> The first part of the oath is a strong affirmation of the basic Catholic truths opposed to Modernism: the demonstrability of God's existence by human reason; the value and suitability of miracles and prophecies as criteria of revelation; the historical institution of the Church by Christ; the inviolable character of Catholic tradition; the reasonableness and supernaturalness of faith.
>
> The second part of the oath is an expression of interior assent to the decree *Lamentabili* and the encyclical *Pascendi* with their contents.[163]

It is a fact of history that Vatican II was largely an exercise in tearing down the disciplinary bulwark Pope St. Pius X had erected, and which had held back the tide of Modernism for nearly sixty years, until the opening of the Council.

Two years after the Council, Paul VI abolished the Oath Against Modernism, along with the Index of Forbidden Books, a decision that Bishop Rudolf Graber rightly described as "incomprehensible."[164] The Church's primary defenses against Modernism were deliberately dismantled, evincing not merely a failure to take action against heresy, but *a positive papal decision not to punish it.*

What do the neo-Catholics have to say about these events in the course of their constant excuses for Rome's failure to reign in the chaos of the postconciliar Church? Nothing.

Yes, it is true that St. Pius X did not excommunicate many people. But would any honest person, in discussing St. Pius X's disciplinary program, leave it at that and make no mention of any of the measures just discussed—the very measures repudiated by the conciliar Popes? What grade would be assigned to a student writing a paper on *Pascendi* whose conclusion, after reading the above, was simply: "St. Pius X did

---

[163]Michael Davies, *Partisans of Error* (Long Prairie, MN: Neumann Press, 1983), pp. 104, 71.
[164]Graber, *Athanasius and the Church of Our Time*, p. 54.

not excommunicate many people"? Yet that is the Pamphlet's conclusion. To call that conclusion misleading would be the mildest thing one could say about it. And what, besides an intention to mislead, could account for this neo-Catholic attempt to present St. Pius X's vast and quite successful campaign against Modernism as if it were an historical example of papal *leniency* in the face of danger to the Church?

We will know when we have a Pope who is serious about reversing the disaster of the past thirty-five years. He is not here yet.

# Chapter 6

# The Charge of "Integrism"

One of the most peculiar aspects of the neo-Catholic system is on display in the Pamphlet: namely, the accusation that traditionalists are "integrists."

There can't be one in a thousand Catholics who have the faintest idea what this word means, so the actual effect of using it—and it is difficult to escape the conclusion that this was in fact the intended effect—is to make traditionalists sound as if they have some kind of clinical disorder. This has been a favorite tactic of the Left for decades now.

What does the term actually mean? The Pamphlet never provides a definition. But an anonymous article about "Integrism" on a website maintained by the Pamphlet's author is helpful in this regard—although not to the Pamphlet's position. The article notes that the word "integrist" was coined by French theologians during the pontificate of St. Pius X to describe those who, in reaction to the rise of Modernism, tended to believe that certain long-standing theological opinions in the Church should be regarded as binding Catholic doctrine in areas where the Church allowed free discussion. For example, an integrist might hold that since Thomistic philosophy was the perennial philosophy of the Catholic Church, it would be heresy to disparage the Thomistic system. While it would be imprudent and wrong to disparage the Thomistic system, and a clear sign of Modernist tendencies (as St. Pius X taught in *Pascendi*), to do so is not heresy, properly speaking. An integrist, therefore, would be someone who makes too great a claim for some element of Catholic truth, such as the preeminence of the Thomistic system — even though what he defends is *true*.

None of this is to suggest that either *The Remnant* or the authors of the Statement are "integrist." Rather, the point here is that the very article the Pamphlet's own author provides to define the key term at issue undermines his position that "integrism" is some sort of grave threat to the good order of the Church and that "integrists" are not orthodox Catholics.

That integrists are neither heretics nor schismatics was affirmed by none other than Dietrich von Hildebrand, whom the Pamphlet rightly praises as an "exemplary churchman." The Pamphlet ignores that it was von Hildebrand who observed in *The Devastated Vineyard* that while an "integrist" may be unduly narrow-minded about certain things, his views "are also *in no way incompatible* with Christian Revelation."[165] In other words, the term "integrist," rightly understood, refers to people who are Roman Catholics in good standing. As von Hildebrand put it: "The narrowness of the integrists may be regrettable, *but it is not heretical*." In fact, integrists are "pious, *orthodox* men." He went on:

> A short while ago, a well-known and important French theologian, who deplores the present devastation of the vineyard of the Lord, said to me that "integrists" were just as bad as "modernists".... *This is obviously a great error.* The narrowness of the integrists may be regrettable, but it is *not heretical. It is not incompatible with the teaching of Holy Church.* Therefore, it is *completely senseless* to place those who hold a philosophic thesis to be inseparable from Christian Revelation...on a level with those who promulgate philosophic theses which are in radical contradiction to the teaching of Holy Church.... [I]t is still *a great mistake* to believe that the integrists, who are pious, *orthodox* men, are just as

---

[165]Dietrich von Hildebrand, *The Devastated Vineyard* (Chicago: Franciscan Herald Press, 1973), p. 16.

dangerous to the Church as declared heretics.... This attack from within is being conducted by all available means and propagated by the mass media; it is an epidemic which is growing more widespread every day. This is *the real danger*, a disintegration of the Church. With the integrists, on the other hand, *there can be no question of such a danger.*

Is this what the Pamphlet means by "integrist" — an orthodox Catholic in good standing with the Church who is simply overzealous in his insistence on certain points? Clearly not. The Pamphlet appears to attribute to the word a meaning held by no one but its author. The term is tossed about so carelessly as to become a mere epithet, applicable to any traditionalist holding any opinion on the postconciliar crisis that is at odds with the neo-Catholic position that all of the Vatican-approved changes in the postconciliar Church must be accepted with docility, and even defended as good.

For example, there is the incident in which the Vicar of Christ kissed a copy of the Koran, the Muslim holy book, presented to him during a visit by a delegation of Iraqi representatives. For this the Pope was praised by the Catholic Patriarch of Iraq, Raphael I.[166] The Koran condemns the Holy Trinity as a blasphemy worthy of eternal hellfire,[167] and denies

---

[166]"On May 14th I was received by the Pope, together with a delegation composed of the Shiite imam of Khadum mosque and the Sunni President of the council of administration of the Iraqi Islamic Bank. At the end of the audience the Pope *bowed to the Muslim holy book the Koran presented to him by the delegation and he kissed it as a sign of respect.* The photo of that gesture has been shown repeatedly on Iraqi television, and it demonstrates that the Pope is not only aware of the suffering of the Iraqi people, he has also great respect for Islam" (*Fides* news agency, Rome, 4 June 1999).

Some neo-Catholics obstinately deny that the incident occurred, while others explain it away. Photographs of the event abound. See e.g, www.garykah.org/html/Popekoran.htm

[167]Surah V, *al-Maa'idah (The Table Spread)*, verses 72-73: "They surely disbelieve who say: Lo! Allah is the Messiah, the son of Mary.... Lo! Whoso ascribeth partners unto Allah, for him Allah hath forbidden paradise. His abode is the Fire. For evildoers there will be no helpers.

that Our Lord was crucified.[168] One can easily imagine a line of Catholic martyrs going to their deaths rather than consenting to kiss that book. Here is what the Pamphlet's own author wrote of the scandal in 1999: "We must pray for the Pope. For gestures are symbolic and, despite disclaimers, suggest a *less-than-Catholic approach* to other religions, especially in the context of worship of a God Who is alleged to guide 'three monotheistic religions' to salvation." The author was right to express this objection. But the same author, having recently embraced the neo-Catholic position, now proclaims in the Pamphlet that such legitimate opinions are "integrist."[169]

Many neo-Catholics invest the term "integrist" with connotations of a formal canonical delict, which it never had in its original usage. According to the Pamphlet, when the "integrist" prescinds from any of the papally approved novelties that have arisen in the Church since 1965, he ceases to be an orthodox Catholic, because he is rejecting "the living Magisterium."

---

They surely disbelieve who say: Lo! Allah is the third of three; when there is no God save the one God. If they desist not from so saying, a painful doom will fall on those of them who disbelieve." Marmaduke Pickthall, *The Glorious Koran* (London: George Allen & Unwin, 1976 ed.).

[168]Surah IV, *al-Nisaa' (Women)*: "They slew him not nor crucified him, but it appeared so unto them…. But Allah took him up to Himself." Ibid.

[169]It seems clear enough that the Pope's gesture was impetuous, and not intended to bless the many errors and blasphemies of the Koran. But if the sedevacantists have made too much of the incident, neither can the scandal be minimized. Gestures like these hardly reinforce the Church's teaching that Christ, and He alone, is the savior of men. It is well-nigh impossible for any Vatican document to counter the impact of such papal conduct, which in this case was exploited to the hilt by the Iraqi mass media. Protestant fundamentalists have also exploited the incident to poison the minds of potential converts. See, e.g., David W. Cloud, *Fundamental Baptist Information Service*, www.abide-in-truth.com.

In particular, the Pamphlet (in another about-face on the author's own earlier views) insists that "Catholic ecumenism" as practiced since Vatican II is part of the "living Magisterium" that "integrists" are obliged to embrace if they would remain Catholics in good standing. On the contrary, "Catholic ecumenism" involves no explicitly stated doctrine requiring religious assent to a specific proposition; it involves, rather, a new ecclesial attitude and program that, as we have demonstrated amply, defy precise definition. Further, there are compelling reasons to prescind from the purely prudential judgments by which "Catholic ecumenism" is animated in practice. Not even the Pamphlet denies that the preconciliar Popes would blanch in horror at what forty years of "Catholic ecumenism" have done to the Holy Catholic Church. (This is not to mention what they would think of the Pope kissing the Koran.)

Let us remember that the chief feature of "Catholic ecumenism" at the papal level consists of elaborate public ceremonies that purport to demonstrate an obviously non-existent "Christian unity" with non-Catholic sects. During these ceremonies, the adamant purveyors of the grossest heresy and immorality are given the false appearance of ecclesiastical dignity, causing enormous scandal and confusion among the faithful. A recent example is the Vicar of Christ pushing open the Holy Door of St. Paul's Outside the Walls together with the "Archbishop" of Canterbury—a layman in a bishop's costume, whose abominable sect teaches that abortion is permissible as a matter of conscience and that women may be ordained as "priests."

Another recent example is the joint Vespers service that the Pope conducted in St. Peter's Basilica with Lutheran "bishops" on November 15, 1999. Two women Lutheran "bishops" were in attendance at this travesty.[170] Like the Anglicans, the mainline

---

[170]"Joint Catholic-Lutheran Vespers at Vatican," CWNews.com, November 13, 1999: "Archbishops G.H. Hammar and Jukka Paarma— the Lutheran primates of Sweden and Finland, respectively—and Bishops Anders Arborelius of Stockholm and Czeslaw Kozon of

Lutherans (including those who negotiated the deplorable "Lutheran-Catholic Accord") preach that abortion is permissible and that women may be priests.   And this is the state of Lutheran doctrine *after* forty years of "ecumenical dialogue." Luther himself would condemn today's Lutherans as heretics! Yet the Pope celebrates Vespers with the very preachers of the culture of death, as if they were authentic clerics who belong to a legitimate church that the Immaculate Bride of Christ should treat as a worthy partner in "ecumenical dialogue."

Such ceremonies reveal "Catholic ecumenism" as a grotesque failure that has descended to the level of self-parody. Obviously, no Catholic is bound to embrace as part of "the living Magisterium" a pastoral program that gives places of honor in public ecclesiastical ceremonies to impostor clerics who condone the murder of children in the womb. Yet this is the very stuff of "Catholic ecumenism" at its highest level.

Then there are Pope John Paul's Lenten apologies in 2000 for sexism, anti-Semitism, crimes against indigenous peoples, violence in the service of truth, lack of respect for other religions — and so on. The papal apologies remind Catholics that John Paul II routinely does things that his admirers would never dream of doing.   Would the neo-Catholics themselves have made these apologies?   Do they really feel the accumulated weight of guilt for the catalogue of sins against liberalism solemnly recited on that shameful day?  What is so intellectually contemptible about the neo-Catholic position is that if we had told a few of our critics a year or two ago that a rank dissident like Fr. Richard McBrien or Hans Küng had proposed that the Church apologize for all these things, we would have had a good laugh together at the inanity of such a suggestion.   But when the Pope suggests *the very same thing* — and even some relatively conservative cardinals were uncomfortable about the whole spectacle — it is suddenly a sign of "integrism" to express outrage or disbelief.

---

Copenhagen joined with the Holy Father for the Vespers service. Several other Lutheran bishops from the Scandinavian countries were present for the ceremony, including two female bishops."

Joe Sobran put it this way: "We must ask: What is the fruit of the hundred or so apologies this Pope has now uttered? Is there any evidence that they have drawn any souls to the Church? Do they not, on the contrary, confirm every malicious common belief about the Church, while discouraging faithful Catholics and confusing weak ones? What on earth is the *point*?" (The desire to ask such questions is the first sign of "integrism.")

Predictably, the apologies were greeted by the squeaking and squawking of the unappeasable—the Pope hadn't gone far enough! "But what, one must ask, did the Holy Father expect?" Sobran wonders. In fact, though, "his list of sins and transgressions was indeed incomplete, from a Catholic point of view; it seems to have been composed with an eye to what modern liberalism regards as evil. In short, it has a fatal whiff of trendiness about it. It's easy to condemn sins of excessive zeal in the past, to which few are now tempted. But what might Catholics of the past (or the future) condemn in the Church today? They certainly wouldn't accuse us of excessive zeal. They might be shocked by our lukewarmness, our cowardice masquerading as tolerance, our laxity, our willingness to countenance heresy, sacrilege, blasphemy, and immorality within the Church itself, our eagerness to ingratiate ourselves with the secular world—of which the papal statement itself is a symptom."

The *American Spectator*'s Tom Bethell had this to say: "The Pope has excused St. Catherine of Siena's involvement in the Crusades by saying that she was a daughter of her times. Well, so is he of his, and his list of errors resembles nothing so much as a catalogue of the things that modern liberals accuse the Church of. They include, to quote [the] *New York Times*, 'religious intolerance and injustice toward Jews, women, indigenous peoples, immigrants, the poor and the unborn....' We now have bishops who have receded to a point where they are inconspicuous in national life, and the Pope might apologize for that. Instead, he apologizes for a time when the Church tried to evangelize the world. But tried too hard." And then the best and most telling line of all: "A priest I spoke to in Washington D.C. the other day said that if the Pope is going to apologize, he should apologize to the elderly conservative priests and nuns who are living out their lives in the wreckage that they find around them."

If objecting to this kind of behavior at the Vatican is "integrism," then no Catholic need fear being an "integrist." Rather, Catholics should fear the consequences of remaining silent about one scandal after another as the damage to the Church continues to mount. The naked emperor was not well served by his subjects in the crowd who marveled at his new suit of clothes. Neither does the neo-Catholic papal apologist well serve the Holy Father by continuing to pretend that the postconciliar *aggiornamento*, with its ruined liturgy, its incessant amiable "dialogue" with enemies of the Faith, its constant papal apologies and self-abasement, has been good for the Church — or even for those outside of her.

The great irony here is that it is actually our neo-Catholic accusers who are "integrists" in their defense of every papally approved novelty as if it were a matter requiring the assent of faith. This classic neo-Catholic position is presented in Likoudis and Whitehead's *The Pope, the Council and the Mass*, the aforementioned apologia for the postconciliar revolution. Like the authors of that unfortunate treatise, the Pamphlet completely obscures the distinction — in terms of the duty of obedience — between the immutable teaching of the Church on faith and morals over two millennia and the papally approved liturgical innovations and novel ecclesial attitudes of the past thirty-five years, whose fruits are the emptying of the pews, the seminaries and the convents, and the rapid dwindling of conversions and vocations from a preconciliar torrent to a postconciliar trickle. Neo-Catholics defend the innovations with all the fervor of the hypothetical traditionalist "integrist" in his defense of something like Thomism, but with this difference: The neo-Catholic "integrist" defends novelties that have obviously done the Church no good, whereas the traditionalist "integrist" defends ancient and venerable things from the Church's patrimony.

It is also important to recall here that the definition of papal infallibility agreed upon at the First Vatican Council (1869-70) was very precise, and for a reason. It declared that the Roman Pontiff,

> when he speaks *ex cathedra*, that is, when carrying out the duty of the pastor and teacher of all Christians in accord with his supreme apostolic authority he explains a doctrine of faith or morals to be held by the universal Church, through the divine assistance promised him in blessed Peter, operates with that infallibility with which the divine Redeemer wished that his Church be instructed in defining doctrine on faith and morals; and so such definitions of the Roman Pontiff from himself, but not from the consensus of the Church, are unalterable.

What is most striking about the Vatican I definition are the strict conditions it imposes upon the charism of infallibility. As Cardinal Newman noted in his discussion of the definition, "these conditions of course contract the range of infallibility most materially."[171] Newman further noted the crucial distinction between the divine *inspiration* of the original Apostles, and the divine *assistance* provided to the Church throughout history: "Hence the infallibility of the Apostles was of a far more positive and wide character than that needed by and granted to the Church. We call it, in the case of the Apostles, inspiration; in the case of the Church, *assistentia.*"

It is hardly an "integrist" error to note, then, that it is only by divine *assistance*, not divine inspiration, that the Pope is protected from any possibility of error—and then only when he defines *a matter of faith and morals* as a doctrine *to be believed by the whole Church*. Lesser matters are subject to the possibility of papal error, however rare and extraordinary that may be. Newman gives the striking example of Pope Nicholas I, whose declaration on the validity of the minister of Baptism (whether it could be a Jew or a pagan), noted in passing (according to Bellarmine) that "Baptism was valid whether administered in

---

[171]John Henry Newman, *Certain Difficulties* (London, 1876), cited in Michael Davies, *Lead Kindly Light: The Life of John Henry Newman* (Long Prairie, MN: Neumann Press, 2001), p. 179.

the name of the three Persons or in the name of Christ only."[172]
Would it be "integrism" to point out that Pope Nicholas I had
taught theological error in a papal pronouncement on an
important doctrinal matter?

There is a reason that the Council decided to define papal
infallibility in such a limited way. There was, at the time, a
strain of thought within Catholic circles that claimed that every
utterance of the Pope was positively infallible.   Thus W.G.
Ward, the editor of the *Dublin Review*, held, according to one
historian, that "the infallible element of bulls, encyclicals, etc.,
should not be restricted to their formal definitions, but run
through the entire doctrinal instructions; the decrees of the
Roman Congregations, if adopted by the Pope and published by
his authority, thereby were stamped with the mark of
infallibility; in short, 'his every doctrinal pronouncement is
infallibly directed by the Holy Ghost.'"[173] A still more extreme
position was reprobated by an American bishop at the Council,
whose concern over the matter led him to suggest the following
canon: "If anyone says that the authority of the Pope in the
Church is so full that he may dispose of everything by his mere
whim, let him be anathema." This position was understood by
the assembled bishops to be so patently ludicrous and unworthy
of the attention of an educated Catholic that the bishop who had
suggested it was told that the bishops had not assembled at
Rome "to hear buffooneries."[174]

This particular buffoonery, though, happens to be the neo-
Catholic position—the very position that Vatican I, under the
guidance of the Holy Ghost, was exceedingly careful *not* to
adopt in its infallible definition. Even Cardinal Ratzinger, who
can hardly be called an "integrist," remarked recently that the
good of the Church demands that this point be appreciated once
again. "After the Second Vatican Council," he writes, "the

---

[172]Ibid., pp. 181-82.

[173]B.C. Butler, *The Church and Infallibility* (London: Catholic Book
Club, 1954), p. 91.

[174]Michael Davies, *Pope Paul's New Mass* (Kansas City, MO:
Angelus Press, 1980), p. 593.

impression arose that the Pope really could do anything in liturgical matters, especially if he were acting on the mandate of an ecumenical council." This idea, vigorously defended by the neo-Catholics, has yielded terrible consequences, Ratzinger insists. "Eventually, the idea of the givenness of the liturgy, the fact that one cannot do with it what one will, faded from the consciousness of the West."[175] All of this happened because of the adoption of an exaggerated view of papal authority nowhere sanctioned by the Church:

> In fact, the First Vatican Council had in no way defined the Pope as an absolute monarch. On the contrary, it presented him as the guarantor of obedience to the revealed Word. The Pope's authority is bound to the Tradition of faith, *and that also applies to the liturgy*. It is not "manufactured" by the authorities. Even the Pope can only be a humble servant of its lawful development and abiding integrity and identity.

In sum, the authority of the Pope "is not unlimited; it is at the service of Sacred Tradition."[176]

The Pamphlet, like the entire neo-Catholic attack on Roman Catholic traditionalism, is based, therefore, upon a patently false premise. To quote the Pamphlet: "Modernists and Integrists are actually twins. Both thrive on opposition to the living Magisterium." The Pamphlet fails utterly to demonstrate how the legitimate grievances of traditionalists concerning a state of ecclesial affairs even the Pamphlet's author deplores constitute opposition to the "living Magisterium" of the Church. What are the *doctrines* of this "living Magisterium" the "integrists" are said to deny—doctrines, we say, as opposed to ill-considered reforms and changes of ecclesial attitude? None are identified, because none exist. Nor does the Pamphlet cite a single statement by any of the "integrists" it condemns by name (i.e., the authors of the Statement) to demonstrate their "integrist"

---

[175]Joseph Cardinal Ratzinger, *The Spirit of the Liturgy*, trans. John Saward (San Francisco: Ignatius Press, 2000), pp. 165-66.
[176]Ibid.

dissent from Magisterial teaching. No statements are provided because none exist.

But the neo-Catholic position depends upon this false equivalence between modernist heretics and faithful traditional Catholics. For if the neo-Catholic critique of Roman Catholic traditionalism involves no Catholic doctrine as such, then traditionalists have the perfect right to state their case. From this it follows that the neo-Catholic position *contra* traditionalism loses all color of authority, revealing itself as a mere opinion among other opinions in the Church, including the opinions of traditionalists.

Sad to say, the unjust equivalence between traditionalists and modernists is advanced not only by the author of the Pamphlet, but also by a Catholic bishop who provided an introduction to it. We are referring to His Excellency Fabian W. Bruskewitz, Bishop of Lincoln, Nebraska.

His Excellency's introduction lauds the Pamphlet's denunciation of the ill-defined "integrists" as a great service to the Church, and warns Catholics to have nothing to do with those sorry traditionalists who would remove an eyeball along with the cinder and then "replace its empty socket with cinders and decayed matters." (Why these poor creatures would *replace* the cinders into their eye-sockets after having just removed them so painfully must remain a mystery.) Equally to be shunned are those who "sometimes say, 'I wish I could cut off my head to cure my headache.'" Horrors!

His Excellency declares that "integrists" are no better than the seventeenth-century Jansenist nuns of Port-Royal, France, described by the Archbishop of Paris as "pure as angels but as proud as devils." Subtle, His Excellency isn't.

More to the point, His Excellency rightly notes (as if anyone did not already know) that "down through the centuries there have been countless sects, denominations, cults and churches which have broken off from the Catholic Church under the pretense of being 'holier than thou.'" His Excellency seems to be suggesting the existence of a present-day analogue of these dissident groups. But it is evidently not present-day Anglicans or Lutherans whom His Excellency has in mind, given that he has presided over an ecumenical prayer service and breakfast together with an Anglican "bishop" and assorted Lutheran "ministers." The Methodists, then? Apparently not, since His Eminence respectfully attended the "consecration" of Methodist "bishop" Joel Martinez, who has publicly recalled (in a sermon on May 21, 2000) the joyous day his mother left the Catholic Church and returned to the Methodist fold, along with Martinez's grandmother. Nor does it appear that His Excellency was thinking of the more obscure local Protestant sects in his own diocese, such as the Congregational Christian Church or the First Congregational Christian Church. One of His Excellency's own parishes conducts what it calls a "Sermon a la Carte" program, in which parishioners are urged to attend sermons by the ministers of these very sects, as well as the local Methodist and Lutheran "churches." Yes, in the Diocese of Lincoln, the sheep are actually being encouraged to go and listen to false shepherds. It is equally clear that His Excellency was not contemplating the modern descendants of the Pharisees, who, in the worst schism of all, cut themselves off from the true religion when they rejected the Messiah in their midst and had Him put to death. Quite the contrary, His Excellency conducted an interfaith Seder Supper with a group of rabbis in his own cathedral during Holy Week.[177]

No, by "sects, denominations and cults" of the present day, His Excellency does not mean the Protestant ministers and rabbis with whom, in true neo-Catholic fashion, he prays, breakfasts and sups in happy concord—even though these false shepherds condone abortion, contraception and divorce, not to mention innumerable gross heresies. His Excellency means the "integrists," and only them. It was only to denounce *his fellow Catholics* that Bishop Bruskewitz lent the weight of his episcopal office to the accusations of the Pamphlet.

The Bishop's leap to public judgment is not surprising. In the neo-Catholic view of things, the "integrists" have committed

---

[177]John Vennari, *Catholic Family News*, January 1999. The authors have examined the original diocesan publications on which this article was based.

the one unpardonable sin in the postconciliar Church: they have refused to cease being what Bishop Bruskewitz himself was only forty years ago, when Catholics were taught to avoid like the plague the very things they are now being told they can embrace without reservation—including such things as the polka Masses that have been featured in at least six parishes in the Diocese of Lincoln.

Let us repeat that neither Michael Matt nor the other traditionalists whom the Pamphlet and *The Wanderer* have condemned are "integrists" in the first place. Nevertheless, the neo-Catholic accusation is impaled on the point driven home by von Hildebrand: that the real danger to the Church (as always) is heresy, not any such thing as "integrism." To recall the words of von Hildebrand, it is a "great error," and "completely senseless," to equate the two. Yet that senseless error is the very foundation of the neo-Catholic critique of the traditionalist position. It is time that foundation was removed, so that the neo-Catholic critique can be allowed to collapse into the uninformed opinion it really is.

# Chapter 7

# Private Judgment?

Perhaps no accusation has been leveled at traditionalists with such frequency and with such undeserved effect as the claim that they engage in "private judgment." As the Pamphlet's own title—*Traditionalists, Tradition and Private Judgment*—suggests, the author advances the basic neo-Catholic thesis that since the Pope is the "sole arbiter" of Tradition, anything the Pope approves or commands is *a priori* consonant with Tradition, regardless of what our memories and our senses may tell us, and that to say otherwise is to engage in "private judgment" of a Protestant character. The same absurd thesis was advanced in *The Pope, the Council and the Mass*.

The thesis is absurd because it deprives Catholic Tradition of objectively knowable content, requiring Catholics to suspend the use of their reason and submit to a kind of ecclesial legal positivism which itself is contrary to Tradition. For example, as the neo-Catholic would have it, even though Paul VI himself referred to his new rite of Mass as "this novelty," "this innovation," "this grave change" in his audience addresses of November 1969, no Catholic may conclude that a novelty of such unprecedented magnitude represents a departure from Tradition, because even novelties must be viewed as consonant with Tradition if they are approved by the Pope. Yet as Cardinals Ottaviani and Bacci noted in their famous *Intervention*, the text and rubrics of the new Mass represented a "striking departure from the theology of the Mass" as taught by the Council of Trent—that is, a departure from Tradition.[178] This was no "private judgment." It was a statement of what was manifest.

Traditionalists, it is alleged, belong in the same category with liberals and even Protestants, because both call certain decisions of those in authority into question. That an obvious qualitative difference separates traditionalist arguments from Protestant ones does not seem to deter our critics from advancing this easily refuted charge. The Pamphlet portrays the neo-Catholic parallel thus: "If the former (our liberal dissidents) are like Judas and prefer their own way to the way of the Master, the latter (the Integrists or extreme Traditionalists who concern us here) are like the nervous disciples in the boat who are scandalized that the Lord sleeps while the boat is whipped in the storms which threaten to plunge them into the deep (Lk. 8:22-25). They forget or hesitate over the divine authority and sovereignty of the Master and would seize control of the Ship themselves if they could—not because they are wicked necessarily, but because, at the end of the day, they do not completely trust the divine 'always' and 'whatsoever.'" The Pamphlet thus asserts that in place of confidence in the "divine 'whatsoever,'" traditionalists substitute their "private judgment."

Let us, therefore, proceed to this central claim with recourse to an initial example. A traditionalist deplores the Vatican's decision to allow Eucharistic ministers, because he believes that by compromising the priest's exclusive custodianship of the Eucharist, they strike at the heart of the meaning and mystery of the holy priesthood, robbing the sacerdotal function of the manliness and awe that entice young men to enter the seminary. Hans Küng, who is no doubt delighted with Eucharistic ministers, does not even believe that Christ instituted the

---

[178]Alfredo Cardinal Ottaviani and Antonio Cardinal Bacci, *The Ottaviani Intervention* (Rockford, IL: TAN, 1992).

Catholic priesthood. By what strange calculus are these two positions in any way equivalent?

We have a Magisterium, the neo-Catholic says, that provides Catholics with a unique source of stability and constancy. Agreed. But with what precisely is the Magisterium concerned? To this question neither the Pamphlet in particular nor neo-Catholics in general are willing to offer a clear answer. Since the neo-Catholic will brook no criticism of any major ecclesial fad that has the support of the Vatican, the neo-Catholic version of the Magisterium seems a quite expansive thing indeed. Is the "ecumenical movement," condemned by Pope Pius XI as a threat to the Catholic faith, a part of Magisterial teaching? Is a Catholic bound in conscience, on pain of mortal sin, to believe against all available evidence that the ceaseless parade of ecumenical gatherings since the Council is a *traditional* Catholic undertaking? (Incidentally, if the neo-Catholics can name one good fruit that has emerged from more than three decades of "ecumenical dialogue" that in any way compensates for the confusion, indifferentism, and theological ambiguities that have been its obvious and quite predictable side effects, we would like to hear what it is.)

The Pamphlet, hewing to neo-Catholic convention, will brook no criticism of papally approved ecumenism. The Pope approved it; therefore it is "private judgment" to object to any of the Pope's ecumenical activities. Some priests doubtless go too far, the author says, but Rome's program is unobjectionable — for, after all, the Pope approved it. In a commentary sent to his supporters, the author even called one of us a "Pharisee" for expressing our objections to the continuing scandal of ecumenical activities with pro-abortion Protestant "bishops" and other bogus clerics in Protestant "ecclesial communities."

At least one Catholic bishop, however, agrees that traditionalists have a right to be heard in opposition to the Pope's ecumenical endeavors:

> There are people who in the face of the difficulties or because they consider that the first ecumenical endeavors have brought negative results would have liked to turn back. Some

even express the opinion that these efforts are harmful to the cause of the Gospel, are leading to a further rupture in the Church, are causing confusion of ideas in questions of faith and morals and are ending up with a specific indifferentism. It is perhaps a good thing that the spokesmen for these opinions should express their fears.

The bishop in question is Pope John Paul II, writing in his inaugural encyclical, *Redemptor Hominis* (1979). It is true that the Pope went on to say that he considered such fears to be misplaced. But it is also fairly significant that the Pope himself says "it is perhaps a good thing" that traditionalists "should express their fears," including the fear that ecumenical activities "are harmful to the cause of the Gospel, are leading to a further rupture in the Church, are causing confusion of ideas in questions of faith and morals and are ending up with a specific indifferentism." Thus, oddly enough, it is the neo-Catholics who are engaging in "private judgment" when they denounce traditionalists for disloyalty to the Pope for voicing precisely that opinion which the Pope is willing to hear. Here, as in many other places, it is the neo-Catholics who reveal themselves as rigorists and "integrists" — though only when it comes to defending postconciliar innovations.

If the previously unheard-of novelties that traditionalists deplore were Magisterial teachings, then we would indeed be in trouble. For starters, the Catechism would have to be produced in disposable missalette form, just to keep up with it all. Thankfully — and, again, quite obviously — this is not the case.

Especially scandalous to the author of the Pamphlet and his neo-Catholic fellows is that traditionalists are not altogether pleased with Vatican II. The central traditionalist criticism of Vatican II, as we have noted, is that it fundamentally changed the Church's orientation in a direction that tended to undermine her divine mission. Again, by what arcane reckoning do neo-Catholics conclude that an *orientation* could itself be a Magisterial teaching? How can an orientation be "true" or "false"? It can only be wise or unwise, fruitful or barren. Thus if the Pope were to declare that the pastoral experiment inaugurated by Vatican II, having produced more dissension and confusion than genuine good, was to be abandoned in favor of the Church's traditional posture, that would be entirely his prerogative. If the optimism of Vatican II has fallen far short of expectations, it can ultimately be rejected by the Church, like any other contingent pronouncement or provision of Popes and councils. For example, in the wake of the Council of Trent and in the face of the Protestant Revolt, the Church granted the request of some of her members that Communion be offered to the faithful under both species. Over time the practice seemed to produce more confusion than piety — some laymen could not be persuaded from the superstitious notion that one receives more grace by receiving under both kinds. And so the very churchmen who had originally requested the Holy See's permission for this experiment finally asked that the previous discipline be restored.

But in matters that truly pertain to the Magisterium — such things as the Holy Trinity, Our Lady's Immaculate Conception, the intrinsic immorality of artificial contraception — the Church can do no such thing. These teachings cannot be revised or rejected no matter what. A pastoral strategy, however, is not a dogmatic definition. There is a fairly obvious qualitative difference between the statement, "Jesus Christ, true God and true man, is the Second Person of the Blessed Trinity," and the statement, "Perhaps the Church should consider a more irenic relationship vis-à-vis other religions." This simple distinction is at the heart of the traditionalist position, and it really borders on the amazing that anyone could actually fail to understand it.

Moreover, it is entirely possible that an ecumenical council can simply fail in its stated goal. The fifteenth-century Council of Ferrara-Florence failed to bring about a lasting reconciliation with the Orthodox. The Second Council of Constantinople (553) seems only to have confused people further about the controversy surrounding Monophysitism. In the present day, Vatican II has manifestly failed to bring about the "new springtime" of Christianity that its proponents predicted. Cardinal Ratzinger himself insisted in late December 1984: "I am repeating here what I said ten years after the conclusion of the work: it is incontrovertible that this period has definitely been unfavorable for the Catholic Church."[179]  If neo-Catholics are going to argue that this disaster has occurred *in spite of* the new orientation advanced by Vatican II, then it is they who are the integrists; for they are asserting, without any Church teaching to support them, that the Church has been given a divine guarantee that she will always follow the soundest and most fruitful pastoral approaches, and that if she recommends them they simply have to work.  Where in any catechism has the Church ever said that she possessed such an assurance?  If nowhere, then why do our critics insist, as if they had Holy Scripture itself behind them, that to doubt the wisdom of the pastoral directives of Vatican II is to cut oneself off from communion with the Church? What Catholics do have is a guarantee that in faith and morals she will not teach error.  That is a far cry from guaranteeing that every suggestion offered even by an ecumenical council will be necessarily successful or wise.

Pope John XXIII set the tone for the postconciliar period when he remarked that it was better to overcome error by putting forth the beauty of the truth in all its radiance than to resort to the iron fist of discipline and punishment.  There is something superficially plausible and even beautiful about such a statement, but it altogether discounts the baneful effects of Original Sin on the human intellect.  John Milton notwithstanding, the truth can rarely be victorious in the free marketplace of ideas without the special assistance of divine grace. The briefest glance at the state of our own civilization should be all the refutation this cliché requires.

The same is true of doctrinal error in the Church.  Error can have a seductive attraction to our fallen nature.  As Pope St. Pius X said of the Modernists: "It is pride which puffs them up with that vainglory which allows them to regard themselves as the sole possessors of knowledge, and makes them say, elated and inflated with presumption, 'We are not as the rest of men,' and

---

[179]*L'Osservatore Romano* (English edition), December 24, 1984.

which, lest they should seem as other men, leads them to embrace and to devise novelties even of the most absurd kind." Rather than be small fish in a big pond, writing books that merely elaborate on what the Church has taught for millennia, the Modernists, thirsting for fame, notoriety, and the applause of the world, chase after errors in order to ingratiate themselves with the Church's influential enemies. St. Pius X would have laughed at the suggestion that in this fallen world truth was its own defense, or that it was somehow uncharitable to have recourse to excommunication and other ecclesiastical penalties. Why, then, is it "private judgment" for traditionalists, with the wisdom of previous Popes behind them, to point out the fallacy behind this postconciliar approach, whose results have been so devastating?

It is blasphemous in the extreme to compare, as the Pamphlet does, the embarrassing and scandalous shenanigans coming out of today's Vatican to Our Lord sleeping in the boat. It is, of course, an extraordinary consolation to recall that Christ is always with us through these terrible trials. But does that mean that we should sit back and let them run their course? One of our peculiar traits, according to the Pamphlet, is that we wish that Church authority might be exercised as it was in generations past. In the author's words, we "demand that it be exercised today as it was yesterday." Guilty as charged. But who in his right mind *wouldn't* like to see that? One must remember what St. Thomas teaches: It is one thing to suffer injustices committed against oneself, following Christ's injunction to turn the other cheek. It is quite another to do nothing while other people suffer injustice. If neo-Catholics wish to delight in the weakness and disciplinary laxity of the past several Popes as a poignant example of the mysterious working of divine providence, that is all very well. The rest of us prefer the rather less narcissistic goal of the salvation of souls, a task made somewhat difficult by the fact that we must reckon with religious orders more concerned with transcendental meditation or massage therapy than with living the Gospel, beautiful sanctuaries and statues replaced with tables and felt banners, bishops who corrupt Catholic youth with sex education—we all know the catalogue of folly, error, and blasphemy that some dare to call "the springtime of Vatican II." So yes, traditionalists cling to their "private judgment" that the Pope really ought to do something about all this.

Can the best approach to the postconciliar debacle really be to say nothing, to do nothing, and to simply allow a veritable revolution that is causing the Church unspeakable damage to proceed unhindered? What kind of loyal son of the Church can watch the Bride of Christ in such agony and remain silent, or, what is worse, engage in the intellectually sterile and egregiously dishonest effort to claim that everything is just fine? What impulse can account for the stoic determination of the neo-Catholic to deny reality?

Now, if Fr. Richard McBrien had quoted favorably from Teilhard de Chardin (on whose works Pope John XXIII placed a *monitum*), held a special meeting with female altar servers, and even publicly *kissed the Koran*, in neo-Catholic eyes this would no doubt constitute still further evidence of the man's perverse delight in dissent. But when the Pope did these very things, the neo-Catholic response was an embarrassed silence.[180] It is heartbreaking to have to speak publicly against some of the practical judgments of the Pope, but to do so is neither without precedent nor a sign of disrespect, either for the person of the Pope or his sacred office. Public correction is the only mechanism available to the concerned Catholic today; it is not possible to remonstrate privately with top churchmen or to receive a lengthy audience with them. As we note elsewhere in this book, St. Thomas Aquinas himself taught that public reproof of a prelate, even including the Pope, can be a requirement in charity in order to avoid scandal to the Faith. For all Catholics are bound together in charity, the highest and the lowest.

---

[180]"The Eucharist is also celebrated in order to offer 'on the altar of the whole earth the world's work and suffering,' in the beautiful expression of Teilhard de Chardin." Pope John Paul II, *Gift and Mystery* (New York: Doubleday, 1996), p. 73.

By far the greater scandal would be to follow neo-Catholic example, making a phony virtue out of doing nothing. How many conservative Protestants turned away in disgust from the Church for good after the Koran episode? The evolution statement? The inexplicable campaign against the death penalty, a punishment obviously sanctioned in Holy Scripture and Tradition? That traditionalists voice their opinions because they love the Catholic Church and can see that certain trends are causing her harm, whereas radicals like Küng write their books because they loathe the Church and want to see her destroyed, would seem to most people to be a fairly significant difference. Why the neo-Catholics pretend not to see this it is impossible to say.

A word about Dietrich von Hildebrand, the revered philosopher whom the Pamphlet claims for the neo-Catholic side: Sorry, but von Hildebrand was a traditionalist. In fact, so much did von Hildebrand lack the neo-Catholic's version of what constitutes "trust" in the Church (which seems to boil down to: be utterly unconcerned with the disciplinary laxity and weekly scandals emanating from Rome, and commit the sin of presumption by blithely insisting that the Holy Spirit will work everything out if only we sit around and do nothing) that he actually secured a private audience with Pope Paul VI, a recourse which a man of his stature could arrange with relative ease. We know that von Hildebrand there pleaded with the Pope (in vain, as it happened) to use his authority as Vicar of Christ to put a stop to the alarming spread of dissent, error and institutional decay within the Church. Later, von Hildebrand would write that when a papal decision "has the character of compromise or is the result of pressure or the weakness of the individual person of the Pope, we cannot and should not say: *Roma locuta, causa finita.* That is, we cannot see in it the will of God; we must recognize that God only permits it, just as He has permitted the unworthiness or weakness of several Popes in the history of the Church.... On account of my deep love for and devotion to the Church, it is a special cross for me not to be able to welcome every practical decision of the Holy See, particularly in a time like ours, which is witnessing a crumbling of the spirit of obedience and of respect for the Holy Father."[181]

In determining to seek out the Holy Father and, yes, correct him to his face, von Hildebrand apparently failed to appreciate the neo-Catholic insight, much on display in the Pamphlet, that papal laxity is like Christ asleep in the boat, and that we ought neither to worry about nor question such a state of affairs. We trust we can be forgiven for being slow to believe that the man whom Pius XII called "the twentieth-century American doctor of the Church," whose brilliance has edified good Catholics for decades, was all this time in need of fraternal correction from the likes of the Pamphlet's author.

Now, not even the Pamphlet's author can be entirely ignorant of previous examples in Church history in which the highest prelates, including the Pope, have been criticized for their failings. The example of St. Catherine of Siena and her rebuke of Pope Gregory XI should come immediately to mind. In addition, the Third Council of Constantinople, held in 680-81, condemned Pope Honorius I as having essentially held the Monothelite heresy (a variation of Monophysitism that claimed that Christ possessed only one will). In confirming the decisions of the Council, Pope Leo II himself sharply criticized his predecessor, but not for actually having held the heresy himself, as the council seemed to suggest, but for having done so little when the heresy was ravaging the Church. In a letter to the Spanish bishops, Pope Leo II explained how he wished the Council's view of Honorius to be understood: "Honorius...did not, as became the Apostolic authority, extinguish the flame of heretical teaching in its first beginning, but fostered it by his negligence." That is, he agreed that "the whole matter should be hushed up."[182]

---

[181]Dietrich von Hildebrand, *The Charitable Anathema* (Harrison, NY: Roman Catholic Books, 1993), pp. 30-31, 32.

[182]Hubert Jedin, *Ecumenical Councils of the Catholic Church: An Historical Survey*, trans. Ernest Graf, O.S.B. (New York: Herder and Herder, 1960), pp. 47-48; Warren H. Carroll, *A History of Christendom*, vol. 2: *The Building of Christendom* (Front Royal, VA: Christendom

The *Catholic Encyclopedia* describes the case in no uncertain terms: "It is clear that *no Catholic has the right to defend Pope Honorius*. He was a heretic, not in intention, but in fact; and he is to be considered to have been condemned in the sense in which Origen and Theodore of Mopsuestia, who died in Catholic communion, never having resisted the Church, have been condemned." Are the neo-Catholics prepared to claim that in rendering such a judgment on a Pope, an ecumenical council of the Church, as well as Pope Leo II, also failed to appreciate the "divine 'whatsoever'"?

The great irony of this whole controversy is that if anything, it is the neo-Catholic who truly partakes of the spirit of Protestantism. Philosophically speaking, Protestants generally are what are known as nominalists, that is, those who assess actions as good not out of their conformity to natural law or the common good, but merely because they flow from the will of the legislator. God, therefore, could, without contradiction, decree tomorrow that murder is a good and holy thing. (This frame of mind, incidentally, helps to account for Calvin's notion of a rigid and absolute predestination both to heaven and to hell—it is just another arbitrary decision of an arbitrary God in an irrational universe.) Nominalism is what neo-Catholics practice every time they intone "obey, obey, obey" in place of reasoned discussion. These are the same people who considered altar girls an abomination in 1980 when the Pope forbade them (in *Inestimabile Donum*), but a potential enrichment to the Church in 1994, when the Pope finally caved in and approved the innovation. That is a central feature of Protestantism: the denial that good and evil, truth and falsehood, are, in the very nature of things, fixed and eternal, and not merely arbitrary designations that Authority may change at its good pleasure.

The nominalism of the neo-Catholics is evident in their approach to the liturgical devastation of the past thirty years. Neo-Catholics routinely advance the argument that it constitutes "private judgment" to claim that the postconciliar liturgical

College Press, 1987), pp. 252-54; "Honorius I, Pope," *Catholic Encyclopedia*, 1913.

reform inaugurated by Paul VI marked a break with ecclesiastical tradition. The Pope alone, so the argument goes, may determine what is and is not in conformity with ecclesiastical tradition. Therefore, whatever liturgical innovation the Pope approves, even altar girls, is *ipso facto* "traditional," and no one may say otherwise. In other words, it would seem that according to the neo-Catholics the Pope is *ontologically incapable* of departing from liturgical tradition.

But consider the text of the traditional papal coronation oath, in existence for many centuries after its introduction by Pope St. Agatho in the seventh century:

> I vow to change nothing of the received Tradition, and nothing thereof I have found before me guarded by my God-pleasing predecessors, to encroach upon, to alter, or to permit any innovation therein;

> To the contrary: with glowing affection as her truly faithful student and successor, to safeguard reverently the passed-on good, with my whole strength and utmost effort;

> To cleanse all that is in contradiction to the canonical order, should such appear;

> To guard the Holy Canons and Decrees of our Popes as if they were the Divine ordinances of Heaven, because I am conscious of Thee, whose place I take through the Grace of God, whose Vicarship I possess with Thy support, being subject to the severest accounting before Thy Divine Tribunal over all that I shall confess;

> I swear to God Almighty and the Savior Jesus Christ that I will keep whatever has been revealed through Christ and His Successors and whatever the first councils and my predecessors have defined and declared.

> I will keep without sacrifice to itself the discipline and the rite of the Church. I will put outside the Church whoever dares to go against this oath, may it be somebody else or I.

If I should undertake to act in anything of contrary sense, or should permit that it will be executed, Thou willst not be merciful to me on the dreadful Day of Divine Justice.

Accordingly, without exclusion, We subject to severest excommunication anyone—be it ourselves or be it another—who would dare to undertake anything new in contradiction to this constituted evangelic Tradition and the purity of the Orthodox Faith and the Christian Religion, or would seek to change anything by his opposing efforts, or would agree with those who undertake such a blasphemous venture.

Note carefully what the Pope is called upon to say here. He solemnly swears that he will uphold the sacred Tradition of the Church and do nothing to the contrary. He is acutely aware of the judgment that awaits him should he act otherwise: "Thou willst not be merciful to me on the dreadful Day of Divine Justice," the oath warns.

Now if the neo-Catholic position—namely, that it is inherently impossible for the Pope to act contrary to Tradition—were correct, the entire papal coronation oath would be rendered nugatory and laughable. Why would the Pope be required to swear not to do something he is inherently incapable of doing?

Nevertheless, this axiom of neo-Catholicism was recently affirmed in an editorial in *The Wanderer*, which declares quite simply: "All approved rites are traditional."[183] It is hardly surprising that both authors of the editorial were born after Pope Paul's suppression of the traditional Latin rite. They are thus chronological as well as intellectual neo-Catholics. For them, the recently concocted Novus Ordo Mass is the Church's primary liturgical patrimony, even though the Novus Ordo (like the authors) is barely thirty years old, and (unlike the authors) is

---

[183]Shawn McElhinney and Pete Vere, "What Makes Us Traditional Catholics?," *The Wanderer*, December 6, 2001, p. 4.

already falling to pieces—"the collapse of the liturgy" is how Cardinal Ratzinger put it.[184]

Now unless, which God forbid, the Catholic faith demands the suppression of the evidence of our senses and indeed of the intellect itself, then surely when an unprecedented new liturgical form manifestly departs from immemorial tradition one ought to be able to say so. Human reason itself tells us that no man's mere *ipse dixit*, no matter what his rank, can compel us to believe that white is black or that what is novel is traditional.

It is helpful, although by no means necessary to this conclusion, that Pope Paul VI himself openly admitted that his new rite was a novelty that represented a startling and bewildering break with the past. As he declared in his audience address of November 19, 1969:

> We wish to draw your attention to an event about to occur in the Latin Catholic Church: the introduction of the liturgy of the *new rite* of the Mass.... This change has something astonishing about it, something extraordinary. This is because the Mass is regarded as *the traditional and untouchable expression of our religious worship and the authenticity of our faith*. We ask ourselves, *how could such a change be made*? What effect will it have on those who attend Holy Mass? Answers will be given to these questions, and to others like them, arising from this *innovation*.

In his audience address of November 26, 1969, only a week later, Pope Paul could not have been more explicit in his intention to depart from the Church's ancient liturgical tradition:

> We ask you to turn your minds once more to the *liturgical innovation* of the new rite of the Mass.... A new rite of the Mass: *a change in a venerable tradition that has gone on for*

---

[184]"I am convinced that the ecclesial crisis in which we find ourselves today depends in great part on the collapse of the liturgy." Ratzinger, *La Mia Vita*, quoted by Michael Davies in *The Latin Mass*, Fall 1997.

*centuries.* This is something that affects our hereditary religious patrimony, *which seemed to enjoy the privilege of being untouchable and settled....* We must prepare for this many-sided inconvenience. It is the kind of upset caused by every *novelty* that breaks in on our habits.... So what is to be done on this special and historical occasion? First of all, we must prepare ourselves. This *novelty* is no small thing. We should not let ourselves be surprised by the nature, *or even the nuisance,* of its exterior forms. As intelligent persons and conscientious faithful we should find out as much as we can about *this innovation.*

Pope Paul's description of what he had decided to do regarding the traditional Latin liturgy would be impossible to believe if he had not said it publicly and for the historical record:

It is here that the greatest newness is going to be noticed, the newness of language. No longer Latin, but the spoken language will be the principal language of the Mass. The introduction of the vernacular will certainly be *a great sacrifice* for those who know the beauty, the power and the expressive sacrality of Latin. *We are parting with the speech of the Christian centuries; we are becoming like profane intruders in the literary preserve of sacred utterance.* We will lose a great part of that stupendous and incomparable artistic and spiritual thing, the Gregorian chant. We have *reason indeed for regret, reason almost for bewilderment.* What can we put in the place of that language of the angels? *We are giving up something of priceless worth.* But why? What is more precious than *these loftiest of our Church's values?*[185]

Pope Paul's answer to his own question—"But why?"—is even more astonishing:

The answer will seem banal, prosaic. Yet it is a good answer, because it is human, because it is apostolic. Understanding of

---

[185]The authors of *The Pope, the Council and the Mass* actually cite this text in an appendix in support of their claim that the new Mass is not novel. Comment would be superfluous.

prayer is worth more than the silken garments in which it is
royally dressed. Participation by the people is worth more—
particularly participation by modern people, so fond of plain
language which is easily understood and converted into
everyday speech.

It is hardly "private judgment" to note, as a purely factual
matter, that there was no evidence whatever to support Pope
Paul's claim that his liturgical innovations were necessary to
accommodate a supposed need of "modern people" for "plain
language." As Cardinals Ottaviani and Bacci observed in their
famous Short Critical Study of the new rite in 1969 (which later
came to be known as *The Ottaviani Intervention*), the people
themselves had never asked for and did not want this change:
"If the Christian people expressed anything at all, it was the
desire (thanks to the great St. Pius X) to discover the true and
immortal treasures of the liturgy. They never, *absolutely never*,
asked that the liturgy be changed or mutilated to make it easier
to understand.    What the faithful did want was a better
understanding of a unique and *unchangeable* liturgy—a liturgy
*they had no desire to see changed.*"[186] In fact, when the liberal
German bishop William Duschak of Calapan proposed in a
speech during Vatican II that there be a new rite of Mass in the
vernacular, he was asked whether his proposal had originated
with the people he served. Duschak replied: "No, *I think they
would oppose it.* But if it could be put into practice, I think they
would accept it."[187]
    And Bishop Duschak, it must be noted, was only suggesting
that a new vernacular rite be implemented on an experimental
basis *alongside* the traditional Latin rite, not in place of it. The *de
facto* abolition of the traditional Mass would have been
unthinkable to the vast majority of Council Fathers. In fact,
when Cardinal Browne expressed to his fellow Council Fathers
the fear that if the Council allowed the vernacular into the
liturgy the Latin Mass would disappear within ten years, he was

---

[186]Ottaviani and Bacci, *The Ottaviani Intervention*, p. 32.
[187]Wiltgen, *The Rhine Flows into the Tiber*, p. 39.

greeted with incredulous laughter. But as Fr. John Parsons notes, "The pessimistic reactionary proved to be more in touch with the flow of events than the optimistic progressives. The Council Fathers' incredulous laughter at Cardinal Browne helps to remind us that a general council, like a Pope, is only infallible in its definitions of faith and morals, and not in its prudential judgments, or in matters of pastoral discipline, or in acts of state, or in supposed liturgical improvements. It is thus false to assert that a Catholic is logically bound to agree with the prudential judgments a council may make on any subject. It is still more illegitimate to extrapolate from the negative immunity from error which a general council enjoys in definitions of faith and morals, to belief in a positive inspiration of councils, as if the bishops were organs of revelation like the Apostles...."[188]

But that is exactly what the neo-Catholic does. The aforementioned *Wanderer* editorial only expresses the basic neo-Catholic position when it contends that "infallibility is *intrinsic* to an ecumenical council," even as to those matters that the Magisterium has not definitively settled or matters of discipline or pastoral prudence. Here again we see that in a manner quite contrary to Catholic teaching, the neo-Catholic obliterates any distinction between the ordinary and extraordinary Magisterium, between the doctrinal and disciplinary decrees of Popes and Councils—it's all infallible.

At any rate, if Pope Paul's own declarations do not describe a break with ecclesiastical tradition, then words have lost their meaning. And for the neo-Catholics, many words *have* lost their meaning—including, as we can see here, the words "liturgical tradition." But while Pope Paul's admissions ought to settle the question as to whether it is "private judgment" to say that the new Mass departs from that tradition, we will nevertheless undertake a further demonstration of what is obvious to everyone but neo-Catholics.

---

[188]Fr. John Parsons, "Reform of the Reform? [Part II]," *Christian Order*, December 2001. Fr. Parsons is a diocesan priest in Australia and a renowned Catholic scholar. His bishop has not, to our knowledge, accused him of "private judgment."

A systematic overview of the new liturgy is well beyond our scope, and in any case has already been undertaken by eminent scholars such as the great Msgr. Klaus Gamber. A single example suffices for present purposes: the new Offertory prayers—or, as the official text has it, the "Prayer over the Gifts." One of the ground rules of the liturgical reform, according to Vatican II, was that "any new forms adopted should in some way grow organically from forms already existing."[189] Let us see to what extent that instruction was observed in this case.

Traditional Catholics are familiar with the beautiful and doctrinally rich words in which the Host is offered in the traditional liturgy:

> Accept, O holy Father, almighty and eternal God, this unspotted host, which I, Thy unworthy servant, offer unto Thee, my living and true God, for my innumerable sins, offenses, and negligences, and for all here present: as also for all faithful Christians, both living and dead, that it may avail both me and them for salvation unto life everlasting. Amen.

This magnificently Catholic prayer has been replaced with:

> Blessed are you, Lord, God of all creation. Through your goodness we have this bread to offer, which earth has given and human hands have made. It will become for us the bread of life.

Quite apart from its utter blandness, this new prayer in no way grows organically "from forms already existing." Quite the contrary, it does not have the slightest relation to the original prayer, which summarized the Catholic teaching so beautifully and concisely. According to Fr. Peter Coughlan in his book *The New Mass: A Pastoral Guide* (1969), it was not even intended to bear such a relation. The new prayer, he says, "is a combination of a prayer taken from the Jewish meal ritual and the concept of

---

[189]Abbott, ed., *The Documents of Vatican II*, p. 147.

man's work consecrated to the Lord, an idea which the Pope himself wanted to be expressed in some way at this point in the Mass."[190]

Therefore, one might think, the new Offertory prayers break radically with ecclesiastical tradition because—as had never happened before—Mass texts were concocted on the spot from borrowed elements cobbled together by a papally appointed committee, Pope Paul's Consilium, to express "ideas" that the Pope wished to include in his new creation. The same is true for the new rite as a whole, including the Consilium's composition of three new "Eucharistic prayers" to supplant the 1,600-year-old Roman Canon, which is now, quite incredibly, reduced to the status of a disused "option"—in favor of texts written in the 1960s.

In view of the wholesale liturgical changes imposed by Pope Paul, that the new liturgy is a dramatic rupture with the Church's entire liturgical past is a matter of simple common sense. Cardinal Ratzinger himself has argued that the imposition of the new rite represents a break with tradition. Clearly commenting on the work of the Consilium, Ratzinger says, "In the place of liturgy as the fruit of development came fabricated liturgy. We abandoned the organic, living process of growth and development over centuries, and replaced it—as in a manufacturing process—with a fabrication, a banal on-the-spot product."[191]

This was also the view of Msgr. Gamber, who explained what would be apparent to any impartial observer when he noted that the new Mass represented not a case of liturgical development but of "fabricating a new liturgy by committee."[192]

---

[190]Davies, *Pope Paul's New Mass*, p. 320. It would strike some as ominous that the new offertory prayer, like the rejected sacrifice of Cain, explicitly offers to God only fruits of the earth, rather than the "firstling of his flock" offered by Abel: "And it came to pass after many days, that Cain offered of the fruits of the earth...." *Genesis*, 4:3.

[191]Gamber, *The Reform of the Roman Liturgy*. Excerpts from Cardinal Ratzinger's preface to the French-language edition appear on the back cover.

[192]Ibid., p. 99.

Gamber, a liturgist of great renown, is a scholar whose authority and credentials are disputed by no one. Beginning in 1962, he headed the liturgical institute in Regensburg, and edited an eighteen-volume monograph series entitled *Studia Patristica et Liturgica,* as well as fifteen volumes of *Textus Patristici et Liturgici.* His devastating critique of the liturgical reform, *The Reform of the Roman Liturgy: Its Problems and Background* (English translation, 1993), for whose French-language edition Cardinal Ratzinger wrote a laudatory preface, merits careful study. (Cardinal Ratzinger describes Msgr. Gamber as "the one scholar who, among the army of pseudo-liturgists, truly represents the liturgical thinking of the center of the Church.")[193]

For Gamber there was no question that the new Mass constituted a clear and tragic break with tradition, and he said so flatly. He observed that while the liturgy had evolved gradually and imperceptibly over time, "there has never actually been *an actual break with Church tradition, as has happened now,* and in such a frightening way, where almost everything the Church represents is being questioned."[194] "We can only pray and hope," he added, "that the Roman Church will *return to Tradition* and allow once more the celebration of that liturgy of the Mass which is well over 1,000 years old."[195] Msgr. Gamber would have been baffled at the anti-intellectual position of the neo-Catholic, whereby radical novelty conforms with tradition as long as ecclesiastical authority says it does, despite all evidence to the contrary and in spite of the very demands of logic itself.

Here is how Gamber viewed our present situation:

> Today, those who out of a sense of personal belief hold firm to what until recently had been strictly prescribed by the Roman Church are treated with condescension by many of their own brothers. They face problems if they continue to

---

[193]Ibid., p. xiii.
[194]Ibid., p. 109.
[195]Ibid., pp. 113-14.

nurture the very rite in which they were brought up and to which they have been consecrated....

On the other side, the progressives who see little or no value in tradition can do almost no wrong, and are usually given the benefit of the doubt, even when they defend opinions which clearly contradict Catholic teaching.

To add to this spiritual confusion, we are also dealing with the satiated state of mind of modern man, who, living in our consumer society, approaches anything that is holy with a complete lack of understanding and has no appreciation of the concept of religion, let alone of his own sinful state. For them, God, if they believe in Him at all, exists only as their "friend."

At this critical juncture, the traditional Roman rite, more than one thousand years old and until now the heart of the Church, was destroyed.[196]

Here we have Gamber at his most devastating. A radical rupture with tradition has taken place, he notes with sadness, and at the worst possible moment. At a time when the spiritual idiocy of modern man has reached appalling proportions, the traditional liturgy, which conveys the sense of tradition and of the transcendent that he so desperately needs, has been vandalized beyond recognition. It is hardly possible to elaborate upon that sentiment.

Gamber in fact went even further than merely stating that the new liturgy constituted a radical break with tradition—that much should be obvious, he thought. More interesting was the question, which Gamber dared to pose, of whether the Pope in fact possessed the authority to change the traditional rite of Mass in such a wholesale manner.

According to Gamber, "It most certainly is not the function of the Holy See to introduce Church reforms. The first duty of the Pope is...*to watch over* the traditions of the Church—her dogmatic, moral, and liturgical traditions."[197] This is a critical point: the Pope's first duty is to *preserve* what has been handed down, not to introduce novelty or to discard what is ancient and

---

[196]Ibid., pp. 98-99.
[197]Ibid., p. 38.

venerable. The fundamentally conservative role of the papal office, as we note elsewhere in this book, was described specifically at the First Vatican Council: it is the Pope's task to *guard* the *depositum fidei*, not to change or augment it.

Gamber concludes: "Since there is no document that specifically assigns to the Apostolic See the authority to change, let alone to abolish the traditional liturgical rite; and since, furthermore, it can be shown that *not a single predecessor of Pope Paul VI has ever introduced major changes to the Roman liturgy*, the assertion that the Holy See has the authority to change the liturgical rite would appear to be debatable, to say the least."[198] As we have already noted, in *The Spirit of the Liturgy* (2000), no less an authority than Cardinal Ratzinger all but endorses this view. "The authority of the Pope," Ratzinger concludes, "is not unlimited; it is at the service of Sacred Tradition."[199]

Likewise, the new Catechism teaches that "Liturgy is a constitutive element of the holy and living Tradition.... Even the supreme authority in the Church may not change the liturgy arbitrarily, but only in the obedience of faith and with religious respect for the mystery of the liturgy."[200] But since the neo-Catholics hold that it is impossible for the Pope to change the liturgy arbitrarily, without the obedience of faith, or without religious respect for the mystery of the liturgy—all papal liturgical innovations being "by definition" traditional—they would no doubt hold this teaching of the Catechism to be quite superfluous, if not in itself an exercise in "private judgment."

Alfons Cardinal Stickler, the retired prefect of the Vatican library and archives, who served as a *peritus* on Vatican II's Liturgy Commission, apparently also concurs in the "private judgment" condemned by the neo-Catholics. After noting that he had never called into question the validity of the Novus Ordo, the Cardinal adds that the juridical question was another matter. Basing his judgment on "my intensive work with the

---

[198]Ibid., p. 39.
[199]See footnote 175.
[200]*Catechism of the Catholic Church*, §§1124, 1125.

medieval canonists," the Cardinal points out that there are certain things so essential to the life of the Church that "even the Pope has no right of disposal" over them, as indeed the Catechism teaches. He suggests that the liturgy should be considered among these essential things.[201]

Cardinal Stickler has distinguished between the two rites by noting that while what he calls the *corpus traditionum* was alive in the old Mass, the new is plainly "contrived."[202] He endorsed Gamber's contention that, in the Cardinal's words, "today we stand before the ruins of a 2,000-year tradition, and...it is to be feared that, as a result of the countless reforms, the tradition is in such a vandalized mess that it may be difficult to revive it."[203]

But according to the neo-Catholics, these eminent churchmen have no right to remark what is obvious, since Catholic fidelity requires us to ignore all empirical evidence and cling to the *a priori* assumption that whatever the Pope approves must be traditional.

Not long after Annibale Bugnini, the head of the Consilium, had finished what observers from across the spectrum have described as the destruction of the traditional Roman rite, he proposed the "renewal" of the Rosary. It was to be shortened and rearranged, with the Our Father recited only once at the beginning, and the Hail Mary edited to include only "the biblical portion of the prayer." The "Holy Mary, Mother of God" would be said "only at the end of each *tenth* Hail Mary." There would also be a new "public" version of the Rosary,

---

[201]Cardinal Stickler's memoirs originally appeared as "Erinnerungen und Erfahrungen eines Konzilsperitus der Liturgiekommission," in Franz Breid, ed., *Die heilige Liturgie* (Steyr, Austria: Ennsthaler Verlag, 1997), pp. 160-95; an English translation appeared as "Recollections of a Vatican II Peritus," trans. Thomas E. Woods, Jr., *The Latin Mass*, Winter 1999, pp. 24-36. All pagination refers to this translation.

[202]Stickler, "Recollections of a Vatican II Peritus," p. 34.

[203]Ibid., p. 36.

consisting of readings, songs, homilies, and "a series of Hail Marys, but limited to one decade."[204]

Paul VI responded to this preposterous proposal through the Vatican Secretary of State: "[T]he faithful would conclude that 'the Pope has changed the Rosary,' and the psychological effect would be disastrous.... Any change in it cannot but lessen the confidence of the simple and the poor."[205] It was a clear sign of the incoherence of the postconciliar program that the very grounds on which the Pope rejected changes to the Rosary were ignored in the decision to make even more radical changes to the traditional rite of Mass.    What about the disastrous psychological effects of changing on a few weeks' notice the rite of Mass that people had known their whole lives and that dated back in Church history to the time of Pope St. Gregory the Great?  How is it "private judgment" to note that a radical change to the foundation of the Church's divine worship has had more serious consequences than Bugnini's rejected plans for a revision of the Rosary?

Certain neo-Catholics even propose the ludicrous thesis that the Mass of Paul VI was completely in line with a supposed "longstanding process" of "liturgical reform" launched by none other than Pope St. Pius X. In *The Pope, the Council and the Mass,* for example, the authors cite St. Pius X's *Divino Afflatu* (which merely rearranged the distribution of the Psalter to restore balance between the Psalms and an increasing number of prayers to saints and blesseds), and his call for "active participation" (i.e., deeper *internal* participation) in the *traditional liturgy.* From these things the authors leap to the conclusion that St. Pius X "was *in favor* [their emphasis] of orderly liturgical change, as required by the times...." The suggestion that St. Pius X would approve of Pope Paul VI's demolition of the traditional Roman rite in favor of a new rite drawn up by a committee cannot be taken seriously by anyone with even a minimal

---

[204]Annibale Bugnini, *The Reform of the Liturgy* (Collegeville, MN: Liturgical Press, 1990), p. 876.
[205]Ibid.

knowledge of the Church's liturgical history. As Michael Davies rightly notes, the attempt to use minor liturgical adjustments by supremely conservative preconciliar Popes to justify the unheard-of Pauline innovations "is not simply unscholarly, but dishonest."[206]

Equally bankrupt, it seems to us, is the neo-Catholic claim that it is "private judgment" to argue that Paul VI never explicitly and *de jure* "banned" celebration of the traditional Latin rite, and that its use has never actually been prohibited by papal command. As the authors of *The Pope, the Council and the Mass* put it: "[W]e cannot conclude other than that the revised Roman Missal with the New Order of Mass has been lawfully established and that the celebration of the Tridentine Mass is forbidden except where ecclesiastical law specifically allows it (aged or infirm priests celebrating *sine populo*, or under special circumstances where a papal indult applies, as in England and Wales under certain special circumstances)."

Leaving aside the *non sequitur* that approval of the new Mass constituted a prohibition of the old Mass, we note that this vintage neo-Catholic claim was demolished by Cardinal Stickler's revelation in 1995 that a commission of nine cardinals convened by Pope John Paul II in 1986 had, by a vote of 8 to 1, agreed that Paul VI *never legally suppressed the traditional Latin rite*, as opposed to simply promulgating his own revised Missal, and that every priest remained free to use the old Missal. (The commission was composed of Cardinals Ratzinger, Mayer, Oddi, Stickler, Casaroli, Gantin, Innocenti, Palazzini, and Tomko.) The Cardinal further disclosed that in view of the commission's findings, the Pope was presented with a document for his signature, declaring that any priest of the Roman Rite was free to choose between the traditional Missal and the new Missal. Cardinal Stickler also confirmed reports that the Pope was dissuaded from signing the document by certain cardinals who claimed it would cause "division."[207] The

---

[206] *Pope Paul's New Mass*, p. 16.

[207] The Cardinal's revelations, to which one of us was an eyewitness, took place at the Christifideles Conference in Fort Lee, NJ,

Pope later settled on the *Ecclesia Dei* indult of 1988, thus in effect granting permission for what had never actually been forbidden in the first place.

Further, Annibale Bugnini admitted in his own memoirs that (long before the cardinalate commission's vote) he had failed in his bid to obtain a definite Vatican ruling that the old Mass had been abolished *de jure*. Bugnini was informed by the Secretary of the Pontifical Commission for the Interpretation of Conciliar Documents that he would not be given permission to seek such a ruling, because to declare the formal prohibition of the Church's own traditional rite of Mass would be "an odious act in the face of liturgical tradition."[208] Yet it is this same "odious act" that neo-Catholics stubbornly ascribe to Paul VI. Are they willing, then, to accuse eight distinguished cardinals of "private judgment" in holding that the odious act of "banning" the Mass of the ages never really occurred?

It is quite a commentary on the current state of the Church that Pope John Paul II needed a commission of cardinals to tell him exactly what his predecessor had done to the traditional Roman rite, but the commission only confirmed what was obvious in the "private judgment" of traditionalists. As we have seen throughout, however, denial of the obvious is basic to the neo-Catholic system.

There appears to be no limit to the audacity with which certain neo-Catholics will defend the inane axiom that any criticism of papally approved innovations constitutes "private judgment." In a *Wanderer* editorial, for example, the authors seriously adduce, in defense of the new liturgy, canon 7 of Session XXII of the Council of Trent, which defended the traditional liturgy *against* innovation: "If any one saith, that the ceremonies, vestments, and outward signs, which the Catholic Church makes use of in the celebration of masses, are incentives

---

on May 20, 1995. The revelations were widely reported in *The Latin Mass* and other organs of the Catholic press and have not been denied by the Vatican.

[208]Annibale Bugnini, *La Riforma Liturgica* (Rome: Ed. Liturgiche, 1983), p. 298.

to impiety, rather than offices of piety; let him be anathema." The cited canon was obviously addressed to the errors of Luther and the other Protestant "reformers," who wanted to see something very much like the Mass of Paul VI offered according to Eucharistic Prayer II, the most commonly used option today, which is practically indistinguishable from an Anglican communion service.

It is typical of the neo-Catholic's selective deference to prior Church teaching (see Chapter 11) that the *Wanderer* editorial fails to mention Trent's declaration in canon 13 of Session VII:

> If any one saith, that the received and approved rites of the Catholic Church, wont to be used in the solemn administration of the sacraments, may be contemned, or without sin be omitted at pleasure by the ministers, *or be changed*, by *any* pastor of the churches whomsoever, into other new ones; let him be anathema.

The editorialists also omit canon 10 from Session XXII:

> If any one saith, that the rite of the Roman Church, according to which a part of the canon and the words of consecration are pronounced in a low tone, is to be condemned; *or, that the mass ought to be celebrated in the vernacular only;* or, that water ought not to be mixed with the wine that is to be offered in the chalice, for that it is contrary to the institution of Christ; let him be anathema.

Also conveniently ignored is the Profession of Faith of the Council of Trent (contained in the Bull *Iniunctum nobis* of Pius IV), which declares as follows: "The apostolic *and* ecclesiastical traditions and *all other observances* and constitutions of that same Church I most firmly admit and embrace."[209]

Even when they are forced to confront the anathemas of Trent, neo-Catholic apologists for the current liturgical ruin will propose the argument that Popes are at liberty to do here what they anathematize in others. That is, the liturgy is sacred and

[209]DZ, 995.

untouchable for every member of the Church *except* the Pope—
the very one who is supposed to act as primary guardian of
liturgical tradition, as Gamber, Ratzinger and the Catechism
note.

In staking out this untenable claim, the neo-Catholic fails to
consider *why* the infallible Magisterium anathematized the
stated liturgical innovations and opinions in the first place. They
were anathematized not merely because they trench upon some
imagined exclusive prerogative of the Pope to indulge in radical
liturgical innovation, but because *such innovation is wrong in
itself*—and thus wrong for everyone. Putting aside, then, all the
wearisome argumentation over whether Paul VI had the raw
power to "abrogate" or "obrogate" St. Pius V's Bull *Quo Primum*
(which canonized the traditional Latin Mass as the norm of the
Roman Rite), one can see in the Tridentine anathemas, and in
like anathemas throughout Church history, the Magisterium's
unwavering intention to protect the Church from any possible
rupture of liturgical tradition, *no matter who causes it.* Surely in
this matter the Pope himself must set the highest example, even
if we assume (as the neo-Catholics do) that a Pope can cast aside
all the liturgical proscriptions of his predecessors. And is this
not why, before Paul VI, no Pope in Church history dared to
concoct a new rite of Mass and impose it upon the Church?

How the neo-Catholics propose to reconcile a Catholic's
obligation to embrace ecclesiastical traditions and observances
with Paul VI's *de facto* suppression of the traditional Roman
liturgy remains a mystery. In fact, the neo-Catholics have a
difficult enough task attempting to reconcile Pope Paul's act
with the teaching of Vatican II in *Sacrosanctum Concilium*: "[I]n
faithful obedience to tradition, the sacred Council declares that
holy Mother Church holds all lawfully acknowledged rites to be
of equal right and dignity; that she wishes to *preserve them* in the
future and to *foster them in every way.*" Surely even the most
determined neo-Catholic proponent of the principle that The
Pope Can Do No Wrong will admit that in suppressing the
traditional Latin rite Pope Paul was not following the Council's

teaching that the traditional rite must be given equal dignity and preserved and fostered in every way.[210]

Nor are the neo-Catholics likely to mention the Church's past solemn condemnations of the very same liturgical innovations approved by Paul VI. Some 200 years after Trent, Pope Pius VI condemned various errors of the illicit Synod of Pistoia in his Apostolic Constitution *Auctorem Fidei*. Among the Synod's many errors, Pius VI identified

> the proposition of the Synod by which it shows itself eager to remove the cause through which, in part, there has been induced forgetfulness of the principles relating to the order of liturgy, "by recalling it [the liturgy] to *greater simplicity of rites*, by expressing it *in the vernacular language or by uttering it in a loud voice*," as if the present order of the Liturgy, received and approved by the Church, had emanated in some part from the forgetfulness of the principles by which it should be regulated.

This proposition Pius VI condemned as "rash, offensive to pious ears, insulting to the Church, favorable to the charges of the heretics...."[211] Also condemned was

> the proposition asserting that "it would be against apostolic practice and the plans of God unless *easier ways were prepared for people to unite their voice with that of the whole Church*"; if

---

[210]*Sacrosanctum Concilium*, 4. On the other hand, as we discuss in Chapter 12, the open-ended ambiguities and "yes-no" style of *Sacrosanctum Concilium* can be used to justify precisely what the document seems to forbid. Thus, in the sentence immediately following the one quoted, we find: "The Council also desires that, where necessary, the rites be *revised* carefully in the light of sound tradition, and that they be given new vigor to meet *the circumstances and needs of modern times*." But "sound tradition" always forbade revising the ancient rites of the Church to suit the "needs of modern times" — least of all the received and approved Latin Mass of the Roman Rite, which Paul VI himself described as "our hereditary religious patrimony, which seemed to enjoy the privilege of being untouchable and settled."

[211]DZ, 1533.

understood to signify introducing *use of popular language* to the order prescribed for the celebration of the mysteries.

Pius VI called this proposition "false, rash, disturbing to the order prescribed for the celebration of the mysteries, *easily productive of many evils.*"[212] Who can doubt the wisdom of that warning after thirty years of bitter experience with the new vernacular liturgy?

It must be noted that Paul VI (citing the Council's liturgical document *Sacrosanctum Concilium*) attempted to justify his liturgical innovations along the very lines condemned by Pius VI, and for the very reasons advanced by the Synod of Pistoia. Defending the sudden abandonment of Latin in the liturgy, for example, Pope Paul declared: "If the divine Latin language kept us apart from the children, from youth, from the world of labor and of affairs, if it were a dark screen, not a clear window, would it be right for us fishers of souls to maintain it as the exclusive language of prayer and religious intercourse?"[213] Pope Paul's discovery that the Latin language was "a dark screen" that obscured the meaning of the Mass from the people would have delighted the Pistoian liberals, but it would also have come as a complete surprise to every one of Paul's predecessors — not to mention the faithful themselves, who had never requested Mass in the vernacular. Nor did Pope Paul seem to notice that perfectly splendid vernacular translations of the traditional Mass had already been printed in Roman Missals in all the principal languages of the world.

*Auctorem Fidei* cannot be dismissed, in the usual neo-Catholic manner (see Chapter 10), as outmoded teaching that has been superseded by a change of ecclesial circumstances. In *Mediator Dei*, his monumental encyclical on the sacred liturgy issued a mere fifteen years before Vatican II, Pope Pius XII cited as authoritative the condemnations by Pius VI we have just quoted. The context was Pius XII's stern rebuke of the

---

[212]DZ, 1566.
[213]Audience Address, November 26, 1969.

innovators of the so-called "liturgical movement" during the immediate preconciliar period.[214] In particular, Pius XII declared that "the temerity and daring of those who introduce novel liturgical practices, or call for the revival of obsolete rites out of harmony with prevailing laws and rubrics, deserve severe reproof." As for Mass in the vernacular: "It has pained Us grievously to note, Venerable Brethren, that such innovations are actually being introduced, not merely in minor details but in matters of major importance as well. We instance, in point of fact, those who make use of the vernacular in the celebration of the august eucharistic sacrifice.... The use of the Latin language, customary in a considerable portion of the Church, is a manifest and beautiful sign of unity, as well as *an effective antidote for any corruption of doctrinal truth.*"[215] Another wise warning disregarded by Pope Paul.

If more proof were needed of the Church's constant abhorrence of liturgical innovation for the first 1,962 years of her history, there is the Apostolic Constitution *Veterum Sapientia,* issued by Pope John XXIII only a few months before the first session of Vatican II. Calling for nothing less than a total restoration of the Church's traditional use of the Latin language in all aspects of her life, Pope John admonished the bishops: "In the exercise of their paternal care, they shall be on their guard lest anyone under their jurisdiction, *eager for revolutionary changes,* writes against the use of Latin in the teaching of the higher sacred studies *or in the liturgy,* or through prejudice makes light of the Holy See's will in this regard or interprets it falsely."[216] As Pope John declared regarding the Latin liturgy, only a few years before his successor suddenly discarded it:

---

[214]*Mediator Dei,* footnote 53.

[215]While the same encyclical allows for the possibility of papal permission for "the use of the mother tongue in connection with several of the rites" — that is, rites other than the received and approved rite of Mass, such as the rite of Baptism in mission countries — it is beyond genuine dispute that Pius XII would have regarded as unthinkable the creation by committee of a new rite of Mass to be offered entirely in the vernacular.

[216]*Veterum Sapientia,* February 22, 1962.

"Finally, the Catholic Church has a dignity far surpassing that of every merely human society, for it was founded by Christ the Lord. It is altogether fitting, therefore, that the language it uses should be noble, majestic, and *non-vernacular*." The almost immediate trampling of *Veterum Sapientia* in the stampede of liturgical destruction following the Council ranks as one of the most remarkable facts of the postconciliar revolution.

In the face of all this evidence, to assert, as the neo-Catholics do, that Paul VI, being himself a Pope, was not bound by the teaching of prior Popes and councils on the Latin liturgy, is to admit implicitly that Paul did depart from his predecessors in what they regarded as the preservation of a vital ecclesiastical tradition. Worse, the neo-Catholic view makes of the Pope an absolute monarch whose teaching on what is prudent and good for the Church applies to everyone but himself. That is precisely what the Pope is not; for (as Ratzinger, Gamber, the new Catechism and our own common sense make clear) the Pope is a servant of the Church's traditions, not their master.

And so, the neo-Catholic would apply the anathema of Trent to traditionalists because they object to the new rite of Mass that the Fathers of Trent, had they seen it, would have viewed with a mixture of horror, disbelief and terrified incomprehension. Trent's condemnation of liturgical innovation is stood on its head to *justify* innovation. Amazingly enough, we are told that it is inadmissible "private judgment" to say that the Pope has departed from liturgical tradition, even when, as in the case of Paul VI, *he expressly states that he has done so.* We are even told that when a Pope approves the very innovations his own predecessors condemned, we must have blind faith that the Pope has acted in conformity with Catholic tradition.

In confronting this neo-Catholic notion of what constitutes "private judgment," we encounter the very core of neo-Catholic thinking. And what one finds there is nothing but a very un-Catholic, and quite unreasonable, demand for willful self-delusion. Ultimately, the neo-Catholic program of sitting back as the destruction takes its course, while blandly dismissing objections to the destruction as "private judgment," might be a nice strategy if Catholics wanted to be perceived as a bunch of quietist morons who smile inanely while the structures of their Faith are being dismantled. But some of us have set our sights a bit higher than that.

# Chapter 8

# Pitting one Pope Against Another?

A corollary of the neo-Catholic axiom that all criticism of the papally approved postconciliar novelties is "private judgment" is the claim that comparisons of recent Popes with earlier ones are also somehow suspect. The Pamphlet, following the neo-Catholic line, condemns the practice as "pitting one Pope against another."

We confess that we do not see what is wrong with such comparisons. The fact is, Popes have differed, and sometimes on fairly significant matters. This does not necessarily make one a heretic and the other an angel, which is how neo-Catholics generally interpret the traditionalist position. It does mean, however, that one may have been right and the other wrong.

Let us take as an example Pope St. Gregory the Great (590-604), one of the most celebrated and revered pontiffs in Church history. His accomplishments were manifold: he arranged for the evangelization of Britain, he codified the chant that bears his name, he stared down the ravaging Lombards and provided for the sick and hungry of Rome. At the same time, it is a fact that he was part of that minority of churchmen who subjected philosophers to withering ridicule and were extremely critical of efforts to synthesize the wisdom of Greek philosophy with the data of divine revelation. In the second century, St. Justin Martyr had used the term "seeds of the Word" to describe the truths that the Greeks, living before Christ, had been able to discover. As Justin saw the matter, it was as though God had prepared the intellectual terrain for the coming of His Son. This intellectual project was carried on by some of the Church's brightest lights: Clement of Alexandria, St. Augustine, the Cappadocian Fathers (St. Basil the Great, St. Gregory of Nyssa, and St. Gregory Nazianzen), and countless others, culminating in the extraordinary philosophical edifice constructed by St. Thomas Aquinas. The angry claim of the likes of Tertullian and Hippolytus that such a synthesis was both pointless and dangerous loses its force when we recall that it was they themselves, and not those Church Fathers who were eager to mine the wisdom of the Greeks, who ultimately fell into heresy. (St. Hippolytus, as we know, died reconciled.)

Yes, we suppose we are "pitting one Pope against another" when we say that Pope St. Gregory the Great, however much we may (rightly) venerate him for his extraordinary accomplishments and personal holiness, was gravely mistaken on this issue and that Pope Leo XIII, to choose just one example, was absolutely correct (cf. *Aeterni Patris*, 1879). So what? In suggesting that "pitting one Pope against another" is a sign of schism or heresy or whatever, the Pamphlet is deliberately stacking the deck against us, ruling out much of our evidence in advance. A neat trick. But we have no intention of playing by the neo-Catholic's arbitrary rules, especially since, as this example reveals so strikingly, they require that we ignore Church history.

Thus, for example, there can be no rational objection when traditionalists compare the tone of optimism apparent in the past several pontificates with the warning and foreboding that characterized the Popes of earlier this century (who lived at a time when the state of civilization was not nearly as bad as it is now). Despite his denunciations of the "culture of death," it is difficult to escape the conclusion that John Paul—and *Gaudium et Spes* before him, whose fatuous optimism even the liberal Eamon Duffy found hard to take—does not fully appreciate the gravity of the situation the Church faces in the modern world. We no longer hear the kinds of constant exhortations of the faithful, so typical of his preconciliar predecessors, that they rally in defense of the Church against her enemies. (This absence is also apparent in the insipid propers of the new Mass. Although standard in the old rite, when was the last time a prayer was heard at the new Mass begging God that by the grace of the Eucharist we might be strengthened against our enemies? That kind of thing is doubtless considered old-fashioned in the age of dialogue and ecumenism.)

Consider John Paul's reflections upon addressing the United Nations Educational, Scientific and Cultural Organization (UNESCO): "At UNESCO, for example, I was amazed by how the Assembly reacted to certain key thoughts and observations that my experience has led me to regard as essential. I felt that there existed in this world a vast accord—though not always conscious—a broad consensus, not only about certain values, but about certain threats. My audience represented countries from all over the world and came from every continent. I felt that it was the representatives of the young nations and of the new states who reacted the most warmly to my elaboration of the meaning of culture and of the conditions for its development. It gave me much to think about."

Such statements can be multiplied many times over. What broad consensus can the Pope possibly have in mind? Decades earlier, when the world was in vastly better shape culturally and morally (though, of course, not perfect by any means), here is how Pope Pius XI perceived the situation: "The two opposing camps are now clearly marked; each man should choose his own. Men of good will and men of evil will face one another. The uninterested and the cowards face their fearsome responsibility. They will have their names changed if they do not change their behavior: they will be called traitors."[217] On another occasion Pius remarked: "Only by being radicals of the

---

[217]Archbishop Arrigo Pintonello, "A Bishop to His Brother Bishops," *Christian Order*, November 1977, p. 671.

right will Catholics have the dynamism to withstand the radicals of the left and to conquer the world for Christ."[218]

Like statements from Pope St. Pius X could be provided almost without end, but we shall confine ourselves to one: "There is no need for Us to remind you that, when the enemy approaches and is at our doors, it is time for the call to arms. But for you, it is not only a question of sounding the alert; the enemy is in the very interior of the Empire.... All the faithful, then, must be gathered together, and especially the most valiant among them. We exhort you to do this with all your strength."[219]

To put it mildly, we are still more persuaded by the preconciliar Popes' posture, and it can hardly be called "integrism" to conclude, based on the evidence, that one position better accords with the objective situation than another. Moreover, can it really be a surprise that in the days when the Church portrayed herself as a standing rebuke to a sinful world, and as the institution that alone could sanctify and transform a world succumbing to decadence, she attracted so many tough, intelligent, and disciplined men to the priesthood? It was precisely the Church's *defiance* of modernity that was at the root of its vibrancy early in the twentieth century. The Church was the one institution that dared to hurl a defiant *no* at the modern world. And people responded, intellectuals among them, for here was something exciting and exhilarating. Hilaire Belloc remarked that "the more powerful, the more acute, and the more sensitive minds of our time are clearly inclining toward the Catholic side."[220] Although St. Pius X found himself the subject of ceaseless ridicule at the hands of many European intellectuals for the vigor with which he battled Modernism, for others this otherwise gentle man's obstinacy seemed to be the mark of a true man of God. In fact it was only *after* the issuance of *Lamentabili Sane* (1907), the list of condemned errors of the

---

[218]Letter to Cardinal Archbishop of Paris, quoted in *The Latin Mass*, Winter 1998, p. 63.

[219]Pius X, *Il Fermo Proposito*, June 11, 1905.

[220]Hilaire Belloc, *The Great Heresies* (1937; repr., Rockford, IL: TAN, 1991), p. 160.

Modernists, that many of the Church's great converts made their way into her fold. In England, for instance, the great historian Christopher Dawson entered the Church in 1914, the former Anglican Ronald Knox in 1917 and G.K. Chesterton in 1922. Dawson vigorously defended Pope Pius IX's *Syllabus of Errors* as an antidote to modern secular liberalism, which denied "the subordination of human society to divine law." As for the United States, Peter Huff notes that the American Church "witnessed such a steady stream of notable literary conversions that the statistics tended to support Calvert Alexander's hypothesis of something suggesting a cultural trend." The pre-Vatican II Catholic Church in the United States was, he argues, "a highly imaginative world of myth, meaning, and ritual, based upon the classical vision of Catholicism's cultural mission."[221] Surveying this cultural phenomenon, historian William Halsey describes pre-Vatican II American Catholicism as constituting a full-fledged "countersociety." His partial listing of Catholic organizations runs as follows:

> In chronological order from 1900 to 1950, Catholics organized: The National Catholic Educational Association (1904), Catholic Press Association (1911), Catholic Writers Guild of America (1919), American Catholic Historical Association (1919), Catholic Library Association (1921), American Catholic Philosophical Association (1926), Catholic Association for International Peace (1926), Catholic Anthropological Association (1928), Catholic Book Club (1928), Catholic Poetry Society of America (1931), Catholic Biblical Association of America (1936), Catholic Art Association (1937), Catholic Theatre Conference (1937), American Catholic Sociological Society (1938), Catholic Renascence Society (1940), Catholic Economic Association (1941), Catholic Commission on Intellectual and Cultural Affairs (1946), and the American Catholic Psychological Association (1947).

---

[221]Peter A. Huff, *Allen Tate and the Catholic Revival: Trace of the Fugitive Gods* (New York: Paulist Press, 1996), pp. 28-29, 23.

And yet, Halsey goes on to argue, although Catholics established an extraordinary array of parallel associations, they did so not because they cherished separateness or exclusion *per se*. What at times was an institutional isolation did not indicate a lack of concern with the nation as a whole; on the contrary, Catholics understood that it was only through cultivating a robust Catholic culture that they could truly serve their country. Catholic culture, he writes, "was an attempt to save middle-class culture from its own decadence. While isolating themselves from disillusionment, these agencies were busy affirming values which were either under attack, forgotten, or going through the disquieting process of transformation."[222]

We have set forth for the reader's consideration numerous examples of papally approved reversals and apparent contradictions of prior Church teaching and practice in the postconciliar Church, taking care to note that none of these changes actually appears in the form of a binding Magisterial pronouncement of Catholic doctrine or an obligatory practice required of all the faithful. To argue that it is "pitting one Pope against another" to point out these discrepancies is nothing but an exercise in begging the question. The question is whether there *are* contradictions and reversals, and, if so, what Catholics are to make of them, given that Rome itself has offered no explanation of how the discrepancies can be reconciled.

The "pitting one Pope against another" argument presumes that lay people are incapable of understanding their own faith and the history of their own Church sufficiently to know whether a given proposition or practice contradicts what they have been taught or what they have practiced before. It makes of the Pope the leader of a kind of gnostic sect, whose members depend upon the latest auguries from Rome in order to know the content of their belief and praxis. And, as is the case with the neo-Catholic claim that papal innovations are "by definition" traditional, the argument presumes *a priori* that no Pope can possibly contradict his predecessors in any matter of

---

[222]William M. Halsey, *The Survival of American Innocence: Catholicism in an Era of Disillusionment, 1920-1940* (Notre Dame: University of Notre Dame Press, 1980), pp. 56-57.

substance. Here it must be noted, however, that some neo-Catholics modify the *a priori* argument by conceding the existence of reversals or contradictions, but holding that since only the Pope can determine if these are necessary "developments" to meet changing conditions, no one may criticize or oppose the changes. The combination of the two arguments renders the neo-Catholic position non-falsifiable; the Pope becomes, for all practical purposes, not merely infallible according to the strict limits of the Vatican I definition, but utterly inerrant—and not just in doctrinal matters, but in all matters.

Thus far we have argued that the novelties of Vatican II and the postconciliar Popes have never actually been imposed as Catholic doctrine. We have also argued that in many cases these novelties defy precise definition and cannot be reduced to distinct propositions to which Catholics are bound to give assent. The difference between Catholic dogma (e.g., the Immaculate Conception, the seven sacraments) and the postconciliar novelties (ecumenism, dialogue, and liturgical innovation) should be obvious enough to the intelligent observer. But let us digress briefly to consider the following. Suppose, in fact, that Vatican II did propose some teaching that seemed to involve Catholics in a contradiction in the area of actual doctrine. What ought Catholics to think? Is such a scenario absolutely impossible?

First of all, as we have indicated elsewhere in this book, and as the Church's highest authorities repeatedly pointed out, Vatican II expressly refrained from issuing doctrinal definitions, and thus prescinded from the exercise of that authority that the Church refers to as her solemn or extraordinary Magisterium. But since, nevertheless, the Council did intend to teach, it must have done so at the level of the ordinary Magisterium.

This is an important point in itself: the Church's Magisterium is exercised in different ways. There is, first and foremost, the solemn or extraordinary Magisterium, which consists of solemn definition or anathema, issued by a Pope or by an ecumenical council confirmed by a Pope, manifestly intended to bind the universal Church on a matter of faith or morals.

There is also the ordinary Magisterium, which involves infallibility in a different way. Thus when a Pope issues a statement that is not in itself infallible as a result of its status — that is, a papal statement on a given subject, rather than a solemn definition invoking the extraordinary Magisterium — it may nevertheless be infallible by virtue of its repetition of a teaching that the Church has held since time immemorial. Such is the general reckoning of the encyclical *Humanae Vitae* (1968) on contraception: while the document itself is not infallible *per se*, the teaching that artificial contraception is intrinsically immoral is infallible because it repeats the constant, uninterrupted moral tradition of the Church.

In an important study of the nature of the Church's ordinary Magisterium, Fr. Paul Nau explained in 1956 that the duty of Catholics toward the ordinary Magisterium was "one of inward assent, not as of faith, but as of prudence, the refusal of which could not escape the mark of temerity, unless the doctrine rejected was an actual novelty or involved a manifest discordance between the pontifical affirmation and the doctrine which had hitherto been taught."[223] Thus Fr. Nau suggests that while the natural Catholic instinct is one of deference and obedience even to the ordinary Magisterium, it is not inherently impossible that there could arise a situation in which assent to a novel teaching, presented in the name of the ordinary Magisterium, might be withheld by a faithful Catholic. If such novelties were impossible and every formulation of the ordinary Magisterium were *ipso facto* infallible, there would be no point in distinguishing between the ordinary and extraordinary Magisterium. In that case, *every* statement would form part of the extraordinary Magisterium, and the distinction between the two would be meaningless.

Germain Grisez made a similar point in the July 1984 *Homiletic and Pastoral Review*:

[223]Dom Paul Nau, O.S.B., "The Ordinary Magisterium of the Catholic Church," in *Pope or Church?: Essays on the Infallibility of the Ordinary Magisterium* (Kansas City, MO: Angelus Press, 1998), p. 29.

Obviously, teachings which are proposed infallibly leave no room for dissent on the part of faithful Catholics. However, other teachings of the Ordinary Magisterium can be mistaken, even though they may require and demand religious submission of mind and will. Such teachings can deserve acceptance inasmuch as they are the Magisterium's current best judgment of what God's word requires of Christians. However, that judgment, on the leading edge of developing doctrine and in truly prudential matters, can be mistaken, and faithful Christians can be led by superior claims of faith itself to withhold their submission to it.[224]

William Marshner, chairman of the theology department at Christendom College, took the same basic position in a special issue of *Faith and Reason* devoted to *Dignitatis Humanae* (DH), the Vatican II document on religious liberty. In spite of the fact that Marshner himself believed that DH could be reconciled with prior teaching, he added the following:

> At the same time, however, I join with all other theologians in saying that the new ground is non-infallible teaching. So when I say that the possibility exists that Vatican II is wrong on one or more crucial points of *Dignitatis Humanae*, I do not simply mean that the Council's policy may prove unfruitful. I mean to signal a possibility that the Council's teaching is false.
>
> But may a Catholic theologian admit that such a possibility exists? Of course he may. The decree [sic] *Dignitatis Humanae* is a non-infallible document, and the teaching which it presents is admitted to be a "new development," hence not something which is already acknowledged dogma *ex magisterio ordinario*. Therefore the kind of religious assent which Catholics owe to that teaching is the kind of assent which does not exclude the logical

---

[224]*Homiletic and Pastoral Review*, July 1984, p. 14; cited in Davies, *The Second Vatican Council and Religious Liberty*, p. 260.

possibility that the teaching is wrong; rather our assent
excludes any probability that the teaching is wrong.[225]

Let us consider an actual example of a teaching of the
ordinary Magisterium that was later found to be false and
actually reversed by a Pope. The fifteenth-century Council of
Florence taught in the name of the Magisterium that the matter
of the Sacrament of Holy Orders was the presentation of the
chalice and the paten, and that the form consisted of the words,
"*Accipe potestatem offerendi sacrificium in ecclesia pro vivis et
mortuis, in nomine Patris et Filii et Spiritus Sancti.*"[226] Pope Pius
XII, in his constitution *Sacramentum Ordinis* (1947), changed this
teaching, on the basis of the findings of sound research into the
Church's ancient practice. Having established to his satisfaction
that the presentation of the chalice and the Host went back no
earlier than the tenth century, the Pope declared "by virtue of
the supreme Apostolic authority" that the matter of the
sacrament was in fact only the imposition of hands, and that the
form was the prayer of the Preface of Ordination.[227] This change
provides a clear example of the difference between the ordinary
Magisterium and the extraordinary Magisterium: the teaching of
the Council of Florence was not what the Church had always
and everywhere believed, and was (for that reason) later found
to be in error.

None of the authors we have cited suggests that withholding
assent from teaching of the ordinary Magisterium could be
justified in any but the most rare and unusual of circumstances,
but neither do they exclude the possibility entirely. The neo-
Catholic system, however, *does* exclude it for all intents and
purposes. The neo-Catholic holds that if an organ of the
Magisterium has made a pronouncement—any pronouncement,
no matter how novel—then *a priori* the pronouncement must be

---

[225]*Faith and Reason*, Fall 1983; cited in Michael Davies, *The Second
Vatican Council and Religious Liberty* (Long Prairie, MN: Neumann
Press, 1992), p. 261.

[226]DZ 701.

[227]Rev. Canon Réné Berthod, "The Infallibility of the Church's
Ordinary Magisterium," in *Pope or Church?*, pp. 60-61.

true. The traditionalist, on the other hand, recognizes (as do the cited theologians) that the confidence Catholics are expected to have in a statement by the "ordinary" Magisterium comes from its objective conformity to what the Magisterium has *always* taught. The neo-Catholic refuses to consider the question of objective conformity to past teaching; his inquiry begins and ends with the confirmation that authority has spoken recently. He is thus unable and unwilling to confront the ruinous effects of the swarm of true ecclesial novelties that has emerged, for the first time, during the postconciliar period.

As mere laymen, we make no claim to have anything like the final or definitive word in this matter. But since Rome has made no effort to explain how apparent contradictions between current novelties and previous teaching can be reconciled, the traditionalist approach seems to us the only way to make sense of the current situation in the Church.[228] The crisis we are

---

[228]On the question of religious liberty, for instance, many Council Fathers expressed their own astonishment at the new teaching and were unable to explain how it could be reconciled with prior statements; it was not only Archbishop Lefebvre who failed to see the compatibility of the two positions. Thus Fr. Yves Congar, a theological celebrity at the Council and afterward, spoke of the tension between the traditional teaching and the conciliar document *Dignitatis Humanae:* "It cannot be denied that a text like this does *materially* say something different from the *Syllabus* of 1864, and even almost the opposite of propositions 15 and 77-9 of that document" (emphasis in original). Since the document also claims that it "leaves intact the traditional Catholic doctrine of men and communities toward the one true religion and the only Church of Christ," even while it goes on to introduce a series of novel ideas in support of which it could appeal to no Church document before 1960, one may well be justified in concluding that *Dignitatis Humanae* is simply too confused to offer any coherent teaching. Professor Oscar Cullmann, one of the Protestant observers at the Council, later remarked that on "far too many occasions" the definitive texts of the Council "juxtapose opposing viewpoints without establishing any genuine internal link between them." See Davies, *The Second Vatican Council and Religious Liberty*, pp. 198-209, 174.

presently enduring may well be the epoch in which the significance of the ordinary/extraordinary distinction was destined to become manifest.[229]

As our previous discussion should make clear, aside from the demolition of the traditional Roman rite, nowhere is the apparent contradiction of prior papal teaching and Church practice more evident than in the "ecumenical venture" launched at Vatican II.

The Pamphlet adopts the neo-Catholic argument that Pius XI's *Mortalium Animos* (1928), which forbade Catholics to participate in the ecumenical movement of the day, condemned only "indifferentist ecumenism" (whatever that may mean), and is therefore quite compatible with the ceaseless ecumenical gatherings and common prayer meetings of the past thirty-five years. This is quite false. Absolutely nothing in the document would lead an impartial reader to such a conclusion. The fact is, though, that even on these grounds the Pamphlet's argument fails, since the major ecumenical initiatives of recent years have *all* been indifferentist.

Before examining a few of these, we note that the Pamphlet, like neo-Catholic sources in general, fails to provide a single concrete example of a successful postconciliar ecumenical initiative. It mentions supposed progress with the Orthodox, who have not moved one inch closer to communion with Rome over the past thirty-five years of "ecumenical dialogue." But (to no one's surprise), the Pamphlet says nothing about the scandalous Balamand Statement of 1993, negotiated by the Vatican's Cardinal Cassidy, which renounces the return of the Orthodox to Rome as "outdated ecclesiology."[230] Likewise, the Vatican's Cardinal Kasper, as we have noted in Chapter 3,

---

[229]Nor do we mean to suggest that there could be such a thing as the "fallible Magisterium," a kind of collection of rare errors existing alongside the infallible Magisterium. Should some pronouncement of a pope or council be false, that statement would, obviously, not really be part of the Magisterium. To hold otherwise would be to adopt a false equivalence between truth and authority, as Fr. Nau notes. It is this false equivalence that is at work in the neo-Catholic system.

[230]See footnote 50.

repudiates prior papal teaching on the return of the Protestants to the one true Church: "today we no longer understand ecumenism in the sense of a return, by which the others would 'be converted' and return to being 'catholics.' This was expressly abandoned by Vatican II." [231]

If the Church's ecclesiological teaching can become "outdated," then why not her other teachings? This is progress? Well, yes, it is—for the Orthodox and the Protestants! The Pamphlet also says nothing about the encouragement of joint worship with non-Catholics, which is indeed quite unprecedented and, as we have discussed, stood condemned by preconciliar Church teaching and canon law. The Pamphlet's entire chapter on ecumenism, in fact, is a series of vapid generalizations about the need to go after the straying sheep—as if the shepherd had hitherto been neglectful in taking the traditional approach: direct evangelization of individual dissidents aimed at their return to Rome.

Ecumenical relations with the Anglicans provide a good first example of how ecumenism has degenerated into an utter debacle in its departure from the preconciliar teaching on the return of the dissidents. In 1966, Pope Paul VI and the Archbishop of Canterbury officially opened channels for dialogue between Catholics and Anglicans. Toward this end, the Anglican-Roman Catholic International Commission (ARCIC) was established. Over the course of the 1970s, this body drew up so-called "Agreed Statements" on the Eucharist, ministry, and authority. Anyone familiar with the liturgical changes that brought us the new Mass would recognize in these "Agreed Statements" the same kind of equivocation regarding sacrifice, the priesthood, and other such issues that seem to be

---

[231] *Adista*, February 26, 2001: "La decisione del Vaticano II alla quale il papa si attiene, è assolutamente chiara: noi intendiamo l'ecumene oggi non più nel senso dell'ecumene del ritorno, secondo il quale gli altri devono 'convertirsi' e diventare 'cattolici.' Questo è stato espressamente abbandonato dal Vaticano II."

present in parts of the new rite. (The whole story is told in Michael Davies' book *The Order of Melchisedech*.) These dreadful and apparently deliberate ambiguities were ultimately repudiated by Rome in the early 1990s. This is to be welcomed. But do we draw any lessons from this? None, apparently. Instead, Pope John Paul II has approved the convocation of yet another Anglican-Catholic "working group," addressing this new collection of Catholic bishops and Anglican "bishops" with these words: "On this significant occasion our minds turn spontaneously to the meeting between Pope Paul VI and Archbishop Ramsey in 1966, from which there came the first Anglican and Roman Catholic International Commission. In their Joint Statement, the Pope and the Archbishop spoke of the need for 'a serious dialogue which, founded on the Gospels and on the ancient common traditions, *may lead to that unity in truth for which Christ prayed.*' Now we can look back and say that that dialogue has continued fruitfully in the years since then."[232] What are the fruits of the Anglican-Catholic "dialogue" since 1996? The Anglicans' ordination of women? Their denial of the torments of hell? Their support for abortion, contraception and divorce? And how does one reconcile John Paul II's statement to the "working group" that Anglican-Catholic dialogue "may lead to that unity in truth for which Christ prayed" with Pius XI's condemnation in *Mortalium Animos* of the very notion that "Christ Jesus merely expressed a desire and prayer, which still lacks its fulfillment"?[233] But there we go, pitting one Pope against another.

---

[232]*Address to Anglican-Roman Catholic Working Group*, November 24, 2001.

[233]*Mortalium Animos*, 7: "And here it seems opportune to expound and to refute a certain *false opinion*, on which this whole question, as well as that complex movement by which non-Catholics seek to bring about the union of the Christian churches depends. For authors who favor this view are accustomed, times almost without number, to bring forward these words of Christ: 'That they all may be one.... And there shall be one fold and one shepherd,' with this signification however: that Christ Jesus merely expressed a desire and prayer, *which still lacks its fulfillment.* For they are of the opinion that the unity of faith and government, which is a note of the one true Church of Christ, has

Perhaps the crisis in the Church is grave enough that the restoration of order within Catholicism itself must take precedence over ecumenical initiatives, if only because, as we have seen time and again, the very liberalism that is wreaking havoc in the Church is also, in the realm of ecumenism, producing distinctly unhelpful and ludicrously ambiguous joint statements. Must we not put our own house in order, remembering that *charity begins at home*? In the meantime, as far as non-Catholics are concerned, there is always the old-fashioned way of missionary work and individual conversion, which used to work pretty well.

Regarding the Orthodox, the Vatican is now actively discouraging proselytism, contrary to the teaching of the preconciliar Popes on the necessity of an Orthodox reunion with Rome. It suddenly transpires that the Catholic and Orthodox Churches are "Sister Churches, responsible together for maintaining the Church of God" — which is apparently something other than the Catholic Church.[234] As we have noted, the quotation comes from the Balamand Statement of 1993, drawn up under the auspices of the Joint International Commission for Theological Dialogue between the Roman Catholic Church and the Orthodox Church. The Vatican's Cardinal Edward Cassidy, who headed the Pontifical Council for the Promotion of Christian Unity until he was replaced by Cardinal Kasper, was part of this commission. The relevant passage goes on: "To pave the way for future relations between the two churches, passing beyond the outdated [!] ecclesiology of return to the Catholic Church connected to the problem

---

hardly up to the present time existed, and does not to-day exist. They consider that this unity may indeed be desired and that it *may even be one day attained through the instrumentality of wills directed to a common end*, but that meanwhile it can only be regarded as mere ideal."

[234]The question has not been resolved with the publication of *Dominus Iesus* in September 2000. We discuss the lingering confusion over the notion of "the Church of God" (also called "the Church of Christ") and the Vatican's backpedaling from DI in Chapter 13.

which is the subject of this document, special preparation will be given the formation of future priests.... In the search for reestablishing unity, there is no question of conversion of people from one Church to the other...." Merely to catalogue the novelty and betrayal in this statement would require a chapter in itself. Was any Catholic ever taught in catechism class that the Catholic and Orthodox Churches were "Sister Churches, responsible together for maintaining the Church of God"?

Much has already been written on the Catholic-Lutheran Joint Statement on Justification that was signed on November 1, 1999, and that has since been praised by the Pope on numerous occasions. A good deal of this criticism has found the text ambiguous (do things ever change?). Conservative Lutherans, for instance, consider the document a lawyers' agreement that can satisfy both sides without really resolving anything. But potentially even more significant in the long run is a statement buried within the text: "Based on the consensus reached," it reads, "continued dialogue is required in order to reach full church communion, a unity in diversity in which remaining differences would be reconciled and no longer have a divisive force." What in the world does that mean? What "remaining differences" would be "reconciled"? And what is meant by "unity in diversity"? Are we to understand that the restoration of "full church communion" between the churches would be characterized by a diversity *of belief*?

And then there is this bombshell, tucked into the final paragraph of the document: "We give thanks to the Lord for this decisive step forward on the way to overcoming *the division of the church*. We ask the Holy Spirit to lead us further toward that visible unity which is Christ's will." Here we find yet another affirmation of the opinion Pius XI condemned in *Mortalium Animos* as the fundamental error of the "ecumenical movement": that the unity of the Church is something yet to be achieved. Again, how are we to reconcile the condemnation by Pius XI with an affirmation of the condemned proposition in the Catholic-Lutheran accord? True, Vatican II's decree on ecumenism, *Unitatis Redintegratio*, declares that "[w]e believe that this unity subsists in the Catholic Church as something she can never lose, and we hope that it will continue to increase until the end of time."[235] But this rather timid restatement of the dogma of the Church's divinely bestowed note of unbreakable unity has been buried in an avalanche of seemingly contradictory Vatican pronouncements since the Council, including the aforementioned statement of John Paul II to the new Catholic-Anglican "working group" that its efforts "may lead to that unity in truth for which Christ prayed." May *lead* to it? The unity in truth for which Christ prayed has always existed in the Catholic Church, which is why the preconciliar Popes unanimously taught that the Protestants and the Orthodox must *return* to that unity.

Happily absorbing the contradiction of "unity in diversity," the neo-Catholic periodical *Pro Ecclesia* expounds and defends the views of Pope John Paul II and his cardinals: "Can there be *church-dividing* differences that are not, ipso facto, heresies to be condemned? Certainly the Joint Declaration shows how. The mutual anathemas regarding the dogmatic expression of justification no longer apply in a meaningful way. There is consensus on the meaning and intention of the biblical teaching of justification, if not on its precise theological formulation. *The paradigm of visible unity as the Church being a communion of communions, one Church in a diversity of churches, is sustained by the acceptance of historically developed differences as mutually edifying diversity within a certain core of the one Church.* We cannot mistake those cultural, historical developments as irreformable truths."

It is bad enough that the agreement could even lend itself to such an interpretation, but is such an interpretation really justified? Unfortunately, it is. In fact, reconciled diversity has been the paradigm for Catholic-Lutheran "reconciliation" for some years now. The pertinent document, signed by representatives of the Pontifical Council for Promoting Christian Unity in 1984, is called "Facing Unity: Models, Forms, and Phases of Catholic-Lutheran Church Fellowship," and includes this passage:

---

[235]*Unitatis Redintegratio*, 4.

There have always been tendencies within the ecumenical movement that aimed at an ecumenical fellowship in which the existing ecclesial traditions with their particularity and diversity would remain in integrity and authenticity.... [T]he model of "unity in reconciled diversity" has recently been developed.... The idea of "unity in reconciled diversity" means that "expression would be given to the abiding value of the confessional forms of the Christian faith *in all their variety*" and that these diversities, "when related to the central message of salvation and Christian faith," and when they "ring out, [are] transformed and renewed" in the process of ecumenical encounter and theological dialogue,..."lose their divisive character and are reconciled to each other...into a binding ecumenical fellowship in which even the confessional elements" are preserved.

It seems impossible that representatives of a pontifical council could endorse such a statement, even if its doctrinal value is nil. An anonymous seminary professor has published a more detailed objection to the self-contradiction of reconciled diversity.[236] It is quite telling that advocates of "reconciled diversity" speak without repercussions even within the Eternal City itself, whereas a seminary professor warning against it has to be published anonymously. So much for the Church of Openness and Dialogue.

"Reconciled diversity" emerged in the pontificate of Paul VI. In Paul's January 23, 1969 speech, he observed: "From theological discussion it can emerge what the essential Christian doctrinal patrimony is, how much of it is communicable authentically and together in different terms that are substantially equal and complementary, and how it is possible for everyone to make the final victorious discovery of that identity of faith, in freedom, and in the variety of its expressions, from which union can be happily celebrated."[237] This is only one

---

[236]R.B., "Full Communion in Reconciled Diversity," *The Latin Mass*, Summer 2000, pp. 24-28. The selection from "Facing Unity" appears on pp. 24-25.

[237]Amerio, *Iota Unum*, p. 553.

of innumerable Vatican statements that create the impression that the differences that separate the Church from the various Protestant sects can ultimately be reduced to mere semantics. Where in statements such as these is there the slightest indication of the undeniable truth that Protestants must change their erroneous beliefs in order to achieve union with us? And since when does the Catholic Church need to engage in theological discussions with Protestants in order to determine "what the essential Christian doctrinal patrimony is"? The Pope's implication that the Magisterium does not already know with infallible certitude what is "essential" to Christianity is staggering.

In early 2000, Bishop (now Cardinal) Walter Kasper declared in *L'Osservatore Romano* that prior to Vatican II the Church "understood the reestablishing of Christian unity exclusively in terms of 'return of our separated brothers to the true Church of Christ...from which they have at one time unhappily separated themselves.'"[238] That is a direct reference to the language of Pius XI in *Mortalium Animos*, which Kasper wishes to make clear has been repudiated. This is no longer the Church's "position," he went on to explain. Kasper thus confirmed what we have been claiming: contrary to all preconciliar papal teaching, ecumenism simply does not seek the return of non-Catholics to the one true Church. "The old concept of the ecumenism of return," he said, "has today been replaced by that of a common journey which directs Christians toward the goal of ecclesial communion understood as unity in reconciled diversity." The old idea of "ecumenism of return" is "no longer applicable to the Catholic Church after Vatican II."

In 2001, Most Rev. Cormac Murphy-O'Connor, Archbishop of Westminster (and recent John Paul II appointee), joined this chorus, noting that "if we look at all the Roman documents in recent years, it is clear that they do not spell a turning back to the 'ecumenism of return,' or 'you-come-inism.' The direction

---

[238]*L'Osservatore Romano*, January 20, 2000; *The Latin Mass*, Summer 2000, p. 7.

and dialogue of convergence were firmly set by the Second Vatican Council and endorsed and confirmed six years ago by *Ut Unum Sint.*"[239] And this prelate is considered "conservative" by postconciliar standards.

Even more disturbing is Cardinal Ratzinger's comment that "the end of all ecumenical effort is to *attain* [?] the true unity of the Church. For the moment, I wouldn't dare venture to suggest any concrete realization, possible or imaginable, of this future Church. We are at an intermediate stage of unity in diversity."[240]

Now note well: Pope John Paul II appointed Cardinal Ratzinger as Prefect of the Congregation for the Doctrine of the Faith. He also appointed Cardinal Kasper, whose orthodoxy was known to be in question, to his current post just last year. He appointed Murphy-O'Connor to be Archbishop of Westminster. Thus, far from condemning the despicable capitulation called "reconciled diversity," John Paul appointed to his council on Christian unity one of its best-known advocates, and Cardinal Ratzinger himself endorses the concept. Note also that Cardinal Kasper made no effort to argue, as the Pamphlet does, that the positions of Pius XI and John Paul II were somehow compatible, and that traditionalists were engaging in "private judgment" and rashly "pitting one Pope against another" when they pointed out the contradiction. Kasper frankly admitted that Pius XI's "model" *no longer applies.* One of the heads of a pontifical council, then, is apparently secure in his job, despite having *pitted one Pope against another.* Maybe the neo-Catholics will raise the same uproar against Cardinal Kasper—a man whose views have implications for Catholics around the world—for committing the very act for which they indignantly condemn traditionalists. Or maybe not.

The Vatican's "ecumenical" policy is today so confused and chaotic that we have to go to Karl Rahner, not an authority to whom we would ordinarily advert, for brutal honesty. "Either recognize the irreconcilability of the different denominations," he said in 1982, "or be content with a merely verbal unity, or

---

[239]De Lubac lecture, Salford University, January 18, 2001.
[240]John Vennari, "Pantheon of the Gods at the Vatican," *Catholic Family News,* December 1999, p. 27.

admit that the different denominations constitute a single faith."[241]

The postconciliar Vatican has not been altogether straightforward regarding the Jews' need for conversion either. The fashionable doctrine these days—again, contrary to all prior papal teaching—is the claim that the Old Covenant that God established with the Jews, far from having been superseded by the New Covenant of Christ and the Church, is in fact still in effect. Thus we have John Paul II telling a Jewish audience: "The first dimension of this dialogue, that is, the meeting between the people of the Old Covenant, *never revoked by God*, and that of the New Covenant, is at the same time a dialogue within our Church, that is to say, between the first and second part of her Bible." "Jews and Christians," he went on to say, "as children of Abraham, are called to be a blessing to the world" by "committing themselves together for peace and justice among all men and peoples."[242] Such statements seem impossible to reconcile with the Church's divine commission to convert the Jews for the salvation of their souls. In fact, Cardinal Kasper, whom the Pope has also made President of the Pontifical Council for Religious Relations with the Jews, has repudiated the conversion of the Jews as explicitly as he has repudiated the return of the Protestant dissidents to the one true Church:

> [T]he old theory of substitution is gone since the Second Vatican Council. For us Christians today the covenant with the Jewish people is a living heritage, a living reality.... Therefore, the Church believes that Judaism, i.e., the faithful response of the Jewish people to God's irrevocable covenant, *is salvific for them*, because God is faithful to his promises.... Thus mission, in this strict sense, cannot be used with regard to Jews, who believe in the true and one God. Therefore—and this is characteristic—there does not exist any Catholic missionary organization for

[241]Amerio, *Iota Unum*, p. 578, n. 77.
[242]Address to Representatives of the Jewish Community in Mainz, West Germany, November 17, 1980.

Jews. There is dialogue with Jews; no mission in this proper sense of the word towards them.[243]

Once again, Kasper received no correction from the Pope or any Vatican dicastery. On the contrary, he has received only a promotion to his current positions of authority. What can one conclude but that the Vatican has *de facto* abandoned the conversion of the Jews, and the return of the Orthodox and the Protestants to Roman Catholic unity? And yet, as in all other areas of postconciliar novelty, we are not dealing with any formal change in binding Catholic doctrine, as opposed to a welter of sub-Magisterial pronouncements, including papal speeches to small groups, which are allowed to create the impression of a real and permanent change.

A fundamental ambiguity is evident everywhere, particularly in the new Good Friday liturgy. *Catholic Family News* editor John Vennari recently compared the papally approved prayer for the Jews in three versions of the Roman liturgy: those of 1954, 1964, and 1974. In 1954, the prayer read:

> We pray for the perfidious Jews: that Our Lord and God may lift the covering off their hearts, so that they may acknowledge Jesus Christ Our Lord. Let us pray. Almighty, eternal God, who does not reject the Jews in Your own mercy: hear our prayers which we offer for the blindness of this people, that acknowledging the truth of Your light which is Christ, they may be pulled out of their darkness. Through the same Christ Our Lord. Amen.

The only difference in the 1964 version of the prayer is that the word "perfidious" has been removed; the remainder of the text is unchanged. The 1974 prayer, however, which is what we have now, reads as follows:

> Let us pray for the Jewish people, the first to hear the word of God, that they may continue to grow in the love of His Name and in faithfulness to His covenant. Almighty and eternal

---

[243]Address at 17th meeting of the International Catholic-Jewish Liaison Committee, New York, May 1, 2001.

God, long ago You gave Your promise to Abraham and his posterity. Listen to Your Church as we pray that the people You first made Your own may arrive at the fullness of redemption. We ask this through Christ our Lord. Amen.

That the language of this prayer is as insipid and uninspiring as we have come to expect from the reformed liturgy is the least of its problems. Does Rome want the Jews to convert to belief in Christ or not? If so, why not just say so, rather than forcing good Catholic priests to repeat every Good Friday the meaningless sentiment that the Jews "continue to grow in the love of [God's] Name and in faithfulness to His covenant"? What does that mean? The appeal to God later in the prayer that the Jews "arrive at the fullness of redemption" is no less vague. Are we praying that the Jews arrive at the fullness of redemption through belief in Christ and membership in His Church? If so, why not just say so? Here, as in so many other areas, the viruses of ambiguity abound, with a resulting debilitation of the teaching Church.

It is a false charity that engages the Jews in irenic dialogue without making clear their need for conversion, a need that extends to the entire human race. *Everyone* needs Christ; what kind of charity wants to deprive anyone of the means of salvation? Christ Himself was clearly not speaking of a people who could be confident of their salvation in their present state when He said, "Jerusalem, Jerusalem, thou that killest the prophets, and stonest them that are sent unto thee, how often would I have gathered together thy children, as the hen doth gather her chickens under her wings, and thou wouldest not? Behold, your house shall be left to you, desolate" (Matt. 23:38-39). The patristic testimony on the matter is unanimous and resounding.[244]

---

[244]On the question of the conversion of the Jews, see Fr. Arthur B. Klyber, *The One Who Is to Come*, ed. Matthew J. McDonald (New Hope, KY: Remnant of Israel, 2000). Fr. Klyber, a Jewish convert to Catholicism, dedicated his life to the conversion of the Jews.

But the new teaching on the religious status of the Jews now appears to be taken for granted. Thus Cardinal Francis George of Chicago, admired as a conservative by neo-Catholics, could write in his diocesan newspaper that "the Church has also sinned against the Jewish people, first of all, in teaching that God's covenant with Israel is no longer valid for them...."[245]

Even *The Wanderer* criticized the late Cardinal John O'Connor, and rightly so, for giving his blessing on national television to a young man who was repudiating his Catholic faith for Judaism. The *Nightline* anchor asked if this young man had the Cardinal's blessing. His Eminence replied, "Oh yes. Oh yes. He doesn't need it, but he has my blessing, if we're going to call it such, because I believe that's what the Church teaches.... Christ came into the world as a Jew. Ethnically, religiously, a Jew. We believe He was the Son of God. But He came for everybody." Toward the end of the program, the Cardinal added: "I would be keenly disappointed if there are Christians, and most particularly Catholics, who watch this at Christmas time and have animosity towards Stephen, towards what has happened. If they want to have animosity, I'd rather they have it toward me.... If they want to consider me wrong, that's fine. But I think that he is happy in his choice. I think that his mother is peaceful in his choice, and I think God is smiling on the whole thing."[246]

In late 2001, the Pontifical Biblical Commission released a book entitled *The Jewish People and the Holy Scriptures in the Christian Bible* that confirmed the radical (but non-Magisterial) drift of Rome's position vis-à-vis the Jews. The book argues that the Jews' continued wait for the Messiah is validated and justified by the Old Testament. "The expectancy of the Messiah was in the Old Testament," papal spokesman Joaquín Navarro-Valls explained, "and if the Old Testament keeps its value, then it keeps that as a value, too. It says you cannot just say all the Jews are wrong and we are right." Asked by reporters whether

[245]Cardinal Francis George, "The Sins of the Church: God's Forgiveness and Human Memories," *Catholic New World*, March 19, 2000.
[246]Vennari, "Cardinal O'Connor Blesses Apostasy," pp. 3, 22.

his statements might be taken to suggest that the Messiah may not in fact yet have come, Navarro-Valls replied, "It means it would be wrong for a Catholic to wait for the Messiah, but not for a Jew." The latest position of the Vatican apparatus (not to be confused with the Church's constant Magisterium) is, in essence, that the Jews are perfectly entitled to live as if Christ had never come. They wait for "their" Messiah and we wait for ours. So much for the objective truth of the matter!

Cardinal Ratzinger put it this way: "The difference consists in the fact that for us, he (sic) who will come will have the same traits of that Jesus who has already come."[247] The *same traits* of *that* Jesus (is there more than one?) — and only "for us"? Would it make the slightest bit of sense to say that, for us, the head of the Congregation for the Doctrine of the Faith has the same traits of *that* Cardinal Ratzinger who occupies the offices of the CDF? What is to account for this apparent dread aversion to the simple, straightforward declaration that the Messiah for everyone, not just "for us," is Jesus Christ crucified in the flesh, and none other than He?

To say the least, the Cardinal's novel locution obscures the fact that when Christ returns it will as be as clear to the Jews as it is to everyone else in the world that this is the One Whom the Pharisees rejected when He walked amongst His people 2,000 years ago — the God Incarnate, Who said to the Pharisees, "Before Abraham was, I am," and Who sternly admonished them that "you shall not see me henceforth till you say: Blessed is he that cometh in the name of the Lord" (Matt. 23:38-39).

Evidently, we are to assume that the Holy Catholic Church was mistaken in the teaching of her traditional Good Friday liturgy. Now we are told that it is suddenly no longer a question of a hardening of the heart or of blindness, but merely a difference of opinion about whether there will be one or two comings of the same Messiah! The Cardinal's implication that

---

[247]The whole matter was reported in Melinda Henneberger, "Vatican Says Jews' Wait for Messiah is Validated by the Old Testament," *New York Times*, January 18, 2002.

the whole question of Jewish conversion can be reduced to the observation that Christ's return will represent His Second Coming for us but only a first coming for the Jews, with no eternal consequences arising from "the difference," dispenses with the entire tradition of the Church.

The response from the neo-Catholic establishment this time was a stony silence. One can hardly blame them; every Catholic instinct must recoil in revulsion at this most recent (and almost unbelievable) display of cowardice. Jewish commentators delightedly hailed it as a marvelous innovation. "This is a total novelty," said Chief Rabbi Joseph Levi of Florence.[248] Rabbi Alberto Piattelli, a professor and Jewish leader in Rome, remarked: "This is something *altogether new*.... It recognizes the value of the Jewish position regarding the wait for the Messiah, changes *the whole exegesis of biblical studies* and restores our biblical passages to their original meaning. I was surprised."[249] And so yet another "surprise" is added to the mountain of surprises we have only attempted to sketch in this book.

But, as always with these postconciliar reversals, no binding Magisterial pronouncement actually obliges us to accept it. Instead, as the *New York Times* report noted, there was a statement from the Vatican's press spokesman: "Everything in the report is now considered part of official church [sic] doctrine, Dr. Navarro-Valls said." Thus a characteristic feature of the postconciliar program of innovation emerges again: the insistence that novel teachings, never presented in such a way as to bind the faithful, constitute "official Church doctrine"—as though the overturning of 2,000 years of biblical exegesis could be accomplished by a lay Vatican spokesman, answering questions at a press conference about a book of theological reflections belatedly discovered by the Italian press in Vatican-area bookstores. Even more ludicrous is that the study in question was released by the Pontifical Biblical Commission, which no longer serves as an organ of the Magisterium (as it did under Saint Pius X), but rather as a kind of theological think-tank whose opinions bind no one. Navarro-Valls thus had no

[248]Zenit, January 18, 2002.
[249]Henneberger, "Jews' Wait for Messiah."

right to describe this embarrassing and despicable capitulation as in any way constituting "official Church doctrine." But as we have shown throughout our presentation, the *impression* that speeches, books, press conferences and other such non-Magisterial statements bind the whole Church is essential to maintaining the neo-Catholic façade of novelty.[250]

In an earlier article in *L'Osservatore Romano,* as if to pave the way for this latest reversal, the Cardinal expressed the opinion that after the Holocaust "a new vision has formed of the relationship between the Church and Israel, a sincere desire to overcome every form of anti-Judaism and to embark on a constructive dialogue for mutual knowledge and reconciliation."[251] Still another "new vision" arises in the postconciliar period, although one will find no proclamation of "new visions" in the constant Magisterium of the Church before the Council. In this "new vision," the Church merely seeks "reconciliation" with "Israel" — whatever that means. There is no longer to be any suggestion that it is individual Jews, along with the rest of humanity, who need be reconciled with Jesus of Nazareth.

Casting the first stone at dead Catholics (as is the fashion these days), Ratzinger further opined in the same article that in former times "Christians considered their mother [i.e., Israel] blind and obstinate," and that the "somewhat insufficient resistance on the part of Christians to these [Nazi] atrocities can be explained by the anti-Judaic legacy of the soul in none too few Christians." Is the traditional Good Friday liturgy now to be viewed as part of this "anti-Judaic legacy of the soul"? Is that why it was abandoned? If so, then why should anyone believe in a Church that could be so mistaken, and so uncharitable, for so long, in the teaching of her universal liturgy? Or is it perhaps this new attitude which is mistaken and lacking in true charity toward the Jews? For how is charity served by abandoning the

---

[250]Ibid.

[251]*L'Osservatore Romano,* Dec. 29, 2000, reprinted in *30 Days* English edition, No. 12, 2000.

Church's public prayer for their conversion, when they are no less in need of the grace of Christ than the rest of humanity?

So we are apparently expected to accept, without the slightest explanation, the sudden disappearance of the Church's perennial approach to the Jews. Yet it was this approach that produced the post-Holocaust conversion to Catholicism of none other than Israel Zolli, the chief rabbi of Jerusalem. Zolli took Eugenio as his baptismal name, in honor of the Pope whose example of true solicitude for the Jews was instrumental in Zolli's gradual conversion, which he had promised God he would complete if he survived the war.[252] As Zolli declared after becoming a Catholic, in answer to the question whether he believed the Messiah has already come: "Yes, positively. I have believed it many years. And now I am so firmly convinced of the truth of it that I can face the whole world and defend my faith with the certainty and solidity of the mountains."[253] Zolli clearly knew nothing of Cardinal Ratzinger's "new vision" of Catholic-Jewish relations that the Holocaust supposedly engendered—and neither did Zolli's dear friend, Pope Pius XII.

Nor would Zolli recognize as at all Catholic the current program of lauding the goodness of decadent Protestant sects and seeking "unity in diversity" with them. When asked why he had not simply joined one of the Protestant denominations, Zolli gave an answer that the current Vatican apparatus would regard as an intolerable breach of ecumenical etiquette: "The Catholic Church was recognized by the whole Christian world as the true Church of God for fifteen consecutive centuries. No man can halt at the end of those 1,500 years and say that the Catholic Church is not the Church of Christ without embarrassing himself seriously. I can accept *only* that Church which was preached to all creatures by my own forefathers, the Twelve (Apostles), who, like me, issued from the Synagogue."

The stirring testimony of Israel Zolli, given only some fifty years ago, is a rebuke to the entire postconciliar program of ecumenism and Christian-Jewish "dialogue," which has gone

---

[252]"Before the Dawn: The Mysterious Conversion of Rome's Chief Rabbi," *Inside the Vatican*, February 1999.

[253]Ibid.

nowhere and produced nothing but embarrassment for the Church. It is hardly surprising that the same Jewish leadership the Vatican futilely attempts to supplicate today denounced Zolli as a traitor and a fraud, even though he had been lauded as a great Old Testament scholar before his conversion.[254]

As we say, the abandonment of the traditional approach to the Jews is too much even for some neo-Catholics to accept. But the view that the Jews are no longer obliged to convert to Christianity, along with the view that the return of the Orthodox and the Protestants to Roman Catholicism was also "abandoned" at Vatican II, are now presented as Catholic doctrine by the Pope's own men. We are to believe, then, that some of the most important and influential cardinals in the world are radically at odds with the Pope in these matters?

In the midst of all of these peculiar developments, the wisdom and foresight of St. Pius X in condemning Modernism with such vigor have been fully vindicated. St. Pius X included quite a number of errors under this heading, but undergirding the whole heresy was a retreat from the idea that God and the truth of the Catholic religion were objectively demonstrable. The Modernists tended instead to focus on the subjective aspect of religion—feeling, emotion, and sentiment—to the exclusion of all else. Hence, religious dogmas were not absolutely true statements of belief presented for our assent by an infallible teaching authority, but merely the inchoate expression of an ineffable religious "sentiment" to be found within all men. As St. Pius X correctly noted, there is no place for religious error in such a calculus, for if religion is based ultimately on subjectivity and sentiment, how can anyone ever really and definitively be wrong? How can we say that one person's *feeling* is true and another's false?

Much of the ecumenical movement in our age, therefore, betrays very strong Modernist influences. In the Modernist schema, religious dogma is not absolute and irreformable, but rather a vague, imprecise reflection of a common religious

---

[254]Ibid.

"feeling" within a human race that is in a constant state of evolution and flux, so it becomes difficult to believe that religious reconciliation could really be based on the "static" formula of the simple return of dissidents to the one true Church and the acceptance of all her doctrines without the slightest alteration. Instead, the ecumenical *apparatchik* imagines a shared spiritual journey, in which the religious sentiment common to the human race comes to its full realization in some new dispensation that is the exclusive possession of no single group.

Returning to the matter at hand, if none of what we have just described qualifies as "indifferentist ecumenism," what on earth does? But it does not end there. Cardinal Ratzinger has said that the Church must be concerned about more than "reconciled diversity" with Protestants, and must look for "ways of conducting ecumenism *across the religions.*"[255] Here we are confronted with such appalling novelties as the pan-religious World Days of Prayer for Peace at Assisi in 1986 and 2002, which have been the source of endless controversy.

In his welcoming remarks at the 1986 event, Cardinal Roger Etchegaray, president of the Pontifical Council for Justice and Peace, stated: "We are here together without any trace of syncretism" — thus providing neo-Catholics with the requisite fig leaf to explain away the whole episode. If there is no trace of syncretism (the attempt to combine or reconcile differing beliefs), why say anything in the first place? Similar disclaimers were repeated endlessly at the 2002 event. The disclaimer is about as effective as a man explaining to his wife and children that while he will be spending the night with the woman next door, they will be "together without any trace of adultery." It might be perfectly true, but how could such conduct fail to undermine the family's confidence in its head?

We have already noted Cardinal Etchegaray's remark at the 1986 Assisi event that "[e]ach of the religions we profess has inner peace, and peace among individuals and nations, as one of its aims. Each one pursues this aim in its own distinctive and

[255]Joseph Cardinal Ratzinger, *Many Religions – One Covenant* (San Francisco: Ignatius, 1999), p. 95.

irreplaceable way."[256] Neo-Catholics call traditionalists all kinds of names for perceiving syncretism in remarks such as these, but it is not easy to understand how this kind of statement coming from a Vatican cardinal could actually *fail* to inspire alarm in an educated Catholic. Can anyone seriously contend that a cardinal expressing such sentiments during the reign of St. Pius X would have escaped censure, or that the Assisi events of 1986 and 2002 would not have been denounced by this great Pontiff?

The Assisi events are too much to swallow even for some of those who could normally be expected to laud John Paul II's innovations. Thus, Vito Messori, the Pope's favored interviewer, was constrained to remark (as summarized by Catholic News Service) that "despite organizers' intentions," the Assisi event of 2002 "sent the message that one religion is as good as another.... The appearance of relativism eroded the Pontiff's authority on moral issues like divorce and abortion." As Messori himself put it, "If the doctrine of every religion is acceptable to God, why persist in following the Catholic one, which is the most severe and rigid of all?"[257]

Messori was merely observing the obvious when he stated that Assisi 2002 implied that the doctrine of every religion is acceptable to God. For example, the invited representative of Voodoo (spelled Vodou by its native practitioners), Chief Amadou Gasseto from Benin, was allowed to sermonize on world peace from a high wooden pulpit suitable for a cathedral, set up in the lower plaza outside the Basilica of Saint Francis. The Chief declared to the Vicar of Christ and the assembled cardinals and Catholic guests: "The invitation to take part in the Prayer for Peace at Assisi is a great honour for me, and it is an honour for all the followers of Avelekete Vodou *whose high priest I am.*" The high priest of Avelekete Vodou then gave the Pope and all the Catholic faithful the Vodou prescription for world peace, which included "asking forgiveness of the protecting

[256]Pontifical Commission "Justitia et Pax," *Assisi: World Day of Prayer for Peace*, 1987, p. 110.
[257]CWNews briefs, February 5, 2002.

spirits of regions affected by violence" and "carrying out sacrifices of reparation and purification, and thus restoring peace."[258] This would involve slitting the throats of goats, chickens, doves, and pigeons and draining their blood from the carotid arteries according to a precise ritual prescription.[259] In other words, the Pope invited a witch doctor to give a sermon to Catholics on world peace.

Among other "representatives of the various religions" who came to the pulpit was one Didi Talwakar, the representative of Hinduism. Talwakar declared that the "divinization of human beings gives us a sense of the worth of life. Not only am I divine in essence, but also everyone else is equally divine in essence...." Talwakar went on to exclaim: "My divine brothers and sisters, from much above the station of life where I am, I dare to appeal to humanity, from this august forum, in the blessed presence of His Holiness the Pope...." While Talawaker acknowledges that the Pope is a holy man, he is only one of many such holy men who lead the various religions. Didi prefers to follow another holy man: the Reverend Pandurang Shastri Athawale, who heads something called the *Swadhyaya parivari*, which teaches "the idea of acceptance of all religious traditions" and the need to "free the idea of religion from dogmatism, insularity and injunctions."[260] Just the thing Catholics of the postconciliar period need to hear.

The spectacle of Assisi 2002 staggers the Catholic mind, and human language fails in its attempt to adequately describe the unparalleled ecclesial situation in which we now find

---

[258]One of us attended the Assisi event as a reporter with a Vatican press credential. The voodoo chieftan's remarks are taken *verbatim* from the Vatican's official booklet for the 2002 Assisi event, entitled "Together for Peace," and can be found at pp. 50, 51 and 52.

[259]A website article describes a typical voodoo session in Benin: "The women kowtow, as Daagbo, a huge man draped in stiff white cotton and necklaces of seashells, lifts a goat to the sky before slitting its throat, draining its blood on an iron altar of rusty car parts, as it bleats for life." http://www.hartford-hwp.com/archives/34/010.html.

[260]"Together for Peace," pp. 56-59.

ourselves—a situation even the Arian heretics of the fourth century would find incredible. Yet, true to form, the neo-Catholic press organs reported the event as if it were a triumph for the Catholic faith—while carefully avoiding any of the shocking images and words that would give scandal to any Catholic who has not been spiritually lobotomized by the postconciliar changes in the Church.

The willful blindness of the neo-Catholic commentators aside, it is not only a Catholic like Messori who can see the deadly indifferentism implied in such gatherings; even the Lutherans recognize it! Twelve days after the September 11 attacks in the United States, Lutheran pastor David Benke took part in an interfaith service at Yankee Stadium, along with a Muslim imam, a rabbi, Sikh and Hindu leaders, and Cardinal Egan. For this he is now at risk of being deposed as president of the Missouri Synod's Atlantic District. As one Lutheran pastor told the *New York Times*,

> When we're dealing with those who are not Christians—Hindus and Muslims—in those cases, St. Paul talks about not being yoked with unbelievers.... The danger there is people see the differences as unimportant. You can't chop up the Christian faith into little departments, and say, "We believe in 9 of 10." If you introduce error in one place, it's going to show up throughout. The Gospel is imperiled by any of these errors. That's something that's required of a Christian, to not just say we agree, but to say we disagree.

Herman Otten, publisher of the Lutheran newspaper *Christian News*, added that Lutherans "don't hate the Muslims, the Jews, the Sikhs. We love them; therefore we want to let them know they are lost, they are eternally lost, unless they believe in Jesus."[261]

---

[261]Daniel J. Wakin, "Seeing Heresy in a Service for Sept. 11: Pastor is Under Fire for Interfaith Prayers," *New York Times*, February 8, 2002, pp. B1, B5.

That is how the Catholic Church, in her solicitude for souls, spoke just a few decades ago, as typified in her public prayer on Good Friday for the conversion of unbelievers. Today, ecumenism and "interreligious dialogue" have placed the Vatican apparatus squarely to the left of the more conservative Lutherans, who happily pose as the unique guardians of Christianity. But the spectacles go on.

At this point in our presentation, we earnestly implore neo-Catholics to examine their consciences and recall how many times they themselves have taken an active part in joint ecumenical liturgies or pan-religious prayer meetings. We retain enough confidence in their good sense to expect that the answer is very few, if any. We can anticipate the objection that these novelties do not, in themselves, amount to a formal contradiction of prior dogmatic teaching, which is certainly true, but they clearly *are* something that Rome very much wants us to be doing. (Thus Cardinal Cassidy has urged Catholics and Lutherans to do as much as possible together without violating their consciences.[262] That Vatican-approved activities now carry the risk of *violation of a Catholic's conscience* does not trouble our neo-Catholic friends in the least.)

Do any neo-Catholics plan to attend any episcopal "consecrations" of our "separated brethren" anytime soon? Our bishops certainly do, and none of them has been censured by the Vatican. Faced with this sorry spectacle, one is forced to wonder: Do these bishops believe or do they not believe that they alone, having been duly consecrated by bishops in apostolic succession from the first days of the Church, are in exclusive possession of the authority and charism that belong to the episcopal office? If so, then what can their presence at the flagrantly invalid "consecration" of a Protestant "bishop" possibly signify? Is it just a gesture of "good will"?

Is the author of the Pamphlet or any of his fellow neo-Catholics planning any public prayer sessions with prominent Anglicans who favor abortion and women's ordination?

---

[262]*L'Osservatore Romano*, English weekly edition, November 24, 1999.

Apparently not.  Yet that is how the Pope opened the Jubilee Year.

Are certain Catholic apologists of the neo-Catholic stripe going to remove from their websites and magazines all the articles aimed at converting Protestants and the Orthodox to Catholicism and having them return to Rome? Are they going to stop publishing the "conversion stories" of Protestants who "came home to Rome" or were "surprised by truth"? It would not seem so.

The neo-Catholics fail to see that by their own avoidance of ecumenical activities and jargon and their persistence in the notion that Protestants should convert to Catholicism and return to Rome, *they themselves are in a de facto state of resistance* to the Pope's entire ecumenical agenda, even as they attempt to defend it against all criticism.

Especially disturbing about the pan-Christian and pan-religious ecumenism is how clearly they repudiate the insistent and tireless teaching of earlier twentieth-century Popes, without ever explaining to the faithful where and why those Vicars of Christ had been mistaken.  Are we really no longer allowed to follow their teaching?  That seems like rather a peculiar demand to make of the faithful, especially in the absence of any effort to point out the deficiencies in the Church's previous posture.  We can easily imagine a neo-Catholic responding that the "signs of the times" call for this radical change; the Pope himself noted that the "tension" existing in the world in 1986 demanded some kind of pan-religious response (hence the Assisi meeting).  But the preconciliar Popes, it should be remembered, *lived through two world wars* without suggesting that a ceremony that could be *misinterpreted* as implying any kind of equivalence between the Catholic Church and other religious communions was at all appropriate.  Philadelphia Archbishop Dennis Dougherty, to offer only one example, was acting as a fairly typical American prelate *when he refused to take part in ecumenical ceremonies marking the end of World War I.*[263] The great Cardinal Mercier, moreover, warned that World War I was a divine punishment visited upon mankind for having placed the Catholic Church at the same level as false religions. And we have already mentioned the refusal of even the Dutch bishops to participate in an ecumenical congress just after World War II, even though the theme of the conference was laudable enough: "The Plan of God and the Disorder of the World." There was no confusion about Catholic identity in those days. These are but three of an endless supply of anecdotes from another world.

And so we freely confess that we *are* pitting one Pope against another. But we are doing so not to convict anyone of heresy. We are doing so because if words still have meaning, the postconciliar and the preconciliar teaching in these matters (and the many others we have mentioned) obviously *are* contradictory, no matter what the neo-Catholics may tell us. Back when the problem was nowhere near as serious as it is now, the preconciliar Popes were terrified by the spread of indifferentism. Within the space of a few years, the view of the preconciliar Popes was completely replaced by a baffling and inexplicable optimism about the same non-Catholic sects, whose conditions *have only degraded* since the ecumenical venture began. What is to account for this paradox of a growing "respect" for non-Catholic sects that are ever less deserving of it?

In the midst of all this, traditionalists are also impertinent enough to ask what has happened to the teaching on the *Social Kingship* of Christ. Has that been abandoned? If so, why? What was wrong with Pope Pius XI's teaching in *Quas Primas* (1925) apart from the fact that it greatly displeased the modern world? We want to know why Rome, having in its official statements beaten a glaring retreat from the call for the enthronement of Christ the King over all human societies, has instead adopted almost exclusively the language of tolerance and human rights. It cannot be a coincidence that in the revised

---

[263]Charles Morris, *American Catholic: The Saints and Sinners Who Built America's Most Powerful Church* (New York: Random House, 1997), p. 172.

calendar the Feast of Christ the King has been moved to the end of the liturgical year, a shift whose clear implication is that the Kingship of Christ is something we await at the end of time and not anything to be established here and now.

These kinds of capitulations are all the more inexplicable in the present spiritual milieu. In our age, it would be difficult to think of an idea that is more prevalent than the basic equality of all religions. Why would we want to do anything that could even inadvertently lend credence to this view? There is nothing that a diehard globalist would like more than to see all the Christian denominations, or indeed all the world's religions, absorbed into a blob that would in consequence be so meaningless and so incapable of commanding the loyalty of its adherents that it would pose no threat whatever to the brave new world they are so eager to impose on us. In this context, it is helpful and even a bit unsettling to recall what we consider one of the most memorable lines of St. Pius X's entire pontificate. We are witnessing, he said, a "great movement of apostasy being organized in every country for the establishment of a one-world Church which shall have neither dogmas, nor hierarchy; neither discipline for the mind, nor curb for the passions...."[264] Apparently, as the neo-Catholics would have it, the situation in the world has improved so much since then that we are no longer in need of such warnings.

By any conceivable interpretation of traditional Catholic teaching, it is dramatically urgent that the members of the Protestant sects and the assembled non-Catholic religions at Assisi convert to the true Faith, and as quickly as possible. Is this urgency so much as hinted at by any of the Catholics involved in ecumenical and pan-religious activities? Here is how Pope Pius IX discussed this issue in his Allocution *Singulari Quadem* (1854), touching on a point that would later appear in his *Syllabus of Errors*: "Not without sorrow we have learned that another error, no less destructive, has taken possession of some

---

[264]*Notre Charge Apostolique*, apostolic letter on the Sillon Movement in France, 1910.

parts of the Catholic world, and has taken up abode in the souls of many Catholics, who think that one should have good hope of the eternal salvation of all those who have never lived in the true Church of Christ." Pius IX taught that the "invincible ignorance" of those who had never known Christ would not be reckoned by God as a sin. He also said, though, that "it must be held by faith that outside the Apostolic Roman Church no one can be saved; that this is the only ark of salvation; that he who shall not have entered therein will perish in the flood.... Truths of this sort should be deeply fixed in the minds of the faithful, lest they be corrupted by false doctrines, whose object is to foster an indifference toward religion, which we see spreading widely and growing strong for the destruction of souls."

This traditional tone and content in papal pronouncements on the one true religion has vanished. In *Ut Unum Sint*, John Paul II wrote: "Along the ecumenical path to unity, pride of place certainly belongs to *common prayer*, the prayerful union of those who gather together around Christ himself. If Christians, despite their divisions, can grow ever more united in common prayer around Christ, they will grow in the awareness of how little divides them in comparison to what unites them." In fact, in its 1949 *monitum* on the "ecumenical movement," the Holy Office warned bishops not to allow any mixed congresses they might approve to be conducted on *"the false pretext that more attention should be paid to the points on which we agree than to those on which we differ [lest] a dangerous indifferentism be encouraged...."*[265] Today, however, we are told that this false pretext provides the very basis for once-forbidden ecumenical prayer meetings. Yet the suggestion that more unites Christians than divides them is clearly false, as demonstrated by the catastrophic collapse of Protestantism into outright liberalism over the course of the twentieth century. But even taking into account the more conservative Protestants, the question can be raised: How can a Faith that teaches us to strive for holiness and to purify our souls through the sanctifying grace we receive from the sacraments be said to be very similar to one that considers such things to be the foulest sins and the grossest

---

[265] AAS 42-152.

presumption?  And how can a Faith that enjoins the absolute sanctity of marriage and life in the womb be very similar to one that teaches that divorce, contraception and abortion are acceptable to God?

Today the doctrine of the one true Church, the Ark of Salvation, gives way to a celebration of diversity.  This development doubtless warms the hearts of the enemies of religion around the world, who are thrilled to see the seriousness and the hard edge of the traditional faith visibly subsiding, but for Catholics with any sense of tradition, it is a repudiation of the efforts and instincts of the whole assembly of saints. And yet the neo-Catholics actually maintain that we have no right to object to any of it.

Surveying the state of Christian and pan-religious ecumenism, Romano Amerio, a *peritus* at Vatican II, had this to say:

> The present temper of ecumenism, involving an effective renunciation of an expansion of the Catholic faith, is clearly evident in John Paul II's speeches in Nigeria in 1982: there is no mention of conversion to Christ, but in a special message to Muslims, which was not actually received by any Muslims or in any way replied to, the Pope hoped for cooperation between the two religions "in the interests of Nigerian unity" and "to make a contribution to the good order of the world as a new civilization of love."  As we have noted, harmony in the world is no longer presented in terms of a single religion, but of a single civilization....[266]

In this connection, it would be well to recall an important teaching of Pope St. Pius X.  In August 1910, the Pope issued his apostolic letter *Our Apostolic Mandate*, directed at the French Sillon.  The Sillon was a social and political organization that sought to base civilization and civic progress exclusively upon human good will and to leave out of the equation those things, religion especially, that divide people.  The Pope quoted one of

---

[266]Amerio, *Iota Unum*, p. 578.

its adherents thus: "Catholic comrades will work between themselves in a special organization and will learn and educate themselves. Protestant and Free-Thinking Democrats will do likewise on their own side. But all of us, Catholics, Protestants and Free-Thinkers will have at heart to arm young people, not in view of the fratricidal struggle, but in view of a disinterested emulation in the field of social and civic virtues."

The Pope answered:

> Here we have, founded by Catholics, an interdenominational association that is to work for the reform of civilization, an undertaking which is above all religious in character, for there is no true civilization without a moral civilization, and no true moral civilization without the true religion: it is a proven truth, a historical fact. The new Sillonists cannot pretend that they are merely working on "the ground of practical realities," where differences of belief do not matter…. But stranger still, alarming and saddening at the same time, are the audacity and frivolity of men who call themselves Catholics and dream of reshaping society under such conditions, and of establishing on earth, over and beyond the pale of the Catholic Church, "the reign of love and justice" with workers coming from everywhere, of all religions and of no religion, with or without beliefs, so long as they forego what might divide them—their religious and philosophical convictions—and so long as they share what unites them—a "generous idealism and moral forces drawn from whence they can." When we consider the forces, knowledge and supernatural virtues which were necessary to establish the Christian State, and the sufferings of millions of martyrs, and the light given by the Fathers and Doctors of the Church, and of the self-sacrifice of all the heroes of charity, and a powerful hierarchy ordained in heaven, and the streams of Divine Grace—the whole having been built up, bound together, and impregnated by the life and spirit of Jesus Christ, the Wisdom of God, the Word made man—when we think, I say, of all this, it is frightening to behold new apostles eagerly attempting to do better by a common interchange of vague idealism and civic virtues. What are they going to produce? What is to come out of this collaboration? A mere verbal and chimerical construction, in which we see, glowing in a jumble, and in seductive confusion, the words of Liberty,

Justice, Fraternity, Love, Equality, and human exaltation, all resting upon an ill-understood human dignity. It will be a tumultuous agitation, sterile for the end proposed, but which will benefit the less-Utopian exploiters of the people. Yes, we can truly say that the Sillon, its eyes fixed on a chimera, brings Socialism in its train.

Compare the teaching of St. Pius X with the "Final Declaration of the Inter-religious Assembly" of October 1999, the Vatican gathering that commemorated the Assisi event of October 1986. This document called on the world's religions to "confront together, responsibly and courageously, the problems and challenges of our modern world (i.e., poverty, racism, environmental pollution, materialism, war, proliferation of arms, globalization, AIDS, lack of medical care, breakdown of family and community, marginalization of women and children, etc.)." Likewise, in an audience address extolling Islam, the Pope declared that the Catholic Church "regards Muslims with respect, convinced that their transcendent faith in God contributes to the construction of a new human family, based on the highest aspirations of the human heart.... Walking together on the path of reconciliation...the two religions [Christianity and Islam] will be able to offer a sign of hope, by reflecting in the world the wisdom and mercy of that one God."[267]

How is this program different from the pan-religious utopianism condemned by St. Pius X? In fact, is it not (considering the pan-religious prayer meetings at Assisi) vastly *worse* than anything St. Pius X had in view? But this, the neo-Catholics will tell us, is "pitting one Pope against another"—an exercise we admit is prompted by our commitment to the Law of the Excluded Middle,[268] that elementary principle of logic to which traditionalists continue to have such stubborn recourse.

The world in which we find ourselves is one that, whether it realizes it or not, needs a tough and militant Catholic Church

---

[267]Vennari, "Pantheon of the Gods," p. 26; Audience Address, May 5, 1999.

[268]The rule of logic that every proposition is either true or false.

more than ever. It was the *militancy* of the Church, and the grace that her sacraments transmit, that gave the saints the strength and fortitude to live lives of truly heroic virtue. It was no conception of the Church as a "joint custodian" of the Church of God with this or that other church that encouraged the saints in their heroism; the Catholic Church *was* the Church of God! It was this conviction that set on fire the souls of the nuns whose self-sacrifice in the Catholic hospitals of the eighteenth century amazed even the freethinking Voltaire, who loathed the Catholic Church, but who admired and could not explain the seemingly superhuman strength of these great women. It was this conviction alone that can account for the great St. Isaac Jogues, a Jesuit missionary who was so horribly mutilated by the Indians in North America that he was not recognized when he returned to Rome, but who nevertheless returned to mission territory two years later, where he met his martyrdom.

The novelties and innovations in the postconciliar years, ecumenism and the new liturgy chief among them, are not irreversible. They constitute a prudential program that, in the name of the Church's welfare, we have the right and duty to oppose. The words of the Dominican theologian Melchior Cano, an important figure at the Council of Trent, could have been written for the neo-Catholics of the postconciliar era: "Peter has no need of our lies or flattery. Those who blindly and indiscriminately defend every decision of the supreme Pontiff are the very ones who do most to undermine the authority of the Holy See—they destroy instead of strengthening its foundations."[269]

The Catholic Church (and not the Union, as Abraham Lincoln foolishly suggested or the United Nations, as Paul VI declared) is truly the last, best hope of earth. Only the Church, with her sacraments and her ancient and compelling rituals and traditions, can sustain us in holiness in a world in which impurity and vice are aggressively and ubiquitously present. Have we not learned from the failed experiments of the

---

[269]Cited in John Jay Hughes, *Pontiffs Who Shaped History* (Huntington, Ind.: Our Sunday Visitor Publishing Division, 1996), p. 11.

postconciliar years that the *traditional Catholic faith alone* can restore a sense of piety, reverence, and humility to a world that is making war on the very idea of the sacred, refusing in its hubris to acknowledge that there might exist any belief, institution, or code of conduct not subject to human revision?

The Catholic Church, wrote the *American Ecclesiastical Review* in 1899, is "the greatest, the grandest, and the most beautiful institution in the world." And so she is. We can only pray that her leaders will start acting like it once again. Meanwhile, do we traditionalists compare the past few pontificates unfavorably with those in the nineteenth and early twentieth centuries? Guilty as charged. And the reason, in a nutshell, is that those great Popes, *at a time when the world was in much better shape than it is today*, sounded the alarm for the faithful to guard against the lures of the modern world and to press on in seeking its conversion to the one true religion.

We can hardly be blamed for advocating a return to the Church's own perennial teaching.

# Chapter 9

# Schism?

Another accusation neo-Catholics frequently hurl at their traditionalist brethren is that traditionalists are "schismatics" on account of their conscientious opposition to certain papally approved conciliar and postconciliar novelties, first and foremost the new liturgy of Paul VI, the new "ecumenism" and the new "dialogue." (In fact, a traditionalist is basically nothing more or less than a Roman Catholic minus this troika of dissolvent novelties, none of which is an article of Catholic faith.) The charge of "schism" is routinely trotted out in place of a substantive response to traditionalist arguments, which are generally left unanswered.

*The Wanderer* and its editor have led the neo-Catholic establishment in denouncing traditionalists as "schismatics." We have mentioned *The Wanderer's* accusation (in its editor's preface to the Pamphlet) that "one can conclude from a careful reading of *We Resist You* that its authors are on a schismatic trajectory that can only have tragic consequences." In the usual mode of this accusation against traditionalists, editor Alphonse Matt fails to give the reader the benefit of his "careful reading" of the Statement, which he neglects to quote even once.

Perhaps the most outrageous example of this neo-Catholic phenomenon is an article by Paul Likoudis published by *The*

*Wanderer* in early 1995.[270] In this article Likoudis lamented the supposed "schism" of certain Roman Catholic traditionalists, including the brilliant convert Gerald C. Matatics, a former Presbyterian minister who became a Catholic in 1986—the first minister of his denomination ever to do so. Horrified to see at work in the Catholic Church the same destructive liberalizing trends he had witnessed and fought against in evangelical Protestantism, Matatics decided in 1993 that he could no longer live at peace with the new liturgy and the other postconciliar novelties, and he committed himself to the traditionalist cause. For this he earned the contempt of the same neo-Catholic establishment that had once lionized him as a prize catch for the Church.

The Likoudis article melodramatically announced that according to *Fidelity* magazine (another neo-Catholic journal), Mr. Matatics "was 'imperiling his own salvation' by leaving the Catholic Church and, more unfortunately, was leading others out of the Church as well." That Likoudis presented no proof that Matatics had "left the Church" or that he had taken others with him—there was only the bare assertion—did not deter *The Wanderer* from publishing this gravest of accusations against a fellow Catholic. Interviewed by Likoudis for the same article, Karl Keating (head of the neo-Catholic apologetics outfit Catholic Answers) offered the equally unsubstantiated denunciation that "Gerry Matatics is a sad example of how schism does lead to heresy very quickly." What schism? What heresy? Keating never produced any evidence for the charges, yet (astonishingly) refuses to retract them.[271]

In fact, Matatics, his wife and eight children were (and remain) registered members of diocesan parishes in communion

---

[270]Paul Likoudis, "What's a Catholic to Do as the Allure of Schism Grows Stronger?", *The Wanderer*, February 16, 1995.

[271]The baseless denunciation of Mr. Matatics remains in EWTN's archives of "expert" answers to theological questions. See www.ewtn.com/library/ANSWERS/WHATTODO.HTM. A complete rebuttal appears at www.gerrymatatics.org/matatics.htm.

with the local bishop, most recently the "indult" Latin Mass parish served by the papally chartered Priestly Fraternity of Saint Peter in Scranton, Pennsylvania. Matatics even taught Sacred Scripture at the Fraternity's diocesan-approved seminary *after* the Likoudis article was published. *The Wanderer's* accusation of "schism" was, quite simply, a gross calumny — but all too typical of the neo-Catholic's approach to his traditionalist brethren.[272] Writing people out of the Church without evidence or a canonical process by Church authorities is something neo-Catholics would never dream of doing with any of the neo-Modernist Church-wreckers who happily infest the hierarchy and the seminaries; but the neo-Catholics cry "schism" with great abandon when it comes to traditionalists.

A more amusing example is a recent article in *The Wanderer* by one Peter Vere. Mr. Vere's own biography reveals that he was a former Catholic, then a former occultist and socialist, then a former Protestant Pentecostal, then a former *traditionalist* (affiliated with the Society of St. Pius X), before arriving at what he now considers home: "a harmonious blend of charismatic action and traditionalist contemplation."[273] While we do not begrudge any man his own spiritual journey back to the Church, we do object to Mr. Vere's rude and noisy arrival, which includes public denunciations of his former Catholic traditionalist friends for holding opinions he himself had vigorously defended only months before.

In his *Wanderer* piece, Vere, now armed with a freshly minted canon law degree, informs us that "I conclude a diocesan bishop may declare as schismatic an author who publicly resists the Second Vatican Council and Pope John Paul II."[274] How

---

[272]One of us personally attended the funeral of the Matatics' ninth child, Felicity Anne, who died in childbirth. The burial took place according to the traditional Latin rite, performed by a Fraternity priest in a Catholic cemetery. Mr. Matatics was not required to renounce the "schism" and the "heresy" publicly declared by *The Wanderer* and Mr. Keating.

[273]"The Trentecost Experience," *New Covenant*, June 2001.

[274]*The Wanderer*, November 22, 2001, p. 4.

exactly does one "resist" the Second Vatican Council? Did the
Council generate some kind of ecclesiastical force field to which
Catholics must submit, as if to the ministrations of a hypnotist?
What *teaching* of Vatican II does Vere claim traditionalists are
"resisting"? What does Vatican II require Catholics to *believe*
that they had not always believed before the Council? The same
questions apply with respect to John Paul II. The answers, of
course, are nothing and none. As we have already demonstrated
abundantly, the things from which traditionalists have
prescinded are novel practices, notions, attitudes and ecclesial
policies of the postconciliar epoch, none of which has actually
been imposed upon Catholics as a requirement of their faith.

For example, there is the "ecumenical venture," an ill-
defined and hitherto unknown ecclesial policy, which no
Catholic can be compelled to believe as if it were an article of
faith. Neo-Catholic authorities like Vere seem unaware of Pope
John Paul II's own teaching in *Redemptor Hominis* (1979),
previously mentioned, that it is "perhaps a good thing" that
traditionalist spokesmen express the concern that ecumenical
activities "are harmful to the cause of the Gospel, are leading to
a further rupture in the Church, are causing confusion of ideas
in questions of faith and morals and are ending up with a
specific indifferentism." But not according to the eminent Mr.
Vere! *He* concludes that to express such concerns is "resistance"
amounting to "schism." That the competent authorities of the
Church have made no such declaration poses no obstacle for
neo-Catholics; they simply arrogate that function to
themselves—while carefully refraining from any application of
the word "schism" to the neo-modernist Church-wreckers who
truly qualify.

If demagogic traditionalist-bashers like Vere would only
think about it for a moment, they would realize that it is quite
impossible for a Catholic to go into "schism" over such things as
the "ecumenical venture," in the sense of breaking all
communion with the See of Peter and thus ceasing to be
Catholic. Are traditionalists less than Catholic because they
strenuously object to and refuse to participate in common

prayer with pro-abortion Protestant ministers or prayer meetings with rabbis, muftis and witch doctors, as the Pope has done? Obviously, this kind of activity can never be imposed upon Catholics as an obligation of their religion. The Holy Ghost would not allow it.

Contrary to what most neo-Catholics assume, schism does not consist in resistance to certain papal commands or policies, but rather a rejection of the Pope's authority *in itself*. As the *Catholic Encyclopedia* notes: "[N]ot every disobedience is schism; in order to possess this character it *must* include, besides the transgression of the commands of superiors, *denial of their divine right to command*."

Thus, for example, there was no schism involved in the refusal of Polycrates of Ephesus and the synods of Asia Minor to obey the command of Pope Victor I that they abandon the quartodeciman Easter. Polycrates and his fellow bishops *resisted* — as in "we resist you" — on the grounds that they had *adjudged* — as in "private judgment" — that the Pope had no right to order them to abandon a custom they claimed was descended from St. John himself. The *Catholic Encyclopedia* makes the very distinction that neo-Catholics recklessly ignore: "The *resistance* of the Asiatic bishops involved no denial of the supremacy of Rome. It indicates solely that the bishops believed St. Victor to be abusing his power in bidding them renounce a custom for which they had Apostolic authority." All the more so today!

Likewise, there was no act of schism when, in 1331, certain French theologians and Cardinal Orsini denounced Pope John XXII as a heretic after he preached and developed in a series of sermons the thesis that there was no particular judgment immediately after death, but that the beatific vision of the saved and the eternal punishment of the damned awaited the final judgment of God on the Last Day. Cardinal Orsini even called for a council to pronounce the Pope a heretic, yet Church history does not record that Orsini or those who agreed with him (including King Louis of Bavaria) were in "schism," even though their motives were evidently more political than religious. On the contrary, history records that when he was *resisted* in his novel teaching, John XXII replied that he had not intended to bind the whole Church, and he impaneled a commission of theologians to consider the question. The commission *informed the Pope that he was in error.*[275]

A well-known modern example of licit resistance, even to papally approved doctrinal novelties, is the public furor over the astoundingly defective definition of Holy Mass in Article 7 of the General Instruction to the Roman Missal, prepared by Bugnini for the promulgation of Pope Paul's new rite of Mass:

> The Lord's Supper or Mass is the sacred assembly or congregation of the people of God met together, with a priest presiding, to celebrate the memorial of the Lord. For this reason Christ's promise applies supremely to a local gathering together of the Church: "Where two or three come together in my name, there am I in their midst" (Mt. 18:20).

Any Protestant would be quite pleased with this definition. It was only after publication of the *Ottaviani Intervention,* which exposed this outrage, that Paul VI was forced to rescind this quasi-heretical definition of the Mass and order it replaced with one that made some mention that the Mass was the unbloody Sacrifice of Our Lord on Calvary, made present on the altar by the priest acting *in persona Christi.* There were no neo-Catholics around in those days to accuse Cardinals Ottaviani and Bacci of "schism" for protesting this atrocious definition of the Mass, not to mention their protest of the new rite in its entirety.[276]

---

[275]Eric John, *The Popes: A Concise Biographical History* (1964; repr., Harrison, NY: Roman Catholic Books, 1994), p. 253.

[276]We do not take up here the alleged "retraction" of the *Intervention* in a letter purportedly signed by Cardinal Ottaviani shortly before his death, when he was virtually blind and gravely ill. We note only that his Secretary, Msgr. (now Cardinal) Gilberto Agustoni, did not deny the public accusation of Jean Madiran that he (Agustoni) had obtained the "retraction" by deception, and/or that the signature, markedly different from others by Ottaviani on recent

One more example may help to illustrate how the *Church* views the crucial canonical and theological difference between schism and simple disobedience in a particular matter: Hans Küng has been quite disobedient to the Pope; he has even condemned John Paul II as a despot who "rules in the spirit of the Spanish Inquisition." Yet the Vatican does not consider Küng a schismatic as such. On the contrary, he remains a priest in good standing in the Diocese of Basle, and Cardinal Ratzinger has referred to him (along with Rahner, Congar and Schillebeeckx) as "a great scholar."[277] Why is this? Because Küng has avoided any explicit denial of *the papal office itself*, so he cannot be convicted of schism, which involves a positive breaking of communion with the See of Peter. Thus, while Küng is supposedly no longer allowed to call himself a Catholic theologian, he *is* allowed to remain a Catholic priest.

By what right, then, do lay neo-Catholics such as Vere and *The Wanderer*'s editor condemn traditionalists as schismatics, when the Vatican regards the likes of Küng as being in communion with the Holy See? By no right at all. The charge is a calumny.

From all of this, it follows that even if the signers of the Statement were wrong in their stated resistance to certain postconciliar novelties, they would not for that reason be guilty of schism, because they have not denied the divine office of the papacy in itself. As we have just shown, the offense of schism does not arise merely because resistance to a particular papal act is not successful or especially well grounded. Rather, the offense depends upon whether the Pope's authority is *generally*

---

documents, was a forgery. Further, the "retraction" is full of flowery praise, quite uncharacteristic of Ottaviani, for the very Mass text whose imposition Ottaviani had only recently denounced as "an incalculable error" and a departure from the theology of the Mass canonized by the Council of Trent. In any case, Cardinal Bacci, Ottaviani's intimate friend, never retracted, and the arguments of the *Intervention* remain valid and unrefuted. See Davies, *Pope Paul's New Mass*, pp. 485-92.

[277]Ratzinger, *Principles of Catholic Theology*, p. 388.

*denied* by the resister. To hold otherwise is to hold that any act of disobedience to any papal command immediately creates a schism and instantly places the one who disobeys outside the Church. Are the neo-Catholics prepared to say this, for example, about all the bishops and priests who for years disobeyed papal liturgical laws against communion in the hand, altar girls and communal penance, or those who openly dissented (and still inwardly dissent) from *Humanae Vitae*? Obviously not. And yet the neo-Catholics suddenly perceive a "schism" when traditionalists object to novelties, many of which, paradoxically enough, were authorized only after *disobedient clerics* demanded them.

Like the faithful Catholics who challenged teachings by John XXII and Paul VI, the signers of the Statement have not generally denied the Pope's authority. To the contrary, they have *appealed* to it:

> Most Holy Father, the Catholic laity who direct themselves to you in this declaration of resistance are among the most ardent supporters of the papacy. For us, the monarchical institution of the Church with the Pope at its apex is the perfect summation of the universe created by God.... And the Pope is the natural link that joins the Glorious Christ with the Church, and the Church with heaven. We recognize, therefore, that there cannot be a more elevated position than that of the Supreme Pontiff, nor one more worthy of admiration. *It is based on this premise that we direct this document to Your Holiness.* We humbly beg the Incarnate Wisdom to illuminate your intelligence, and guide your will to do what should be done for the glory of God, the exaltation of Holy Mother Church, and the salvation of souls.

Schismatics do not beg the Pope to exercise his supreme authority; they do not recognize that authority in the first place. This passage from the Statement completely extinguishes the frivolous charge of schism—not only as to the authors, but also as to all other traditionalists of like mind and action.

Today our beloved Church is infested with scandal and neo-modernist heresy, and heterodox literature denying or undermining dogmas and doctrines of the Faith abounds in Catholic seminaries and universities, while the neo-Catholics say nothing of schism. But the same neo-Catholics cry "schism" as loudly as possible upon the appearance of a Statement signed by four traditional Catholics, and *The Wanderer* devotes *seven issues* to the tract—while managing to avoid any real discussion of its contents!

And what is so exquisitely ironic here is that the signers of the Statement, and traditionalists in general, are denounced as "schismatics" because they propose an intellectual resistance to novelties that have served to undermine the papacy itself—as, for example, the Pope's shocking invitation to Protestant theologians in *Ut Unum Sint* to help him seek a new way of exercising the papacy that they might find acceptable, without sacrificing anything "essential" to the primacy.[278] (The invitation was followed by the creation of a papal commission, including Protestants, to "study" the "question" of the papal primacy. But if nothing "essential" to the papacy is to be sacrificed, then this exercise, like the rest of the "ecumenical venture," is a waste of time, since Protestants adamantly reject the very essence of the primacy: the Pope's supreme governance of the Church in matters of faith and morals.) To the neo-Catholic mind, then, it is an act of "schism" to *defend papal authority* by raising the objection that even if this "study" of the papal primacy comes to nothing (as it surely will), the divinely instituted office of the papacy can only be debased when the Pope himself allows it to be scrutinized for possible changes by Protestant dissidents who reject the primacy but *accept murder in the womb.*

---

[278]"I am convinced that I have a particular responsibility in this regard, above all in acknowledging the ecumenical aspirations of the majority of the Christian Communities and in heeding the request made of me to find *a way of exercising the primacy* which, while in no way renouncing what is essential to its mission, is nonetheless open to *a new situation.*" *Ut Unum Sint*, 95.

As the present controversy demonstrates, it is the very existence of a large body of quiescent neo-Catholics that has allowed the postconciliar revolution to advance as far as it has into the structure of the Church. The basic function of the neo-Catholic in the dynamic of the revolution has been the marginalization of traditionalists, whom neo-Catholic leaders helpfully denounce for their simple refusal to cease being what neo-Catholics were only thirty-five years ago. In his book *The Remaking of the Catholic Church*, arch-liberal Richard P. McBrien noted this very phenomenon: "Criticism of the extreme right by moderate conservatives is far more effective than by moderate progressives."[279] How right he is. With the traditionalists safely marginalized, the soft wood of the neo-Catholics is the only resistance the termites have encountered. The results speak for themselves.

This is not to say that neo-Catholics as a group are subjectively complicit in the advances of the postconciliar revolution. Most neo-Catholics have accepted all the changes in good faith, hewing to the false notion of holy obedience peddled by their prominent spokesmen, who serve as *de facto* apologists for the revolution, which they find a hundred ways to minimize and explain away. With the preconciliar past now hazy at best, most neo-Catholics do not recognize that in the Church's long history we have seen time and again a principled resistance by loyal Catholics to sudden changes in the Church, even in relatively trivial matters. Just as it was licit for the Asian synods to refuse Pope Victor's direct command to change the date on which they observed Easter, so also is it licit to resist the hugely destructive changes being imposed upon us in the postconciliar period, and to work and pray for the ultimate reversal of these changes. We certainly do not advocate here anything approaching the violent (and successful) resistance of the people of Milan to papal efforts to eliminate the Ambrosian rite of

---

[279]Richard P. McBrien, *The Remaking of the Catholic Church* (New York: McGraw-Hill, 1973), p. 146.

Mass.[280] But even these violent resisters of an abuse of papal power are not viewed as schismatics by Church history.

* * *

If we may be permitted to indulge in a bit of amateur psychology, we would venture that the strange preoccupation of certain neo-Catholics with the "schism" of traditionalists — whom they denounce far more often and far more harshly than they do any true enemy of the Church — is but a reflection of an inner conviction that traditionalists legitimately oppose the ruinous postconciliar changes they themselves should have opposed, but did not. Neo-Catholic leaders understand, at least implicitly, that the very existence of a traditionalist movement *within* the Church demonstrates that they too could have resisted the changes without ceasing to be Catholics, yet history will record that they did absolutely nothing. It would be very convenient indeed if traditionalists could somehow be declared non-Catholics, so that the neo-Catholics' failure to act could thus be seen as exemplary "trust in the Church" and the only Catholic way to behave.

And so, just as liberals in secular society employ epithets — "anti-Semite," "homophobe," "racist" — to marginalize and destroy people whose arguments they are unable to answer and do not wish to be heard, prominent neo-Catholics hurl the epithet "schism" to marginalize and destroy traditionalists. But worse than the secular liberals, neo-Catholics use this demagogic trick against their own brothers in the Faith.

We can think of no other answer to the mystery of why neo-Catholics are so eager to accuse traditionalists of the crime of schism, yet so loath to make the same accusation against any of the neo-modernists who are dismantling the Church before their very eyes, often in direct disobedience to explicit papal

---

[280]See *Catholic Encyclopedia* (1913), "Ambrosian Liturgy and Rite."

commands to refrain from what they are doing. If there is another explanation for the mystery, we would like to hear it.

# Chapter 10

# A Question of Resistance

It can no longer seriously be denied that the unprecedented barrage of ecclesial novelties since Vatican II has induced a crisis whose scope equals and even exceeds the Arian crisis. Even a perceived "moderate," Msgr. Gamber, confirms the traditionalist view of the crisis:

> Great is the confusion! Who can still see clearly in this darkness? Where in our Church are the leaders who can show us the right path? Where are the bishops courageous enough to cut out the cancerous growth of modernist theology that has implanted itself and is festering within the celebration of even the most sacred mysteries, before the cancer spreads and causes even greater damage? What we need today is a new Athanasius, a new Basil, bishops like those who in the fourth century fought courageously against Arianism when almost the whole of Christendom had succumbed to heresy.

Gamber was right. Despite the appearance of order and regularity in the Church's merely logistical functioning, today we find ourselves in a situation little different in substance from that faced by the victims of the Arian onslaught. In his treatise *On Consulting the Faithful in Matters of Doctrine*, Cardinal Newman provided a description of the Arian wasteland in the Church that cannot fail to remind us of the postconciliar wasteland:

The body of bishops failed in their confession of the Faith....
They spoke variously, one against another; there was nothing,
after Nicea, of firm, unvarying, consistent testimony, for
nearly sixty years. There were untrustworthy Councils,
unfaithful bishops; there was weakness, fear of consequences,
misguidance, delusion, hallucination, *endless, hopeless,
extending into nearly every corner of the Catholic Church.* The
comparatively few who remained faithful were discredited
and driven into exile; the rest were either *deceivers or
deceived.*[281]

The point of Cardinal Newman's treatise was that it was the
laity, clinging to the defined dogma of the faith, along with a
few good bishops such as Athanasius, who kept the faith alive
during the Arian crisis. Today, as Gamber notes, we do not
even have an Athanasius or a Basil to guide us. As any
traditional Catholic parent who has had to remove his children
from the corrupting influence of a *Catholic* school will attest, we
are more or less on our own in the great ecclesial darkness
observed by Gamber.

As we noted in the Introduction, *The Wanderer's* decision to
publish the Pamphlet's scattershot critique of Roman Catholic
traditionalism was what prompted us to write the essays that
became this book. We also noted that *The Wanderer* justified its
decision as a response to the *We Resist You* statement of
traditionalist opposition to papally approved novelties. In view
of all the considerations we have thus far presented, we can now
return to the Statement and confront its most controversial
aspects from the proper perspective—the perspective of an
ecclesial crisis almost beyond imagining.

The signers of the Statement declare:

In the face of the situation described...the lay Catholics who
direct this document to Your Holiness are obliged in

---

[281] John Henry Newman, *On Consulting the Faithful in Matters of
Doctrine* (Kansas City: Sheed and Ward, 1961), p. 77.

conscience to declare themselves in a state of resistance relative to the teachings of Vatican Council II, Popes John XXIII and Paul VI, and your teachings and actions that are objectively contrary to the prior ordinary and extraordinary papal Magisterium.

In conjunction with this, the signers also declare a "suspension of obedience to the aforementioned progressivist teachings and the authorities who desire to impose them upon us."

It would be easy, if one were malicious, to extract these statements from their total context—and from the entire historical context of the crisis itself—and use them to indict the signers for "schism" or some other trumped-up delict. That is precisely what *The Wanderer*'s editor did in declaring that the signers (including the editor's own cousin, Michael Matt) "are on a schismatic trajectory that can only have tragic consequences." But this exercise of publicly writing fellow Catholics out of the Church involves deliberately overlooking the crucial point, made perfectly clear by the signers: that they are resisting only certain postconciliar novelties and have not rejected papal authority in itself, but rather *appeal to papal authority* for the undoing of the novelties. (It is yet another indication of neo-Catholic inconsistency that *The Wanderer* paid less attention to the actual text of the Statement than the Vatican does in dealing with texts published by outright heretics.)

Despite the signers' obvious intention to elicit discussion and debate with a highly provocative title, upon close examination the Statement advocates nothing more than we have endeavored to present here: a balanced approach to the crisis that seeks to account for, rather than ignore, the empirical evidence of an ecclesial disaster. While the vast conciliar and postconciliar program of innovation tends *materially* to oppose the perennial teaching of the Church in a number of areas, it does not involve any *formal* contradiction of an article of divine and Catholic faith. The postconciliar novelties have not been imposed upon the universal Church as matters of Catholic doctrine and belief, so that the indefectibility of the Church has not been implicated in the new teachings and practices. The conciliar Popes are valid Popes. All of this the signers of the Statement have affirmed, both publicly and privately to us.

As this entire discussion should make clear, moreover, the posited "suspension of obedience" operates largely in the potential. If one thinks about it for a moment, one can see that there is no doctrinally binding papal command that the signers are actually disobeying at present. For example, no Catholic is required to participate in any of the scandalous activities that are the staple of "Catholic ecumenism." But let us suppose that the Pope were to order everyone in the Church to attend joint liturgical services with pro-abortion Protestants, such as the Vespers service His Holiness conducted with Lutheran "bishops" (including women "bishops") in St. Peter's Basilica. Any reasonable Catholic would agree that such a command would have to be resisted.

As for those cases in which the signers are referring to an actual teaching they see as "objectively contrary to the prior ordinary and extraordinary papal Magisterium," the resistance still operates in the potential, since none of these teachings has been imposed upon the universal Church. For example, no Catholic is obliged to believe, with Pope John Paul II, that altar girls are an enrichment of the liturgy, that the new liturgy as a whole is a joyously accepted liturgical "renewal," that Protestant ministers are (as *Ut Unum Sint* repeatedly calls them) "disciples of Christ," that God has not revealed whether any human beings at all will ever be in hell, or, concerning the death penalty, that "the dignity of human life must *never* be taken away, even in the case of someone who has done great evil." Likewise, the Pope's assurance to a hypothetical grieving mother in *Evangelium Vitae* that her aborted child is now "living in the Lord" — an opinion that would appear to abolish Limbo — was binding on no one, and was in fact later struck from the definitive Latin text.[282] Nor is any Catholic bound to adhere to Pope Paul VI's repeated references to the Anglican sect as a "sister Church" or his teaching that the new liturgy was a great improvement over the old, or, for that matter, Blessed Pope John XXIII's departure from the repeated teaching of his predecessors on the moral duty to avoid any collaboration with Communist-led or Communist-inspired movements. The examples of such dubious novelties, which we have only partially indicated in this book, would require a multi-volume study to discuss fully. As far as the Pope's novel view on the death penalty is concerned, both Supreme Court Justice Antonin Scalia and columnist Patrick J. Buchanan have publicly stated the obvious: that the current pope has no power to abolish the Church's 2,000-year-old approbation of capital punishment as a matter of natural justice. As Buchanan put it in a column defending Scalia's "dissent" from the Pope's opinion: "For Scalia had not contradicted or defied any Catholic doctrine. Rather, it is the Holy Father and the bishops who are outside the Catholic mainstream, and at odds with Scripture, tradition and natural law."[283]

Integrists! Schismatics!—so the *Wanderer* would proclaim were this remark to come from the editor's cousin, Michael Matt, and his fellow signers of the Statement. But since Buchanan has written for *The Wanderer*, and since Justice Scalia is, well, Justice Scalia, *The Wanderer* will doubtless save those epithets for hurling at safer targets, like the editor's cousin. Yet here we see a Supreme Court justice with many children and a son in the priesthood, and alongside him one of America's staunchest Catholic commentators, doing precisely what the Statement's lowly signatories have done: *resisting* a "progressivist teaching" which obviously has no warrant in Scripture, tradition or natural law. But what else should a Catholic do when faced—as we have been so often since the Council—with an apparent departure from what the Church has always taught?

Concerning other "progressivist teachings" from which the Statement's signers prescind (with no less cause than Scalia and Buchanan), they are careful to note that the sheer volume of postconciliar Vatican pronouncements, in so many varied places

---

[282]Msgr. John F. McCarthy, Living Tradition, July 1996, www.rtforum.org/lt/lt65.html

[283] WorldNetDaily, February 8, 2002.

and forms and on so many different subjects, makes it impossible to know for certain which are doctrines for the Church and which are the opinions of a private doctor. Consequently, the signers rightly note that "the clarity of the degree of obedience has been lost." Let the Church, then, and not the neo-Catholic establishment, tell the signers (and us) what is the degree of obedience, if any, owed to each of the pronouncements in the *ten linear feet* of shelf space occupied by the writings and speeches of John Paul II alone.

That the "suspension of obedience" does not relate to any identifiable binding Catholic doctrine is the very reason the author of the Pamphlet failed to answer our challenge to identify exactly where the signers were guilty of "opposition to the living Magisterium." There is no question, however, that the phrase "suspension of obedience" served to highlight the gravity of the current situation and to act as the vehicle by which the signers gained wide publicity for their contention that the postconciliar program of innovation should be resisted. That resistance, however, really involves nothing more than prescinding from—that is, not attaching oneself to—certain novelties that Catholics have never been clearly bound to embrace as doctrine or practice in the first place. The resistance also involves presenting arguments against the novelties and petitioning for their rescission. In the process, neither the signers nor any other traditionalist whom we would defend has denied any Catholic doctrine, violated any law of the Church or broken communion with the Roman Pontiff.

But is even such limited "resistance" justifiable for a Catholic? In Chapter 8 we demonstrate that resistance to the Pope or bishops in *particular matters* involving the postconciliar novelties does not constitute schism, since even if traditionalist resistance were unfounded, traditionalists do not deny, but rather affirm and appeal to, the authority of the hierarchy. Granted that resistance in particular matters is not strictly schismatic, does that make it right? Quite obviously, we believe the answer is yes. Further, we believe that Catholics have a *duty* to oppose the damage that is being done to the Church, even if it is being done with Vatican approval and in the name of the Second Vatican Council.

The Pamphlet, in line with neo-Catholic thinking in general, ignores the unanimous teaching of Catholic theologians, including Doctors of the Church, that the members of the Church, like the citizens of any commonwealth, have the natural right and even the duty to resist unjust actions by their rulers that threaten harm to the common good. The notion that every papal command must be obeyed blindly, without resistance or open objection under any circumstances, is not a Catholic notion. The *Catholic* position was stated classically in the oft-quoted passage from St. Robert Bellarmine's work on the Roman Pontiff:

> Just as it is licit to resist the Pontiff that aggresses the body, it is also licit to resist the one who aggresses souls or who disturbs civil order, or, above all, who attempts to destroy the Church. I say that it is licit *to resist him by not doing what he orders and by preventing his will from being executed*; it is not licit, however, to judge, punish or depose him, since these acts are proper to a superior.[284]

It must be noted that St. Robert Bellarmine presented the case for licit resistance to papal commands in order to refute the Protestant contention that the Pope is some sort of absolute despot whom Catholics were never allowed to resist, no matter what he said or did. Thus the neo-Catholic position on papal authority is very much in line with the Protestant caricature.

The eminent sixteenth-century theologian Francisco Suarez explained the same principle thus:

> And in this second way the Pope could be schismatic, if he were unwilling to be in normal union with the whole body of the Church, as would occur if he attempted to excommunicate the whole Church, or, as both Cajetan and Torquemada observe, if he wished to *overturn the rites of the Church based on Apostolic Tradition*.... If [the Pope]...gives an order contrary to

---

[284]St. Robert Bellarmine, *De Romano Pontifice*, Book II, Chapter 29.

right customs, he should not be obeyed; *if he attempts to do something manifestly opposed to justice and the common good, it will be lawful to resist him*; if he attacks by force, by force he can be repelled, with a moderation appropriate to a just defense.[285]

It is remarkable that in the sixteenth century an esteemed theologian would matter-of-factly discuss the possibility that a *Pope* could be guilty of schismatic acts that his own subjects would be forced to resist. We have no intention of suggesting that the conciliar Popes were guilty of schism, but we do note that there were no neo-Catholics in the sixteenth century to denounce Suarez as an "integrist" or "extreme traditionalist" for discussing the possibility of a Pope taking schismatic actions in the abuse of his authority.

Does any of this mean, however, that there can be a *duty* to resist the harmful actions of a Pope, as opposed to a mere excuse from culpability if one does so? On this question we need go no further than the teaching of St. Thomas Aquinas. In the *Summa Theologica*, under the question "Whether a man is *bound* to correct his prelate," St. Thomas teaches as follows: "It must be observed, however, that if the faith were endangered, a subject *ought* to rebuke his prelate even publicly. *Hence Paul, who was Peter's subject, rebuked him in public, on account of the imminent danger of scandal concerning faith....*" (Peter had scandalized potential converts and threatened the mission of the Church by continuing to follow Mosaic dietary laws and refusing to eat with Gentiles.) St. Thomas here observes that the public rebuke of a prelate "would seem to savor of presumptuous pride; but *there is no presumption in thinking oneself better in some respect,* because, in this life, *no man is without some fault.* We must also remember that when a man reproves his prelate charitably, it does not follow that he thinks himself any better, but merely that he offers his help to one who, 'being in the higher position among you, *is therefore in greater danger,*' as Augustine observes in his Rule quoted above."[286]

---

[285]*De Fide*, Disp. X, Sec. VI, N. 16.
[286]ST, Q. 33, Art. V, Pt. II-II.

In a rather desperate bid to deny that the teaching of St. Thomas refers to the first Pope as an example of legitimate resistance to prelates, one of the authors of *The Pope, the Council and the Mass* actually defended an absurd "exegesis" of Galatians 2:11, according to which the Cephas rebuked by St. Paul was not Peter, but some other Cephas. Thus the neo-Catholic becomes a scriptural revisionist, if that is what it takes to defend the current novelties.[287]

That even a Pope may have to be resisted if he takes actions against the common good of the Church is, after all, just a matter of common sense; for the Pope more than any other ruler must show himself to be subject to the requirements of justice and charity. Thus, when traditionalist members of the Church's commonwealth raise objections to the Pope's behavior or his lackluster administration of commonwealth affairs, no reasonable man concludes from this that traditionalists are thereby denying that the Pope is, in fact, the Pope. The reasonable interpretation of traditionalist grievances is that we, too, love the commonwealth of the Church and are simply petitioning its ruler — because he *is* the ruler — to address urgent problems with its governance and threats to its common good. This, we are convinced in conscience, is our duty. It would take

---

[287]James Likoudis, "Were the Apostle Peter and Cephas of Antioch the Same Person?", *Serviam* Newsletter, Jan./Feb. 1996 and March 1997; credo.stormloader.com/Doctrine/cephas.htm. In this article Mr. Likoudis admits: "There is no question that mainstream opinion in the Church has held that the Apostle Peter and the Cephas whom St. Paul rebuked in Galatians were the same person." By "mainstream opinion," Likoudis means the Church's constant belief as seen in the teaching of the Doctors and Fathers, including St. Jerome and St. Thomas. Against this overwhelming weight of Church authority, Likoudis pits one Fr. Pujol, a nineteenth-century French Jesuit! Notice how Likoudis, true to neo-Catholic form, demotes traditional Church teaching to "mainstream *opinion*" when it gets in the way of the neo-Catholic system — in this case, the neo-Catholic view of the Pope as irresistible, absolute monarch. Likoudis takes the position that the papal *primacy* depends on showing that it was not Peter who was rebuked by Paul. He thus confuses primacy with irresistibility.

malicious intent, and a great deal of effort, to arrive at any other interpretation of our position.

We offer here one key example of why we believe there is not only a right, but a duty, to resist the postconciliar novelties: the incalculable damage they have caused to the sacred liturgy, and thus the entire life of the Church—and indeed the world!

The "traditionalist" position regarding the liturgy in particular was expressed in 1969 by Cardinal Ottaviani (former Prefect of the Holy Office) and Cardinal Bacci in their famous "intervention" against the new Mass, which we have discussed already. As the Cardinals warned with prophetic accuracy:

> The innovations in the Novus Ordo and the fact that all that is of perennial value finds only a minor place, if it subsists at all, could well turn into a certainty the suspicions already prevalent, alas, in many circles, that truths which have always been believed by the Christian people, can be changed or ignored without infidelity to that sacred deposit of doctrine to which the Catholic faith is bound forever. Recent reforms have amply demonstrated that fresh changes in the liturgy could lead to nothing but complete bewilderment on the part of the faithful, who are already showing signs of restiveness and of an indubitable lessening of faith.

Rather than submitting with docility to the destruction of the Roman rite, traditionalists have been guided by the axiom of moral theology stated in the *Intervention*: that subjects of a legislator, even subjects of the Pope, "have always had the right, nay the duty, to ask the legislator to abrogate the law, should it prove to be harmful." Traditionalists have never ceased to exercise that right and duty, and to this day have never embraced the postconciliar reforms—above all, the reform of the liturgy, which they regard in conscience as an abuse of papal authority which no Pope before Paul VI would have dared to impose upon the Church.

We have mentioned more than once in this book Klaus Gamber's view that we have witnessed the destruction of the Roman rite, and Cardinal Ratzinger's opinion that the consequences of Paul VI's radical liturgical reform could only be tragic. Ratzinger, furthermore, has stated that the Pope is not an absolute monarch, but rather is bound by liturgical tradition.

If all this is true—and it obviously *is* true—then is it not obvious that the Pope's subjects had not only the right but the *duty* to use all licit means, short of judging or deposing him, to resist the incalculable damage that was about to be inflicted upon the Church? A simple analogy should suffice to bring this point home for even the most determined neo-Catholic defender of the fallacy of irresistible papal authority: Suppose a Pope were to order the immediate destruction of every marble altar in every church, chapel and cathedral in the world. Only a lunatic would insist that such a command must be obeyed; on the contrary, one would have a duty to impede its execution. What, then, is more important to the Church: *the form of the altar or the form of the Mass*? If one could rightly resist a papal command to destroy altars, by what tortured logic would one be forbidden to resist a papal command to destroy the traditional Roman rite itself?

For traditionalists, licit resistance to the Pope has meant simply refusing to abandon the traditional rite of Mass in favor of the new liturgy, or to practice any of the other novelties that suddenly appeared in the Church during the 1960s. One of the aims of this book has been to show that history has already proven that traditionalists were right to do so, as Cardinal Ratzinger's own statements about the new liturgy would tend to prove, even if he himself would not embrace the traditionalist position.

In finally disposing of the neo-Catholic argument against any resistance to papally approved acts of ecclesial destruction, we need only note that the Pamphlet's author is guilty of precisely what he condemns in traditionalists. We have mentioned that in Part 3 *of his own tract against traditionalists*, the author declares as follows: "I myself consider the new rite of Mass *inferior* so far (we expect improvements to come) to the traditional Latin Mass." And on his own Internet site, he further declares: "[O]ur real crisis today focuses on the liturgy and in the *dangerous ambiguity* of Conciliar texts and events."[288]

Thus, the same neo-Catholic commentator who demands absolute obedience to "the living Magisterium" publicly declares that the Church is in crisis because the conciliar Popes imposed an *inferior* rite of Mass on the Church and an ecumenical Council promulgated *dangerously* ambiguous texts. The author of the Pamphlet fails to recognize that he himself, along with millions of other Catholics, is more or less in a state of resistance, explicit or implicit, to the postconciliar debacle. As the author's entire position extinguishes itself in this fatal self-contradiction, we may bid him goodbye. He provided a useful provocation with his tract, but we may now say of him what Newman said of Kingsley: "And now I am in a train of thought higher and more serene than any which slanders can disturb. Away with you, Mr. Kingsley, and fly into space. Your name shall occur again as little as I can help, in the course of these pages. I shall henceforth occupy myself not with you, but with your charges."

---

[288]http://www.geocities.com/Athens/Itahaca/3251/ecumod. html.

# Chapter 11

# A Nest of Contradictions

From all that we have presented thus far, it should be apparent that what we call neo-Catholicism is essentially *a defense of novelty* in the Church.  Never before in Church history have Catholics felt obliged to defend ecclesial novelty on a vast scale, because ecclesial novelty on a vast scale was never attempted (or even imagined) by any Pope before Paul VI.  On the contrary, as we have noted, the counsel of all the preconciliar Popes was unanimous: Catholics should abhor novelty.  To recall the words of St. Pius X in *Pascendi*: "[F]or Catholics nothing will remove the authority of the second Council of Nicea, where it condemns those 'who dare, after the impious fashion of heretics, to deride the *ecclesiastical traditions*, to invent *novelties of some kind*...or endeavor by malice or craft to overthrow *any one of the legitimate traditions* of the Catholic Church'.... Far, far from our priests be the love of novelty!"

Yet the neo-Catholics have counseled blind acceptance of novelties that would have elicited righteous fury from all the great preconciliar Popes.  In adopting this mentality, they have become what fellow neo-Catholic George Sim Johnston contentedly describes as "progressive Catholics."  That is, the neo-Catholic is nothing more or less than a kind of liberal, even if he conforms to the moral teaching of the Church and espouses no formal heresy as such.  As we have shown, the generality of neo-Catholics has accepted or acquiesced in many of the propositions condemned in the *Syllabus of Errors* (#13, #16, #17, #18, #24, and #77-80). In many respects, the neo-Catholic fits Pius X's description in *Pascendi* of "the modernist as reformer," i.e., one who disparages the Thomistic system, favors dramatic liturgical reform, the decentralization of power in the Church (collegiality), abolition of the Index of Forbidden Books and the Holy Office, and the Americanist emphasis on the active virtues, which is the very hallmark of Vatican II's call for an "open" and activist Church, engaged in dialogue with the world. (Once again, we stress that we are speaking here only in the objective realm of ideas, without presuming to judge the subjective faith of any individual—even if neo-Catholics are only too happy to pronounce judgment on the traditionalists they denounce publicly by name as "schismatics" and "integrists.")

Neo-Catholicism, being a moderate form of liberalism, cannot avoid the self-contradictions that inevitably arise from the internal conflict between true and false principles in liberal thinking. Mindful of the true principle that Catholics are obliged to preserve the Church's patrimony, yet clinging to the false principle that whatever a Pope approves is traditional, many neo-Catholics seek ways to relieve the insupportable tension of their own position. The result is a series of self-contradictions and inconsistencies in the neo-Catholic system. We will examine a few of them here.

We note, first of all, that while neo-Catholics may agree that *priests, bishops and cardinals* (outside of the Vatican) may be rebuked when they take actions that harm the common good of the Church, they somehow conclude that the Pope and his collaborators in the Vatican apparatus are exempt from the same basic principle of natural law. Hence neo-Catholics may often be seen criticizing high-ranking prelates for doing *what the Pope does.*

For example, *The Wanderer* recently lambasted Cardinal Keeler for conducting a public prayer for forgiveness of the alleged historical sins of Catholics in the Archdiocese of Baltimore, including their supposed "racism."[289] Yet this

---

[289]*The Wanderer*, Jan. 11, 2001, "From the Mail."

ceremony was no different in kind from the Pope's own Day of Pardon liturgy, in which he begged forgiveness for the historical "sins" of deceased Catholics in every nation, including "acts of discrimination on the basis of racial and ethnic differences," "sins against the dignity of women" and "sins against love, peace and respect for cultures and religions."[290] *The Wanderer* even featured an irate letter of protest to Cardinal Keeler from a layman, *reciting precisely the same theological objections raised by traditionalists* against the Pope's substantially identical ceremony—including the objection that it is outrageous to accuse the dead of sins when they cannot defend themselves, or that it is theologically impossible to ask forgiveness from God for the sins of departed souls who have already been judged. Likewise, in 1997 *The Wanderer* complained about "churchmen who publicly issue 'apologies,' not for their own sins, but for the alleged sins of dead men who obviously cannot defend themselves."[291]

So the neo-Catholic will publicly rebuke a cardinal and other churchmen for *following* the Pope's example, while defending the Pope when he engages in precisely the same activity! Such is the confusion of the neo-Catholic mind.

In like manner, certain neo-Catholics spend a great deal of time decrying the abysmal state of the liturgy, without ever seeming to notice that it results from practices fully permissible under Vatican guidelines. Without exceeding a single Vatican

---

[290]See *Solemn Prayer of the Faithful Confessing Sins and Requesting God's Pardon.* EWTN's website happily reported: "There was a confession of sins in general, of sins committed in the service of truth, of sins that have harmed Christian unity, of sins against the people of Israel, of sins against love, peace and respect for cultures and religions, of sins against the dignity of women and the unity of the human race, and of sins related to the fundamental rights of the person. Each category was introduced by representatives of the Roman Curia and was followed by the Holy Father's prayer and the chanting of a triple Kyrie eleison." See, www.ewtn.com/library/papaldoc/ jp2dyprd.htm

[291]"Catholics Protest Apologies for 'Sins' of the Past," December 11, 1997, p. 11.

permission, any local bishop can authorize the repellent spectacle of a charismatic guitar Mass with babbling parishioners speaking "in tongues," altar girls, female "lectors," communion in the hand, and even readings by a Protestant minister—all conducted in a church used jointly by a Catholic parish and a Protestant sect, as allowed and even encouraged by the utterly astounding 1993 Directory on Ecumenism.[292]

To give another example of blaming middle management for what the boss allows, neo-Catholics can often be heard complaining about the scandal of "sex education" in Catholic schools; for decades *The Wanderer* has been condemning the local bishops who allow it to go on. Yet neo-Catholics never seem to notice that for thirty years the Holy See has been well aware of the pornographic content of "Catholic" sex-ed curricula and has taken no action to remove them from Catholic classrooms, much less punish the bishops, priests and nuns who force this filth upon innocent children.[293] On the contrary, despite the preconciliar papal condemnation of any form of "sex education"[294]—yet another preconciliar teaching given the

---

[292]See *Directory for Application of Principles and Norms on Ecumenism*, n. 138, which authorizes shared ownership of church premises if the Bishop deems it financially or otherwise appropriate, and there is "a good ecumenical relationship" with the Protestant co-owners—whatever that means. In such case, "*consideration*" should be given to removal of the Blessed Sacrament from the *jointly owned sanctuary*, in order to accommodate the "sensitivities" of "those who will be using the building" (n. 139). In his encyclical *Ut Unum Sint,* Pope John Paul II confirms that the Directory was "issued with my approval" as the basis for applying ecumenism in "the pastoral sphere" (*Ut Unum Sint*, n. 16).

[293]One of us served as legal counsel to Catholic parents whose ten-year-old daughter was expelled from a "Catholic" school in the Archdiocese of Miami because the parents refused to allow their little girl to study the details of sexual intercourse in the classroom—including descriptions of private parts and sexual actions so explicit that a local TV news reporter *could not read them on the air.*

[294]See, for example, Pius XI's 1929 encyclical *Divinis Illius Magistri*, condemning all forms of classroom sexual instruction, and cautioning

heave-ho since 1965—Cardinal Ratzinger refused to put a stop to the disgusting "New Creation" sex-ed program in American Catholic schools, declaring that "anxiety about doctrinal aspects of the program...would seem to be without foundation." Ratzinger passed the matter over to Cardinal Baum, then head of the Pontifical Council for the Family, who likewise approved it and sent it back to America, where "New Creation" has been destroying the innocence of children ever since.[295] While the Vatican goes on allowing little children to be scandalized in Catholic classrooms around the world, the neo-Catholics heap lavish praise on a toothless 1995 Vatican document, issued thirty years too late, which contains the laughable advice that "it is *recommended* that respect be given to the right of the child...to withdraw from any form of sexual instruction imparted outside the home."[296] Recommended? It is an intolerable outrage in the first place that a Catholic child should have to withdraw from a Catholic classroom in order to preserve his innocence.

The same curiously selective indignation is seen in the neo-Catholic's approach to papal collaboration with the very forces of secularism the preconciliar Popes condemned. Thus, certain neo-Catholic luminaries (among them Mother Angelica) condemned Ted Turner—quite rightly—for donating a billion dollars to the increasingly evil United Nations.[297] Yet the neo-

---

that if "some instruction" is to be given *in private,* that it not descend to details.

[295]"The Sodomization of Innocence: Homo Church Invades the Catholic Kinergarten," by Randy Engel, www.dotm.org/r-engel.htm. The postconciliar Vatican's shameful failure to put an end to the scandal of "Catholic" sex education has been exhaustively documented by the redoubtable Mrs. Engel—another of those "private judgment" Catholics who finds herself forced to oppose Vatican policy.

[296]*The Truth and Meaning of Human Sexuality,* n. 120.3 (1995).

[297]In anticipation of dishonest criticism of this book, we hasten to reiterate here that our entire discussion of neo-Catholicism relates to *ideas,* not to the personal holiness of those who, in our opinion, are associated with the neo-Catholic phenomenon. Thus, there is no

Catholics will hear no criticism of the Vatican's staunch support of the U.N., where it enjoys permanent observer status and subscribes, with useless "reservations," to U.N. documents that only advance the organization's godless agenda.[298] Neither will neo-Catholics tolerate criticism of the conciliar document *Gaudium et Spes*, which called for establishment of a world government,[299] or any opposition to papal endorsements of the U.N. Thus, while condemning the U.N. out of one side of their mouths, out of the other the neo-Catholics will defend Paul VI's speech in tribute to the United Nations, in which he called the Tower of Babel on the Hudson "this lofty institution" and "the best hope of the world," declaring: "May unanimous trust in this institution grow; *may its authority increase*...."[300] Nor will the neo-Catholics hear any objection to the pro-U.N. policy of Pope John Paul II, a major contributor to *Gaudium et Spes*. In his own speech to the General Assembly, the current Pope proclaimed the "esteem of the Apostolic See and of the Catholic Church for this institution" and pronounced the U.N. — worldwide promoter of contraception, abortion and atheistic humanism — "a great instrument for *harmonizing and coordinating* international life." The Pope even declared that the U.N. "has the historic, even momentous, task of promoting this qualitative leap in international life, not only by serving as a center of effective mediation for the resolution of conflicts, but also by fostering values, attitudes and concrete initiatives of solidarity...."

How can neo-Catholics condemn Ted Turner for giving a billion dollars to the United Nations, while defending lavish papal praise and support for the same utterly corrupt institution? But one cannot expect consistency from neo-

intention here to question the Catholic fidelity of Mother Angelica or anyone else, but simply to discuss the implications of objective words and deeds of persons who participate in what we call the neo-Catholic system in the postconciliar Church.

[298]For example, the Vatican is a signatory "with reservations" to the deplorable U.N. Convention on the "Rights of the Child."

[299]*Gaudium et Spes*, nn. 77 and 82.

[300]Address to United Nations, October 4, 1965.

Catholics on this score, given their adherence to the axiom that The Pope Can Do No Wrong—even when he is doing what neo-Catholics condemn in others.

It seems, moreover, that even some of the UN's population-control propaganda has taken its toll on certain individuals within the neo-Catholic ranks. Pope Pius XII taught that large families point to "the physical and moral health of a Christian people; a living faith in God and trust in His Providence; the fruitful and joyful holiness of Catholic marriage."[301] But Fr. Stephen F. Torraco, who answers questions on morality for EWTN's website, argues that those who do not use Natural Family Planning (NFP) and "leave procreation in the hands of God" are following a "deficient" and "less than human" approach. Fr. Richard Hogan, who answers questions specifically pertaining to NFP, contends that "it is better to have 2 or 3 children you can educate all the way than 7 or 8 you can only take so far."[302] It would take an entire book to address all the implications of this position, but suffice it to say that one of the most influential neo-Catholic sources has somehow transformed the concession allowed by Pius XII and Paul VI into a positive obligation, the neglect of which constitutes dereliction of duty.

Another indefensible disparity in the neo-Catholic system is its whole approach to the question of schism—a term neo-Catholics no longer apply to real schismatics, but only to Roman Catholic traditionalists! While neo-Catholics harshly condemn the putative schism of Archbishop Marcel Lefebvre, they observe a strange silence regarding the blatant schism of the Communist-controlled Catholic Patriotic Association (CPA) in Red China, yet another of the series of contradictions and double standards that our critics have adopted.

---

[301]Pius XII, Address to the Directors of the Associations for Large Families of Rome and of Italy, January 20, 1958.

[302]"John Galvin Responds to the Commentaries," *The Latin Mass*, Winter 2002, p. 24.

On June 30, 1988, Archbishop Lefebvre consecrated four bishops without a papal mandate — an offense that, under Canon 1382, carries the penalty of excommunication, subject to various excuses from culpability under Canons 1321-23. One of these excuses is that the offender acted out of necessity or to avoid grave inconvenience. Another is that the offender sincerely believed, however mistakenly, that his action was justified, and he was thus not subjectively culpable for the offense. Given the current chaotic state of the Church, Lefebvre argued that his action was necessary to preserve some semblance of Catholic tradition. We do not take up that defense here, but merely note three things:

- First, that the defense of necessity was raised by the Archbishop, and that, right or wrong, His Eminence no doubt acted with a good intention, as envisioned by Canons 1321 and 1323.

- Second, the penalty for illicit episcopal consecrations under Canon 1382 is *latae sententiae* — that is, automatic and without need of a formal declaration by ecclesiastical authority. However, the effects of the penalty become much more severe if the penalty is then declared by ecclesiastical authority (Canon 1331). For one thing, the declared penalty cannot be remitted by a confessor in situations of urgency, outside of the danger of death (Canon 1357).

- Third, the 1983 Code of Canon Law nowhere provides that an illicit episcopal consecration constitutes in itself the canonical crime of schism. In fact, Cardinal Castillo Lara, President of the Pontifical Commission for the Authentic Interpretation of Canon Law, admitted to *La Repubblica* that "the act of consecrating a bishop (without a papal mandate) is not in itself a schismatic act...."[303] (Cardinal Lara claimed that Lefebvre was guilty of schism before the 1988 consecrations, for which claim he offered not the slightest proof.)

As we know, the Vatican's reaction to the Lefebvre consecrations was immediate: On July 2, 1988, only two days later, the Pope issued his *motu proprio Ecclesia Dei*, which declares that "Archbishop Lefebvre and the priests Bernard Fellay, Bernard Tissier de Mallerais, Richard Williamson and Alfonso de Galarreta have incurred the grave penalty of excommunication envisaged by ecclesiastical law." The *motu proprio* went even further than what the cited canon provides, declaring that "such disobedience—which implies in practice the rejection of the Roman primacy—constitutes a schismatic act." Yet the canonical admonition sent to Lefebvre before the consecrations had contained no warning that his action would be deemed schismatic; the only possible penalty cited was that of *latae sententiae* excommunication. The result was rather like being charged with only one offense, but then convicted of two. The *motu proprio* also warns that "formal adherence to the schism is a grave offense against God and carries the penalty of excommunication decreed by the Church's law." But the term "formal adherence" is nowhere defined. (Later, however, the Vatican made it clear in particular decisions that mere attendance at an SSPX chapel in Arizona is not an act of schism, nor even recourse to an SSPX bishop for the sacrament of Confirmation at an independent chapel in Hawaii.)

While the *motu proprio* applied the excommunication and the delict of schism by name only to Lefebvre and the four priests he consecrated, since then, true to form, neo-Catholic commentators at EWTN, *The Wanderer* and elsewhere have with great alacrity denounced as "schismatic" not only Lefebvre and the four SSPX bishops, but all the priests of the Society, any member of the faithful who frequents their chapels, and anyone who defends Lefebvre's actions. The neo-Catholics have even

---

[303]*La Repubblica*, October 7, 1988.

coined the terms "Lefebvrist" and "Lefebvrism" to stigmatize "extreme traditionalists" in general.

Thus, in the case of Lefebvre, we have the following: an immediate declaration of excommunication, and, going beyond what the express terms of the Church's law provide, the declaration of a schism; the unauthorized extension of those delicts by neo-Catholic organs to an entire class of Catholics who are not at all embraced in the original *motu proprio*; and, for good measure, the demonization of Archbishop Lefebvre and all his followers and sympathizers. Yet there is no question that those whom the neo-Catholics denounce as "Lefebvrists" — including the bishops, priests and laity actually affiliated with the SSPX — possess the Catholic faith and follow the moral teaching of the Church, as even Cardinal Castrillón admitted in the course of the recent negotiations toward "regularization" of the SSPX. Further, "Lefebvrist" priests and bishops profess their loyalty to John Paul II and pray for him at every Mass, along with the local ordinary.[304]

We now consider the events of January 6, 2000. On that date, the Catholic Patriotic Association (CPA) illicitly consecrated five bishops — one more than Lefebvre — without a papal mandate. The Red Chinese regime created the CPA in 1957 to replace the Roman Catholic Church in China, which it declared illegal and drove underground, where loyal Chinese Catholics have been forced to worship ever since, following the example of their spiritual father, the great martyr Cardinal Ignatius Kung. Including the five bishops illicitly consecrated on January 6, 2000, since 1957 the CPA has illicitly consecrated *one hundred bishops* without a papal mandate. What is more, unlike the four SSPX bishops consecrated by Archbishop Lefebvre, the CPA

---

[304]In fact, the Vatican's private approach to SSPX would indicate that the "Lefebvre schism" is illusory, and is really nothing more than an internal disciplinary problem of the Church. For example, as Cardinal Cassidy admitted in a letter of March 25, 1994, the Pontifical Council for Christian Unity "is not concerned with the Society of St. Pius X. The situation of the members of this Society is an internal matter of the Catholic Church. The Society is not another Church or Ecclesial Community in the meaning used in the Directory."

bishops dare to assert territorial jurisdiction over sees from which the Communists drove the legitimate bishops of the Catholic Church.

The CPA constitution requires express disavowal of allegiance to the Roman Pontiff. As the Kung Foundation website points out: "The Patriotic Association's own fundamental and explicit principle is autonomy from the Pope's administrative, legislative, and judicial authority" — the very definition of schism under Canon 751. By comparison, the SSPX professes its acceptance of papal authority and has entered into papally ordered negotiations for regularization as an apostolic administration directly under the Holy Father. (As Cardinal Castrillón told the press, Bishop Fellay said to him that "when the Pope calls, we run.") And while there is no question that Archbishop Lefebvre's acts constituted disobedience to a particular papal command, disobedience in particular matters is not in itself schism — which, as we discussed in Chapter 9, is defined by rejection of the papal office itself. But since denial of the Pope's right to command is the founding principle of the CPA, it is undeniably schismatic by definition. CPA bishops swear their allegiance not to the Pope, but to Premier Jiang and the Red Chinese regime, of which they are pawns. Thus, in 1994, the CPA bishops issued a "pastoral letter" calling upon Chinese Catholics to support China's population control policies, including forced abortion, and, as the Cardinal Kung Foundation notes, "the Patriotic bishops passionately denounced the Holy Father's canonization of the 120 Chinese martyrs on Oct. 1, 2000."

The CPA, therefore, is a Communist-created, Communist-controlled, blatantly schismatic, pro-abortion organization founded by the devil himself, acting through Mao Tse-Tung and the Red Chinese regime, now headed by "President" Jiang. Accordingly, in the performance of his apostolic duty, Pope Pius XII issued an encyclical denouncing the CPA as an assault on the integrity of the Catholic faith and the Mystical Body. "For under an appearance of patriotism," the Pope wrote, "which in reality is just a fraud, this association aims primarily at making

Catholics gradually embrace the tenets of atheistic materialism, by which God Himself is denied and religious principles are rejected." Pius XII went on to condemn the CPA's illicit consecration of bishops as "criminal and sacrilegious," declaring that CPA bishops had no authority or jurisdiction whatsoever, and were subject to a *latae sententiae* excommunication, reserved to himself.[305]

Now, what was the reaction of the neo-Catholic establishment to news of the CPA's five illicit episcopal consecrations on January 6, 2000? According to the Zenit news agency, Vatican spokesman Joaquin Navarro-Valls "criticized Beijing's decision, expressing 'surprise' and 'disappointment,' and stating that 'this gesture will raise obstacles that certainly hinder the process' of normalization of relations between the Vatican and China." Surprise and disappointment! A hindering of the process of normalization! But no declared penalty of excommunication. No declaration of schism. Not even a statement to the faithful in China that, as Pius XII warned even before the CPA condoned forced abortion, the CPA has the aim of "making Catholics gradually embrace the tenets of atheistic materialism, by which God Himself is denied and religious principles are rejected." That indeed is why the "underground" Catholics in China, following the example of Cardinal Kung, have endured fierce persecution rather than join the CPA.

Ironically enough, the ecclesiastical public law reflected in Canon 1382, under which Lefebvre and the four bishops were punished, originated with the preconciliar Holy Office's announcement in 1957 of a *latae sententiae* excommunication for illicit consecrations in Communist China. That is, the penalty envisioned by Canon 1382 arose to address Communist interference with the Apostolic Succession.[306] But far from

---

[305]Pius XII, *Ad Apostolorum Principis*, June 29, 1958.

[306]The decidedly neo-Catholic commentary on Canon 1382 by the Canon Law Society of America (CLSA) dishonestly suggests that Canon 1382 was "perhaps" enacted as the result of the "increasingly intense Holy See-Archbishop Lefebvre conflict in the late 1970s and early 1980s." This is a complete fabrication of canonical

declaring the excommunication or schism of the CPA bishops, the Vatican apparatus has assiduously courted them, to the applause of the neo-Catholic gallery. In September of 2000, some nine months after the five illicit consecrations, Cardinal ("Spirit of Assisi, come upon us all!") Etchegaray went to China to attend a conference on "Religions and Peace" (which is rather like attending an Herbalife rally on death row). During his trip, Etchegaray was shuttled around by CPA bishops, while being denied access to underground bishops loyal to Rome. CWNews.com (another neo-Catholic organ) favorably reported Etchegaray's remark that "Basically it is a question of one Church, and one common faith, trying bit by bit to overcome the unhappy separation into 'underground' and 'official.'"[307] So, the CPA, which condones abortion, rejects submission to the Pope and denounces his canonization of Chinese martyrs is part of the same Church as the loyal Catholics who have been driven underground because they refused submission to the CPA. To demonstrate this view, the Cardinal celebrated Mass in a Marian shrine the Communists stole from the Catholic Church and turned over to the CPA "hierarchy."

What about the five illicit episcopal consecrations the previous January? According to Etchegaray, "This is a very serious fact that affects ecclesiology. If it is repeated, there is a risk of impeding the rapprochement among Catholics." A mere *risk* of "impeding rapprochement" — if it is *repeated*? Well, it *has* been repeated — a hundred times! Etchegaray added: "I had the opportunity to say it clearly to the official bishops of Beijing and

---

legislative history, since there was not the slightest suggestion at that time that Lefebvre would consecrate bishops some eight or nine years later. Clearly, Canon 1382 was carried over from the 1957 Holy Office penalty directed at communist-controlled episcopal consecrations. In typical neo-Catholic fashion, a footnote to the commentary argues that there could be an exemption from the penalty in the case of the Chinese consecrations due to "extreme governmental pressure." That is, the CLSA is willing to give communist schismatics the benefit of the doubt, but not Archbishop Lefebvre.

[307]Catholic World News, September 25, 2000.

Nanjing. The question of the ordination of bishops is a crucial point for the Church and state; it can neither be avoided nor easily resolved, given the *differences and points of view*. However, history shows that reasonable solutions can be found in all political climates." So, when it comes to the illicit episcopal consecration of abortion-condoning Communist puppets, the Vatican's representative speaks of "differences and points of view" and says that "reasonable solutions can be found in all political climates." But as for Archbishop Lefebvre, it took the Vatican only 48 hours to cast him and all his supporters into outer darkness, while warning the faithful to have nothing to do with him or his Society.

Cardinal Etchegaray wished to make it clear, however, that "none of my steps should be interpreted as an approval of the structures of the official [state-approved] church." (What would give anyone that idea?) Notice the careful hedging: the Cardinal does not approve the structures of the CPA, but as for its adherents, Etchegaray clearly rejects the notion that they are schismatics: "The fact that I recognized *the fidelity to the Pope* of the Catholics of the official church [i.e., the CPA] can in no way diminish my recognition of the heroic fidelity of the silent Church."[308] Let us see if we can make sense of this remark: The adherents of an organization whose very constitution rejects submission to the Pope and which condones forced abortion are *faithful* to the Pope. But the underground Catholics have *heroic* fidelity to the Pope because they suffer persecution—for refusing to join the *faithful* Catholics of the CPA! It seems we have reached a new height of postconciliar absurdity.

Cardinal Etchegaray is not just a lone wolf in this matter. The Kung Foundation notes that Cardinal Tomko, one of the Pope's closest advisors, has been quoted as saying that the "'two groups in the Church in China' (the underground Roman Catholic Church and the CPA) are 'not two Churches because *we are all one Church*,' and that the 'true enemy' of the Church is 'not inside the Church but outside the Church.'"[309] Even more telling

---

[308]Zenit, September 28, 2000.
[309]Kung Foundation online newsletter, July 2001.

is the Kung Foundation's Open Letter of March 28, 2000, addressed to Cardinal Sodano, Archbishop Re, Cardinal Ratzinger and other members of the Vatican apparatus, which notes that CPA priests have been trained in American seminaries, given faculties in American parishes with Vatican approval (according to Archbishop Levada and other American prelates) and are being supported by Catholic charities, while loyal seminarians and priests of the underground Church receive no support. The Vatican's answer to the Open Letter has been a resounding silence.

It is only typical of neo-Catholic thinking that they would find a way to endorse the Vatican's disgraceful pandering to the CPA. Catholic World News, for example, has adopted the line that adherents of the CPA "while openly loyal to the government association, secretly pledge allegiance to the Pope."[310] CWN seems to have forgotten Our Lord's teaching about the impossibility of serving two masters. Cardinal Kung spent thirty years in solitary confinement rather than utter one word dictated to him by his Communist persecutors. But it seems the neo-Catholics have invented a new standard of Catholic fidelity—"secret loyalty"—to go along with all the other novelties they have embraced.

We are familiar enough with the phenomenon in the political realm whereby liberals praise and lionize butchers like Mao Tse-Tung as benevolent "agrarian reformers," while savagely attacking such comparatively harmless right-wing figures as Joe McCarthy. The disparity of treatment between the PCA and the members of the Society of Saint Pius X is but one of innumerable examples of the close parallel between this kind of behavior in secular politics and the double standard that neo-Catholics follow in the Church. For Catholics of the "extreme Right," there is uncompromising rigor, fierce denunciation and ostracism, while putative Catholics of the extreme Left are shown every possible indulgence and given every benefit of the doubt, even where no doubt exists.

---

[310]CWN news report, June 20, 2001.

This is a tale of two schisms: the one illusory or at best technical, the other very real and very deadly to souls; the one incurred in an effort (however misguided some may think it to be) to defend Catholic Tradition, the other incurred to subject the Catholic Church to Communist domination. Sad to say, we are not in the least surprised to see which schism the neo-Catholics condemn, and which they ignore.

Another example of the tendency to self-contradiction in the neo-Catholic system is the program being advanced by those neo-Catholics who advocate a "reform of the reform" in the liturgy—that is, a revision of Paul VI's Missal more in line, supposedly, with the intentions of Vatican II. The leader of this neo-Catholic constituency group, an organization called *Adoremus*, announced some six years ago that it was launching "a new liturgical movement" for a "reform of the reform," declaring with a fanfare of bulletins and advertising that "Our work will be guided by the intention of the Second Vatican Council as expressed in its decree on liturgy, *Sacrosanctum Concilium*."[311] *Adoremus* did not seem to notice the repeated teaching of both Paul VI and John Paul II that they themselves *have already carried out* the "intention of the Second Vatican Council." As we noted earlier, Paul VI insisted that his new rite of Mass was *precisely* what the Council intended, and that he was imposing it on the Church in obedience to the Council's "mandate";[312] and on the twenty-fifth anniversary of the conciliar document on the liturgy, *Sacrosanctum Concilium*, John Paul II lauded the "liturgical renewal" begun by his predecessor as "the most visible fruit of the work of the Council," observing that "for many people the message of the Second Vatican

---

[311]*Adoremus Bulletin*, December 1995, p. 2.

[312]"This change has something astonishing about it, something extraordinary. This is because the Mass is regarded as the traditional and untouchable expression of religious worship and the authenticity of our faith. We ask ourselves: How could such a change be made? Answer: *It is due to the will of the Ecumenical Council held not long ago....* It is an act of obedience." Audience Address of November 19, 1969.

Council has been experienced principally through the liturgical reform." His Holiness later added altar girls to boot.

Thus, while condemning traditionalists for declining to accept the new liturgy with utter docility, these same neo-Catholics implicitly accuse two Popes of erring gravely in their implementation of the supposed conciliar "mandate" for liturgical reform, and they announce to the whole Church that *they* will seek to fulfill the Council's true intention. No "private judgment" there!

A further example of neo-Catholic self-contradiction concerning the liturgical debacle is to be found in the Pamphlet, whose author declares: "Now it is important to insist here that Catholics may legitimately criticize aspects of the new rite of the Mass, and seek for its improvement, just so long as they do not question its validity. There have been hosts of well-balanced Catholics, ranging from Dietrich von Hildebrand to Una Voce to the traditional Mass orders to Joseph Cardinal Ratzinger himself, who have, each in their own way, responsibly criticized the new rite on various grounds, and this is perfectly legitimate if done constructively, without polemics.... *I myself consider the new rite of the Mass inferior as a rite* so far (we expect improvements to come) to the traditional Latin Mass and to certain Eastern Catholic rites.... But we are not allowed to say it is not a genuine rite of the Church!"

A great deal can be said about this paragraph. For one thing, it seems rather arbitrary, and a bit too convenient, that the one significant disagreement the author has with the current Vatican regime, namely the liturgy, just happens to be the one area in which the author (along with a goodly number of neo-Catholics) concedes that criticism of papal decisions is permissible. Also, was Dietrich von Hildebrand (whom the author claims to admire) writing "without polemics" when he penned a book entitled *The Devastated Vineyard*, in which he declared: "Truly, if one of the devils in C.S. Lewis' *The Screwtape*

*Letters* had been entrusted with the ruin of the liturgy, he could not have done it better"?[313]

We also find in this passage of the Pamphlet the neo-Catholic's self-contradictory admission that the new Mass is an "inferior rite" compared with the traditional Latin liturgy. Pope Paul VI certainly did not think so, and neither does John Paul II. Here the author forgets himself and openly dissents from papal proclamations that the new Mass represents a marvelously successful "liturgical renewal," even as he castigates traditionalists for doing the same. Moreover, if, as these same neo-Catholics insist, "all approved rites are traditional," what Catholic tradition favors the replacement of a received and approved ancient rite of Mass with what they themselves admit is an inferior substitute?

We next consider what we believe to be the single most important self-contradiction in the neo-Catholic system. As we have seen, the neo-Catholic demands blind adherence to the postconciliar novelties simply and only because they enjoy papal approval; but this demand puts the neo-Catholic at odds with the teaching of the preconciliar Popes against the same novelties. Faced with this conflict of authority (which the Vatican has made no real effort to resolve), the neo-Catholic will think nothing of disparaging the teaching of preconciliar Popes wherever it appears to conflict with the postconciliar program of innovation.

A telling case in point is neo-Catholic luminary Alan Schreck, a professor of theology at the Franciscan University of Steubenville, which has somehow acquired a reputation for uncompromising orthodoxy. In discussing the *Syllabus of Errors* of Pius IX, which orthodox theologians regard as a probably infallible condemnation of the false principles of modern liberty and Church-State relations, Schreck remarks: "Unfortunately, the *Syllabus* condemned most of the new ideas of the day and gave the impression that the Catholic Church was against everything in the modern world.... The Catholic Church looked

---

[313]Von Hildebrand, *The Devastated Vineyard*, p. 71.

like it was becoming a fortress Church, standing in opposition to the modern world and rejecting all new ideas."[314]

But a fortress against "new ideas" is what the Catholic Church is meant to be by her divine Founder. The Church has no need of the world's "new ideas" (which are really old heresies with new faces), since she is the repository of everything that has already been revealed to us by God for our salvation. Schreck's slighting of the *Syllabus* is in stark contrast to the obsequious submission neo-Catholics demand toward the novelties and fallible pastoral directives of the postconciliar era.

Schreck's assessment of the definitive acts of Pius X against the modernists is even more revealing of this self-contradiction within the neo-Catholic system: "It is probably true that Pius X overreacted against the threat of Modernism, which led to the stifling of creative Catholic research, especially in the area of biblical and historical studies, over the next fifty years...."[315] In other words, Schreck castigates Pope St. Pius X for having *succeeded* in suppressing the "creative" theology that afflicts the Church today.

So Pope St. Pius X, perhaps the greatest Pope in Church history and the only Pope to be canonized in the past 450 years, is blithely accused of "overreacting" by Professor Schreck of Steubenville. Yet Schreck would never dream of accusing Pope Paul VI of "overreacting" in his quest for "Christian unity" when he suddenly imposed upon the entire Church a new rite of Mass concocted with the aid of six Protestant advisors—under the guidance of a suspected Mason who was later dismissed and packed off to Iran![316]

It almost goes without saying that Schreck and his neo-Catholic colleagues discount the anti-modernist decisions of the Pontifical Biblical Commission during the reign of St. Pius X (another example, we suppose, of the sainted Pope's

---

[314]Alan Schreck, *The Compact History of the Catholic Church* (Ann Arbor: Servant Books, 1987), p. 95.

[315]Ibid., p. 105.

[316]See Davies, *Pope Paul's New Mass*, chapter 24.

"overreaction" to "creative Catholic research"). Under St. Pius X the Commission was an organ of the papal Magisterium. Among other decisions against the modernists, the Commission (and thus St. Pius X himself) forbade a modernist reading of the first three chapters of Genesis that would deny "the special creation of man; the formation of the first woman *from* the first man" and "the transgression of the divine command through the devil's persuasion under the guise of a serpent." The Commission answered in the *negative* the query whether "the literal and historical sense can be called into question" where these elements of the Genesis account were concerned, since they are *"facts...*which pertain to the foundations of the Christian religion."[317]

Today, however, neo-Catholic commentators blithely dispense with the special creation of man and the formation of Eve from Adam, generally citing John Paul II's favorable opinion of evolution in his 1996 speech to the Pontifical Academy of Sciences, which (unlike the decisions of the Pontifical Biblical Commission) was addressed to a few people rather than the universal Church. For example, in an article entitled "The Pope and Evolution," George Sim Johnston (a critic of "materialistic" evolution) declared that "It makes no difference whether man is descended biologically from some ape-like creature, so long as we understand that there had to be what the Pope calls an 'ontological leap' to the first human person"—a direct reference to the 1996 papal speech. Johnston offers no metaphysically or scripturally plausible scenario for how an ape—by an "ontological leap"—suddenly became a man with an immortal human soul. Given that Catholics may not hold (consistent with the dogma of Original Sin) that there was more than one first man (cf. Pius XII, *Humani Generis*), did God instantaneously transform one existing ape into a man, thus doing violence to the order of His own creation, like some mischievous god of Greek mythology? If so, why doesn't Genesis mention this transmogrification of an ape into Adam, which would have been no more difficult to convey in simple

---

[317]DZ, 2123.

language than the special creation of Adam from the dust of the earth? Or would Johnston say instead that Catholics are free to believe that God *gradually* created Adam by "evolving" a line of apes into one human body with an animal soul, and that God then "swapped out" the animal soul for a human soul in a kind of metaphysical software upgrade? If so, why are these things not revealed in Genesis? And what about Eve? Neo-Catholics seem to think they can just forget St. Pius X's teaching on the necessity of believing that Eve was created from the flesh of Adam, such that woman is of one flesh and bone with man.

In any case, neo-Catholic thinkers generally see no problem with the grotesquery that Adam (and Eve) had animal parents — which would mean that *Christ Himself* is descended from animals. But if even Christ stands in the line of evolutionary development, who is to say where that line will end? Will man always be man as he is at this stage of evolution — a unity of physical body and spiritual soul — or will he finally "ascend" to the ultimate convergence of all things at Teilhard's Omega Point, the terminus of evolutionary "complexification" at which the "arbitrary" distinction between matter and spirit will no longer be seen? It should not be surprising at this point that Cardinal Ratzinger (when he was Father Ratzinger) dabbled in this very notion: In his *Introduction to Christianity*, Ratzinger, after several favorable references to Teilhard's "thought," speculates: "If the cosmos is history and if matter represents *a moment in the history of spirit*, then there is *no such thing* as an eternal, neutral combination of matter and spirit but a final 'complexity' in which the world finds its omega and unity." Thus Ratzinger openly declares: "Paul [St. Paul] teaches *not the resurrection of physical bodies* but of persons...."[318] But it was the

---

[318]Joseph Ratzinger, *Introduction to Christianity* (San Francisco: Ignatius Press, 1990), p. 277. Defenders of the Cardinal will protest (without citing any proof) that the views of Father Ratzinger are no longer the views of Cardinal Ratzinger. Yet this book was republished with his knowledge and consent in 1990. To our knowledge, the

*physical Body* of Our Lord that was gone from the Tomb after the Resurrection, the same Body that had died on the Cross, the same Body whose wounds could be seen and touched by doubting Thomas. This was no *illusion* of corporeality. Indeed, the *bodily* Assumption of Mary into heaven anticipates the resurrection of our own physical bodies, which is likewise an article of the Catholic faith.[319]  Moreover, there is probably a reason that for 2,000 years Catholics have buried their dead rather than cremating them—possibly something having to do with the resurrection of the body.

As even this passing discussion shows, neo-Catholics are quite content to allow the corrosive acid of evolutionary thinking to be poured over the joints and ligaments of Catholic theology, paying no heed to anything as inconsequential as the decisions of the Pontifical Biblical Commission of St. Pius X. But great is their outrage at anyone who dares to question the thinking of Cardinal Ratzinger or the current Pope's opinion on evolution in a speech to a group of scientists.

We shall provide one further instance of the neo-Catholic's amazingly cavalier attitude toward the teaching of the preconciliar popes. This is found in *The Pope, the Council and the Mass*. Back in 1978, the authors asserted that Catholic fidelity required us to accept even the abominable ICEL translation of the Mass into English approved by Vatican bureaucrats—even though the Vatican is now (thirty years too late) calling for correction of the very translations it approved![320] The authors concede that the Catechism of the Council of Trent clearly teaches that the words of Our Lord over the Chalice of His Blood are to be translated *pro vobis et pro multis*—for you and for

---

Cardinal has yet to retract any of the questionable opinions that fill his books, interviews and addresses.

[319]For example, the Fourth Lateran Council declared that on the Last Day all the dead "will arise with their bodies *which they now bear*, that they may receive according to their works..." DZ, 429. The state of the transfigured bodies in heaven and the suffering bodies in hell is open to theological debate, but they *will* be physical bodies united to spiritual souls.

[320]See *Liturgiam Authenticam*.

*many*—because the Church has always taught that the fruits of the Sacrifice of the Mass benefit only the elect, not all men.[321] Yet ICEL mistranslates "for many" as "for all," even though not even Protestant versions of the Bible, nor even the Anglican Book of Common Prayer, have ventured such a falsification of Our Lord's words at the Last Supper.

Faced with an undeniable conflict between a solemnly promulgated Catechism of the universal Church and a currently approved vernacular translation of the Mass, the authors give the Catechism the heave-ho: "[I]t [the Catechism] was not issued by the Council of Trent, but was only prepared afterwards at the request of the Council."[322] But the authors fail to mention that the Tridentine Catechism was promulgated by the authority of Pope Pius V, a canonized saint!

In further support of a mistranslation that alters the very theology of the Mass and contradicts Trent, and which Msgr. Gamber rightly calls "truly scandalous," the authors cite a lone theologian who claimed in 1963 that "Christ had no intention of establishing a rigid formula."[323] Thus, the neo-Catholics will even pit the opinion of a single theologian against the Catechism of a sainted Pope in order to justify the innovations of the postconciliar period. What happened to their abhorrence of "private judgment"?

In their defense of current novelties against the Church's own past, neo-Catholics do not hesitate to engage in the most audacious denigration of the preconciliar Church as a whole. We have already seen neo-Catholic George Sim Johnston's tribute to his fellow "neo-conservative Catholics" as the champions of Vatican II's deliverance of the Church from her own legalism, clericalism and Jansenism of forty years ago. In the same vein is *The Pope, the Council and the Mass*, which informs us: "It was providential, then, that the Council later

---

[321]*Catechism of the Council of Trent* (Hawthorne, CA: Christian Book Club, 1829), p. 220.
[322]PCM, p. 106.
[323]Ibid., p. 103.

under the guidance of Pope John XXIII and Pope Paul VI clearly addressed itself to the removal of some of the past Church patterns of externalism, legalism, and formalism which in some ways had served to paralyze the evangelizing efforts of priests, religious and lay people in spreading the Gospel among the peoples of the modern world already undergoing vast cultural and technological changes."[324] What an insult to all the great preconciliar Popes, who (despite the threat of modernism and neo-modernism) delivered a robust Church into the hands of the Fathers of Vatican II!

The neo-Catholic myth of a moribund preconciliar Church is exploded by none other than Blessed Pope John XXIII himself, who declared in the very document convoking the Council that the Church was in the midst of "the rise and growth of the immense energies and of the apostolate of prayer, of action in all fields. It has seen the emergence of a clergy constantly better equipped in learning and virtue for its mission; and of laity which has become ever more conscious of its responsibilities within the bosom of the Church, and, in a special way, of its duty to collaborate with the Church hierarchy."[325] Likewise, during the debate on the schema concerning the bishops, a prominent Council Father declared that "the Church, notwithstanding the calamities that plague the world, is experiencing *a glorious era*, if you consider the Christian life of the clergy and of the faithful, the propagation of the faith, and the salutary universal influence possessed by the Church in the world today."[326] That assessment is completely confirmed by the empirical data on rising conversions, baptisms and vocations before the Council—all of which underwent a sudden and unparalleled decline during the "springtime of Vatican II."

---

[324]Ibid., p. 27.

[325]Apostolic Constitution *Humanae Salutis*, December 25, 1961.

[326]Wiltgen, *The Rhine Flows into the Tiber*, p. 113, quoting the Armenian Patriarch of Cilicia, who spoke against the forces determined to diminish the authority of the Roman Curia, then led by Cardinal Ottaviani.

Evincing that avoidance of reality that is such an important element of the neo-Catholic system, the authors of *The Pope, the Council and the Mass* venture the hypothesis—supported by no evidence whatsoever—that the vigorous condition of the Church in America just before the Council was only a "façade" that hid great weakness: "No greater proof of the weakness underlying much *traditional Catholic observance and practice* can be found than in the amazingly quick collapse of the formerly imposing *façade* of American Catholicism that has been manifested since the Second Vatican Council and the rapid changes which followed in its wake."[327] The authors resolutely refuse to consider that the "rapid changes" in "traditional Catholic observance and practice" which they themselves note might have had something to do with the "amazingly quick collapse" of the "façade" of a Church into which converts had been flocking in record numbers before the changes began. And now that the "façade" has collapsed, what do the authors claim to see standing in its place—the "real" Church? As some thirty-five years of bitter experience have shown us, it was only *after* the Council that a great façade was erected—the façade of the postconciliar "renewal."

Even more insulting to the preconciliar Church, if that were possible, are the remarks of prominent neo-Catholic (and former '60s liberal) Michael Novak, who is positively giddy over Pope John XXIII's fabled liberation of the Church from its hidebound Scholastic tradition—that is, from the teaching of a long line of preconciliar Popes: "He cast the church free from *the island of Latin Scholasticism on which she has for some centuries been marooned,* and launched her once more on the currents of human history with hope, with courage, with joy, with the exhilaration proper to those who see in the darkness the star of eternal life. So doing, he made it possible for Catholics to speak of good news to their companions who do not see, and to learn from those who do not see the humility of the human situation."[328]

---

[327] PCM, p. 24.
[328] *Commonweal*, August 11, 2000, p. 16.

Had this been the exuberant soliloquy of a naïve '60s observer who had not yet seen the catastrophe that would follow, we would not have embarrassed him by resurrecting this passage. But these words were written *in the year 2000*, long after such sentiments could still be uttered even jokingly.

Thus according to Novak, thanks to Scholasticism the Holy Catholic Church had become pretty much useless for proclaiming the Gospel, until her great liberation at Vatican II. Here Novak happily incurs the condemnation of the *Syllabus*, which listed among the condemned propositions (proposition 13) the claim that "the method and principles according to which the ancient scholastic doctors treated theology are by no means suited to the necessities of our times and the progress of the sciences." Novak also incurs the condemnation of St. Pius X in *Pascendi*, which, citing the *Syllabus*, teaches that "the passion for novelty is always united in them [the Modernists] with hatred of scholasticism, and *there is no surer sign that a man is on the way to Modernism than when he begins to show his dislike for this system.*"[329] But, as we can see, neo-Catholics feel no sense of obedience to preconciliar papal teaching perceived to be at odds with the reigning novelties, nor any sense of wonderment over the disappearance of that teaching into the postconciliar memory hole.

Novak's suggestion that the Church was "marooned" during the pontificates of such great Popes as St. Pius V, Gregory XVI, Leo XIII, Blessed Pius IX, St. Pius X, Pius XI and Pius XII is completely outrageous. Yet no neo-Catholic complains about his blithe indictment of centuries of Church teaching. It never occurs to the neo-Catholics that this kind of talk has helped to undermine the faith of millions of Catholics in their own Church. But when traditionalists offer comparatively mild critiques of the contingent novelties of the past *forty years*, they are loudly denounced as "schismatic" by the neo-Catholic establishment, led by such organs as *The Wanderer* and EWTN. One can easily imagine the neo-Catholic furor that would arise if some prominent traditionalist were to declare that the Church

---

[329]*Pascendi Dominici Gregis*, n. 42.

needs a new Pope to free her from the "island of ecumenism" on which she has been "marooned" since Vatican II, so that the Church can be "launched once more on the currents of human history."

This neo-Catholic denigration of the Church's entire past is hardly peculiar to Novak. An entire book could be devoted to similar examples in neo-Catholic writings. Neo-Catholic luminary Janet E. Smith, for another, writing in the neo-Catholic organ *Catholic Dossier*, declared: "The faithful Catholics of my generation have rushed to the intellectual ramparts. We have been determined to do so not in any *pre-Vatican II formulaic fashion*, but to do so by *reformulating the basics in terminology more accessible to our times* and to draw upon the best of modern thought [especially that of John Paul II] to deepen our understanding and the understanding of others."[330] The casual disparagement of the teaching of the preconciliar Church as "formulaic" is a staple of neo-Catholic thinking. As for Smith's grand project of "reformulating" Catholic teaching to make it "more accessible to our times," it is hard to think of a time (except perhaps the Arian crisis) in which Catholic truth has been *less* accessible, and less heeded, than our own.

Smith's call for greater reliance on "the best of modern thought" and the "*thought* of John Paul II," rather than the perennial Magisterium, is another common form of neo-Catholic disparagement of the Church's past. For many neo-Catholics, the current Pope is viewed as if he were an oracle of new insights, ignoring the fact that he should be instead a faithful custodian of what has been handed down by his predecessors. Neo-Catholic leader Helen Hull Hitchcock summarizes this attitude in one pithy phrase: "Whatever the Pope thinks, and whenever he thinks it."[331] Likewise, Smith marvels at "the kids" who "look like the rest of their age group, slovenly and even sometimes sporting earrings and colorful hair," but who "follow

---

[330]*Catholic Dossier*, Nov.-Dec. 1997, p. 60.
[331]*The Catholic Register*, week of November 17, 1997, p. 21.

the Pope and His Church *wherever he goes.*"[332] Here we see the neo-Catholic notion of the Pope as a kind of mobilist guru who "goes" places to which everyone must follow, as opposed to an occupant of the Chair of Peter, who does not *go* anywhere but rather stays firmly seated in traditional teaching.

The Pamphlet provides another example of this disparagement of the "formulaic" Church of the preconciliar dark ages. The author presents the standard neo-Catholic explanation of "the reasons" for the Second Vatican Council. One of these reasons, he claims, was "a desire to understand and speak to modern man."

It is amazing that neo-Catholics never perceive the implications of this bromide, which they repeat so dutifully. How could the Church, commissioned by Our Lord Himself to save souls, lose for even a moment her divinely endowed capacity to understand man and speak to him in any age? Who knows more about man than the Holy Catholic Church? The very term "modern man" is an unwarranted concession to the *Zeitgeist*, since it implies the very claim the Church has always rejected: that man could somehow progress by evolution to a point at which he becomes ontologically superior to his predecessors and thus truly and objectively "modern" with respect to all of the men who have gone before.

Besides the capacity to sin hugely with the aid of high technology, what was so different about the "modern man" of the 1960s that an ecumenical council was needed to "understand" him and learn how to "speak" to him of the Gospel? The Pamphlet offers another staple of neo-Catholicism when it claims that a Council was needed because "more and more laymen in the modern age were able to avail themselves of postsecondary school education, and...they were asking more penetrating and sophisticated questions than was ever the case in the largely peasant cultures of times past."

Here we must pause and admire this neo-Catholic perspective on Church history. Surveying all of the epochs and ages in which the Church has pursued her divine mission for the

---

[332]*Catholic Dossier*, Nov.-Dec. 1997, p. 61.

past 2,000 years—from the Roman Empire to the time of the
Arian heresy and the barbarian invasions; from the Gregorian
epoch to the rise of Islam; from the Age of Charlemagne and the
Greek schism to the Age of Hildebrand and the emerging
Christian commonwealth of Europe; from the Crusades to the
rise of the great medieval heresies; from the glorious thirteenth
century of Aquinas and Dante to the Babylonian captivity of the
Popes and the great Western Schism; from the Renaissance to
the Protestant Revolt; from the French Revolution to the First
Vatican Council—surveying this panorama in all its vastness,
the author detects one common factor to explain why it was not
until the 1960s that the Church encountered any special
difficulty in dealing with contemporary man: "largely peasant
cultures."

As the author sees it, for most of her history the Church had
only ignorant peasants to contend with, whose feeble
theological objections (if they even dared to raise them) could be
parried effortlessly by the local parish priest.   As for the
occasional uppity intellectual, he could easily be burned at the
stake. Back in the days of "largely peasant cultures," the Church
could make do with the likes of St. Thomas Aquinas in dealing
with challenges to her teaching. But the Angelic Doctor was no
match for the "penetrating and sophisticated questions" of
people with college degrees obtained in the Sixties.  Some of
these "modern men" even had doctorates in theology from
major universities! And what penetrating and sophisticated
questions these "modern men" of the Sixties were posing! Let us
recall several of them:

Is God dead?

Where have all the flowers gone?

What's new, pussycat?

Faced with questions like these—not to mention those posed
by such theological titans as Teilhard de Chardin and Hans

Küng—the Church had no choice, so the neo-Catholic fable goes, but to Do Something Extraordinary. The only way out of this crisis of very sophisticated questions by people with college degrees was...an ecumenical council. No matter that there had been little demand for a council by anyone but the modernists. In fact, as Pope John told it, the whole idea had sprung into his head while he was strolling in the Vatican gardens. "Like a flash of heavenly light, shedding sweetness in eyes and hearts," is how he put it.

The Pamphlet goes on to observe: "As a consequence, it was apparent that high metaphysical abstractions—even though surely true—needed to incarnate themselves, as it were—make themselves more amenable to—the language of the twentieth century." Here again we see the neo-Catholic bromide expressed by Janet Smith: that the very teaching of the Magisterium down through the centuries had somehow crystallized into a set of dry abstractions that no longer had any real meaning for people. But if that were really so, then how would the neo-Catholics explain the great harvest of converts and vocations drawn by the Church's "high metaphysical abstractions" and ancient customs before the Council, as compared with the precipitous decline in conversions and vocations immediately after the Church adopted the "language of the twentieth century" and abandoned her ancient liturgy in the postconciliar *aggiornamento?*

Neo-Catholics do not seem to recognize that their denigration of the Church's past makes them far harsher critics of the Church's human failings than any traditionalist. The traditionalist merely says, with St. Peter Canisius, Doctor of the Church, that "it behooves us unanimously and *inviolably* to observe the ecclesiastical traditions, whether codified *or simply retained by the customary practice of the Church.*" This perennial Catholic attitude of perfect conservatism—a fierce protection of all things that are good, not merely apostolic Tradition with a capital T—only reflects the perfect conservatism of the immutable God Who founded the Church. The typical neo-Catholic, however, is perfectly prepared to argue, alongside the very modernists who have always agitated for revolutionary reforms, that the Church needed the Council in order to *cast off* numerous ecclesiastical traditions and customs, and even her traditional way of speaking, because they had become actual impediments to the Church's very mission on earth.

The neo-Catholic has thus swallowed whole the modernist critique of the Church as a visible institution.  And if the Church had become obscured throughout the centuries by mere accretions of useless and dispensable things, if her ancient and always untouchable liturgy had gone wrong after 1,965 years and needed to be thrown off to make the Church more appealing to her suddenly respectable Protestant critics, then perhaps the Church, having gone wrong in so many of her ancient features, was wrong about many other things as well.  And if that is the case, then perhaps (as Küng and the other neo-modernists contend) the Church is not the divinely founded institution she had always claimed "triumphally" to be.  At least that is what many of the faithful in the pews concluded when they wandered out of the Church at around the same time evangelism became "dialogue," Latin became English, and the altar became a table.

And here it must be asked: By what peculiar standard of Catholic discourse do neo-Catholics claim the right to denigrate the supposed "formalism," "externalism," "legalism," "clericalism," and so forth, of the preconciliar Church, while at the same time questioning the loyalty of traditionalists who mention the liberalism, false irenicism and indifferentism that have invaded the Church since Vatican II?   At least traditionalists can point to Paul VI's own admission that the Council's "opening to the world became a veritable invasion of the Church by worldly thinking. We have perhaps been too weak and imprudent." Which Pope, on the other hand, sustains the neo-Catholic thesis of a preconciliar dark age in the Church?

There is another irony here: While the Pamphlet claims that the Council was needed to address the problem of "high metaphysical abstractions" getting in the way of the Gospel, is it not obvious that the proliferation of vague abstractions *since* the Council has caused untold confusion in the Church and in the

preaching of her message? What inspirations of faith has the
world received from preaching laden with such slogans as
"ecumenism," "dialogue," "ecumenical dialogue,"
"interreligious dialogue," "collegiality," "inculturation,"
"solidarity," "the civilization of love," "the spirit of Assisi," and
so forth? The drastic decline in the Church's vital statistics since
this lingo was adopted answers that question.

Another very recent example of this kind of thinking is the
book *Triumph: The Power and Glory of the Catholic Church* by one
H.W. Crocker III. While Crocker admits to the "inarguably
disastrous results"[333] of Vatican II and does a great deal to dispel
myths about the Church's past (papal apologies
notwithstanding), he nonetheless faithfully adheres to the neo-
Catholic line when he says that at the Council "Catholic
triumphalism was erased at its borders so that the Eastern
Orthodox churches and Protestant sects were recognized as
containing important aspects of the truth."[334]

What is this "Catholic triumphalism" the neo-Catholics and
the neo-modernists are always deriding? The term appears to
connote the Church's perennial claim that she alone is the ark of
salvation, or as Pope Pius XI put it in *Mortalium Animos* (quoting
an ancient Church Father): "The Catholic Church is *alone* in
keeping the true worship. This is the fount of truth, this the
house of Faith, this the temple of God: if any man enter not here,
or if any man go forth from it, he is a stranger to the hope of life
and salvation." So much for that! Now we are solemnly
assured that the Orthodox and Protestant creeds contain
"important aspects of the truth" — as if a heretic's possession of
part of the truth were a luminous conciliar insight hidden for

---

[333]Crocker's admission represents something of a breakthrough.
Traditionalists have been writing and speaking about the Council's
disastrous results for more than thirty-five years, bearing the brunt of
condemnation by the neo-Catholic establishment for the offense of
remarking the obvious. Crocker appears to be the first neo-Catholic
commentator to recognize explicitly that the Council caused an
ecclesial disaster.

[334]H.W. Crocker III, *Triumph: The Power and Glory of the Catholic
Church* (New York: Random House, 2001), pp. 420-21.

2,000 years, rather than a statement of the obvious about heretics. Obviously, non-Catholic "believers" (as they are now called) accept certain truths of Revelation, while rejecting others. The question, however, is whether non-Catholic religions, all of which corrupt truth by mixing it with error, are objectively adequate unto salvation. If so, then who needs the Catholic Church? If not, then *what is the point* of emphasizing that non-Catholics possess "important aspects of the truth"? What of it? Would a doctor tell a man with a potentially fatal disease that he possesses "important aspects of health," without warning him that he will die unless he immediately receives the proper treatment? Is it now "triumphalism" for Catholics to say to non-Catholics, in union with Pius XI and all the preconciliar Popes, that actual membership in the Catholic Church is, objectively speaking, the only known way to heaven?

In splendid neo-Catholic fashion, Crocker praises Pope John Paul II because "he saw that the old altar-and-throne model of Catholicism had died with the Hapsburg Empire after World War I, though the Church had never conceded this." Foolish Church, refusing to concede to reality! And what vibrant, modern thing has the current Pope preached in place of the "altar-and-throne model of Catholicism"? The table-and-pluralist model, perhaps? And since the neo-Catholics (along with the neo-modernists) are now talking about "models of Catholicism," it might be asked: How will we know when this new model has become obsolete? Must we have another Council for the rolling out of the next model?

Crocker further enthuses: "When the Council decided to put the liturgy into the vernacular" — a decision the Council never in fact made — "the future Pope [John Paul II] saw springs of popular renewal." If "springs of popular renewal" means the most precipitous decline in Mass attendance in Church history and widespread loss of faith in the Real Presence, then the future Pope's vision was quite accurate.

Now, when neo-Catholics contradict themselves by disparaging the preconciliar Church, its outdated teaching and its outmoded liturgy — while condemning traditionalist criticism of a few current novelties — they are not conducting some sort of rogue operation disapproved by the Vatican. We have already discussed how Vatican-level prelates, with at least the tacit approval of Pope John Paul II, have openly declared the abandonment of prior papal teaching on the Church's relation to non-Catholics, and how the postconciliar Popes departed from the teaching of their predecessors on the grave duty to preserve the Latin liturgical tradition. And when it comes to repudiating the teaching of the anti-liberal and anti-modernist Popes of the preconciliar period, it is not any lay neo-Catholic commentator, but none other than Cardinal Ratzinger, who provides the most striking example.

In his *Principles of Catholic Theology*, republished five years after he became Prefect of the Congregation for the Doctrine of the Faith, Cardinal Ratzinger all but declared that Blessed Pius IX's *Syllabus of Errors* and St. Pius X's *Pascendi* were officially abandoned at Vatican II. Before discussing this claim, some further details concerning the *Syllabus* are in order.

The *Syllabus of Errors* (1864), together with the appended encyclical *Quanta Cura*, comprised Blessed Pius IX's systematic condemnation of the errors of liberalism, which already stood at the heart of modern societies and were threatening the integrity of the Catholic faith. The propositions Blessed Pius IX condemned (along with his predecessors in various encyclicals and other papal pronouncements) include the following:

- so-called "liberty of worship" for all sects, even in Catholic countries (propositions 15, 77 and 78);
- unbridled freedom of the press (proposition 79);
- abandonment of all legal penalties for external violations of the Catholic religion in Catholic societies (*Quanta Cura*);
- proclamation by law of liberty of conscience and of worship as the inalienable right of every man (*Quanta Cura*);
- strict separation of Church and state (proposition 15);
- secularization of public education (propositions 40, 45 and 48);
- abolition of the Pope's civil power (proposition 76);

- reconciliation and adaptation of the Pope to progress, liberalism and modern civilization (proposition 80);
- the claim that the Church has no right to use force, and that she has no temporal power, either direct or indirect (proposition 24);
- the claim that it is no longer expedient that Catholicism should be the religion of the state to the exclusion of all others (proposition 77);
- the claim that Protestantism is just another form of the true Christian religion in which it is possible to serve God as well as in the Catholic Church (proposition 18);
- the claim that salvation is possible in the practice of any religion (proposition 16);
- the claim that we must have at least good hope for the salvation of all those who are not in the Catholic Church (proposition 17);

In short, the *Syllabus* condemns the founding principles of modern, post-Christian civilization and Liberal Catholicism, whose ruinous results are manifest everywhere today.

In his classic little work *Liberalism Is a Sin* (1899), Fr. Felix Sarda y Salvany noted that faithful Catholics had hailed the *Syllabus* "with an enthusiasm equaled only by the paroxysm of fury with which the Liberals received it," while "Liberal Catholics thought it more prudent to strike at it indirectly by overwhelming it with artificial interpretations [and] emasculating explanations."[335] It is a sad indication of the difference between then and now that when a liberal Spanish priest, a certain Fr. de Pazos, submitted Father Sarda's book to the Sacred Congregation for the Index for what he hoped would be a condemnation, the Congregation responded by commending Fr. Sarda's book and condemning the writings of de Pazos! Today, traditionalists who take Fr. Sarda's position in defense of the *Syllabus* are derided as "integrists" and "schismatics," while neo-Catholics who embrace the views of

---

[335]Felix Sarda y Salvany, *Liberalism Is a Sin* (Rockford, IL: TAN, 1993), p. 52.

the liberal Spanish priest are considered exemplars of responsible orthodoxy. The results of this radical reversal speak for themselves.

Abandoning all pretense of deference to the perennial Magisterium, certain neo-Catholics and neo-modernists alike now seek to relegate the *Syllabus* to the dustbin of history. Yet history has demonstrated that the very errors Blessed Pius IX condemned have led to the total collapse of the moral order in the secularized, pluralist regimes that are enslaved by them, as well as a loss of faith and discipline in the Church, in which many of the condemned propositions are now considered received wisdom by a thoroughly liberalized clergy and laity.

No one has done more to neutralize the teaching of the *Syllabus* with "emasculating explanations" than Cardinal Ratzinger. In *Principles of Catholic Theology*, Ratzinger opines as follows concerning the conciliar document *Gaudium et Spes*: "If it is desirable to offer a diagnosis of the text as a whole, we might say that (in conjunction with the texts on religious liberty and world religions) it is *a revision of the Syllabus of Pius IX, a kind of countersyllabus.*" The Cardinal goes on to say that

> the *one-sidedness* of the position adopted by the Church under Pius IX and Pius X in response to the situation created by the new phase of history inaugurated by the French Revolution was, to a large extent, *corrected via facti*, especially in Central Europe, but there was still no basic statement of the relationship that should exist between the Church and the world that had come into existence after 1789. In fact, *an attitude that was largely pre-revolutionary continued to exist in countries with strong Catholic majorities.* Hardly anyone will deny today that the Spanish and Italian Concordat strove to preserve *too much of a view of the world that no longer corresponded to the facts.* Hardly anyone will deny today that, in the field of education and with respect to the historico-critical method in modern science, anachronisms existed that corresponded closely to this adherence to *an obsolete Church-state relationship.*[336]

---

[336]Joseph Ratzinger, *Principles of Catholic Theology* (San Francisco: Ignatius Press, 1989), pp. 381-82.

Having pronounced the "pre-revolutionary attitude" and "position adopted by the Church under Pius IX and Pius X" to be one-sided and passé, and the Catholic confessional state exemplified by Spain and Italy "obsolete" because it no longer corresponds to "the facts," Ratzinger reiterates his opinion that "the text [*Gaudium et Spes*] serves as a *countersyllabus* and, as such, represents, on the part of the Church, an attempt at an official reconciliation with the new era inaugurated in 1789."[337] That is, according to the Cardinal, the Church must reconcile with the new order of things simply because *the Church's enemies have succeeded in overthrowing Catholic social order.*

But this very capitulation to "the facts" was condemned by the *Syllabus* itself, in which Blessed Pius IX enumerated as condemned proposition #80 the following: "The Roman Pontiff can and ought to reconcile himself and come to terms with progress, liberalism and modern civilization." Moreover, why should the Church even desire an "official reconciliation" with the "new era inaugurated in 1789," when the "new era" constitutes the worst moral, spiritual and social debacle in human history? Has it not occurred to the Cardinal that the very errors condemned in the *Syllabus* have something to do with the state of the world today?

Lest there be any doubt that he considers the *Syllabus* a dusty relic, Ratzinger adds that *"there can be no return to the Syllabus,* which may have marked the first stage in the confrontation with liberalism but cannot be the last stage."[338] Obviously, to say that there can be no *return* to the *Syllabus* is to say that the *Syllabus* is no longer the teaching of the Catholic Church. In nearly 2,000 years of preconciliar Church history, one will find no example of this kind of repudiation of a solemn papal teaching by a Vatican prelate.

As for the Cardinal's claim that the *Syllabus* represents only an outmoded early stage in the confrontation with liberalism,

---

[337]Ibid., p. 381.
[338]Ibid., p. 191.

the suggestion that the Church's "opening to the world" at Vatican II is a more advanced strategy ignores reality. The abandonment of the *Syllabus* has been accompanied by the triumph of Liberalism in all its forms (from Chinese Communism to American pluralist democracy) throughout the world, and Liberalism has made huge inroads into the Church itself. We have noted that as early as 1973 none other than Pope Paul VI admitted that "the opening to the world has become a veritable invasion of the Church by worldly thinking." In the very same year Dietrich von Hildebrand observed that "the poison of our epoch is slowly seeping into the Church herself, and many have failed to see the apocalyptic decline of our time."[339] That failure of vision certainly seems to afflict the current Vatican apparatus.

And one can only shudder at Cardinal Ratzinger's recommendation of a future strategy for the Church's confrontation with the forces of the world: "The fact is, as Hans Urs von Balthasar pointed out as early as 1952, that 'the demolition of bastions' is a long-overdue task.... She [the Church] must relinquish many of the things that have hitherto spelled security for her and that she has taken for granted. *She must demolish longstanding bastions* and trust solely the shield of faith."[340] The advice that the Church which has already undergone a process of auto-demolition (as Paul VI lamented) now get busy "demolishing bastions" would be dismissed as neo-modernist ranting if it came from anyone else. What bastions, exactly, are left to demolish? And how long can the Church hold on to "the shield of faith" without the sword she laid down at Vatican II? Cardinal Ratzinger's proposed advance beyond the condemnations of the *Syllabus* looks very much like a retreat from the field of battle. Is it not the grand delusion of Vatican II that there is no battle with the world at all, but only dialogue?

It is not as if the Cardinal's repudiation of the Church's entire preconciliar posture toward Liberalism is limited to a

---

[339]Von Hildebrand, *The Devastated Vineyard*, p. 75.
[340]Ratzinger, *Principles of Catholic Theology*, p. 391.

book of theological reflections. In 1990, the Congregation for the Doctrine of the Faith issued an "Instruction on the Theologian's Ecclesiastical Vocation." In explaining the Instruction to the press, Cardinal Ratzinger asserted that certain teachings of the Magisterium were "not considered to be the final word on the subject as such, but serve rather as a mooring in the problem, and, above all, as an expression of pastoral prudence, a kind of *temporary disposition.*" As examples of these "temporary dispositions," Ratzinger cited "the statements of the Popes during the last century on religious freedom, as well as the anti-modernist decisions at the beginning of this century, especially the decisions of the Biblical Commission of that time."[341] (The Cardinal thus dispenses with St. Pius X's injunctions against an evolutionary reading of Genesis, which we discussed earlier.)

Ratzinger went on to say, "Their core remains valid, but (speaking of the anti-Modernist decisions of the Church during the reign of Pius X) "the details of the determination of their content were later superseded once they had carried out their pastoral duty at a particular moment." The Cardinal did not elaborate on the precise meaning of this elusive and rather strange remark, or explain how a statement's "core" can remain valid while its details pass away. How does His Eminence propose to disentangle what exactly constitutes the "core" of the *Syllabus,* as opposed to its time-bound details, especially since Blessed Pius IX appeared to be defending universal principles, not bound by time and place? No answer is provided.

We are not told which particular aspects of these prior teachings are "temporary dispositions" and which still bind the faithful. No specific preconciliar papal document is labeled as "expired." The precise expiration date for the "temporary provisions" in major preconciliar encyclicals is likewise not provided. But at least as of 1990, according to Cardinal Ratzinger's non-binding opinion at a press conference, theologians are now free to disregard some or all—and who knows which?—of the *Syllabus* of Blessed Pius IX, *Pascendi* by St.

---

[341]*L'Osservatore Romano,* English Weekly Edition, July 2, 1990, p. 5.

Pius X, along with the decisions of his Biblical Commission, and (it would appear) the anti-liberal encyclicals of Leo XIII, Gregory XVI and any other preconciliar Pope whose teaching does not comport well with the novel attitudes and programs of the conciliar *aggiornamento*.

An example of how such a principle may work in practice occurred in mid-2001 when the Congregation for the Doctrine of the Faith declared "superseded" the 1887 condemnations of the writings of Fr. Antonio Rosmini (1797-1855). The condemned statements of Rosmini, available at DZ 1891, certainly appear erroneous, including references to the "natural" state of the soul after death and a frankly apparent pantheism. But the CDF now claims that the intellectual milieu in which Rosmini's propositions had been condemned was one in which his arguments could not be properly understood. In other words, Pope Leo XIII and his Holy Office got it wrong. "The adoption of Thomism," the CDF explains, "created the premises for a negative judgment of a philosophical and speculative position, like that of Rosmini, because it differed in its language and conceptual framework from the philosophical and theological elaboration of St. Thomas Aquinas." Conceding that Rosmini's system contained "concepts and expressions that are at times ambiguous and equivocal," the CDF document nevertheless explains away Pope Leo XIII's 1887 condemnation as the result of "historical-cultural and ecclesial factors of the time." Having argued that the prior Magisterium had misunderstood Rosmini, however, the CDF nowhere explains precisely how the interpretations of Rosmini held by Leo XIII's Holy Office were mistaken, or how Rosmini's system could be given a Catholic meaning. The document simply concludes by declaring that "the plausibility of the Rosminian system, of its speculative consistency and of the philosophical and theological theories and hypotheses expressed in it remain entrusted to the theoretical debate."[342]

---

[342] See Congregation of the Doctrine of the Faith, *Note on the Force of the Doctrinal Decrees Concerning the Thought and Work of Fr. Antonio Rosmini Serbati*.

Liberal theologian Gregory Baum was delighted at this development. "Never before," he wrote, "has the Magisterium applied the historical-critical method to its own teaching." Ratzinger, according to Baum, "has shown that the condemnation of Rosmini's propositions in 1887...[was] justified in terms of the Church's pastoral policy and hence could be lifted without inconsistency later. Yet *he does not raise the truth question*." That is, people who had read the condemnation "were made to believe that these propositions *were erroneous*: They were not told that they were erroneous only when read from a neo-Thomist perspective....."[343]

But what, then, is a Catholic to do? How are Catholics to know which solemn condemnations in papal encyclicals and other pronouncements were only "temporary dispositions" or "moorings in the problem," and which are still binding? How can one tell whether a given condemnation was based on "historical-cultural and ecclesial factors of the time," as opposed to an objective error in the proposition itself? Will there be periodic bulletins from the CDF on which condemned errors were not really errors at all, but only misunderstandings that can now be cleared up?

Further, if Pope Leo XIII and his Holy Office got it wrong because they viewed the Rosminian propositions from within a Thomistic "conceptual framework," then how do we know that Cardinal Ratzinger has gotten it right from within his *non*-Thomistic framework? And if papal condemnations of theological error are now to be judged according to the "conceptual framework" in which they were issued, how indeed will we ever get to what Baum calls the "truth question" — namely, whether a proposition is simply *wrong*, always and everywhere, regardless of the "framework" in which the proposition is judged?

There is really no cause for alarm, however. As with all the other novel Vatican pronouncements that have been issued since

---

[343]Gregory Baum, "Ratzinger Explains How Condemnation Was Right Then, Wrong Now," *National Catholic Reporter*, January 25, 2002.

the Council, Cardinal Ratzinger's opinions at the 1990 press conference and his historical-critical methodology in the Rosmini matter do not bind the universal Church, any more than they can actually overrule the teaching of Bl. Pius IX or Leo XIII. There has been no encyclical or other definitive statement by the Pope confirming the reputed expiration of the *Syllabus* or any other formal papal condemnation of error. Once again the faithful are left with the impression, but not the reality, of an official retraction of what the Church taught before the Council. And so it has gone for the past forty years.

With all due respect to the Cardinal, we believe his approach in this area represents the neo-Catholic contradiction at its most extreme. For if the Cardinal can declare that the teaching of prior popes was "one-sided," a mere "position adopted by the Church" but rendered obsolete in the "new era" following the French Revolution, a collection of "temporary dispositions," a time-bound artifact of past "historical-cultural and ecclesial factors" or the product of a superseded "conceptual framework," on what ground can traditionalists be attacked for their critique of novelties that were unheard of in the Church before 1962? As we have endeavored to demonstrate throughout this book, unlike the solemn condemnations of the *Syllabus*, such things as the "ecumenical movement" are clearly historically contingent pastoral experiments rather than Catholic doctrines. Ratzinger himself describes an "attempt" by the Council to reconcile the Church with "the new era inaugurated in 1789." By what standard of Catholic fidelity, then, is the Council's *attempt* to teach something held to be immune from traditionalist criticism, while the solemn and definite teaching of a whole line of preconciliar Popes is dismissed by neo-Catholics as temporary and outmoded? The answer is: by the neo-Catholic standard.

To be perfectly fair, and for the sake of completeness, it needs to be said that some neo-Catholic commentators at least make an effort to demonstrate that the *Syllabus* and other anti-liberal teachings of the preconciliar Popes have not expired or been "countered" or "corrected," but have rather been "developed" by the Council's teaching, especially *Dignitatis Humanae*.

Avery Dulles, for example, suggests that this "development" was needed because the earlier Popes

> were speaking within the relatively narrow horizon of Catholic Europe and Latin America, where traditional religion was under attack from militant secularist liberalism represented by the Jacobinism of the French Revolution and the Italian laicism typified by Count Cavour. Gregory XVI in his encyclical *Mirari Vos* (1832) condemned the extreme liberalism of Félicité de Lamennais, which would allow all kinds of unfounded, libelous, and subversive opinions to be circulated without any legal restrictions. In this context he characterized as "insanity" (*deliramentum*) the view "according to which freedom of conscience must be asserted and vindicated for everyone whatsoever." Pius IX in his encyclical *Quanta Cura* (1864) repeated this condemnation.[344]

But Dulles fails to notice at least three things: First, the attack of "militant secularist liberalism" has hardly abated since the nineteenth century, but rather has become an institutionalized feature of so-called democracies. Second, the "extreme liberalism" of Lammenais is now the norm in Western democracies. Third, the nineteenth century secularist regimes condemned by Popes Leo, Pius and Gregory were *far more conservative of the moral order* than the secularist regimes (either Communist or democratic) of the conciliar and postconciliar period. Abortion, for example, was a criminal offense in the nineteenth century, as were the sale of contraceptives, the publication of pornography, obscene public speech and adultery.

Thus, if anything, the condemnations of liberalism by the preconciliar Popes, especially in the *Syllabus*, ought to apply with even more force today. Granted, the harshest aspects of

---

[344]"Religious Liberty: Innovation and Development," *First Things*, December 2001.

overt repression of the Church in, say, Jacobin France or Cavour's Italy have been replaced by the modern notion of "religious liberty," but the papal condemnations were not limited to overt persecution of the Church. The nineteenth-century Popes condemned *moral and philosophical errors* that are now accepted as the foundational truths of modern democracy.

Further, Dulles himself concedes that modern "religious liberty" is largely a sham:

> The greatest threat to religion, in my estimation, is the kind of secularism that would exclude religion from the public forum and treat churches as purely private institutions that have no rightful influence on legislation, public policy, and other dimensions of our common life. When churches speak out on issues such as abortion, euthanasia, marriage, and divorce, they are accused of transgressing the barrier between Church and State. Even the courts often interpret the non-establishment provision of the First Amendment so as to prevent any public role for religion, thereby inhibiting the free exercise of religion. Legal, fiscal, and regulatory pressures render it difficult for Catholic charitable and educational institutions to maintain their distinctive identity.

Dulles describes a state of affairs in which, despite the appearance of "religious liberty," the Church now has even less influence over society than she did in the post-revolutionary republics of nineteenth-century Europe. That fact, combined with the utter depravity of contemporary public law, makes the *Syllabus* more relevant than ever—at the very moment in history when the neo-Catholics, joining the neo-modernists, pronounce it a dead letter!

Confronted with Cardinal Ratzinger's frank repudiation of the *Syllabus*, some neo-Catholic commentators trot out the reliable "what the Cardinal [the Pope, the Council] *really* means to say" defense. Neo-Catholicism has developed a cottage industry of lay and clerical commentators who inform us what the Pope and Vatican prelates "really" intended by a given statement or gesture[345] — as if the members of the upper hierarchy were somehow incapable of accurately expressing their own thoughts.

In an article entitled "The Counter-Syllabus Canard," one I. Shawn McElhinney, who maintains a website decrying the errors of "ultra-traditionalists," concedes that Cardinal Ratzinger's reference to a "counter-syllabus" is "unfortunate." But, McElhinney assures us, "the *intended meaning* of the Cardinal Prefect was that the condemnation of errors in the *Syllabus* could logically be seen as being countered by positive teaching in GS [*Gaudium et Spes*] that encapsulates the elements of truth contained in the aforementioned errors. Seen in this light, the negative element of the summary condemnations, complimented [sic] by the later positive and elaborated teaching encapsulating what elements of truth the previously condemned errors contained, results in the climate moving from negative and reactive to positive and pro-active...."[346]

That explanation — if anyone can follow it — at least has the merit of being no more contorted than other efforts to explain how a teaching that is "counter" to another can be "complementary" to it. As for McElhinney's thesis that the errors condemned by Blessed Pius IX contained "elements of truth," this is about as sensible as the claim that the proposition $2 + 2 = 5$ contains elements of truth. Errors are errors and truths are truths. The two may be mixed together into a series of propositions, the whole of which contains both true and false statements (e.g., "$2 + 2 = 5$, and $5 + 5 = 10$"), but Blessed Pius IX condemned errors singly, in a numbered list, not some combination of true and false propositions.

---

[345]Concerning the Pope's kissing of the Koran, neo-Catholic historian Warren Carroll asserted on the EWTN website that "In kissing the Koran...the Pope was not blessing their errors; he was recognizing common ground among those who, in our secular 'God is dead' age, still share our belief in one God." The papal kiss, however, was not accompanied by any such disclaimer.

[346]http://matt1618.freeyellow.com/syllabus.html

At any rate, in the usual neo-Catholic manner of covering up embarrassing discrepancies between pre- and postconciliar thinking at the Vatican, McElhinney neglects to mention Cardinal Ratzinger's further statements, which we have just quoted, that the *Syllabus* was "one-sided," "obsolete," represented "a view of the world that no longer corresponded to the facts," and was "corrected" by historical events, and that "there can be no return to the *Syllabus*." How these things can be said of a document that McElhinney claims is *complementary* to the Council's teachings is one of the many problems neo-Catholic apologists encounter in their vast enterprise of denying the obvious.

In the end, the efforts of neo-Catholics like Dulles to harmonize the *Syllabus* of Pius IX with the "counter-Syllabus" of Cardinal Ratzinger only devolve into the same objection raised by the neo-modernists: that prior papal condemnations of error are limited to their "historical context." The authors of *The Pope, the Council and the Mass* are quite explicit in their claim that the *Syllabus* is no longer applicable: "When Pius IX condemned the proposition that it was no longer expedient that the Catholic religion should be held as the only religion of the state, this was no doubt a valiant attempt to recall the governments of Catholic countries to their plain duty; today, however, *hardly a government exists any longer in the world that would recognize that it has any such duty to Catholics or to the Church.* This fact does not make Pius IX's teaching any less true, but it does mean that *there is no longer any situation in the world to which Pius' particular teaching applies.*"[347] So, if Catholic countries reject their duty to God by becoming secularized "democracies," then Church teaching on that duty no longer "applies" to them.

The authors are equally dismissive of Pope Leo XIII's teaching in *Libertas* that "Since, then, the profession of one religion is necessary in the State, that religion must be professed which alone is true, and which can be recognized without difficulty, especially in Catholic states, because the marks of

---

[347]PCM, p. 188.

truth are, as it were, engraven upon it."[348] According to the authors, "There is nothing at all wrong with Leo XIII's teaching; it is as true as ever; it even applies to individuals today with the same force as it ever did. *Once again, however, it doesn't apply to the conditions of today as far as the state is concerned....* Not even in Ireland, Portugal, or Spain does there exist any government which any longer seriously heeds the Church's insistence that the state has a duty to uphold true morality and true religion."[349]

So, when governments no longer "seriously heed" Church teaching, the teaching ceases to apply to governments, but still applies to individuals! But then, why would the teaching apply even to individuals, if they too no longer "seriously heed" it? It would be hard to find a neo-modernist whose abandonment of solemn papal teaching is more cavalier than that of the authors of *The Pope, the Council and the Mass*—who, paradoxically enough, see themselves as defenders of strict loyalty to the Magisterium as opposed to the traditionalists' "disobedience."

It must be noted that in both *Libertas* and *Immortale Dei* Pope Leo condemned the very notion that the State could somehow exempt itself from the moral duties owed to God by individuals; for, after all, society is ordained by God as a collective in which individuals can be better enabled to carry out their duties to Him.[350] From this it follows that there must be an organic *union*

---

[348]*Libertas* (1888), N. 21.

[349]PCM, p. 189.

[350]*Libertas*, 8: "What has been said of the liberty of individuals is no less applicable to them when considered as bound together in civil society. For, what reason and the natural law do for individuals, that human law promulgated for their good, does for the citizens of States." See also *Immortale Dei*, n. 6: "As a consequence, the State, constituted as it is, is clearly bound to act up to the manifold and weighty duties linking it to God, *by the public profession of religion.*" See also *Vehementer Nos* (1906) by Pope St. Pius X, who, citing Pope Leo, declared: "That the State must be separated from the Church is a thesis absolutely false, a most pernicious error...for the creator of man is also the Founder of human societies, and preserves their existence as he

between Church and State, which is not to be confused with a *co-penetration* of the two powers. Pope Leo XIII described the proper Church-State relation as follows:

> But, inasmuch as each of these two powers has authority over the same subjects, and as it might come to pass that one and the same thing—related differently, but still remaining one and the same thing—might belong to the jurisdiction and determination of both, therefore God, who foresees all things, and who is the author of these two powers, has marked out the course of each in right correlation to the other.... There must, accordingly, exist between these two powers a *certain orderly connection, which may be compared to the union of the soul and body in man.*[351]

Clearly Leo was right: the severance of the soul of the Church from the body of the State produces a morally dead, soulless State—like that which afflicts America today. The proper relation existed, Pope Leo noted, in the Christian commonwealths of pre-"reformation" Europe:

> There was once a time when States were governed by the philosophy of the Gospel. Then it was that the power and divine virtue of Christian wisdom had diffused itself throughout the laws, institutions, and morals of the people, permeating all ranks and relations of civil society. Then, too, the religion instituted by Jesus Christ, established firmly in befitting dignity, flourished everywhere, by the favor of princes and the legitimate protection of magistrates; *and Church and State were happily united in concord and friendly interchange of good offices.* The State, constituted in this wise, bore fruits important beyond all expectation, whose remembrance is still, and always will be, in renown, witnessed to as they are by countless proofs which can never be blotted out or ever obscured by any craft of any enemies.

---

preserves our own. We owe Him, therefore, not only a private cult, *but a public and social worship* to honor Him."
[351]*Immortale Dei*, 13-14.

Moreover, in his encyclical letter to the American hierarchy, *Longinqua Oceani* (1895), Pope Leo rejected the notion that the American pluralistic regime represented the best situation for the Church, and he reaffirmed the Catholic ideal of an organic Church-State union in a Catholic confessional state: "[I]t would be very erroneous to draw the conclusion that in America is to be sought the type of the most desirable status of the Church, or that it would be universally lawful or expedient for State and Church to be, as in America, dissevered and divorced." Pope Leo taught that notwithstanding the Church's liberty in America, "she would bring forth more abundant fruits if, in addition to liberty, she enjoyed *the favor of the laws and the patronage of public authority.*"

The same neo-Catholic commentators who lambaste traditionalists for their alleged "rejection of Vatican II" — whatever that means — make bold to say that Pope Leo's teaching on Church-State relations is purely dispensable, even though it is based on that of his predecessors (Gregory XVI in *Mirari Vos* and Blessed Pius IX in *Quanta Cura* and the *Syllabus*) and was affirmed by his successors St. Pius X (in *Vehementer Nos*) and Pius XI (in *Quas Primas*, on the Social Kingship of Christ). Neo-Catholic historian James Hitchcock is typical of this dismissive attitude toward a whole corpus of preconciliar papal encyclicals: "The lingering belief…that *Catholic theory required the union of Church and state* has been finally laid to rest. It was a skewed way of looking at the world and an albatross that impeded Catholic influence."[352] The suggestion that the Church has *greater* influence today because she has abandoned the "theory" of Gregory XVI, Blessed Pius IX, Leo XIII, St. Pius X and Pius XI can hardly be taken seriously.

Surprisingly enough, the very teaching on Church-state relations dismissed by neo-Catholics as outdated or merely

---

[352]"The Real Post-Conciliar Reforms," *Catholic Dossier*, Nov.-Dec. 1997, p. 50. Within the ellipsis is the phrase "that the Church would suppress religious liberty if it had the chance" — a caricature of Catholic teaching we do not address here.

provisional was affirmed by Vatican II itself. Article 1 of DH states that the Council "leaves untouched traditional Catholic doctrine on the moral duty of both men *and societies* toward the true religion and the one Church of Christ."[353] That the Council had to assure everyone it was leaving the traditional teaching "untouched" was in itself without precedent in conciliar documents. Such assurances were no doubt deemed necessary, however, in view of DH's surprising announcement that there was a *natural right* to immunity from coercion by the State in any religious matter, including the *public* activities of false sects—a right never mentioned in the extensive preconciliar teaching of the Church on the nature of liberty in society and the Christian constitution of states.[354]

---

[353]*Dignitatis Humanae*, n. 4.

[354]Ibid., n. 2: "[T]he human person has a right to religious freedom. This freedom means that all men are to be immune from coercion on the part of individuals or social groups and of any human power, in such wise that in matters religious no one is to be forced to act in a manner contrary to his own beliefs." This much is clearly in line with prior teaching, since the Church has always taught that no man may be forced to embrace a religion not his own. However, DH goes further and states: "Nor is anyone to be restrained from acting in accordance with his own beliefs, whether privately *or publicly*, alone or in association with others, within due limits.... The Synod further declares that the right to religious freedom has its foundation in the very dignity of the human person." Subject only to "due limits," then, DH announces a natural right not to be restrained from propagating a false religion even publicly. No Pope before Vatican II even hinted that there could be such a natural right, as opposed to a revocable civil right of *tolerance* of the public propagation of religious error, conceded by the State for prudential reasons. See, e.g., *Libertas*, n. 33: "For this reason, while not conceding *any right* to anything save what is true and honest, she does not forbid public authority to *tolerate* what is at variance with truth and justice, for the sake of avoiding some greater evil, or of obtaining some greater good." But Pope Leo warned that this tolerance must be "*strictly confined* to the limits which its justifying cause, the public welfare, requires. Wherefore, if such tolerance would be injurious to the public welfare, and entail greater evils on the State,

Equally surprising was DH's announcement that even when "special legal recognition is given in the constitutional order of society to one religious body," government must still ensure that "equality of citizens before the law...is *never* violated for religious reasons, whether openly or covertly. Nor is there to be *any* discrimination among citizens."[355]

How the State can profess and protect Catholicism as the one religion of the State under the "untouched" traditional teaching, while avoiding *any* discrimination among citizens based on religion, is one of the many mysteries the Council has left everyone to ponder. For one thing, a Catholic confessional state cannot long remain such if no barrier is erected to the holding of public offices and judgeships by those who reject and seek to undermine Catholic teaching as reflected in public law. The great Garcia Moreno, President of Ecuador, was assassinated by the Masons precisely because he took bold measures to restore Catholic social order in Ecuador, including amendments to the 1869 constitution that made Catholicism the religion of the State and required that both political candidates and voters be Catholic. Moreno predicted his own assassination, which occurred in 1875.[356] Blessed Pius IX ordered a solemn Requiem Mass to be celebrated in the Church of Santa Maria in Trastevere and had a monument built in Rome whose inscription praised Moreno's Catholic fidelity and obedience to the Holy See.[357] Nothing more needs to be said about Blessed Pius IX's view of Moreno's implementation of the Catholic teaching reflected in the *Syllabus*—which the neo-Catholics (and the neo-modernists)

---

it would not be lawful; for in such case the motive of good is wanting" (n. 34).

[355]*Dignitatis Humanae*, n. 6.
[356]See "Gabriel Garcia Moreno," *Catholic Encyclopedia* (1913).
[357]*Religionis integerrimus custos*
*Auctor studiorum optimorum*
*Obsequentissimus in Petri sedem*
*Justitiae cultor; scelerum vindex.*

now tell us no longer "applies." We can all see the results of the *Syllabus'* supposed inapplicability to present-day societies.[358]

Volume upon volume has been written to "demonstrate" how DH can be reconciled with prior papal teaching—an exercise that was never seen as necessary with any other conciliar document in the entire history of the Church.[359] But it is

---

[358]Obviously, we are speaking here of the Catholic *ideal* defended in preconciliar papal teaching discussed above, which presupposes a Catholic body politic that would have the right to remain such through appropriate legal measures, not excluding legitimate control of immigration. Indeed, the notion that non-Catholics coming to Catholic countries should be allowed the public profession of any form of worship was condemned in the *Syllabus* (proposition 79). We are obviously not suggesting that such measures be forcibly imposed on apostate populations today. But the duty to strive to *restore* Catholic social order remains: "First and foremost, it is the duty of all Catholics worthy of the name...to endeavor *to bring back all civil society to the pattern and form of Christianity* which We have described" (*Immortale Dei*, n. 46). Nations, no less than individual Catholics, are objectively obliged to embrace the true religion. The nation/individual distinction in this prime duty toward God is rank Protestantism, and is now also a feature of neo-Catholicism.

[359]Abbé Basil of St. Madeleine de la Barroux has written six volumes on the subject. The estimable Fr. Brian Harrison, O.S., has devoted an entire book and numerous articles to a demonstration of DH's compatibility with the teaching of Blessed Pius IX, Leo XIII and St. Pius X. In the March-April 2000 issue of *Catholic Dossier*, Fr. Harrison concluded that although "the conciliar Church has indeed *departed from tradition here*" (as to the public exercise of non-Catholic religions in predominantly Catholic societies), DH involves "discarding a traditional *policy*, not a traditional *doctrine*." Even if that is so, in our view Fr. Harrison and others have not shown how DH's enunciation of a *natural right* to immunity from state coercion in the *public* activities of non-Catholic sects can be reconciled with prior papal teaching, which allows the mere *tolerance* of such activities by the State as an *exception* that must be "strictly confined." (See footnote 350.) The preconciliar Popes say absolutely nothing about a generalized natural right to *be* tolerated. Thus, DH seems to take the prior exception and turn it not only into the rule, but also into a rule grounded in a natural right of which the preconciliar Popes were

neither our wish nor our task to enter deeply into the endless debate over whether DH and the rest of Vatican II's ambiguous "counter-syllabus" proposes a formal or material contradiction of the *Syllabus* and the related teaching of the preconciliar Popes. Only the infallible Magisterium can resolve the issue.[360] Our aim here is only to demonstrate the self-contradiction involved in the neo-Catholic's less-than-deferential approach to prior papal teaching, as compared to his slavish defense of present-day novelties.

As we have shown, the neo-Catholic's deference to papal authority is drastically skewed in favor of the postconciliar innovations of the Church, including "the ecumenical movement," "dialogue with the world" and "the liturgical renewal," even though these clearly provisional matters are what truly belong in the category of "temporary dispositions" into which Cardinal Ratzinger would place the *Syllabus* and *Pascendi*. In a flagrant self-contradiction, the neo-Catholic dissents as readily as any modernist from prior papal teaching, and on the same grounds condemned by the preconciliar Popes—that solemn encyclicals condemning error are limited to their "historical context."

The neo-Catholic's adherence to what he asserts is the "living Magisterium" is therefore not *diachronic*—extending throughout time—but merely chronologic, focusing on the

---

apparently unaware. Only the Magisterium, not commentators, can definitively demonstrate DH's harmony with prior teaching. That so much commentary has been generated only demonstrates the need for a Magisterial resolution of the problem.

[360]Even if there were an actual doctrinal contradiction between DH and preconciliar teaching—and DH seems far too ambiguous to allow that conclusion—it cannot be forgotten that the Church has never claimed to be infallible in all her pronouncements, but only in what she has constantly taught (always, everywhere and by everyone) or solemnly and explicitly defined as binding Catholic doctrine. See discussion in Chapter 8. As we discussed in Chapter 2, this distortion of Catholic teaching only plays into the sedevacantist argument that Vatican II is a "false council" and the conciliar Popes "false Popes."

*recency* rather than the *constancy* of a given pronouncement or practice in the Church. In the neo-Catholic system, the distinction between fallible and infallible exercises of the Magisterium, and between Magisterial and non-Magisterial pronouncements as such, is allowed to be asserted *only* as to preconciliar teaching perceived to be at odds with the prevailing novelties. As for current Vatican pronouncements, no such distinctions are allowed to traditionalists—or anyone else. We believe it is quite literally the case that if, *per impossibile*, the Vatican were to announce tomorrow that contraception was permissible, at least some neo-Catholics would feel compelled to defend the new teaching, just as they discovered the virtue of altar girls after the Pope revoked not only a 2,000-year-old tradition, but also his own teaching, in approving the innovation.

We stress once again that none of this is to suggest that the neo-Catholic is not a true Catholic. Rather, we mean to say that he is a true Catholic who, in our opinion, has fallen into self-contradiction because a misguided sense of loyalty to Church leaders counsels him to defend novel notions and practices that run counter to the Church's traditions. As Blessed Pius IX himself observed concerning Catholics of this tendency: "Assuredly these associations [of Catholics] are not wanting in the obedience due to the Church...but they might be pushed into the slippery path of error by the force of those opinions called Liberal; opinions accepted by many Catholics *who are otherwise honest and pious*, and who, *even by the very influence which gives them piety*, are easily induced to profess the most pernicious maxims."[361]

The only difference today is that many of the liberal opinions condemned by Blessed Pius IX in the *Syllabus* now appear to have the approval of the Vatican itself, and certainly

---

[361]Address to Bishop of Quimper, quoted in Sarda, *Liberalism Is a Sin*, p. 49.

the approval of most of the hierarchy and laity at large. This is why the Church is now undergoing the most profound crisis in her long history—the invasion of the Church by the worldly thinking rued by Paul VI. It is our conviction that we would not be witnessing this crisis were it not for rise of the neo-Catholic system with its self-contradictory approach to Church teaching.

# Section III

# Toward A Solution

# Chapter 12

# Returning to the Council?
# A Case Study

*"Considering the results of the Second Vatican Council,
perhaps it is time the Holy Father called for
a second Council of Trent."*
–Patrick J. Buchanan

Among the neo-Catholic commentators who at least admit that the Church is in the midst of a grave crisis, the received wisdom is that we must "go back to the Council" and implement its ambiguous decrees according to their "true intention." Why the Council's "true intention" has proven to be so elusive over the past forty years is never explained. But Janet Smith, in a typical expression of this longing after the Council's lost intention, proclaims: "Those of us who have labored in the trenches are most grateful for and appreciative of the reinforcements and new troops the Holy Spirit is raising up, for soon we may see the Church the Council envisioned."[362]

What is meant by "the Church the Council envisioned"? Smith cannot say exactly—and neither, it seems, can anyone else. But Smith does observe that

> perhaps the time for weeping is coming to an end. The ravages of ICEL are being reconsidered, the U.S. bishops are revisiting norms for building churches, *permission for Latin liturgies is*

---

[362]"The Wake of Vatican II," *Catholic Dossier*, November 2000.

*being extended,* Eucharistic adoration is becoming an *underground movement* [!] of immense proportions. It is a good sign that at the University of Dallas, the students *have spontaneously begun to sing the ordinary of the Mass in Latin* at some of the liturgies. It is now a truism to say that *the more traditional orders and dioceses are attracting by far the greater number of vocations.*

It seems, then, that the Church "envisioned" by Vatican II involves something strangely reminiscent of the Church *before* Vatican II. Perhaps, in time, the neo-Catholics will admit explicitly that a return to integral Catholic tradition is what is needed. Meanwhile, they continue to speak of an indescribable conciliar apotheosis, which is always—just there!—on the horizon.

In the same vein is neo-Catholic luminary George Weigel: "Unlike other ecumenical councils, Vatican II did not provide 'keys' to its teaching in the form of creeds, canons or anathemas." In other words, one cannot learn what Vatican II teaches simply by reading its documents. Understanding the Council requires a set of "keys" that the Council itself did not provide. Weigel claims that these "keys" have been provided by John Paul II: "It has been left to the pontificate of John Paul II to provide an authoritative interpretation of the council...." That the teaching of Vatican II is so obscure as to require an "interpretation" seems to trouble no one in the neo-Catholic camp.

But, in any event, what *is* the "authoritative interpretation" of the Council? Weigel proposes the following, based upon his understanding of the thinking of John Paul II:

Like Blessed John XXIII, John Paul II thinks of the Second Vatican Council as a new Pentecost—a privileged moment in which the Holy Spirit prepared the Church for a springtime of evangelization. Contrary to the conventional readings of the meaning of Vatican II proposed by both Catholic traditionalists and Catholic progressives, John Paul II has insisted that the council was not primarily about the distribution of authority and jurisdiction inside the Church.

Rather, the council was meant to revivify within the Church a profound sense of itself as the sacrament of the world's salvation: the "communio" in which we experience, here and now, a foretaste of what God intends for humanity for all eternity. In Karol Wojtyla's experience of the council as one of its most active Fathers, and in his authoritative interpretation of the council as Pope, Vatican II was meant to prepare the Church, theologically and spiritually, to rediscover itself as a great evangelical movement in history, proclaiming to the world the truth about the human person, human community, human origins and human destiny.[363]

So, as Weigel understands it, the "authoritative interpretation" of Vatican II developed in the teaching of John Paul II is as follows:

- Vatican II was a new Pentecost,

- to prepare for a springtime of evangelization;

- it was not about distribution of authority in the Church, but rather was meant to:

- revivify the Church's profound sense of itself,

- provide a foretaste of what God intends for humanity for all eternity, and

- prepare the Church to rediscover itself as a great evangelical movement in history.

As we can see, this "interpretation" of Vatican II requires an interpretation of its own. The neo-Catholic explication of "the real meaning" of Vatican II never amounts to much more than the rhetorical equivalent of tinted steam. But this is not the fault of the neo-Catholic commentators; the nebulosity of their subject matter makes anything approaching concreteness impossible.

---

[363]Zenit interview, March 8, 2002.

Nevertheless, the misty search for the Council's true intention goes on. Cardinal Ratzinger, with reference to the postconciliar crisis, has written: "Does this mean the Council itself must be revoked? Certainly not. It means only that the real reception of the Council has *not yet even begun*. What devastated the Church after the Council was not the Council but the refusal to accept it.... The task, therefore, is not to suppress the Council but to *discover the real Council* and to deepen its *true intention* in the light of present experience."[364]

But what is meant by "the real Council"? And why, nearly forty years after the Council ended, are we still seeking to divine its "true intention"? Like Smith, Cardinal Ratzinger cannot really say, although he does give an indication of why "the real Council" has been so difficult to "discover." Speaking of the preface to *Gaudium et Spes*, the Cardinal writes that "the history of its influence is not to be separated from the spirit of this preface and is, to a large extent, stamped with its *ambiguity*." And speaking of the need for present-day "diagnoses" of *Gaudium et Spes* and the other key conciliar texts, Ratzinger observes that "*the lack of clarity* that persists even today about the *real meaning of Vatican II* is closely associated with such diagnoses."[365]

Let us state the point as frankly as possible: Observations like Smith's and Ratzinger's only confirm what has long been known: that the documents of Vatican II are a hopeless muddle of ambiguity from which it is impossible to discern the "real Council," let alone the fabled "Church the Council envisioned." To "discover the real Council" is, therefore, only to return to the source of our current difficulties, and we will find there no more guidance than was to be had forty years ago. The fact is that wherever the Council did not simply repeat the constant teaching of the Church, it offered nothing definite in the way of Catholic doctrine. The "real Council" is, therefore, a chimera.

Here it is apropos to note a proposition neo-Catholic commentators seem never to have entertained: that it was

[364]Ratzinger, *Principles of Catholic Theology*, p. 390.
[365]Ibid., pp. 378, 379.

*Vatican II*, not the preconciliar Popes, that gave us a "one-sided" (to recall Cardinal Ratzinger's assessment of the *Syllabus* and *Pascendi*) and a "skewed" view of the world that ought now to be discarded. No one has made this point more tellingly than Fr. Stanley Jaki, whose membership in the Pontifical Academy of Sciences ought to squelch neo-Catholic objections to this assessment of the Council: "Do not the texts of Vatican II bespeak of a *lopsided optimism*, at least in the sense that they contain *no appropriate presentation of mankind's fallen predicament* and of the chain of ongoing historical tragedies implied therein?... They [the conciliar *periti*] looked forward to the emergence of a new humanism most sympathetic to the most cherished cultural objections of the Church. Such a hope proved itself very hollow when the legalization of rank immoralities made great strides in such Catholic countries as Ireland and Poland...."[366] (These are the very same countries in which the *Syllabus* and the teaching of Pope Leo XIII "no longer apply," according to neo-Catholic commentators.)

Jaki is only remarking the obvious, but the obvious is something the neo-Catholic establishment refuses to admit. Here yet again we see the recurring double standard in neo-Catholic thinking: Neo-Catholics see nothing wrong with declaring outmoded the teaching of a whole line of preconciliar Popes, but they instantly denounce as disloyal to the Church any traditionalist who holds that it is the worldview of Vatican II, rooted in the false optimism of the 1960s, that is hopelessly passé.[367]

---

[366]Stanley L. Jaki, *Newman's Challenge* (Grand Rapids, Michigan: Eerdmans, 2000), p. 11.

[367]As Cardinal Ratzinger recalled, "[S]omething of the Kennedy era pervaded the Council, something of the naïve optimism of the concept of the great society. We can do everything we want to do, if only we employ the right means. It was precisely the break in historical consciousness, the self-tormenting rejection of the past, that produced the concept of a zero hour, in which everything would begin again, and all those things that had formerly been done badly would now be done well. The dream of liberation, the dream of something totally different, which, a little while later, had an increasingly potent

The Council's ambiguity could simply be allowed to pass into memory were it not a continuing source of enormous problems in the Church. As Msgr. George A. Kelly put it in *The Battle for the American Church*: "Gregory Baum, who was at the Council, once thought that Pope John smiled in two directions. Critics of Pope Paul suggest that he prayed the same way. The problems of the postconciliar Church reflect this predicament. The documents of the Council contain enough *basic ambiguities* to make the postconciliar difficulties understandable."[368] And, as Fr. Jaki has observed: "In adopting this non-dogmatic, or attenuatedly dogmatic approach, Vatican II unintentionally opened the floodgates to vagueness, ambiguity, and indecision (all, of course, in the disguise of 'pastoral' solutions) that do not cease to take a heavy toll on the Catholic life—priestly, religious and lay."[369]

Nowhere is this more apparent than with the Council's document on the sacred liturgy, *Sacrosanctum Concilium* (SC). We will discuss it here at some length, as a prime example of why we (and so many others) believe the Council is a cause of such great havoc in the Church.

For the better part of thirty years, traditionalists have listened to neo-Catholics argue that the postconciliar devastation of the Roman rite has nothing whatever to do with the language of SC. To the contrary, they argue: SC actually contains the solution to the current liturgical crisis. If only SC were implemented "as the Council intended," they claim, we would finally have the "authentic reform" of the liturgy that the Council really intended. (We have mentioned that the neo-Catholic liturgical group *Adoremus* has been the leading exponent of this thesis.)

As we have noted, it is one of the many self-contradictions of the neo-Catholic system that those who advocate a "correct"

---

impact on the student revolts, was, in a certain sense, also attributable to the Council; it was the Council that first urged man on and then disappointed him...." *Principles of Catholic Theology*, p. 372.

[368]Kelly, *The Battle for the American Church*, p. 20.

[369]Jaki, *Newman's Challenge*, p. 9.

implementation of SC as the solution to what Cardinal Ratzinger has called "the collapse of the liturgy" are themselves engaging in the same sort of "private judgment" they condemn in traditionalists.   That is, they are implicitly contradicting Pope Paul VI's declarations in November 1969 that the new Mass is what SC authorized and therefore what the Council intended. They also contradict Pope John Paul II's address on the twenty-fifth anniversary of SC, in which he praised SC and "the reforms which it has made possible," declaring that "the liturgical reform is the most visible fruit of the whole work of the Council." These facts are very difficult for certain neo-Catholics to acknowledge. For if both Paul VI and John Paul II agree that the provisions of SC warranted the creation of the very liturgy we see today, then the neo-Catholic must either agree with the Popes' reading of SC, in which case the "authentic reform" of the liturgy has already occurred, or they must accuse two Popes of erring gravely in their authoritative interpretation of a conciliar document. Quite a quandary.

Putting this neo-Catholic difficulty aside, we ask: is the solution to the liturgical crisis—which after all is at the heart of the postconciliar crisis as a whole—really to be found in some new implementation of SC, or what *Adoremus* has called "a reform of the reform"? We are convinced the answer is in the negative. To read SC attentively, line by line and word by word, is to understand that SC is *part* of the liturgical crisis, not its solution. In light of our actual experience with the document, anyone with a modicum of perspicuity can see (if only in retrospect) that SC was designed by its principal draftsman, Annibale Bugnini, to authorize a liturgical revolution, while giving the appearance of liturgical continuity. It is a nest of deadly ambiguities that the Council Fathers can only have approved in the confidence that the liturgical tradition of the Roman Rite could not possibly suffer a dramatic rupture, because it had never happened before.  As we have earlier mentioned, Cardinal Browne was subjected to incredulous laughter when he worried aloud that SC's ambiguous permission for vernacularization of the Mass might lead to abandonment of the Latin liturgy within a few years. Who's laughing now?

A lawyer knows that the dangers in a contract from his client's perspective lie not so much in what the terms of the contract provide as in what they permit the other party to do. The danger is in the loopholes. Quite simply, SC permits all manner of drastic things to be done to the Roman liturgy. It is one long collection of loopholes. If a lawyer entrusted with the task of protecting the Roman liturgy from harmful innovation had drafted this document, he would be guilty of gross malpractice. It is amazing that anyone who claims to have read SC thoroughly could still maintain that its "true" interpretation precludes the liturgical innovations that have been inflicted upon us. If Paul VI and John Paul II did not think so, why should the neo-Catholics?

We present here a brief discussion of what can be called the "conservative" and "liberal" norms of SC. Two themes in SC are apparent from the provisions we shall quote: the first is an open-ended authorization for liturgical reform on what is potentially a vast scale, but without requiring that any particular reform of the liturgy be enacted or avoided; and the second is "democratization" of the liturgy by ceding effective liturgical control to the "ecclesiastical territorial authority" of each country, and the liturgy commissions to be established in each diocese. These two themes are couched in language that seems to inhibit the scope of potential reform in the light of tradition, but does so in a way that always admits of immediate exceptions to suit local needs, conditions and circumstances as determined by "territorial ecclesiastical authority," subject only to Rome's approval or *ex post facto* confirmation—which has rarely been withheld. The playing out of these two themes over the past thirty years has meant nothing less than what Msgr. Klaus Gamber called "the real destruction of the Roman rite," with the consequent loss of unity of cult in the Western Church. Yet again, the results speak for themselves.

The careful reader of SC will readily observe a characteristic typical of the other ambiguous documents of the Council: an interplay between "conservative" and "liberal" phraseology, the latter serving to undermine and even negate the former. In reading SC's "liberal" norms, one wonders how the Council Fathers, including the late Archbishop Marcel Lefebvre, could have been induced to approve such an open-ended document. As Msgr. Gamber observed in *Reform of the Roman Liturgy:* "The Council Fathers, when publishing the *Constitution on Sacred Liturgy,* simply did not expect to see the avalanche they had started, crushing under it all traditional forms of liturgical worship, even the new liturgy they themselves had created...."[370] As we have seen, today's neo-Catholics evince a similar blindness, even though they, unlike the Council Fathers, have had the benefit of seeing the document interpreted and implemented by two Popes, with disastrous results.

Let us examine first the "conservative" norms in SC.

> **Art. 4 –** ...Holy Mother Church holds all lawfully recognized rites to be of equal right and dignity; ...she wishes to *preserve them in the future and to foster them in every way.*

Undoubtedly this norm went a long way toward persuading the Council Fathers to adopt SC, despite the swarm of liberal norms that follow in the document. Assuming SC is still operative, traditionalists are certainly entitled to rely on this norm to support a return to the traditional liturgy by preserving and fostering the traditional rite of Mass, still untouched by the reform, in every way.

Yet, in typical conciliar fashion, the quoted sentence is followed by a disclaimer: "The Council also desires that, where necessary, the rites be revised carefully in the light of sound tradition, and that they be given new vigor to meet the circumstances and needs of modern times." But the "sound tradition" of the Church is entirely contrary to the revision of ancient rites in order to suit "the circumstances and needs modern times" — whatever that means — much less a radical alteration of the Roman rite as a whole, which would have been unthinkable to any Pope before Vatican II.

---

[370]Gamber, *The Reform of the Roman Liturgy,* p. 23.

**Art. 23** …[T]here must be no *innovations* unless the good of the Church genuinely and certainly requires them, and care must be taken that any *new forms adopted* should in *some* way grow organically from forms already existing….

To say that there will be no innovations "unless," means, of course, that there will be innovations. And there *were* innovations — lots of them. This "conservative" norm introduces two novel concepts into the liturgical discipline of the Church: "innovations" in the liturgy and the adoption of entirely "new forms" of liturgy, as opposed to the gradual, almost imperceptible liturgical refinements of preceding centuries. The requirement that "any new forms adopted should in some way grow organically from already existing forms" opens the way to entirely new liturgy, whose resemblance to the preceding immemorial form is vestigial at best.

To follow the language of this "conservative" norm: Is not the Mass of Paul VI an "innovation" that he deemed to be "genuinely and certainly required" for the good of the Church, a "new form adopted" that grew "in some way" from the existing form of the Mass? At least that is how Pope Paul VI presented it to the faithful.

Certainly, this norm can also be given a strict interpretation, prohibiting any revisions to the preconciliar Mass whatsoever; and traditionalists are entitled to promote this strict interpretation as against the neo-Catholic interpretation, which assumes the existence of some hypothetical "authentic reform" yet to be discovered. This presupposes that SC is still an operative document. But now that two Popes have told us that SC has been faithfully implemented, why do certain neo-Catholics constantly refer back to SC as though it provides a mandate for still more liturgical change? Is SC to be viewed as a permanent charter for liturgical innovation? So much, then, for the "authentic reform" of the liturgy supposedly envisioned in SC.

Art. 36 - ...(1) The use of the Latin language, *with due respect to particular law,* is to be preserved in the Latin rites.

Certain neo-Catholics argue that this norm has been "violated" by a "liberal faction" of reformers in the Church, and by some liberal bishops — by which they mean to say (but do not have the candor to say) two Popes and nearly the entire hierarchy. But has Art. 36 really been violated by the postconciliar reforms? As two Popes have told us: not at all.

In the first place, the norm provides only that *use* of the Latin language is to be preserved, not the traditional Latin Mass or even the Roman Canon. More important, this qualified protection for the Latin liturgy is undermined by the phrase "with due respect to particular law." The framework of "particular law" erected under SC's liberal norms completely negated this conservative norm *ab initio* by permitting extended use of the vernacular in the Mass and adaptation of the liturgy to local customs and conditions, as deemed "useful" by "territorial ecclesiastical authority."

Regarding this disastrous effect of SC, the omnipresent Bugnini declared in triumph:

> For four centuries all power has been reserved to the Holy See in liturgical matters (Canon 1257). The bishops' role was limited to seeing that the liturgical laws were observed.... *The Constitution has broken down this centuries-old barrier.* The Church is now in the process of restoring to the competent territorial authorities — *the word "territorial" is decidedly elastic —* many problems pertaining to the liturgy, including...*the introduction, the use and the limits to the use of the vernacular in certain rites.*[371]

In 1964, only a year after SC was enacted, Pope Paul VI issued his *motu proprio Sacram Liturgiam.* Article 9 of *Sacram Liturgiam* authorized all national hierarchies to approve vernacular translations of the Mass, subject only to Rome's *ex post facto* approval, which was given in every case.

---

[371]Quoted in Davies, *Pope Paul's New Mass,* p. 25.

So much for the "use of Latin" in the Roman liturgy. The "particular law" exception swallowed up this much-vaunted conservative norm within a year, as Bugnini clearly anticipated it would. Anyone who says that Article 36 of SC has been "violated" and the Council "disobeyed" by reason of the all-vernacular new liturgy either has never read SC in its entirety, or is pretending that two Popes and nearly the entire hierarchy have not already shown us that SC freely authorizes (even if it does not mandate) Mass entirely in the vernacular.

> **Arts. 114-116** - [114]...The treasury of sacred music is to be preserved and cultivated with great care. [Art. 116] - ...*Other things being equal* [Gregorian chant] should be given pride of place in liturgical services....

The phrase "other things being equal" partially undermines the phrase "pride of place," and the remaining provisions of SC (discussed below) complete the undermining by vesting "territorial ecclesiastical authority" with total control over the adaptation of church music to "local needs," along with the rest of the liturgy.

And now we come to SC's "liberal" norms, from which most of the subsequent mischief flowed.

> **Art. 1** - The sacred Council has set out to impart an ever-increasing vigor to the Christian life of the faithful; *to adapt more closely to the needs of our age* those institutions which are subject to change; to foster whatever we can *to promote union among all those who believe in Christ....* Accordingly, it sees *cogent reasons for undertaking a reform...*of the liturgy.

This norm actually cites "Christian unity" and adapting Church institutions to the "needs of our age" — whatever that means — as "cogent reasons" for revising the immemorial and hitherto sacrosanct liturgy of the Roman Rite. That the Council authorized unspecified reforms to our 1,500-year-old rite of Mass for these reasons is almost incredible. It is widely known that Paul VI later confided to his intimate friend Jean Guitton that the new Mass was specifically designed to resemble as closely as possible a Calvinist communion service, evidently with this norm in mind.[372]

> **Art. 4** - ...The Council also desires that, where necessary, the rites be revised carefully in the light of sound tradition, and that they be given new vigor to meet present-day circumstances and needs.

As Michael Davies has noted, the Council did not explain how a rite can be revised "in the light of tradition," when all tradition is against revision of our ancient rites, especially the rite of Mass. Nor did the Council give the slightest indication of which "present-day circumstances and needs" would suggest a revision of the liturgy, as opposed to the "circumstances and needs" of any other time in Church history.

> **Art. 14** - ...In the restoration and promotion of the sacred liturgy, the full and active participation by all the people is the aim to be considered *before all else*, for it is *the primary and indispensable source* from which the faithful are to derive the true Christian spirit.

This norm exalts participation by the people above every other consideration in the Mass. Although this norm does not relate to liturgical revision as such, but rather to the "promotion and restoration" of the liturgy, its elevation to the paramount concern in the liturgy certainly impacts on those norms governing liturgical reform at Article 21, *et seq.*

---

[372] "[T]he intention of Pope Paul VI with regard to what is commonly called the Mass, was to reform the Catholic liturgy in such a way that it should almost coincide with the Protestant liturgy.... [T]here was with Pope Paul VI an ecumenical intention to remove, or at least to correct, or at least to relax, what was too Catholic in the traditional sense, in the Mass, and, I repeat, to get the Catholic Mass closer to the Calvinist mass" (Dec. 19, 1993), *Apropos*, #17, pp. 8f; quoted in *Christian Order*, October 1994.

> **Art. 21** - In order that the Christian people may more certainly
> derive an abundance of graces from the sacred liturgy, holy
> Mother Church desires to undertake with great care *a general
> restoration of the liturgy itself.* For the liturgy is made up of
> unchangeable elements divinely instituted, and of *elements
> subject to change.* These latter not only may be changed but
> *ought to be changed with the passage of time,* if they have suffered
> from the intrusion of anything out of harmony with the inner
> nature of the liturgy *or have become less suitable.* In this
> restoration both *texts and rites should be drawn up so as to express
> more clearly the holy things which they signify.*

The phrases "general restoration of the liturgy" and "texts
and rites should be drawn up" imply that the "experts" to be
"employed" under Article 25 are to undertake a totally
unprecedented (and completely unspecified) wholesale revision
of the Roman liturgy, "drawing up" new texts and rites as they
see fit. And that is what the Consilium did, giving us a new
Mass and rites for the other sacraments, all with the full
approval of Pope Paul VI.

This norm clearly implies that the reason for the "general
restoration" and the drawing up of new texts and rites is that
the existing rites for the Mass and sacraments in the Roman Rite
do not express clearly enough "the holy things which they
signify." It also suggests constant adaptation of the liturgy
whenever any of its elements become "less suitable" — but "less
suitable," like all the other terms in SC, receives no definition
whatsoever.

> **Art. 25** - The liturgical books are to be revised as soon as
> possible. Experts are to be employed on this task, and bishops
> from various parts of the world are to be consulted.

This norm, for the first time in Church history, authorizes
the simultaneous revision of all the liturgical books of the
Roman Rite by unknown "experts," without providing any
specific guidelines whatsoever for their work. The "experts,"
with the full approval of Paul VI, quickly proceeded to do
exactly what the Council had permitted, with this open-ended

license: to revise all the liturgical books in consultation with the bishops of the world. The bishops' own liturgical "experts" then proceeded to ruin the Roman liturgy with vernacular translations and other local adaptations they were empowered to make under the following norms of SC.

> **Art. 34** - ...The rites should be distinguished by a noble simplicity. They should be short, clear, and free from useless repetitions. They should be within the people's powers of comprehension, and normally should not require much explanation.

Does not this norm imply that the Damasian-Gregorian-Tridentine liturgy of 1,500 years' standing—the Roman Rite's greatest treasure—was too long and complicated and should be "simplified" in some *completely unspecified* manner? (This is not to mention the rites for the other sacraments.) What is meant by such terms as "noble simplicity," "short" and "clear"? Which repetitions are "useless"? The Council defined absolutely nothing in this "time-bomb" of a norm; it delegated "experts" in Article 25 to interpret these open-ended terms after the Council.

Also, what was to be done to the Mass to bring it within the "people's powers of comprehension," given that Pius XII had taught only *fifteen years earlier*, in his definitive liturgical encyclical *Mediator Dei*, that those who could not comprehend the Roman Missal could still actively and fruitfully participate at Mass by praying the Rosary or engaging in other prayers and devotions? The Council did not answer this question either. But the "experts" did answer it, by giving us the new, stripped-down, easily comprehended, vernacular Mass of Paul VI.

> **Art. 36 (2)** - But since the use of the vernacular, whether in the Mass, the administration of the sacraments, or in other parts of the liturgy, may frequently be of great advantage to the people, *a wider use may be made of it,* especially in [but not limited to!] readings, directives and in some prayers and chants.... [I]*t is for the competent territorial ecclesiastical authority mentioned...to decide whether, and to what extent, the vernacular language is to be used.* Its decrees have to be approved, that is, *confirmed,* by the Apostolic See.

This norm gave the bishops the power to introduce as much vernacular into the Mass as they liked, subject only to Rome's confirmation after the fact. This norm is reflected in Article 9 of *Sacram Liturgiam,* under which Rome soon approved the all-vernacular national liturgies we now have, which shattered the unity of liturgical cult in the Roman Rite.

> **Art. 38-40 -** [38] Provided that the substantial unity of the Roman rite is preserved, provision shall be made, *when revising the liturgical books,* for legitimate *variations and adaptations to different groups, regions and peoples,* especially in [but, again, not limited to!] mission countries. This should be borne in mind when *drawing up the rites and determining rubrics.* [39] Within the limits set by the typical editions of the liturgical books, *it shall be for the competent territorial ecclesiastical authority to specify adaptations,* especially in the case of *the sacraments, the sacramentals, processions, liturgical language, sacred music, and the arts;* but according to the fundamental norms laid down in this Constitution. [40] In some places and circumstances, however, *an even more radical adaptation of the liturgy is needed....*

These norms flung open the door to the winds of change in the Roman rite. They authorized a complete transformation of the face of Catholic worship by "adaptation" of the liturgy—even *radical* adaptation—to suit local customs and preferences, as the bishops saw fit. They empowered the bishops to alter virtually every aspect of the liturgy, including the "liturgical language" to be used in celebrating Mass.

Has not the Holy See approved this radical transformation of the liturgy at every step of the way, according to the "fundamental norms" of SC—norms that posed no real impediment to what Gamber rightly called the "avalanche they [the Council Fathers] had started"?

> **Art. 40 (1), (2) -** ...(1) The competent territorial ecclesiastical authority mentioned in Article 22:2 must, in this matter, carefully and prudently consider which elements from the traditions and cultures of individual peoples might

appropriately be admitted into divine worship. Adaptations which are considered useful or necessary should then be submitted to the Holy See, by whose consent they may be introduced. (2) To ensure that adaptations may be made with all the circumspection necessary, the Apostolic See will grant power to this same territorial ecclesiastical authority to permit and to direct, as the case requires, the necessary preliminary experiments over a determined period of time among certain groups suitable for the purpose.

Are not these "certain groups" launched by SC among the prime causes of the destruction of the Roman rite and its replacement by a vernacular, inculturated liturgy, constantly being adapted to the "present-day circumstances and needs" referred to in Art. 4?

Art. 50 - The rite of the Mass is to be revised in such a way that the intrinsic nature and purpose of its several parts, as well as the connection between them, may be more clearly manifested, and that devout and active participation by the faithful may be more easily achieved.... For this purpose the rites are to be simplified, due care being taken to preserve their substance. Parts which with the passage of time came to be duplicated, or were added with little advantage, are to be omitted. Other parts which suffered loss through accidents of history are to be restored to the vigor they had in the days of the holy Fathers, as may seem useful or necessary....

How exactly does the traditional liturgy of the Roman Rite fail to manifest clearly the nature and purpose of its parts and the connection between them? Which parts of the Mass have been "added with little advantage" over the past 2,000 years? Which parts are "duplicated" — any part involving a repeated prayer or gesture, or only some repeated prayers or gestures? Which parts have "suffered loss" or must be restored to "vigor"? And what is the "substance" of the rites that should be preserved during all the revisions suggested, but not specified, by this norm?

The Council provided no answers to these questions. It simply turned the Roman liturgy over to the Article 25 "experts" for their decisions, as approved by the Pope. The only standard given for their work is, incredibly, whatever "may seem *useful* or necessary." The result was the Mass of Paul VI. In fact, in his Audience address of November 19, 1969, Pope Paul relied expressly on Article 50 to justify his imposition of the entirely new rite devised by Bugnini's Consilium.

> **Art. 54** - *A suitable place may be allotted to the vernacular* in Masses which are celebrated with the people, especially in the readings and "the common prayer," and also, as local conditions may warrant, in those parts which pertain to the people, according to the rules laid down in Article 36 of this Constitution…. *Wherever a more extended use of the vernacular in the Mass seems desirable,* the regulation laid down in Article 40 of this Constitution is to be observed….

This norm opened the way to "a more extended use of the vernacular" than just in the readings and "common prayer," as long as it "seems" desirable to the "territorial ecclesiastical authority" under Article 40. Under this norm and the previously cited norms, and *Sacram Liturgiam*, which proceeded from these norms, Rome very quickly approved the decision of each national hierarchy that it would be "desirable" to extend the vernacular to the entire Mass.

> **Art. 63** - Because the use of the vernacular in the administration of the sacraments and sacramentals can often be of very great help to the people, *this use is to be extended* according to the following norms: (a) In the administration of the sacraments and sacramentals the *vernacular may be used* according to the norm of Article 36. *The competent territorial ecclesiastical authority*…shall forthwith prepare, in accordance with the new edition of the Roman Ritual, *local rituals adapted linguistically and otherwise to the needs of the different regions.* These rituals, on authentication by the Apostolic See, are to be followed in the regions in question….

This norm opened the way to vernacular rites for the other sacraments to go along with the all-vernacular Mass, with both

RETURNING TO THE COUNCIL?

to be adapted to local customs and needs as the local bishops would see fit.

> Art. 81 - Funeral rites should express more clearly the paschal character of Christian death, and should correspond more closely to the circumstances and traditions found in various regions. This also applies to the liturgical color to be used.

This norm suggests the inculturated funeral Masses we see today, in which a white-vested priest assures us that the departed soul is a saint who will have a glorious resurrection like Our Lord's.

> Art. 107 - The liturgical year is to be revised so that the traditional customs and discipline of the sacred seasons shall be preserved or restored to suit the conditions of modern times.... If certain adaptations are necessary because of local conditions, they are to be made in accordance with the provisions of Articles 39 and 40.

This norm authorized a complete revision of the Church's ancient liturgical calendar, but provided absolutely no guidance on how it was to be done. It opened the way to destruction of the traditional liturgical cycle of readings of over 1,300 years' standing — to "suit the conditions of modern times." And, like all other aspects of the liturgy, the liturgical year was subjected to local variations under Article 40. Was not the loss of the traditional liturgical year, an integral part of our liturgical home, a prime cause of the confusion and loss of faith after the Council, as Gamber demonstrates in *Reform of the Roman Liturgy* and as Cardinal Stickler recalls in his memoir of the Council?[373]

> Art. 119 - In certain countries, especially in mission lands, there are people who have their own musical tradition, and this plays a great part in their religious and social life. For this reason *their music should be held in proper esteem and a suitable*

---

[373]Gamber, *Reform of the Roman Liturgy*, pp. 99-100; Stickler, "Recollections of a Vatican II Peritus," p. 32.

*place is to be given to it,* not only in forming their religious sense but also *in adapting worship to their native genius....*

This norm permits the introduction of folk music into the sacred liturgy of the Mass, and the "adaptation" of the Mass to such music in any country with "its own musical tradition" and "native genius." Are not the "folk Masses" and African tribal liturgical dancing exactly what this norm has produced in practice? With good reason did Pope St. Pius X, Pope Pius XII and all their predecessors forbid any secular music whatever at Holy Mass. This norm casts off that wise proscription and invites the profane melodies and rhythms of the world into the holy sanctuary.

> Art. 120 - ...But other instruments [besides the traditional pipe organ] also may be admitted for use in divine worship, in the judgment and with the consent of the competent territorial authority....

This norm opened the way to the introduction of pianos, guitars and other profane instruments into the sacred liturgy, as long as the newly empowered "competent territorial authority" judges them acceptable. Has not the result been "lounge music" during Holy Mass? This norm casts off the explicit proscriptions on the use of profane musical instruments such as guitars (as opposed to bowed instruments) which were found in the Holy See's preconciliar instructions on sacred music, up to and including the pontificate of Pius XII.

> Art. 123 - ...*The art of our own times from every race and country shall also be given free scope in the Church,* provided it bring to the task the reverence and honor due to the sacred buildings and rites....

This norm encouraged the intrusion of modern art into the Church, including grotesquely distorted images of Our Lord and the detested and ridiculous felt banner. The most widely recognized example of this is the hideous "Resurrection of

Christ" by Pericle Fazzini, a diabolically grotesque image of Our Lord that disfigures the stage of the Paul VI Audience Hall at the Vatican.

> **Art. 128** - The canons and ecclesiastical statutes which govern *the provision of external things* which pertain to sacred worship *should be revised as soon as possible*, together with the liturgical books.... These laws refer especially to the worthy and well-planned construction of sacred buildings, *the shape and construction of altars, the nobility, placing, and security of the Eucharistic tabernacle, the suitability and dignity of the baptistery, the proper ordering of sacred images, and scheme of decoration and embellishment.* Laws which seem less suited to the reformed liturgy should be amended or *abolished....* In this matter, especially as regards the material and form of sacred furnishings and vestments,...powers are given to territorial episcopal conferences *to adapt such things to the needs and customs of their different regions.*

Notice how this norm anticipates a massive liturgical upheaval, which Bugnini was already planning before the Council. This norm is a rather lawyerly "catch-all" provision opening the way to an iconoclastic revision of *every Church law regarding the externals of Catholic worship.* This norm gave the territorial bishops' conferences complete authority (subject only to Rome's rubber stamp) to adapt all of the ancient, traditional externals to "the needs and customs of their different regions," and to *abolish* all traditional tabernacles, altars, vestments, statues, church furnishings and *church structures* if they merely seem "less suited to the reformed liturgy" — which reformed liturgy was not even specified to begin with!

Are we not afflicted today by all the things this norm permitted? Consider: a liturgy nearly devoid of traditional sacred images, vestments, music and rubrics; the marble high altar replaced by a wooden table because the altar "seems less suited to the reformed liturgy" in the judgment of the bishops; the tabernacle relegated to the side of the sanctuary or to a different room altogether, under the bishops' authority to determine its "placing"; and the sanctuary itself subject to gutting at the architectural pleasure of each bishop, with the

Holy See upholding the bishop's iconoclasm in practically every instance.

In conclusion, SC is a case study of why "a return to the Council" is no solution to the crisis in the Church. No one who reads SC carefully in the light of our experience since the Council can deny that it constitutes a blank check for liturgical reform, with the amount to be filled in depending entirely upon who wields the pen in the postconciliar period. The few neo-Catholic norms that seem to limit the possibility of liturgical change were clearly overwhelmed by the far more numerous and pervasive liberal norms, which create an almost unlimited potential for destruction of the liturgy.

Yet, except for restoring the prayer of the faithful in Article 53, *SC does not actually mandate a single specific change in the text or rubrics of the traditional Order of Mass.* This would appear to be the main reason the Council Fathers were induced to vote for the document, since in containing virtually no outright mandates, it did not threaten any apparent harm to the Latin liturgical tradition. And it is also the reason that neither the neo-Catholics nor anyone else can determine from a reading of SC "the authentic reform" supposedly intended by the Council.

We believe the same is true concerning the effort to "discover the real Council" as a whole. All the key conciliar documents are marked by the same sort of vagueness and open-endedness that made SC a recipe for liturgical disaster.

What, then, do we propose? We propose that the time has come to consider whether the Church ought simply to close the book on Vatican II, thus beginning the process of forgetting that this confusing and divisive Council ever happened. It is a process that we believe will occur sooner or later. Why not sooner?

Here we are not without historical precedent. There was a roughly analogous situation much earlier in the Church's history, of which traditionalists and neo-Catholics alike are possibly unaware: the Second Council of Constantinople, held in 553. In 1934, historian Msgr. Philip Hughes described it as "the strangest of all the general councils."[374] It was indeed strange. This was an ecumenical council, the fifth of the twenty-one the Church has convoked from Nicea to Vatican II. Strictly speaking, it taught nothing erroneous. Yet, as Vatican II has proven to be, Constantinople II was an unmitigated disaster, and was recognized as such by a great many contemporary observers. Neo-Catholics who condemn traditionalist critics of Vatican II ought to become familiar with this ill-starred council.

The roots of this council extend at least to the Council of Chalcedon, held just over a century earlier, and even to the Council of Ephesus, which condemned the Nestorian heresy. The primary purpose of the Council of Chalcedon (451) had been to render judgment on the Monophysite heresy that denied Christ's human nature. The orthodox formula of two natures (human and divine) in one Person is what Chalcedon, under the direction of Pope Leo the Great, ultimately decreed.

The Monophysites were not so easily dispensed with, however, and continued to have a strong presence throughout the Christian world, particularly in the East. Church and secular rulers alike deplored this unfortunate situation. The Emperor Justinian was particularly concerned about overcoming the heresy and reestablishing a unified Christian world.

Toward this end, Justinian put forward a suggestion that a confidant had offered to him: he would uphold the teaching of Chalcedon, but he would condemn the writings of three theologians whose work offended the Monophysites—the so-called "Three Chapters." Theodore of Mopsuestia, whose work was fatally imbued with Nestorianism, was to be condemned personally and in his writings. Some of the writings of Theodoret of Cyrrhus, who had played an important role at Chalcedon, would likewise be condemned, as would a famous letter of Ibas of Edessa to the Persian bishop Maris, giving his account of the Council of Ephesus. Yet all three of these authors

---

[374]For the many details of this bizarre controversy, a kind of antitype of the present confusion, see Philip Hughes, *A History of the Church*, vol. 1: *The Church and the World in Which the Church Was Founded* (1934; London: Sheed and Ward, 1979), p. 282.

had died in the good graces of the Church. Thus began the raging "Three Chapters" controversy.

Justinian hoped that a solemn condemnation of the Three Chapters would mollify the Monophysites, without actually retreating from the positions adopted by the Council of Chalcedon. That the condemnation of three dead Catholics was not the most straightforward way of handling the problem of lingering Monophysitism is something of an understatement. A good many Catholics at the time had serious misgivings about this approach. According to the *Catholic Encyclopedia,* "There were no good precedents for thus dealing harshly with the memory of men who had died in the peace of the Church." Moreover, the condemnation "was not demanded to crush a heresy, but to conciliate heretics who were implacable enemies of the Council of Chalcedon."[375]

At first, Pope Vigilius absolutely refused to condemn the Three Chapters. But as time went on he gradually warmed to the idea, and in 548 he issued a public condemnation of these celebrated writings. But he again hedged in 553, the year of the Council, and it was months after the Council had closed that he definitively approved the condemnation once and for all—thus issuing three contradictory statements in the span of five years.

A number of bishops later protested to Justinian that the Pope's condemnation of the Three Chapters had been done "to give satisfaction to the Monophysites."[376] Msgr. Hughes shared this assessment: the condemnation of the Three Chapters was a "tricky attempt to conciliate the Monophysites."[377] Rather than reiterating or elaborating upon the irreformable teaching of Chalcedon, Constantinople II sought *both* to uphold Chalcedon *and* to call to account three long-dead theologians—two of whom had been intimately associated with Chalcedon! How could such a strategy *not* have generated confusion and discord among the faithful? As the great historian W.H.C. Frend

---

[375]Ibid., pp. 279-80.

[376]Charles Joseph Hefele, *A History of the Councils of the Church,* vol. IV, trans. William R. Clark (Edinburgh: T&T Clark, 1895), p. 352.

[377]Hughes, *A History of the Church,* vol. 1, p. 280.

described it: "At the council itself the bishops turned intellectual somersaults in their efforts to uphold Chalcedon yet condemn the Three Chapters."[378]

For all that, the desired reconciliation with the Monophysites was not achieved. Still another great historian, Henry Chadwick, concludes that the "painful affair of the Three Chapters did nothing to reconcile even moderate Monophysites, and actually had the reverse effect to that intended." As for the segment of the Catholic world that was fully orthodox and supported the Council of Chalcedon, "the immediate effect was to produce temporary schisms in the West; and the *successive contradictory utterances* of [Pope] Vigilius did not enhance the authority of the Roman see."[379] Would our neo-Catholic friends care to denounce these eminent historians for "private judgment" in their disparaging references to Pope Vigilius and the Council?

Rome's attempts to heal these various schisms supply us with some useful insights. The situation in Milan is especially apt. Bishop Lawrence II of Milan reestablished communion with the Holy See in 571. Unfortunately, we do not possess his correspondence with Pope John III, but based on correspondence between his successor, Archbishop Constantine, and Pope St. Gregory the Great, we can infer at least something about the terms on which he was welcomed back into the unity of the Church. According to Charles Hefele, one of the great historians of the Church's ecumenical councils, Bishop Lawrence was instructed that, if asked, he must not swear that he had refused to condemn the Three Chapters. This proviso leads Hefele to conclude: "There must, therefore, have been a concession contained in it [the letter] in regard to the anathema on the three chapters."[380] Perhaps the Bishop had been told that while he did not necessarily have to subscribe to the anathema, neither could he swear that he had not.

---

[378]W.H.C. Frend, *The Rise of Christianity* (Philadelphia: Fortress Press, 1984), p. 853.

[379]Henry Chadwick, *The Early Church* (New York: Penguin, 1993), p. 210.

[380]Hefele, *A History of the Councils*, p. 357.

That the Popes were in fact counseling silence in this matter becomes clearer during the pontificate of Pope St. Gregory the Great. As noted, Lawrence's successor in Milan was Archbishop Constantine. Shortly after his consecration, Constantine found himself deserted by three of his suffragan bishops as well as by the Lombard Queen Theodelinda, all of whom withdrew from communion with him because they believed he had anathematized the Three Chapters. Pope St. Gregory responded by conveying a letter to Constantine to be delivered to Theodelinda, in which the Pope himself vouched for the orthodoxy of the Second Council of Constantinople, as well as of Archbishop Constantine, to whom he urged Theodelinda to return.

Not long afterward, Archbishop Constantine wrote back to Pope St. Gregory to say that he had not in fact delivered the letter to the Queen, since it mentioned the Second Council of Constantinople! Archbishop Constantine wanted to know: Would the Pope agree to send another letter, this one assuring the Queen of his (Constantine's) orthodoxy without making any reference whatever to Constantinople II? This Gregory did, mentioning only the first four ecumenical councils in his next letter. (It does not appear that Gregory denounced Archbishop Constantine as a "schismatic" or "integrist" for declining to deliver the Pope's letter because of its reference to a widely rejected council.)

Further, Pope St. Gregory recommended that Constantine deal with the inhabitants of Brescia (who were demanding that he swear that he had not condemned the Three Chapters) simply by not mentioning Constantinople II at all. Instead, explains Hefele, Constantine ought to "declare to them in a letter that he neither infringed upon the faith of Chalcedon himself in the least degree, nor would receive into his communion anyone who should venture to infringe it; that he condemned all who condemned the Council of Chalcedon, and recognized all who had recognized that." "The Pope, therefore," Hefele points out in conclusion, "not only himself was silent to the Lombardian Queen on the fifth [council], and on the three chapters, but he requested that Constantine also should be silent on the subject, and that he should direct his efforts to one point, 'restoration of union with Rome.'"[381] This prelate, then, was instructed by no less than Pope St. Gregory the Great simply to *remain silent* about the fifth ecumenical council of the Catholic Church. Gregory could see that Archbishop Constantine possessed the Catholic faith; what more was necessary? We have no record of anyone accusing Constantine of having thwarted "the spirit of Constantinople II."

A Catholic has to be free to say of the Second Council of Constantinople what is obvious to anyone who has ever studied it: it did nothing to bring back the Monophysites into the bosom of the Church, and in fact alienated many of them still further. Given the confusing nature of what the Council was attempting to do, orthodox Catholics, for their part, could not help but be perplexed and demoralized by this Council, and for decades afterward whole areas of the West refused to acknowledge it as an ecumenical council at all, convinced that it had in some way repudiated or vitiated the teaching of Chalcedon. Basing ourselves, therefore, on the testimony of human reason, we are surely free to conclude that this council, although it taught nothing certainly erroneous, was an appalling catastrophe that ought never to have been convoked. It is not possible to imagine any grounds on which even the most hardened neo-Catholic could describe this fifth ecumenical council as a boon to the Church.

The example of the Second Council of Constantinople serves to demonstrate not only the confusion that an ecumenical council can introduce into the Church, even without teaching dogmatic error, but also that the entire life of the Church need not be organized around the decrees of the most recent council. Yet today, after nearly forty years of bitter postconciliar experience, we still hear exhortations that the entire life of the Church must be reordered in conformity with Vatican II's decrees, that all the Church's activity must take place in light of "the Council." Following Constantinople II, on the other hand,

---

[381]Ibid., p. 363.

when churchmen could see that the most recent council had caused only division, confusion, and strife, we hear no such exhortations. As we have shown, Pope St. Gregory the Great actually counseled a bishop troubled by the Council to remain silent on the matter, holding fast to the Catholic faith as expounded at the Council of Chalcedon. Gregory and the other Popes of the sixth and seventh centuries were intelligent enough to see that an obsessive emphasis on "the Council" would have perpetuated schism and continued to demoralize the orthodox party. Whenever possible, then, Church leaders simply ignored it. "Subsequent leaders of the western churches," writes historian Judith Herrin, "often excused Pope Vigilius's apparent support for the council and *consigned its decisions to oblivion*."[382]

If Pope St. Gregory could advise silence about the fifth ecumenical council, it cannot be inherently unlawful to advise a similar approach to an ambiguous council of our own time. Certainly it was legitimately convoked, and holds the status of an ecumenical council. Everyone recognizes that. But if it has introduced only confusion and discord, why insist on treating it as an idol, emphasizing it to the exclusion of all else, when history proves such an attitude to be neither necessary nor desirable?

In the same way, without denying the validity of the new Mass, we may legitimately hope and pray that the "renewal of the liturgy" is forgotten, and that the traditional Roman rite of Mass returns to preeminence in the Church. This, too, is far from an historical impossibility. As Msgr. Gamber has observed:

> All this, of course, has happened before! Levitin-Krasnov tells us about a similar attempt at reform in the Russian Orthodox Church during the years following the October Revolution. At that time, different attempts were made to no longer celebrate within the sanctum of the altar room, but instead in the center

---

[382]Judith Herrin, *The Formation of Christendom* (Princeton: Princeton University Press, 1987), p. 124. Herrin adds that Pope Gregory the Great "on occasion advised acceptance of the first four ecumenical councils only." Ibid.

of the Church. The liturgy was translated into modern
Russian, and prayers were supplemented by using parts from
other liturgies. The private prayers of the priest were recited
publicly so that the faithful could hear them. The singing of
church hymns by the faithful was introduced to replace the
traditional chants sung by the choir, and so on and so forth.
The liturgical crisis in Russia has now passed and the
traditional forms of liturgy have been restored.[383]

Why not also in the Holy Catholic Church? Is it really
impossible for Catholics to admit that the conciliar *aggiornamento*
is a wreck that should be allowed to collapse of its own weight?
Can the victims of Vatican II not move on to the next chapter in
the Church's history, as did the victims of Constantinople II?
Can we not simply *stop talking* about the Second Vatican
Council?

Meanwhile, the continued neo-Catholic pursuit of "the
Church envisioned by the Council" and the "authentic reform of
the liturgy" only demonstrates that unless this incessant
recourse to the Council's ever-elusive "true intention" is finally
abandoned, the postconciliar crisis will not end. Turbulent
demands for "renewal" by neo-modernists on the one hand, and
for "authentic renewal" by neo-Catholics on the other, will
continue to swirl about the Council's problematical documents,
so long as they continue to serve as a warrant for the perpetual
reformist mentality that Vatican II unleashed upon the Church.

---

[383]Gamber, *Reform of the Roman Liturgy,* pp. 93-94.

# Chapter 13

# *Dominus Iesus*:
# An Ambiguous Answer to Heresy

The publication of Cardinal Ratzinger's *Dominus Iesus* (DI) on September 5, 2000, is one of the most important events in the history of the postconciliar Church, although not for the reasons neo-Catholics suggest. True to neo-Catholic form, *The Wanderer* heaped nearly hysterical praise upon the document, pronouncing it "a new Syllabus of Errors." In this we see yet another self-contradiction in neo-Catholic thought. As we discussed in Chapter 11, certain neo-Catholics openly dismiss the *Syllabus* as outmoded. In Chapter 5 we observed that other neo-Catholics have argued that the reason the Vatican no longer issues "harsh" condemnations of error like those found in the *Syllabus* is that in "modern" circumstances they would only be counterproductive, perhaps even leading to a schism, which John Paul II is trying to avoid by refraining from strict measures for the universal Church. Yet when the neo-Catholics perceive in DI what they believe to be a return to the firmness of preconciliar condemnations of error, they suddenly reverse position and joyfully proclaim the arrival of a new *Syllabus*. They thus reveal their implicit recognition that the Church desperately *needs* a new *Syllabus*, along with a general restoration of her former rigor in exposing and condemning errors against the Faith.

Is DI a roadmap out of the postconciliar crisis? Is it, like the *Syllabus*, a major corrective measure that will shore up Catholic orthodoxy in a time of peril to the Faith? Unfortunately, the suggestion that DI is a new *Syllabus* does not correspond to reality. As we showed in Chapter 11, it is none other than DI's principal author, Cardinal Ratzinger, who has assured us that "there can be no return to the *Syllabus*" and that the documents of Vatican II are "a countersyllabus," whose aim is to attempt "an official reconciliation" with an era whose institutions are now founded on the very errors the *Syllabus* condemns. To expect anything like a new *Syllabus* from the current Vatican apparatus is to indulge in fantasy.

To begin with, Catholics have been perplexed by DI's use of the ancient Nicene-Constantinopolitan Creed (381), which refers to the procession of the Holy Spirit from the Father (see DI 1). Although there is obviously nothing wrong with this early creed *per se*, the Council of Constantinople was merely concerned with affirming the divinity of the Holy Spirit against the Pneumatomachians, who denied it. (It should be mentioned, however, that the *filioque* does appear in the version of the Nicene-Constantinopolitan Creed by Dionysius Exiguus.) Subsequent councils, however, (Lyons and Florence) explicitly affirmed the *filioque* (the procession of the Holy Spirit from the Father and the Son together) as a *de fide* teaching of the Church against the Greek schismatics. As the Council of Lyons declared: "In faithful and devout profession, we declare that the Holy Spirit proceeds eternally from the Father *and* the Son, not as from two beginnings but from one beginning, not from two breathings, but from one breathing. The most Holy Roman Church, the mother and teacher of all the faithful, has up to this time professed, preached and taught this; this she firmly holds, preaches, declares and teaches; the unchangeable and true opinion of the orthodox Fathers and Doctors, Latin *as well as Greek*, holds this."[384]

---

[384]DZ, 460.

But in DI, the *filioque* is suddenly dropped in favor of a fourth-century creed that did not address that theological question. So much for the "development of doctrine" that neo-Catholics are always citing! Neo-Catholics are constantly wavering between "development of doctrine" and "return to antiquity" in defending the current unexampled novelties (which follow neither principle).

At any rate, the pointed omission of the *filioque* from DI is curious in a document promulgated to defend the salvific role of the Son. Why diminish the Catholic teaching about the Son even slightly by omitting the *filioque*? Evidently, the Vatican did not wish to offend present-day Greek schismatics by being as forthright as the Council of Lyons about what the Catholic Church teaches. "Ecumenism" strikes again.

Now, it cannot be denied that DI refutes some very basic errors against the Faith: that Christ is not the sole mediator between God and man, but only one of many faces of the divine Logos; that His revelation is not complete and definitive; that there is an economy of salvation outside the Word Incarnate; that the salvific action of the Word is separable from the human nature of Christ; that one religion is as good as another. But while it is certainly a good thing to refute such errors, they are so obvious as to be little more than theological straw men. No self-respecting neo-modernist of the Third Millennium would traffic in such crudities.

DI delivers whopping roundhouse blows at these straw men, but nary a jab at the most subtle error in postconciliar thinking: not that all religions are equal, but rather that all religions are *good enough* for salvation, given the proposed action of God's grace through all religions. Instead of refuting that proposition, which renders actual membership in the Catholic Church irrelevant to salvation, DI announces the commencement of a vast theological project to demonstrate that "other religions" (i.e., all religions) participate, more or less, in the one mediation of Christ, *whether or not their followers know it*:

> Bearing in mind this article of faith [the unique mediation of Christ], theology today, in its reflection on the existence of *other religious experiences and on their meaning in God's salvific*

*plan*, is invited to explore *if and in what way the historical figures and positive elements of these religions may fall within the divine plan of salvation.* In this undertaking, theological research has a vast field of work under the guidance of the Church's Magisterium. The Second Vatican Council, in fact, has stated that "the unique mediation of the Redeemer does not exclude, but rather gives rise, to a manifold cooperation which is but a participation in this one source." The content of this participated mediation should be explored more deeply, but...those solutions that propose a salvific action of God beyond the unique mediation of Christ would be contrary to Christian and Catholic faith.

Accepting Cardinal Ratzinger's invitation, the neo-modernists can now recycle their pan-religious heresies by the simple expedient of incorporating the phrase "participation in the unique mediation of Christ," or something equivalent. Thus, the religion of Islam, which explicitly *rejects* the unique mediation of Christ, could be said to *participate* in that mediation to the extent that it contains what DI calls "positive elements." But how is the invited thesis different from Karl Rahner's "anonymous Christianity"? Some may see in this aspect of DI what lawyers call a distinction without a difference.

Rahner held that, thanks to "modern theological developments," the Christian "will regard non-Christians...*not as having no part in Christianity, but rather as anonymous Christians, who do not realize what they truly are in virtue of grace in the depths of their own consciences; what they are, namely, in virtue of something that they achieve at a level which is perhaps wholly unadduced, but is nonetheless real....*"[385] Rahner accordingly viewed missionary work not as a process of making converts who are delivered from Original Sin and the snares of the devil through the sanctifying grace of Holy Baptism, but rather of presenting to "anonymous Christians"

---

[385]Karl Rahner, *The Content of Faith* (New York: Cross Road, 1999), pp. 393; excerpting from *Theological Investigations* X, trans. David Bourke (New York: Herder and Herder, 1973), pp. 14-24.

that which *they already possess*: "[W]hen the Christian preaches Christianity to the 'non-Christian,' he will take as his starting point not so much the basic attitude of wanting to make the other something which he simply has not been hitherto. Rather he will attempt to *bring him to himself....* God, in his grace, and because of his will to save all human beings universally, has already long before *offered* [Rahner's emphasis] *the reality of Christianity in its truest and deepest essence* to the individual, and...it is perfectly possible, *and even probable,* that the individual *has already freely accepted this reality* without consciously adverting to it."[386]

Note well: Rahner claims it is probable that Christianity in "its truest and deepest essence" is present in non-Christians *without baptism, without any adherence to Christian doctrine, and without even an explicit act of faith in Christ.* Obviously, this notion spells the death of the missions, no matter what one may say to the contrary. Fr. Giovanbattista Mondin, the vice rector of the Pontifical Urban University, observed that "[w]hat is taking place today is actually a 'demissionization' of the Catholic Church." He noted that the "suicide of the missions" began at the end of the 1960s, a development he attributes to Rahner's "anonymous Christianity" and "the salvific function of the non-Christian religions."[387]

Is DI inviting theologians to attempt a vindication of Rahner's view that non-Christian religions are really in some measure *Christian* religions that can, accordingly, suffice unto salvation? If so, *what is this point of this exercise?* If the Church has never taught this thesis in 2,000 years, if the so-called "participation" of non-Christian religions in the mediation of Christ has not already been revealed by God, how could the Church now adopt this novelty as binding Catholic doctrine?

We are saved from disaster by the single word "*if*" in Cardinal Ratzinger's phrase "*if* and in what way the historical figures and positive elements of these religions may fall within the divine plan of salvation." Since DI identifies this subject as a matter of free debate, we believe it is our right and duty to say

---

[386]Ibid., p. 399.
[387]*Fatima Crusader,* issue 29 (1992), p. 22.

that it would be a serious mistake to encourage the notion that false religions and their false prophets can be said to "participate," even partially, in the mediation of Christ.

Meanwhile, however, what, if anything, does DI do to arrest "the suicide of the missions"? The good news is that DI does affirm, after a long silence on the matter, that objectively speaking the followers of other religions "are in a gravely deficient situation in comparison with those who, in the Church, have the fullness of the means of salvation" (DI 22). But by the time DI is through *praising* other religions, one wonders why anyone should be very concerned about the "gravely deficient" situation of their adherents, let alone risk his life as a missionary to bring about their conversion to Catholicism. The very phrase *"fullness* of the means of salvation" suggests, at least to us, that non-Christian religions already possess the means of salvation, even if they are not as "full" as those possessed by the Catholic Church. So far as we can see, DI does nothing to negate this impression.

Concerning what it calls the "sacred books of other religions," DI 8 asserts that "it must be recognized that there are some elements in these texts which may be *de facto* instruments by which *countless people throughout the centuries have been and still are able today to nourish and maintain their life-relationship with God.*" DI 8 also declares: "Nevertheless, God, who desires to call all peoples to himself in Christ and to communicate to them the fullness of his revelation and love, does not fail to make himself present in many ways, not only to individuals, but also to entire peoples through *their spiritual riches, of which their religions are the main and essential expression,* even when they contain gaps, insufficiencies and errors. Therefore, the sacred books of other religions, which *in actual fact direct and nourish the existence of their followers,* receive from the mystery of Christ *the elements of goodness and grace* which they contain" (internal quotations omitted).

DI 10 likewise speaks of "the manifold gifts—especially the spiritual treasures—that God has bestowed on every people"; while DI 22 states: "Certainly, the various religious traditions contain and offer religious elements which come from God, and which are part of what 'the Spirit brings about in human hearts and in the history of peoples, in cultures, *and religions.'"*

If "other religions" (without distinction) all contain spiritual riches and treasures bestowed by God as part of what "the Spirit brings about in human hearts"; and if the "sacred books of other religions" (also without distinction) all contain "elements of goodness and grace" from Christ that sustain "countless people" in a "life-relationship with God," then what becomes of the "gravely deficient" situation of Muslims, Hindus and so forth? Further, is there any substantial difference between DI's praise for the "positive elements and historical figures" of other religions and what Pius XI in *Mortalium Animos* condemned as "that *false opinion* which considers all religions to be more or less good and praiseworthy, since they all in different ways manifest and signify that sense which is inborn in us all, and by which we are led to God and to the obedient acknowledgment of His rule"? (We recall here that Pius XI condemned this false opinion as to nominally Christian sects; all the more would it apply to non-Christian sects.)

Moreover, how does one reconcile DI's esteem for the value of "other religions" (again, without distinction) with two propositions condemned in the *Syllabus:*

In the worship of any religion whatever, men can find their way to eternal salvation, and can attain salvation (Proposition 16).

We must have at least good hope concerning the salvation of all those who in no wise are in the true Church of Christ (Proposition 17).

Does DI in its teaching on the value of other religions deny either of these propositions, or does it not tend to favor them, even if it does speak of a "grave deficiency" in the same religions it describes as possessing riches and treasures bestowed by God?

It is impossible to ignore the stark contrast between DI's praise for the riches and treasures of other religions and the critical view of all the preconciliar popes, as exemplified by the teaching of Blessed Pius IX in his encyclical *Quanto conficiamur moerore*. While making due allowance for the unknowable subjective state of the invincibly ignorant, the Pope makes it perfectly clear that there is no prospect of salvation in the "positive elements" of false religions or in their "historical figures," who are nothing but false prophets:

> Here, too, our beloved sons and venerable brothers, it is again necessary to mention and censure *a very grave error* entrapping some Catholics who believe that *it is possible to arrive at eternal salvation although living in error and alienated from the true faith and Catholic unity.* Such belief is *certainly opposed to Catholic teaching.* There are, of course, those who are struggling with invincible ignorance about our most holy religion. Sincerely observing the natural law and its precepts inscribed by God on all hearts and ready to obey God, they live honest lives and are able to attain eternal life by the efficacious virtue of divine light and grace. Because God knows, searches and clearly understands the minds, hearts, thoughts, and nature of all, his supreme kindness and clemency do not permit anyone at all who is not guilty of deliberate sin to suffer eternal punishments.
>
> Also well known is the Catholic teaching that no one can be saved outside the Catholic Church. Eternal salvation cannot be obtained by those who oppose the authority and statements of the same Church and are stubbornly separated from the unity of the Church and also from the successor of Peter, the Roman Pontiff, to whom "the custody of the vineyard has been committed by the Savior." The words of Christ are clear enough: "If he refuses to listen even to the Church, let him be to you a Gentile and a tax collector"; "He who hears you hears me, and he who rejects you, rejects me, and he who rejects me, rejects him who sent me"; "He who does not believe will be condemned"; "He who does not believe is already condemned"; "He who is not with me is against me, and he who does not gather with me scatters." The Apostle Paul says that such persons are "perverted and self-condemned"; the Prince of the Apostles calls them "false teachers...who will

secretly bring in destructive heresies, even denying the Master...bringing upon themselves swift destruction."

It must be said that DI's generous praise for the "positive elements" of "other religions" — all of them! — is not shown by DI to have any roots in the Church's traditional teaching. Not one of the sources cited in support of this optimism is older than the Second Vatican Council. The amazing thing is the emergence of such optimism at a time when, as Pope Pius XII declared even before the worldwide legalization of abortion, "the wickedness of perverse men has reached a degree of impiety that is *unbelievable and absolutely unknown in other times."*[388]

We do not deny that whatever limited truth there is in false religions comes from God, who is the ultimate source of all truth. The problem arises, we believe, with DI's invitation to an optimism which, with Rahner, would view virtually any religion that teaches something true as an adequate (if only barely so) vehicle of salvation—by "participation" in the one mediation of Christ. That concern does not appear to us to be allayed by DI's declaration that the Church's mission is "announcing the necessity of conversion to Jesus Christ and of adherence to the Church through Baptism and the other sacraments, in order to *participate fully* in communion with God, the Father, Son and Holy Spirit" (DI 22). Is the Church still in the business of saving souls from hell, or does she now offer only *"full* participation" in "communion with God"?

All told, it appears to us that DI forcefully restates, but then substantially undermines, three neglected truths of the Faith:

First, DI affirms the distinction between the saving supernatural virtue of theological faith in our religion and mere natural belief in "other religions" (DI 7), but then asserts a "life relationship with God" which is "nourished" in "countless people throughout the centuries" by the "elements of grace and goodness" in the "sacred books of *other religions"* (DI 8, 12, 21).

Second, DI affirms that only the Old and New Testaments can be considered divinely inspired texts (DI 8), but then asserts that the "elements of *grace* and goodness" in the "sacred books"

---

[388]Letter of February 11, 1949.

of other religions come from "the Mystery of Christ" and are part of what *"the Spirit brings about in human hearts* and in the history of peoples, in cultures, and *religions"* (DI 8, 21).

Third, DI notes the "gravely deficient" condition of the followers of other religions (DI 22), but then praises the spiritual "riches" and "treasures" to be found in the religions of "every people" (DI 8, 10), and the elements of grace and goodness in their sacred books, by which the aforesaid "countless people throughout the centuries" are able to "maintain their life-relationship with God."

We cannot see how the followers of other religions would have any idea from reading DI as a whole that they (like we) are objectively in need of the helps that only the Catholic Church provides in order to save their souls from hell. The overall impression is quite to the contrary. We recall that Blessed Pius IX (in *Singulari Quadem*) declared the question of the salvation of those objectively outside the Catholic Church a matter so fraught with danger that it ought not to be pursued ("It is unlawful to proceed further in inquiry," he said). But the great research project that Ratzinger outlines for theologians in DI – namely, if and in what way the "historical figures and positive elements" of other religions "may fall within the divine plan of salvation" – not only disregards this papal warning, but also raises fairly serious questions. Is it conceivable that the "spiritual treasures" of other religions could "fall within the divine plan of salvation" in such a way as to provide good assurance of the salvation of their adherents? If so, then the Catholic Church serves no indispensably salvific purpose, particularly if one can be saved though the "positive elements" of a religion that allows its members to give free rein to libertinism and license. On the other hand, if, in spite of their "spiritual treasures," the various religions nevertheless cannot provide sufficient means of salvation, then, again, what is the point of attempting a theological demonstration of their *insufficient* "participation" in Christ's mediation? With the unceasing missionary work of countless generations of martyrs and saints a dramatic testimony against this novel view (why would these heroes have wasted their time and even risked their lives?), is it not better to restate without ambiguity the Church's traditional position, rather than give a false sense of security to people at risk of losing their souls?

The traditional tone of pessimism regarding the prospects of eternal bliss for those objectively outside the Catholic Church is hardly a dispensable adjunct of the Catholic faith; our need for the sacraments in order to keep our souls in a state of sanctifying grace, and hence pleasing to God, is a fundamental truth of our religion. We also acknowledge that without the aid of the sacraments it is much more difficult to remain in the state of grace. Even the saints, the Church's holiest members, were terrified of hell and the prospect that they themselves might merit its punishments.[389] Thus the conclusion is inescapable that in a state of nature, so to speak, in which a man has embraced either a false religion or none at all, he is at much greater risk of being damned. Why not say so, as a matter of prudence and honesty? And if this conclusion is not true – if in fact one may just as easily cling to the state of grace in a state of nature – then why be a Catholic? Is not the principal reason for membership in the Church, namely, having recourse to the means by which God purifies souls in order that they might spend eternity with Him, thereby fatally vitiated?

Characteristic of the confusion in the Church since Vatican II is that Ratzinger himself, in 1966, clearly recognized both the novelty and the danger of this kind of optimism:

In the meantime, a teaching had gained more and more acceptance, although it was previously regarded as only a marginal thesis, namely, that God wills and is able to save outside the Church, though, in the end, not without her. Thereby, an optimistic understanding of the world religions was recently brought forth, the consideration of which once again makes clear that not all of the favorite thoughts of modern theology are at the same time biblically sound. For if anything may be called foreign, yes, even opposed to Sacred Scripture, then it is the current optimism with regard to the

[389]Cf. Fr. Martin von Cochem, O.S.F.C., *The Four Last Things* (New York: Benziger Brothers, 1900), p. 175.

world religions which, in fact, conceives these religions as means of salvation, a view which can hardly be reconciled with their standing in biblical perspective.[390]

Ratzinger's misgivings were well-founded. A year before the publication of DI, neo-Catholic author Stratford Caldecott revealed where such thinking inevitably led:

> As the Church teaches, a member of another religion may be saved without hearing of Christ, and without converting. At the same time we are obliged by our fidelity to Christ and our love to proclaim Christianity to all. And once we have done so, the other may find himself in a radically new situation. He may be at a stage where he could only understand conversion to Christianity as a betrayal of the truth he knows. But if he is at the point where he could integrate the truth he knows with the truth that is proclaimed to him, and chooses not to; if his rejection of our words is in any way due to his own closure to truth, rather than to our own sins and inadequacy; then his own religion is no longer such a safe refuge, and his salvation is no longer so certain. It is God who obliges us to put him into this state of spiritual danger, for the sake of his soul and our own.[391]

This is where the conciliar and postconciliar optimism regarding other religions ultimately takes us. Pause for a moment to consider the radicalism of what Caldecott is saying, bearing in mind that this is a neo-Catholic, rather than a professed liberal, who is speaking. According to Caldecott, missionary activity, though binding on us by Christ's command, may well place souls in spiritual danger, in comparison with

---

[390]*Die letzte Sitzungsperiode des Konzils* (Cologne, 1966), p. 60; cited in Fr. Johannes Dörmann, *Pope John Paul II's Theological Journey to the Prayer Meeting of Religions in Assisi*, Part I: *From the Second Vatican Council to the Papal Elections* (Kansas City, MO: Angelus Press, 1994), p. 29.

[391]Stratford Caldecott, "Christianity and Other Religions," *The Sower*, September 1999.

their spiritual "safety" (through blissful ignorance) in other religions. Our Lord's promise that "ye shall know the truth and the *truth* shall set you free" is thus negated, for whether he knows it or not, Caldecott implicitly presumes (in keeping with the new optimism) that those who do *not* know the truth are already free. Although Caldecott and like-minded neo-Catholic commentators commend missionary activity because Christ tells us it is a good work, according to their own logic it no longer makes much sense, and might actually be dangerous. For if followers of other religions will acquire the truth in the next life anyway, no one is doing them a favor by burdening them with the truth and its many obligations during this life. That is the conclusion Caldecott demonstrates (unwittingly or not) in an article filled with conciliar and postconciliar references. Such is the confidence of the postconciliar establishment in the salvific power of the "positive elements" of other religions – a confidence that the *Syllabus* of Pope Blessed Pius IX forbade us to have even about Protestants and schismatics, let alone non-Christians. What more can one say?

In light of all this, it should come as no surprise that while DI is subtitled "On the Unicity and *Salvific* Universality of Jesus Christ," not once does the main text of the document mention what it is that the Savior saves us *from*. Salvation from hell is mentioned only in footnote 45. To us, this says a great deal. In DI, as in the postconciliar Church at large, hell has become a mere footnote to the Church's teaching; yet the threat of hell has never loomed larger in human history.[392]

While Cardinal Ratzinger claims "there can be no return to the *Syllabus*," is it unreasonable to suggest that a return to the kind of teaching represented by Blessed Pius IX is exactly what the Church needs at a time of unparalleled worldwide depravity? Can even the neo-Catholics seriously contend that Blessed Pius IX or St. Pius X, looking at the world today, would issue an invitation to theologians to demonstrate exactly how "the historical figures and positive elements" of Islam,

---

[392]While DI begins with a citation to Mark 16:15-16—"He who believes and is baptized will be saved; he who does not believe will be condemned"—the verse is never discussed or even mentioned again.

Hinduism, Buddhism and Zoroastrianism "may fall within the divine plan of salvation" or that such Popes would be praising the "riches" and "treasures" of pagan religions and their adherents' "life-relationship with God"?

Unfortunately, DI's approach to the status of Protestants and the Orthodox appears to be as ambiguous as its teaching with respect to non-Christian religions. DI clearly continues along the lines of the same "ecumenical venture" that has led to open repudiation of the preconciliar teaching on the return of the dissidents to the Catholic Church, a development we discussed in Chapter 7.

Here we note first of all that DI contains a number of propositions to which it attaches such admonitions as "must be *firmly believed*" or "must be firmly held." Each of these propositions must indeed be firmly believed and held, for each is a statement of the constant teaching of the Magisterium. One of these is DI 16, which teaches that "the unicity of the Church founded by him must be *firmly believed* as a truth of Catholic faith. Just as there is one Christ, so there exists a single body of Christ, a single Bride of Christ: 'a single Catholic and apostolic Church.'" As far as this goes, DI is a strong reaffirmation of a basic Catholic truth.

DI, however, contains many statements that appear *between* the teachings proposed as binding, including its optimistic statements about other religions. To these statements are attached no admonition requiring an assent of faith.  This omission is consistent with our basic thesis that not a single one of the theological novelties of the past forty years has ever been imposed upon the faithful as Catholic doctrine. It is here, in what could be called the theological interstices of DI, that we encounter what we believe is an *attempt* by Cardinal Ratzinger to demonstrate how the novel, optimistic, "pastoral" formulations of Vatican II can be harmonized with the preconciliar teaching on the identity between the Mystical Body of Christ and the Roman Catholic Church, and the return to the one true Church by those outside her as the *only* means of achieving true Christian unity.

As our brief discussion of DI's teaching on non-Christian religions would suggest, what is said in the interstices of DI tends to undermine what is said in its principal headings—in much the same fashion as the documents of Vatican II themselves do. In particular, the just-quoted teaching of DI 16 on the unicity of the Church, which the faithful are instructed they must embrace, seems to be undermined by the teaching on the ecclesial status of the Orthodox and Protestant confessions at DI 17, which the faithful are *not* instructed they must embrace. DI 17 teaches as follows:

> Therefore, there exists a single Church of Christ, which subsists in the Catholic Church, governed by the Successor of Peter and by the Bishops in communion with him. The Churches which, while not existing in perfect communion with the Catholic Church, remain united to her by means of the closest bonds, that is, by apostolic succession and a valid Eucharist, are true particular Churches. Therefore, the Church of Christ is present and operative also in these Churches, even though they lack full communion with the Catholic Church, since they do not accept the Catholic doctrine of the Primacy, which, according to the will of God, the Bishop of Rome objectively has and exercises over the entire Church.

Before proposing our concerns, we stress that of course we recognize that, as mere laymen, we have no right to pronounce theological judgments on DI. But DI itself does not deny to the faithful the right to pose questions that clearly arise from DI's obvious effort to integrate the ambiguous "pastoral" formulations of Vatican II with the far more precise teaching of the preconciliar Popes. We pose those questions here, and submit ourselves to the judgment of the Church, should it ever be rendered.

By way of background on this issue, we note that when Cardinal Ratzinger was still Father Ratzinger, a former *peritus* at the Council, he provided in his *Theological Highlights of Vatican II* the following explanation of the Council's teaching on Christian unity and Church membership:

The new text describes the relationship between the Church and non-Catholic Christians without speaking of "membership." By *shedding this terminological armor,* the text acquired a much wider scope.... The Catholic has to recognize that his own Church is not yet prepared to accept the phenomenon of multiplicity in unity; *he must orient himself toward this reality....* Meantime *the Catholic Church has no right to absorb the other Churches.* The Church has not yet prepared for them a place of their own, but this they are legitimately entitled to.... A basic unity — of Churches that remain Churches, yet become one Church — *must replace the idea of conversion,* even though conversion retains its meaningfulness for those in conscience motivated to seek it.[393]

This remarkable text, which Cardinal Ratzinger has never repudiated, declares that the Magisterium can "shed" its own established terminology on membership[394] in the Church, that the Bride of Christ had neglected to "prepare" itself for acceptance of the "reality" of non-Catholic confessions, that organizations indisputably founded by mere men in a rebellion against divine authority have a positive right to exist and be given "a place" by the one true Church, and that Protestants *need not convert to Catholicism* unless they are "motivated" to do so. In all candor, we do not see how Father Ratzinger's opinions here could have avoided censure during the reign of any preconciliar Pope.

---

[393]Joseph Ratzinger, *Theological Highlights of Vatican II* (New York: Paulist Press, 1966), pp. 61, 68.

[394]Pius XI, *Mortalium Animos*: "[I]t were foolish and out of place to say that the mystical body is made up of *members* which are disunited and scattered abroad: whosoever therefore is not united with the body is *no member* of it, neither is he in communion with Christ its head"; Pius XII, *Mystici Corporis*: "Actually *only* those are to be included as *members* of the Church who have been baptized and profess the true faith, and who have not been so unfortunate as to separate themselves from the unity of the Body, or been excluded by legitimate authority for grave faults committed."

As we have already demonstrated abundantly, these opinions are quite in line with the current thinking of Cardinal Ratzinger's fellow German bishop, Cardinal Walter Kasper, the new head of the Pontifical Council for Christian Unity. We have noted that in the Italian journal *Adista*, Kasper declared that "today we no longer understand ecumenism in the sense of a return, by which the others would 'be converted' and return to being 'catholics.' This was expressly abandoned by Vatican II."[395] Any Catholic should be horrified to see the head of a pontifical council ostensibly devoted to "Christian unity" placing contemptuous quotation marks around the very words *converted* and *Catholics*. According to Cardinal Kasper, Vatican II "abandoned" what the Holy Office in 1949 described as "the teachings of the encyclicals of the Roman Pontiffs on the return of the dissidents to the one true Church" and "the Catholic truth regarding...the only true union by the return of the dissidents to the one true Church."

And yet the context of Kasper's remarks in *Adista* was a *defense* of DI against Protestant critics! Nor did Cardinal Ratzinger offer any correction of Kasper's opinion, which Kasper expressed within days of his elevation to the rank of cardinal. These facts do not inspire confidence that DI represents a major course correction in the Church's postconciliar drift from her prior clarity of teaching about the condition of the dissidents who need to return to the one true Church.

Before Vatican II, it was perfectly obvious that there could never be Christian unity unless the Orthodox and the Protestants assented to every single point of Catholic doctrine, thus *becoming Catholics* themselves. It is just as obvious that anyone who prescinds from even the least point of Catholic doctrine can never be united with us. As Pope Leo XIII taught in *Satis Cognitum*: "The practice of the Church has always been the same, as is shown by the unanimous teaching of the Fathers, who were wont to hold as outside Catholic communion, and alien to the Church, whoever would recede *in the least degree*

---

[395]See footnote 231.

from *any* point of doctrine proposed by her authoritative Magisterium."

Equally obvious is that to embrace the whole of Catholic doctrine without reservation is necessarily to turn away from the human institutions in which that doctrine was more or less corrupted, and to turn instead toward the Catholic Church, in which the Deposit of the Faith has always been preserved undefiled. That is what *conversion* means. Even in today's ecumenical confusion, we still hear about the "conversion stories" of ex-Protestants.

How, for example, could any Lutheran come to an acceptance of the whole of Catholic teaching under the influence of God's grace, yet continue to insist upon belonging to an organization named after a psychotic, foul-mouthed, womanizing drunkard of a monk, who ran off and married a nun, indeed the greatest arch-heretic in Church history, who referred to the Vicar of Christ as an "ass-head"? What could the husk of Luther's decrepit human organization possibly offer any Lutheran that is not found in superabundance in the Roman Catholic Church? Could anyone who would cling to the notion of belonging to Luther's version of a church ever be in union with us? On the other hand, if the Lutherans, by some miracle of grace, all suddenly decided to abjure every one of Luther's errors — in which case, why would they wish to be associated any longer with the name of Luther? — the Catholic Church would have no reason, much less a *duty*, to make "a place" for Luther's "church." It would simply cease to exist as a separate organization, the Lutherans having become Catholics. Is this really something that is debatable today? Apparently so.

That Christian unity can somehow be accomplished without all Christians becoming Catholics is one of the Zen-like notions that abound in postconciliar thinking. But not only has Cardinal Ratzinger never retracted Father Ratzinger's opinions, we also now find that they have become Vatican policy at the Pontifical Council for Christian Unity. Nor does it appear that DI in any way reproves Kasper's opinions. To the contrary: in discussing DI with the press, Cardinal Ratzinger affirmed his own support for the novel notion of "reconciled diversity" that we discussed earlier:

> **Question**: So then, after the publication of your document, is the ecumenical formula of "reconciled diversity" still valid?

> **Ratzinger**: *I accept the concept of a reconciled diversity,* if it does not mean equality of content and the elimination of the question of truth so that we could consider ourselves one, even if we believe and teach different things. To my mind this concept is used well, if it says that, *despite our differences,* which do not allow us to regard ourselves as mere fragments of a Church of Jesus Christ that does not exist in reality, *we meet in the peace of Christ and are reconciled to one another,* that is, we recognize our division as contradicting the Lord's will and this sorrow spurs us *to seek unity* and to pray to him in the knowledge that we all need his love.[396]

Notice that Ratzinger acknowledges that we could not consider ourselves one with Protestants unless we all believed the same things. But in the meantime he proposes that "despite our differences" we can all be "reconciled to one another" as we "seek unity." Ratzinger does not explain—because quite obviously he *cannot* explain—how we can ever "find" unity with Protestants without their return to the one true Church. Nor does he explain what it is that Catholics are "seeking" in terms of "unity," given that they already have the true Faith in the unity of the one true Church. Perhaps this is why Ratzinger has declared that "for the moment, I wouldn't dare venture to suggest any concrete realization, possible or imaginable, of this future Church. We are at an intermediate stage of unity in diversity."

Thus, according to Cardinal Kasper and (it would appear) Cardinal Ratzinger, there are no longer any dissidents who must return to the one true Church, but only "Christians" engaged in a joint ecumenical "search for unity." The notion that the conversion and return of non-Catholics to the Catholic Church has suddenly been replaced by some other (as yet undefined)

---

[396]*Frankfurter Allgemeine*, September 22, 2000.

"model" of unity obviously has important implications for our understanding of DI. For if a return to the one true Church is no longer seen as necessary for Christian unity, then it can hardly be necessary for salvation as such. This would mean that the members of heretical and schismatic confessions are presumed by DI to be adequately secured in their salvation, without need of formal membership in the Catholic Church and recourse to her sacraments.

How can DI's apparent abandonment of the return of the dissidents to the one true Church be reconciled with the perennial Magisterium? As recently as 1943, Pope Pius XII declared in his monumental encyclical *Mystici Corporis*:

> They, therefore, walk in the path of dangerous error who believe that they can accept Christ as the Head of the Church, while not adhering loyally to His Vicar on earth. They have taken away the visible head, broken the visible bonds of unity and left the Mystical Body of the Redeemer so obscured and so maimed *that those who are seeking the haven of eternal salvation can neither see it nor find it.*

For this reason, Pius XII implored all who would call themselves Christians "to correspond to the interior movements of grace, and to seek to withdraw from that state in which they cannot be sure of their salvation." Pius XII was warning heretics and schismatics as charitably as he could that they were risking eternal damnation if they did not *correspond to grace* and enter the Catholic Church. Where do we find this teaching affirmed in DI 17 or anywhere else in the document, or, for that matter, anywhere in the vast "ecumenical venture" as a whole? And is it not this very teaching that needs affirming, in view of the moral decrepitude of the Protestant sects?

In short, *what has happened to the Church's perennial concern for the danger to souls lost in error?* Where do we see today anything like the solicitude for souls expressed by Bl. Pius IX in *Quanto Conficiamur Moerore*:

God forbid that the children of the Catholic Church should even in any way be unfriendly to those who are *not at all united to us* by the same bonds of faith and love. On the contrary, let them be eager always to attend to their needs with all the kind services of Christian charity, whether they are poor or sick or suffering any other kind of visitation. First of all, *let them rescue them from the darkness of the errors into which they have unhappily fallen and strive to guide them back to Catholic truth* and to their most loving Mother, who is ever holding out her maternal arms to receive them lovingly back into her fold. Thus, firmly founded in faith, hope, and charity and fruitful in every good work, *they will gain eternal salvation.*

As laymen, we are mystified that today's Vatican apparatus expresses no concern about the eternal fate of souls who, by every objective measure, are in far greater danger of damnation than the comparatively upright Protestants Bl. Pius IX had in view — Protestants, moreover, who would regard their own pro-abortion, pro-"gay rights" descendants as worthy of hellfire.

Turning to the particular language of DI 17 we pose some additional concerns:

First, how is it possible that the schismatic churches of the East can be "united to her [the Catholic Church] by the closest of bonds"? Here it seems we are facing yet another novelty of postconciliar thought: the concept of *unity in schism.* How can this be anything but an oxymoron?

As Pope Leo taught definitively in *Satis Cognitum,* there can be no unity in the Mystical Body without *visible* unity under its earthly head, the Vicar of Christ. This is because the visible and invisible aspects of the Church are as inseparably united as the body and soul in human nature, and the divine and human nature in Christ Himself:

The connection and union of both elements is as absolutely necessary to the true Church as the intimate union of the soul and body is to human nature. The Church is not something dead: it is the body of Christ endowed with supernatural life.... The union consequently of visible and invisible elements because it harmonizes with the natural order and by God's will belongs to the very essence of the Church, must necessarily remain, so long as the Church itself shall endure.... Furthermore, the Son of God decreed that the Church should be His mystical body, with which He should be united as the Head.... As He took to Himself a mortal body, which He gave to suffering and death in order to pay the price of man's redemption, so also He has one mystical body in which and through which He renders men partakers of holiness and of eternal salvation.... Scattered and separated members cannot possibly cohere with the head so as to make one body.

Now the neo-Catholics have no problem affirming this doctrine most strongly when it comes to "extreme traditionalists," including members of the Society of St. Pius X, whom they denounce as "schismatics" with great relish, as they piously intone the necessity of strict communion with Peter for membership in the Church. But when it comes to the Protestants and the Orthodox, who are objectively guilty of both schism and heresy, the neo-Catholics, along with DI, retreat into the ambiguities of Vatican II.

According to DI 17 (which refers to *Lumen Gentium*'s use of the term *subsistit*), the Church of Christ *subsists* in the Catholic Church but is also *"present and operative"* in the Orthodox churches as *true* particular churches, even though they lack "full communion" with the Catholic Church. This goes even beyond what is said of the Protestant sects—i.e., that they possess "ecclesial elements," though they are not proper churches. But as we know, in *Humani Generis* 27, Pope Pius XII taught that the Catholic Church and the Mystical Body of Christ are identical: "Some say they are not bound by the doctrine, explained in Our Encyclical Letter of a few years ago,[397] and based on the Sources of *Revelation*, which teaches that *the Mystical Body of Christ and the Roman Catholic Church are one and the same thing* [quae quidem docet corpus Christi mysticum et Ecclesiam Catholicam Romanam unum idemque esse]."

---

[397] That is, *Mystici Corporis*.

This leads to further questions: If the Church of Christ can *subsist* in the Catholic Church while also being *present and operative* in Orthodox churches, does this not mean that the Church of Christ is an entity greater in scope than the Roman Catholic Church, and therefore not identical to it as Pius XII taught? If the Church of Christ can be present and operative in the Orthodox churches *at the same time* the Orthodox churches lack communion with the *Catholic* Church, then how can the Church of Christ and the Catholic Church be one and the same thing?

For the past thirty-five years, traditionalists have been claiming that the term "subsists" was inserted by the conciliar liberals to imply that the Church of Christ is "larger" than, and thus not identical to, the Roman Catholic Church, whereas our neo-Catholic brethren insisted that "subsists" was merely a more powerful way of expressing that the Church of Christ *is* the Roman Catholic Church. Well, it appears that at least as far as the principal author of DI is concerned, we were right and they were wrong. In an extensive interview in the German newspaper *Frankfurter Allgemeine* following publication of DI, Cardinal Ratzinger addressed various non-Catholic objections to DI's teaching on the nature of the Church. Here is what the Cardinal said about the Council's use of the term *subsistit*:

> When the Council Fathers replaced the word "is" with the word "subsistit," they did so for a very precise reason. The concept expressed by "is" (to be) is far broader than that expressed by "to subsist." "To subsist" is a very precise way of being, that is, to be as a subject, which exists in itself. Thus the Council Fathers meant to say that *the being of the Church as such is a broader entity than the Roman Catholic Church*, but within the latter it acquires, in an incomparable way, the character of a true and proper subject.[398]

---

[398]*L'Osservatore Romano*, Italian edition, October 8, 2000, p. 4: "Quando i Padri conciliar sostituirono la parola 'è' con la parola 'subsistit' lo fecera con un scopo ben preciso. Il concetto espresso da 'è' (essere) è piu ampio di quello espresso da 'sussistere.' 'Sussitere' è un modo ben preciso di essere, ossia essere come soggeto che esiste in

If the Mystical Body of Christ and the Roman Catholic Church are one and the same thing, then what exactly is this

---

sé. I Padri conciliari dunque intendevano dire che l'essere dlla Chiesa in quanto tale è un entità piu ampia dell Chiesa cattolica romana."

The L'Osservatore translation, however, curiously omits several key words from the Cardinal's remarks to Frankfurter Allgemeine. The original German reads, "...die Konzilsväter das *von Pius XII gebrauchte* Wort 'ist' durch 'subsistit' ersetzten" — literally, "...the Council Fathers replaced the word 'is,' *used by Pius XII,* with 'subsistit.'" This apparently deliberate omission is of great importance. L'Osservatore's translation makes it appear that the word "is," as in the Mystical Body of Christ *is* the Catholic Church, was simply a way of speaking that had somehow become part of the Church's intellectual milieu. But the Cardinal's German words reveal an acknowledgment that the use of the word "is" in this context *can be traced directly to a pope,* and a recent one at that: Pius XII. Excising these words obscures the degree of novelty contained in Ratzinger's position.

The L'Osservatore translation is also deficient in another regard: In the last sentence of this passage, the original German reads, "So wollten die Väter sagen: Das Sein der Kirche als solches *reicht viel weiter* als die römisch-katholische Kirche," — literally, "Thus the Fathers meant to say: the being of the Church as such *extends much further* than the Roman Catholic Church." The L'Osservatore translation, above, which translates this phrase to say that "the being of the Church as such is a broader entity than the Roman Catholic Church," once again plays down the radical nature of what Ratzinger is saying. "Extends much further" is a fairly startling statement, certainly more troubling than the admittedly problematic "is a broader entity."

The entire passage in the original German reads: "Als die Konzilsväter das von Pius XII gebrauchte Wort 'ist' durch 'subsistit' ersetzten, hatte dies einen sehr genauen Sinn. Der Begriff 'ist' (sein) ist weiter als der Begriff 'subsistieren.' 'Subsistieren' ist eine bestimmte Weise des Seins, nämlich Sein als eigenes in sich stehendes Subjekt. So wollten die Väter sagen: Das Sein der Kirche als solches reicht viel weiter als die römisch-katholische Kirche, aber in ihr hat sie in einzigartiger Weise den Charakter eines eigenen Subjekts." *Frankfurter Allgemeine,* September 22, 2000.

"Church of Christ" whose "being as such is a broader entity than the Roman Catholic Church," and which subsists in the Roman Catholic Church while also being present and operative in the Orthodox churches? How can there be an ecclesial entity broader than the Mystical Body itself? As Catholic laymen who believe they understand their Faith, we do not see how Cardinal Ratzinger's opinion can be reconciled with the teaching of Pius XII; and we also believe we have the right to ask how it *can* be reconciled.

It might be argued that what Ratzinger means to teach is that the Church of Christ is identical to the Mystical Body, and that the Mystical Body (being identical to the Church of Christ) subsists in the Catholic Church. But if the Church of Christ is identical to the Mystical Body, and if Pius XII taught that the *Roman Catholic Church* is identical to the Mystical Body, then the Church of Christ and the Roman Catholic Church must likewise be identical, since if A=B and C=B, then A=C. But in the *Frankfurter Allgemeine* interview, Cardinal Ratzinger explicitly denies that the Church of Christ and the Roman Catholic Church are identical:

> In his Encyclical, Pius XII said: The Roman Catholic Church "is" the one Church of Jesus Christ. This *seems* [!] to express a complete identity, which is why there was no Church outside the Catholic community. However, this is not the case: according to Catholic teaching, which Pius XII obviously also shared, the local Churches of the Eastern Church separated from Rome *are authentic local Churches.*

Cardinal Ratzinger provided no proof that what "seems" to be the complete identity between the Roman Catholic Church and the Church of Christ in the teaching of Pius XII is "not the case." Further, Ratzinger's *Frankfurter Allgemeine* interview provides no demonstration that Pius XII "shared" the teaching of DI 17 that the Orthodox churches are "authentic local churches." If Pius XII or the other preconciliar Popes had ever taught such a thing, one supposes their teaching would have been cited rather prominently in DI to show its continuity with the perennial Magisterium. To the contrary, in *Satis Cognitum,*

Leo XIII taught the following about the ecclesial status of non-Catholic sees:

> [I]t must be clearly understood that Bishops are deprived of the right and power of ruling, if they deliberately secede from Peter and his successors; because, by this secession, they are *separated from the foundation* on which the whole *edifice* must rest. They are therefore *outside the edifice* itself; and for this very reason they are *separated from the fold*, whose leader is the Chief Pastor; they are *exiled from the Kingdom*, the keys of which were given by Christ to Peter alone.

Likewise, in his letter on reunion with the Eastern churches, St. Pius X declared as follows:

> Let, then, all those who strive to defend the cause of unity go forth; let them go forth wearing the helmet of faith, holding to the anchor of hope, and inflamed with the fire of charity, to work unceasingly in this most heavenly enterprise; and God, the author and lover of peace, will hasten the day when the nations of the East shall *return* to Catholic unity, and, united to the Apostolic See, *after casting away their errors*, shall *enter the port of everlasting salvation*.

There is an urgent need for the Church to explain, in a definitive and binding pronouncement, how churches that lack all jurisdiction, are separated from the very foundation of the Church, are outside the edifice of the Church, not within the fold, exiled from the Kingdom, and not yet in the port of everlasting salvation, can be "true particular churches" or "authentic local churches."

It is not enough to say that *individual members* of the schismatic Orthodox churches may be inculpable of the personal sin of schism. That is not the point here. The point is that, according to every preconciliar papal pronouncement on the subject, the Orthodox churches, *as institutions*, are in a state of schism — cut off from Peter, the very foundation of Christian unity. (Again, neo-Catholics have no problem saying this when it comes to the alleged schism of the Society of St. Pius X.) The departure of the Orthodox churches from a number of Catholic doctrines and their permission for the sin of divorce and remarriage demonstrate the dire consequences of that cutting off.

Granted, the Orthodox churches would *become* true particular churches the moment they abjured their errors, submitted to the Vicar of Christ and thereby entered "the port of eternal salvation," to recall the words of St. Pius X. But then any Jew would become a Christian the moment he was baptized and professed the Faith. The *potential* state of churches or individual people is not the same as their actual state. But it seems to us that confusion between the actual and the potential is at the heart of ecumenism, and that DI 17 only perpetuates the confusion.

Indeed, if Leo XIII and St. Pius X were not addressing their teaching to the actual, objective condition of Orthodox churches and their adherents, what was the point of their teaching? Are we to suppose that these two great Popes lamented an ecclesial condition from which no one was actually suffering any longer, merely because the Orthodox schism had perdured for centuries and all the Orthodox could be presumed to be in good faith? Or has the ecclesial standing of the Orthodox somehow been elevated since the pontificates of Leo and Pius?

Furthermore, one must ask: Of *which* Church are the Orthodox churches said to be "true particular churches"? Are they true particular churches of the Catholic Church? This is obviously untenable. Are they, then, true particular churches of the posited Church of Christ, which DI says is "present and operative" in Orthodox churches despite their lack of communion with the Catholic Church? In that case, the Church of Christ would have to be regarded as an entity capable of being present and operative without the Catholic Church also being present and operative—meaning, once again, that the Church of Christ and the Catholic Church are distinct from each other, a conclusion whose harmony with Catholic teaching is not apparent.

Then again, if the Orthodox churches are said to be particular churches of *neither* the Catholic Church nor the Church of Christ, but merely particular churches standing alone, how can use of the phrase "particular churches" be justified, since the concept of a particular church has meaning only with reference to the universal church?  By analogy, if one of the American states had permanently seceded from the Union before the Civil War—say, Virginia—would we still call it a state today, or would it not simply be the independent commonwealth of Virginia?

More questions present themselves: If the Orthodox churches are said to be "true particular churches," does this mean that they are part of the Mystical Body of Christ?  But how could this be true, in view of the solemn teaching of Pius XII in *Mystici Corporis* that churches not in communion with the Pope are not part of the Mystical Body, since they are not part of the visible Catholic Church?  Pius teaches:

> Actually, *only* those are to be included as members of the Church who have been baptized and profess the true faith, and who have not been so unfortunate as to separate themselves from the unity of the Body, or been excluded by legitimate authority for grave faults committed.... It follows that *those who are divided in faith or government cannot be living in the unity of such a Body*, nor can they be living the life of its one Divine Spirit.

Here, Pius XII was repeating the teaching of his predecessor, Pius XI, in *Mortalium Animos*:

> For since the mystical body of Christ, in the same manner as His physical body, is one, compacted and fitly joined together, it were foolish and out of place to say that the mystical body is made up of members which are disunited and scattered abroad: *whosoever therefore is not united with the body is no member of it*, neither is he in communion with Christ its head.

Pius XII clearly meant his teaching to apply to the schismatic churches of the East, whose members he described in his encyclical *Orientalis Ecclesiae* as "those who are wafted *towards* her [the Catholic Church], as it were, on wings of yearning desire"—the same yearning and desire Pius attributed to morally upright, good-faith Protestants in *Mystici Corporis*. In *Orientalis Ecclesiae*, Pius also spoke of "promoting the *reunion* of all our separated sons with *the one Church of Christ*." Obviously, the Orthodox churches cannot be part of the Mystical Body if they are wafting *toward* the Catholic Church and need to be *reunited* with "the one Church of Christ," which Pius XII clearly identifies with the Catholic Church. And if the Orthodox churches need to be *reunited* with "the one Church of Christ" referred to by Pius XII, how can "the Church of Christ" referred to by Cardinal Ratzinger *already* be "present and operative" in the Orthodox churches as "true particular churches"? Furthermore, how can the Orthodox churches "remain united" to us "by the closest of bonds," as DI asserts, if, as Pius XII taught, there must be a *reunion* of the Orthodox with the one Church of Christ, i.e., the Catholic Church? What sense does it make to speak of the Church being united with those who have not yet *reunited* with her?

These questions all arise from the conundrum caused by the postconciliar "optimism" that refuses to view heretics and schismatics, even *objectively* speaking, as outside the Church—as in the defined dogma that *outside the Church there is no salvation*. Yet the Council of Florence was surely speaking about the *actual* state of *somebody* when it declared infallibly that the Church "firmly believes, professes and proclaims that those not living *within the Catholic Church*, not only pagans, but also Jews, heretics and schismatics, cannot become participants in eternal life, but will depart 'into everlasting fire which was prepared for the devil and his angels,' unless before the end of life the same have been added to the flock...." If that was true of pagans, Jews, heretics and schismatics in the fifteenth century, it holds all the more today, in an age of moral depravity that even the likes of Luther would find unbelievable.

On the other hand, if it is admitted that the Orthodox churches are *not* part of the Mystical Body and thus are *outside* the one true Church, then how can they possibly be "true particular churches"? Can there be a true particular church outside the visible aspect of the Mystical Body, which is inseparable from its invisible aspect? How is this possible? DI offers no apparent answer to any of these questions.

Perhaps the difficulties we have noted here explain why DI contains not a single reference to the Catholic doctrine of the Mystical Body of Christ. DI 16 does refer to "a single body of Christ," but makes no mention of the *Mystical* Body of preconciliar teaching, consisting of a visible Church inseparably united to its soul, the Holy Ghost, and identified so precisely with the Roman Catholic Church by Pius XII and Leo XIII. Are we witnessing the "shedding" of more "terminological armor" for the sake of ecumenism?[399]

It is our sincere conviction as laymen that the attempted integration of Vatican II's ambiguities with the teaching of the preconciliar Popes is completely bewildering, and seems to leave the doctrine of the Mystical Body in shambles. As a consequence, the whole concept of *membership* in the Church — the very term Father Ratzinger disparaged as "terminological armor" — is almost completely lost, and with it the teaching that Church membership is objectively necessary for salvation. Fifty years almost to the day after publication of Pius XII's *Humani Generis,* the publication of *Dominus Iesus* finds us in what seems to be the very state of affairs Pius XII condemned in his encyclical:

> Some say they are not bound by the doctrine, explained in Our Encyclical Letter of a few years ago, and based on the Sources of Revelation, which teaches that the Mystical Body of Christ and the Roman Catholic Church are one and the same thing.

---

[399]*Mystici Corporis* is relegated to a footnote in support of a reference unrelated to the doctrine of the Mystical Body. See DI, footnote 92.

*Some reduce to a meaningless formula the necessity of belonging to the true Church in order to gain eternal salvation.*

Beyond its fundamental points of doctrine, which no Catholic can dispute, we believe DI raises more questions than it answers. Only the infallible Magisterium can explain what has happened to the teaching on the Mystical Body of Christ, and how that teaching can be integrated with a "Church of Christ" that is not identical to the Roman Catholic Church. Our own conviction is that such a pronouncement will never come. Rather, we believe that sooner or later we will see an end to the exercise of attempting a merger between the perennial clarity of the Magisterium and the ambiguous terminology of a council that departed from Scholastic theological precision, only on the assurance that the resulting novel formulations were not meant to serve as statements of binding Catholic doctrine.

Having said all this, we are not here denying that DI is a positive development in certain respects. Not only does it refute some blatant theological errors, but it also affirms two key doctrinal points that have been obscured in the haze of ecumenical and interreligious dialogue: that the salvation of every man is through Christ and Him alone, and that Protestant sects are not churches in the proper sense because they lack Holy Orders and the Holy Eucharist. Jewish and Protestant leaders have loudly objected to these teachings. Thus, for the first time in a long time, a Vatican document has at least proclaimed enough of the truth to give serious offense to Jews and Protestants. That, at least, is something. But even here the benefit has already been lost through Vatican backpedaling and equivocation.

Incensed by DI's teaching that all salvation comes through Christ, the chief rabbi of Rome, Elio Toaff (in whose synagogue John Paul II infamously appeared), announced that Jewish representatives would not be attending the "day of Judeo-Christian friendship" at the Vatican on October 3, causing the event to be canceled.[400] As for the Protestants, the World Alliance of Reformed Churches expressed "dismay and

---

[400]Zenit news account, September 26, 2000.

disappointment" over DI's long-overdue affirmation that Protestant sects were not churches.[401]    Manfred Kock, head of the Council of Evangelical Churches in Germany, complained that DI was "a step backward in ecumenical dialogue," while the "Archbishop" of Canterbury, George Carey, huffed that DI failed to reflect "the deeper understanding that has been achieved through ecumenical dialogue and cooperation during the past thirty years."[402] Carey insisted that his pro-abortion debating society of lay people in clerical costumes "believes itself to be part of the one, holy, catholic, and apostolic Church of Christ."[403]

That Jews and Protestants were put off by DI's affirmation of such basic truths raises an obvious question: What on earth has the Vatican been *discussing* during the past thirty-five years of ecumenical and interreligious "dialogue"? After more than three decades of palaver about our respective religions, it seems that, as of the date of DI's publication, the Vatican's experts in dialogue had not reached matters as fundamental as the one mediation of Jesus Christ and the ecclesial status of Protestant sects. What better evidence is there that the interminable dialogues launched by Vatican II are an exercise in futility? Obviously, the Vatican's Jewish and Protestant interlocutors have not advanced even one millimeter toward an acceptance of the divine claims of the Catholic Church.    Rather, they are outraged to learn that the Catholic Church has not advanced as far as they had thought toward *their* positions. How long will it take for the Vatican to recognize that non-Catholics view "dialogue" with the Church in the same way the Soviets viewed "peaceful coexistence" with the West—as a means to wear down the opposition while strengthening their own position?

From the Jewish and Protestant perspectives, it has appeared, at least in the immediate aftermath of DI's publication, that the whole process of "dialogue" has been

---

[401]Catholic News Service, September 25, 2000.

[402]*Avvenire* On Line, September 27, 2000.

[403]CWNews.com report, September 5, 2000.

nothing but a protracted tease, suggesting a result that could never really have occurred—namely, that the Catholic Church would finally admit that Judaism and Protestantism were divinely recognized co-equals of herself. But let us be honest where the neo-Catholics are not: It is Pope John Paul II's own actions and pronouncements over the years that have contributed mightily to these false expectations.

We cannot forget that this is the only Pope to enter a synagogue in 2,000 years—in tribute, not to preach conversion to Christ. We have noted that in various speeches, exhortations and addresses of a non-Magisterial character, John Paul II and his Vatican collaborators have referred to the Jews as "our elder brothers" and "the people of the Covenant," proclaiming their "irrevocable calling" and pronouncing the Old Covenant "irrevocable," without placing any qualification on these affirmations. His Holiness has prayed at the Wailing Wall that God would forgive the putative sins of Christians against "the people of the Covenant," as if that place were a locus of communion with God, rather than an alleged remnant of the very temple God destroyed to mark the passing of the Old Covenant.[404] Not once in the past twenty-three years, to our knowledge, has His Holiness even suggested, much less explicitly taught, that the mission of the Church to make disciples of all nations extends to the Jews. The same is true of the Vatican apparatus as a whole and virtually the entire postconciliar hierarchy, as we have shown by various examples.

As for Protestant expectations, throughout his pontificate John Paul has been conducting joint liturgical services and administering public blessings side by side with Anglican, Lutheran and other Protestant ministers, even in St. Peter's Basilica itself, and in *Ut Unum Sint* he repeatedly refers to these false prophets as "disciples of Christ," despite their preaching of all manner of gross heresy and immorality. Were the Protestants expected to infer from these activities and pronouncements that they were *not* the ministers of true churches?

---

[404]See, for example, *Discourse at the Rome Synagogue*, April 13, 1986; General Audience of April 28, 1999.

Given these facts, it is hardly surprising that Jewish and Protestant leaders would perceive a double-cross when the same Pope suddenly affirmed (via Cardinal Ratzinger) that all salvation was through Christ and that Protestant sects were not true churches. We would venture to say that this is why DI was issued by Cardinal Ratzinger instead of the Pope himself. Would it not have been impossibly awkward for John Paul II to sign a document that signaled at least a partial retreat in principle from what his entire pontificate has implied in practice?

Thus we think it is fair to say that DI is intended at least in part to put the brakes on a situation largely of John Paul II's own making, even though anonymous theologians from Asia have been assigned all the blame. The proof is in the pudding: *No document of John Paul II regarding Christ, ecclesiology, salvation or non-Catholic religions has ever provoked protests like those elicited by DI.* That is because Jews and Protestants have been uniformly pleased, even delighted, with the Pope's pronouncements and innovations in these areas. It does no good to deny the obvious.

As the flap over DI illustrates, the novelty of postconciliar "dialogue" exists in tension with the Church's divine commission to preach to non-Catholics, by the peremptory authority of God Himself, in order to convert souls to the one true religion. The past thirty-five years of meandering ecumenical and interreligious dialogue do not square well with Our Lord's injunction: "And whosoever shall not receive you, *nor hear your words*: going forth out of that house or city shake off the dust from your feet. Amen I say to you, it shall be more tolerable for the land of Sodom and Gomorrah in the day of judgment, than for that city" (Matt. 10:14-15). What are the conciliar "dialogues" if not interminable conversations with those who will not hear His words? Considering their promotion of abortion alone, are not the adamant unbelievers of today also headed for a fate worse than that of Sodom and Gomorrah?

This tension between "dialogue" and the Church's perennial mission of converting souls has produced a kind of institutional schizophrenia in the Church. Churchmen who are supposed to proclaim the truth are also compelled *not* to proclaim it, lest the dialogue come to a screeching halt, as it did with Toaff and his fellow rabbis in the protest over DI. This institutional schizophrenia became frankly symptomatic in Cardinal Cassidy's attempt to induce Toaff to come back to the dialogue table. Within a few weeks of DI's publication, the Cardinal offered to the press the very revealing excuse that DI "is not directed to the ecumenical and interreligious realm, but to the academic world." Cassidy criticized the "scholastic" nature of the text, which requires it to say: "this is true and this isn't."[405] Well, we can't have that!

In a slap at Cardinal Ratzinger, Cassidy said that "those of us whose ears are more attuned to the nuances of dialogue" would have written a different document—that is, a document that does a better job of obscuring the truth.[406] Cassidy minimized the importance of DI by claiming it was really meant for "theology professors in India, because in Asia there is a theological problem over the oneness of salvation."[407]

Cassidy's comments demonstrate that in order to accommodate "dialogue" the institutional Church has given itself a split personality: one personality engages in dialogue, while the other (at least in theory) sets forth Catholic doctrine. This is a kind of Dr. Jekyll and Mr. Hyde arrangement. Dr. Jekyll (Cardinal Cassidy) inhabits the realm of ecumenical and interreligious dialogue, while Mr. Hyde (Cardinal Ratzinger) inhabits the "scholastic" realm. In the case of DI, both personalities made their appearance at the same time, causing great commotion among the Church's "dialogue partners."

The backpedaling from DI continued when the official theologian of the papal household, Fr. Georges Cottier, OP, as much as stated that its publication to the world was all a big mistake—like Mr. Hyde escaping from the laboratory. "To be

[405]"*Dominus Iesus* Not an Ecumenical Document, Cardinal Says," CWNews.com, September 26, 2000.
[406]Ibid.
[407]"Cardinal Cassidy Appeals to Jews to Renew Dialogue," Zenit news story, September 26, 2000.

sure," Cottier said, "*Dominus Iesus* was not addressed to a Jewish audience.... However, it would be an illusion to think that today such a document could remain exclusively in the hands of the particular audience to which it was addressed. With the international press coverage, a statement like this is immediately brought to the attention of the general audience."[408]

Just a moment: DI was introduced *at a press conference called by the Vatican* on September 5, 2000. Why, then, would Cottier imply that the "international press coverage" of DI was an accident the Vatican regrets? In any event, the problem as Cottier saw it was that because of press coverage the Jews *found out* what the Church still teaches about the sole mediation of Christ! Do we need more proof that the conciliar "dialogues" depend upon hiding as much of the truth as possible, lest it offend the other party? Bushel basket, anyone?

Soothing ruffled feathers, Cottier assured Jewish leaders that "while [DI] repeats that the Church 'possesses' the fullness of the means of salvation, it does not exclude salvation for the Jews." What does that mean? Did Fr. Cottier intend to suggest that the Jews have sufficient means of salvation without faith in Christ or baptism, even if the Church can offer them the "fullness" of means? Cottier did not explain himself. Perhaps this was intentional, given that the very fuel of "dialogue" is unresolved ambiguity.

Cardinal Ratzinger himself began backpedaling almost immediately at the September 5 press conference itself. According to the Italian bishops' newspaper *Avvenire,* when asked whether DI taught that the Jews could not be saved without faith in Christ, Ratzinger offered the following non-answer: "Every Catholic theologian recognizes the salvific role of that people."[409] Granted that "salvation is of the Jews," as our Lord taught us (John 4:22), but as He says immediately

---

[408]"Vatican-Jewish 'Misunderstandings' Seen," CWNews.com, September 26, 2000.

[409]"Ogni teologo cattolico riconosce il ruolo salvifico di quel popolo."

afterward: "But the hour is coming, *and now is*, when the true adorers shall adore the Father in spirit and in truth" — that is, the Messiah has arrived and shall be adored by those who worship truly. Having rejected the Messiah, however, what "salvific role" does modern Israel play today? When pressed on whether an *individual* Jew could be saved without recognizing Christ, the Cardinal replied that "it is *not necessary* that he recognize Christ the savior, and it is not given to us to explore how salvation, the gift of God, can come even for him."[410] Ratzinger went on to say that "Christ is a reality that changes history, even for those who do not recognize him." Are we to take from this that Christ saves the Jews whether they recognize him or not, simply because His existence "changes history"?

However, it appears that at the same press conference Ratzinger gave a more nuanced answer, apparently in response to another questioner:

> [W]e are in agreement that a Jew, and this is true for believers of other religions, *does not need to know or acknowledge Christ as the Son of God in order to be saved*, if there are insurmountable impediments, of which is he not blameworthy, to preclude it. However...Christ in history affects us all, even those who are opposed or cannot encounter Christ. This is a reality that transforms history; it is something important for others, without violating their conscience.[411]

Now, which is it—that a Jew need not recognize Christ in order to be saved, or that a Jew need not recognize Christ *if* there is an "insurmountable impediment"? Note also that Cardinal Ratzinger here repeats the suggestion that the mere presence of Christ in history "affects" Jews who reject him. What does this *mean*? One thing all these remarks mean is a diminution of the impact of DI's teaching that Christ is the sole

---

[410]"Non è necessario che riconosca Cristo salvatore e non ci è dato di esplorare come la salvezza, dono di Dio, possa venire anche per lui."

[411]"Are Believers of Other Religions Saved?" Zenit news story, September 5, 2000.

mediator and the only way of salvation for all men—a teaching DI itself nuances nearly to the point of irrelevance.

Since the publication of DI was supposed to be the occasion for clarifying confusion about Christ and salvation, why not end a long period of postconciliar confusion by stating forthrightly what the Church always taught before the Council: "Yes, *objectively* speaking, a Jew must come to Christ and be baptized in order to be saved, just like everyone else in the human race; for Christ is God and He commissioned His Church to make disciples of all nations. This is what the Catholic Church has always taught and always will teach." Instead, Cardinal Ratzinger immediately focused on "insurmountable impediments." And what is an "insurmountable impediment" in the first place? Is this notion something even broader than the ever-expanding category of "invincible ignorance"? Cardinal Ratzinger gave no indications. However, if one of Rabbi Toaff's own predecessors as chief rabbi of Rome, Rabbi Israel Zolli, was able to follow God's grace into the Roman Catholic Church immediately after World War II, then why not Rabbi Toaff himself or any other Jew alive today—especially after thirty-five years of "Jewish-Christian dialogue," which was supposed to engender greater understanding of the Church on the part of Jews?

Or is the mere fact of *being* a Jew, immersed in Jewish religion and culture and facing ostracism if one converts, now to be considered an "insurmountable impediment" to conversion? If so, then no Jew from St. Paul to the present day has ever been subjectively obliged to join the Church; nor has anyone else in religious, emotional or cultural circumstances that would make conversion difficult. But this would mean that the only people obliged to become Catholics are those who would not find conversion unduly burdensome. Everyone else has an "insurmountable impediment." That is the very thesis being promoted by some of the more liberal exponents of "invincible ignorance," who speak of "unconscious psychological blocks" and other elaborate pseudo-scientific excuses for not becoming a Catholic that have proliferated since Vatican II. There is very little place for the power of God's grace in this kind of semi-Pelagian thinking. We are not here contending that Cardinal Ratzinger himself actually teaches anything like this, but in view of the veiled nature of his remarks it is difficult to know what he *is* teaching. A clarification of DI's "clarifications" is already urgently needed.

Cardinal Ratzinger's lack of clarity persisted at an October 6 press conference to promote the publication of his new book, *God and the World*. When asked if "Jews must, or should, acknowledge Jesus as the messiah," Ratzinger answered:

> We *believe* that. That does not mean that we should force Christ upon them. The fact remains, however, that our *Christian conviction* is that Christ is also the Messiah of Israel. Certainly it is in the hands of God how and when the unification of Jews and Christians in the people of God will take place.[412]

The duty of the Jews to embrace Christ is a truth that God has revealed to all men, including the Jews. Yet Cardinal Ratzinger, in the manner of all postconciliar churchmen, seems instinctively to present revealed truth as merely the belief or conviction of Christians—which is obviously so, but hardly what the question required. Surely Cardinal Ratzinger understands as well as anybody that to modern ears the words "we believe" mean only one thing: "That's what *we* believe, but you don't necessarily have to believe it." Why do modern churchmen insist on presenting divine truths necessary for salvation as if they were merely the consensus of a group of people called Catholics? The Church does not teach that Jews are obliged to convert because the Church "believes" this; the Church teaches this *because God has revealed it and thus it is true*. If one is asked whether 2 + 2 is equal to 4, one does not say, "I *believe* that." One says *yes*. When will today's churchmen recover the ability to say *yes* in response to a simple question about what is true? "Let your speech be yea, yea, no, no. But that which is over and above these is of evil" (Matt. 5:37).

---

[412]*National Catholic Reporter*, October 6, 2000.

It should also be noted that Ratzinger subtly shifted from what the questioner wished to know—i.e., whether individual Jews have a duty to embrace the Messiah—to "the unification of Jews and Christians in the people of God"—not in the Catholic Church, of course!—at some unknown point in the hazy future. The question of individual conversion to Christ for *salvation* was obscured and avoided by yet another vague conciliar-style reference to "unity" and communal activity, as opposed to the eternal fate of individual souls, which is the Church's primary concern.   In keeping with Vatican II's novel focus on the collective, and its equally novel *loss* of focus on the Last Things (a development John Paul II himself has admitted), Ratzinger stated that "we wait for the instant in which *Israel* will say 'yes' to Christ, but we know that it has a special mission in history now...which is significant for the world."[413] Here is yet another exercise in distraction: the question is the eternal salvation of *individual Jews* through faith in Christ, not some unidentified "special mission" for Israel in today's world.  At any rate, what "special mission" does the Cardinal mean, and what does it have to do with the salvation of Jews as individual people who have as much need of the grace of Christ as any Catholic?

As things now stand, Cardinal Ratzinger has yet to give a direct answer to one of the most important questions the public has about DI: Putting aside all the excuses one can conjure up for particular cases of subjective inculpability, are the Jews under the same *objective* obligation as the rest of humanity to believe in Christ the Savior and join His Church in order to be saved? *Yes or no?*

With the publication of *The Jewish People and the Holy Scriptures in the Christian Bible* (which we discussed in Chapter 8), the post-DI backpedaling on the question of Jewish conversion has turned into a complete rout of the Church's traditional teaching, as evidenced by the universal expressions of delight over the book, which Rabbi Joseph Levi called "a total novelty."  And this is the state of affairs which obtains after

---

[413]Ibid.

promulgation of what was supposed to have been a monumental reaffirmation of the sole and unique mediation of Jesus Christ as the Savior of all men, including the Jews.

Cardinal Ratzinger's post-DI equivocations concerning the Lutherans represent another apparent retreat from the Church's traditional claims. When asked what DI teaches about the salvation of Luther's followers, Ratzinger said:

> We all recognize objectively that the Church should be one, and we should all desire to find ourselves in a renewed Catholic Church on the road toward the future. However, *this objective necessity must be distinguished from the state of conscience of persons who learn their faith in their community and are nourished by the Word of God in it.*[414]

What does Cardinal Ratzinger mean by "learn *their* faith"? What about *the* Faith? And what does the Cardinal mean by "nourished"? Are we to understand that merely because Protestants "learn their faith" and feel "nourished" by the grossly corrupted version of "the Word of God" provided in their pro-abortion, pro-contraception, pro-divorce "ecclesial communities," they are *ipso facto* in a state of conscience that exculpates them from their failure to enter the one true Church? How is this different from saying that contented Protestants are not obliged to become Catholics? Cardinal Ratzinger might not have meant to suggest this, but how can the tenor of such remarks do anything but confirm Protestants in their errors?

Here, as with the Jews, Cardinal Ratzinger casts the conversion of Lutherans solely in terms of the objective necessity "that the Church should be one." Once again, in typical postconciliar fashion, the concepts of unity and communal activity obscure the duties owed to God by individual men. In any case, the Church is already one, and the Lutherans are not in it. The true objective necessity is — as it has always been — that the Lutherans abandon Luther's religion and return to the one true Church.

---

[414]Ibid.

Ratzinger's backpedaling continued in an interview on October 9 in the German newspaper *Frankfurter Allgemeine*. Here Ratzinger observed that when the Council stated that the true Church "subsists" in the Catholic Church, which DI repeats, the Council "wished to say also that, although the Lord maintains his promise, *an ecclesial reality exists outside the catholic community*, and it is just this contradiction [?] which is the strongest impulse to pursue unity."[415] So while DI states that Protestant sects are not churches in the proper sense, we are evidently to understand this to mean that there is nonetheless an "ecclesial reality" in these sects outside the "catholic community" that somehow presents an unacceptable "contradiction" to the Church's unitary existence.

An "ecclesial reality" is apparently something less than a true church, but something more than no church at all. What the Protestants are supposed to infer from this notion is anybody's guess. Does it mean they already possess enough "church" to be saved? If they do, then why should any Protestant become a Catholic? And if they do not, then what is the point of stressing an "ecclesial reality" that is not a true church sufficient for salvation?

Ratzinger also declared that "the Catholic Church acknowledges that other Christians participate in the life of *the Church*."[416] Which Church? The Catholic Church? The Church of Christ? Or the "ecclesial reality" outside the "catholic community" that we must make part of the Church? How do the members of the pro-abortion Lutheran World Federation, for example, participate in "the life of the Church"?

Minimizing the doctrinal import of his own document, Ratzinger protested that "the ecclesiological and ecumenical questions" in DI "take up only a small portion of the document" and that "the real point of the statement was to invite all Christians to rededicate themselves to Jesus Christ in this

---

[415]Quoted in *L'Osservatore Romano*, Italian daily edition, October 8, 2000; translation ours.

[416]CWNews.com, October 9, 2000.

Jubilee."[417] So DI was not intended primarily as "a new *Syllabus*," as the neo-Catholics proclaim, but rather as a kind of theological pep talk for the great ecumenical family of Christians we have all become, thanks to "ecumenical dialogue." We are apparently supposed to overlook the fact that many of the "Christians" in this ecumenical family insist that mortal sins are positive goods and that the Catholic Church is a medieval invention.

Finally, the Pope inevitably took his own turn at backing away from DI. It happened as follows:

It seems that the aforementioned World Alliance of Reformed Churches (WARC) was very upset that DI declared that "the church of Christ...continues to *exist fully* only in the Catholic Church." The Church is now so tightly bound by the chains of "ecumenical dialogue" that our "dialogue partners" object if the Vatican rattles the chains by attempting to defend even the ambiguities of Vatican II. Does the phrase "exist fully" imply that the Church of Christ exists *partially* in other places, such as WARC? If not, then why use the phrase "exist *fully*" at all, as opposed to saying simply, "the Church of Christ continues to exist only in the Catholic Church"? The use of the phrase "*continues* to exist" is also problematic. Could the situation change?

The Secretary of WARC fired off a letter to Cardinal Cassidy, complaining that "when statements in that declaration seem to contradict commitment to ecumenical cooperation within the Christian family, or *even to take us back to a pre-Vatican II spirit,* we are concerned.... Among other things, it raises questions concerning how we can continue in dialogue with integrity — trusting and respecting one another." But WARC need not have worried about any return to the dreaded "pre-Vatican II spirit," otherwise known as the traditional attitude of the Catholic Church. The mere threat that WARC was going to walk prompted a personal appearance by the Vicar of Christ at the all-important meeting of the "dialogue commission" of Catholics and WARC. The Pope assured WARC that "the

---

[417]Ibid.

commitment of the Catholic Church to ecumenical dialogue is irrevocable."

A few days later the Pope assured all the Protestants in the world that DI "does not mean to express little consideration for other churches and ecclesial communities." His Holiness declared that far from being a retrenchment, DI "expresses once again the same ecumenical passion which is at the core of my encyclical *Ut Unum Sint*."[418] The message was clear: Rest easy, all you Protestants: DI changes nothing.

With all due respect to the Pope, after more than thirty-five years of utterly fruitless ecumenical activity, have we not heard enough of this sort of thing? Why should the Immaculate Bride of Christ have *any* consideration for "ecclesial communities" that are nothing but human organizations arising from the rebellion of the King of England and the monk of Wittenberg? How can the Bride of Christ have anything other than *righteous contempt* for "communities" whose doctrines are an ever-deepening pit of theological and moral decay? And how much longer must we endure the postconciliar paradox of increasing "respect" for decreasingly respectable organizations?

It is also legitimate to ask how it is possible for the Pope to make "ecumenism" into something "irrevocable" when it was unheard of before 1965, and when, according to the neo-Catholics, not even the 1,500-year-old received and approved rite of Mass could be made irrevocable by the most solemn papal decree of St. Pius V. And what does the Pope mean by "ecumenical passion"? Is it his desire for Christian unity? If so, then why does the Holy Father not call the dissidents home to Rome in the manner of every one of his predecessors, including Pius XI in *Mortalium Animos*:

> Let them therefore return to their common Father, who, forgetting the insults previously heaped on the Apostolic See, will receive them in the most loving fashion. For if, as they continually state, they long to be united with Us and ours, *why*

---

[418]VIS news report, October 1, 2000.

*do they not hasten to enter the Church,* "the Mother and mistress of all Christ's faithful"?

Why indeed?

As far as Jews and other non-Christians are concerned, the Holy Father let it be known in his Message to Cardinal Cassidy on September 21, 2000, that "interreligious dialogue" will continue just as before DI, because interreligious dialogue is a "providential gift for our time." How do we know this? Because the pan-religious prayer meeting at Assisi in 1986 "had an explosive *spiritual force*: It was like a spring from which new *energies of peace* began to flow. For this reason, I hoped that the 'spirit of Assisi' would not be extinguished, but could spread throughout the world and inspire new witnesses of peace and dialogue. Indeed, this world, marked by so many conflicts, misunderstandings and prejudices, has the utmost need for peace and dialogue.... You [Cardinal Cassidy] know well that dialogue does not ignore real differences, but neither does it deny *our common state as pilgrims bound for a new heaven and a new earth.* Dialogue is also an invitation to strengthen that friendship which neither separates nor confuses. We must all be bolder on this journey, so that men and women of our world, to *whatever people or belief* they belong, can discover that they are *children of the one God* and brothers and sisters to one another...."

What can one say? In view of papal statements like these, DI's declaration that the followers of other religions are in a "gravely deficient" situation will surely not be interpreted to mean that they are actually facing eternal damnation unless they enter the Church. Rather, as we mentioned earlier, DI itself concludes by stating that baptism and membership in the Church are necessary, not for salvation as such, but "in order to participate fully in communion with God." No salvation outside the Church seems to have become no *full participation* outside the Church.

At the Day of Prayer for Peace in Assisi in 2002, which Vito Messori rightly criticized for promoting religious indifferentism, the Vatican arranged for representatives of the religions of the world to ride on a "peace train" from Rome to Assisi and pray for world peace at the Pope's invitation, according to their various "traditions." No one seemed especially concerned about their "gravely deficient" condition. Indeed, what other impression can one take from this event than that the Vatican apparatus now views all religions as passengers on the same train—the train of "participation in the one mediation of Christ" (cf. *Dominus Iesus*)—even if they ride in different cars? As always, it seems, Cardinal Ratzinger frankly confirmed the traditionalist diagnosis. The Zenit news agency uncritically reported the Cardinal's remarks on the pan-religious "peace train" as follows:

> Cardinal Joseph Ratzinger described the train that took religious leaders from the Vatican to Assisi as "a symbol of our pilgrimage in history.... *Are we not all, perhaps, passengers on the same train?*... Is not the fact that the train chose as its destiny peace and justice, and the reconciliation of peoples *and religions*, a great inspiration and, at the same time, a splendid sign of hope?"[419]

Such remarks hardly reflect a pressing concern about the "gravely deficient" condition of the followers of "other religions." The apparent lack of such concern is remarkable, given that the Assisi event itself brought modern-day pantheists and polytheists into close proximity with the Vicar of Christ and into the Vatican itself. *What possible claim of "invincible ignorance" of the true religion can exist for these people,* who fly on jet planes to attend peace conferences with the Pope and have access to computer technology that puts the Gospel and the entire teaching of the Catholic Church at their fingertips—if only they will lift a finger? A modern-day witch doctor who attends Vatican gatherings and makes use of the Internet hardly qualifies as the hypothetical blissfully ignorant pagan on a desert isle. Will no one at the Vatican warn these people that eternal punishment awaits those who do not follow Christ once they learn of Him and His Church?

---

[419]Zenit news report, February 21, 2002.

A mere thirty-seven years before the "springtime of Vatican II," Pius XI directed the entire Church to pray publicly the following prayer on the Feast of Christ the King:

> Be Thou King of those who are deceived by erroneous opinions, or whom discord keeps aloof, and call them back to the harbor of truth and unity of faith, so that soon there may be but one flock and one shepherd. Be Thou King of all those who are still involved in the darkness of idolatry or of Islamism and refuse not to draw them all into the light and kingdom of God. Turn Thine eyes of mercy toward the children of that race, once Thy chosen people. Of old, they called down upon themselves the Blood of the Savior, may it now descend upon them a laver of redemption and life.

That the present-day Vatican would regard this prayer as unthinkable, even though it was promulgated within the lifetime of John Paul II, says a great deal about the nature of the current crisis. *After 2,000 years, the Church has suddenly stopped calling for the conversion of non-Catholics to save them from hell.* It is that simple. Masses are no longer being offered for the conversion of Protestants, Jews, Muslims and other non-believers, although a single papal Mass for that intention would accomplish infinitely more for the cause of true spiritual unity than endless "dialogue" or pan-religious prayer meetings at Assisi. But the Church has laid down such spiritual arms, lest the parties to "dialogue" be offended by their use.

It is self-evident that in the postconciliar period the Church's traditional solicitude for the salvation of individual souls outside her visible confines has been suppressed. DI's slight movement toward a recovery of that tradition has been downplayed by the Vatican itself in response to Jewish and Protestant howls of protest. This is why the publication of *Dominus Iesus* is such an important event: the Vatican's response to the document's hostile reception demonstrates that we are nowhere near the end of the postconciliar crisis. In fact, the crisis continues to deepen.

Little more than two years after the publication of *Dominus Iesus*, we seem to have arrived where we started: the Vatican is no longer willing to say forthrightly to the world that Jews, Protestants and the followers of other religions are *obliged* to belong to the one true Church, or even to have explicit faith in Christ, in order to save their souls. The Jews have a "special mission" until "Israel" decides to join the Church. The Protestants are "nourished by the Word of God" in the "ecclesial reality" of their "ecclesial communities." The followers of other religions possess "spiritual riches," "spiritual treasures" and "sacred books" that "sustain their life relationship to God," and they are united with us as "pilgrims bound for a new heaven and a new earth" in the spirit of Assisi. It appears that the only people who must be Catholics are Catholics—unless they decide to convert to Judaism, in which case prelates like the late Cardinal O'Connor (may God rest his soul) will give them a blessing on national television.

The good points presented in DI have done nothing to change a situation in which the defined dogma *extra ecclesiam nulla salus* has become in practice the empty formula condemned by Pius XII in *Humani Generis*. Weakened by the viruses of ecumenism and dialogue, the human element of the Church hobbles along on an ecumenical and interreligious road to nowhere—an enfeebled caricature of what it was less than forty years ago, publicly arguing with itself over how the world should take its own pronouncements.

*Dominus Iesus* has not proven to be the answer to the postconciliar crisis. No Vatican document will be. It is our conviction that the only way out of the crisis is *the full restoration of Roman Catholic ecclesiastical tradition, classical theology, classical preaching and Scholastic philosophy.* That is, a restoration of the Church to her basic condition a mere forty years ago. We are also convinced that such a restoration is no nostalgic dream, but an inevitable provision of God's providence, for the current abysmal state of the Church's liturgy, preaching and general discipline cannot possibly serve as the foundation for her mission in the future. Sooner or later, God will intervene, if those who govern the Church will not do what has to be done to bring her back to health.

In the next chapter we consider one way, perhaps the only way, that this restoration can be accomplished, humanly speaking, in the present epoch.

# Chapter 14

# The Great Façade

Where do we traditionalists stand today, and where do we go from here? With Msgr. Gamber, we ask: "Is this the spring people had hoped would emerge from the Second Vatican Council? Instead of a genuine renewal in our Church, we have seen only novelties. Instead of our religious life entering a period of new invigoration, as has happened in the past, what we see now is a form of Christianity that has turned towards the world."[420]

Despite a mountain of evidence that the current novelties have been ruinous for the Church, the search for the conciliar apotheosis goes on, with the Vatican staging one novel publicity stunt after another aimed at demonstrating the emergence at last of the "new humanity" extolled in *Gaudium et Spes* and the "new advent of the Church connected with the approaching end of the second millennium" proclaimed by John Paul II in *Redemptor Hominis*. More than thirty-five years after the Council, we are still bobbing in its tempest of ineffable intuitions, passed off as "developments" of Catholic doctrine.

The spirit of Vatican II continues to prowl about the Church, seeking some epochal manifestation of itself—a kind of lost soul in search of its body. Since 1985, we have been told that the World Youth Days the Pope invented are just such a

---

[420]Gamber, *The Reform of the Roman Liturgy*, p. 102.

manifestation. At World Youth Day 2000, Cardinal Stafford pointed to the throngs of youngsters gathered in Saint Peter's Square and declared: "Here are the children of Vatican II!" Here indeed they are. But how many of these "children of Vatican II" could answer correctly ten basic questions about the Catholic faith? And how many of the "children of Vatican II" from the first World Youth Day in 1985 are practicing the Faith today, including the Church's teaching on marriage and procreation, now that they have reached adulthood?

Behind the façade of these great spectacles lurks the reality of an entire generation deprived of anything approaching a solid formation in the Catholic faith; these youngsters are practically defenseless against the forces of the world. A striking demonstration of this is a recent fundraising piece published by Catholic Answers, whose president, Karl Keating, notes with alarm that *"Thousands* of Catholic teenagers are in danger of *losing their faith* at the Pope's 'World Youth Day' in July [2002] (his emphasis)." The dire threat to the faith of thousands of young Catholics is the anti-Catholic literature of Chick Publications, which Protestant fundamentalists plot to distribute at all the World Youth Days. Keating cites as the worst example of this "vicious anti-Catholic propaganda" a ludicrous comic book in which a faceless Christ, sitting in the Judgment Seat, sends a Catholic to hell because the poor man thought that he could be saved by going to Mass and confession and praying his Rosary, "just like the Pope does." Keating urgently requests donations so that he and his organization—not the priests who have charge of these youngsters, not their bishops, not the Pope—can save the faith of thousands of World Youth Day attendees. This will be done by handing out a Catholic Answers pamphlet to counter the Jack Chick comic books.

Without denying that this is a worthy and even necessary undertaking that Catholics should support, it must be observed that its very necessity reveals the utter bankruptcy of the conciliar "renewal." These "children of Vatican II," surely among the Pope's most fervent admirers and the very future of the Church, are apparently so ignorant of Roman Catholicism that one must be afraid that a *comic book* could suddenly persuade *thousands* of them that the very pillars of their religion—the Mass, the sacraments, devotion to the Blessed Virgin Mary—are damnable inventions that will cause them to go to hell! In which case, one must ask: What exactly do these youngsters think they are doing when they travel to the World Youth Days in such vast numbers? Are they going to show their loyalty to the Vicar of Christ and the Church he heads, or merely to attend a festival presided over by a beloved celebrity, whose actual influence over their lives is less than that of an asinine comic book? How can they be said to be followers of the Pope at all, if they could be so easily persuaded that the Pope and the Church have usurped Christianity with false and damnable claims? Is there no one in their Catholic schools, no one in their parishes, who has armed them against such silly propaganda? Did they not receive the Sacrament of Confirmation? Were they not told what that Sacrament means and the obligations it imposes upon them? Where, in short, is their Catholic faith and their Catholic militancy in the midst of the "great renewal" of Vatican II?

Such questions do not seem to trouble the promoters of these spectacles. For them, the emotion engendered by cheering crowds who make the Pope happy is sufficient evidence of ecclesial well being. The gushing over World Youth Day 2000 at a neo-Catholic website is typical of this mentality:

> As Pope John Paul II looked out at the vast throng of joyful youth, hearing their shouts of "Viva il Papa" and "Giovanni Paulo" and "JP II, we love you!" ringing in the air—everywhere they gathered with the Holy Father—no wonder he wiped tears from his eyes, swayed with the young as they sang, waved his arms in the air, and let a glorious smile break through, again and again. Here he saw, before his very eyes, the fulfillment of the words of Vatican II to the young, in its blossoming and growth (since the first World Youth Day, over 15 years ago).[421]

So an ephemeral outpouring of mass sentiment from a boisterous crowd is "the fulfillment of the words of Vatican II."

---

[421]http://www.praiseofglory.com/childrenvat2.htm

The crowd sways. The Pope sways with them. All is well. The phenomenon of *feelings* is the triumph of Vatican II. All empirical evidence of the actual condition of the Church is ignored in favor of a phenomenal event.

It is not merely facile to say that World Youth Day is the Catholic version of Woodstock. We have heard the same extravagant claim for both events: that the world can be changed for the better if only vast numbers of young people — just because they are young — can be gathered together in one place for the promotion of love and peace. Cardinal Stafford, quoting one youngster, enthused that WYD 1997 in Paris was nothing less than "a revolution of love." But the "revolution of love" in Paris was evidently not accompanied by a revolution of honesty. According to the Catholic World News service (CWN), the French bishops' conference was left with $5 million in debts because only about 100,000 of the 500,000 participants in WYD 1997 paid the registration fee. (Oddly enough, the proportion of gatecrashers at Woodstock was about the same.) As Bishop Michael Dubost complained: "I see many of the youngsters buying T-shirts, Coca-Cola, and numerous unnecessary objects, but not [registration] badges, which shows they are not prepared to help." Neither was this revolution in love accompanied by a revolution in generosity to the Church. A collection taken up from the 1.3 million people who attended the Pope's outdoor Mass at a racetrack yielded $330,000 — an average of 33 cents per congregant.[422] The same people undoubtedly expended vastly more money for souvenirs of Paris. Could one find a more graphic representation of the "fruits of Vatican II"?

Nevertheless, WYD '97 was pronounced a "papal triumph" by CWN, the neo-Catholic press organ.[423] Had not the Pope attracted a huge, cheering crowd? What is more, "400,000 young people took to the streets of Paris, spreading out across the roads, and at precisely 10:50 a.m. joined their hands in a human

---

[422]"French Bishops Mull Debts Following World Youth Day," CWN report, August 26, 1997.
[423]"World Youth Day Concludes in Papal Triumph," CWN report, August 25, 1997.

chain that stretched over twenty miles." What was the point of this human chain? According to CWN, the chain faced *away* from the center of Paris, because "the organizers had sought to demonstrate the commitment of young people to be 'open to the world,' and a press statement explained that this was 'a symbol of friendship, of gathering, and an overture to the five continents—a universal appeal for peace.'"[424] Openness to the world, friendship, gathering and peace. Secular aims for what was, in essence, a secular festival. As CWN notes: "Tolerance was also the theme of the papal message on Saturday. In the morning at the Church of St. Etienne du Mont, speaking to delegates of the World Youth Day crowd—representing the 140 countries which sent contingents to Paris—the Pope said: 'The Spirit of God sends you forth, so that you can become, with all your brothers and sisters throughout the world, builders of a civilization of reconciliation, founded on brotherly love.'"[425]

It should be evident from everything we have shown that this "civilization of reconciliation" does not mean anything like the Catholic social order presented as the ideal in the teaching of the preconciliar Popes. That ideal has been replaced by something quite different. As the Pope would later observe in his Message for World Day for Peace 2001:

> Dialogue leads to a recognition of diversity and opens the mind to the mutual acceptance and genuine collaboration demanded by the human family's basic vocation to unity. As such, dialogue is a privileged means for building *the civilization of love and peace* that my revered predecessor Paul VI indicated *as the ideal* to inspire cultural, social, political and economic life in our time.... *The different religions too can and ought to contribute decisively to this process.* My many encounters with representatives of other religions—I recall especially the meeting in Assisi in 1986 and in St. Peter's Square in 1999—have made me more confident that mutual openness between the followers of the various religions can greatly serve the cause of peace and the common good of the human family.

---

[424]Ibid.
[425]Ibid.

There is no question here of making converts of the followers of other religions in order to save their souls, nor any mention of Our Lord's admonition about the consequences of the world's rejection of His Gospel and His Church: "Do not think that I came to send peace upon the world: I came not to send peace but the sword" (Matt. 10:27). Also forgotten is the teaching of Pius XI in *Quas Primas* that there can be no peace worthy of the name without the Social Kingship of Christ over every man and every nation. That is not what World Youth Day and the "civilization of love" are all about. As we have seen throughout this book, that is not the program of the postconciliar Vatican apparatus.

Yes, World Youth Days are filled with exhortations that young people who are already baptized Catholics "follow Christ," but only in the context of a pan-religious brotherhood in which the beliefs of others are respected and even admired, not viewed as forms of darkness from which souls must be rescued. And while there are outdoor Masses with pop-rock liturgical music, and an opportunity to go to confession, trendy Mass liturgies and even confession can be had at any local parish. Clearly, it is not these things that draw the vast World Youth Day crowds. The rock music, the camaraderie, the chance to be close to a great celebrity—the *Woodstock* of it all—are what attract so many of the same youngsters who would, with equal alacrity, attend a performance of heavy-metal rock music.

There is great danger in this use of pop culture to entice Catholic youngsters to attend huge festivals in faraway places. Putting aside the temptation that arises when thousands of immodestly clad teenage girls are thrown together in a bivouac with thousands of teenage boys, there is the incalculable potential for sacrilege. Gerry Matatics attended WYD '93 in Denver. The enactment of the Stations of the Cross with a woman in the role of Jesus was nothing compared to what he saw at the outdoor papal Mass:

> We had camped out the night before on the ground to be sure that we would have a place for the papal Mass. We all had grimy faces and "sleeping-bag" hair. The assisting priests who were to distribute Holy Communion, implementing

enculturation, accommodated themselves to the heat and humidity by wearing tee shirts, shorts, flip-flops and baseball caps along with their stoles. Priests similarly attired were listening to confessions beforehand.

The crowd had been roped off into quadrants, about a hundred of us in each one. When the time came for reception of Holy Communion I knelt at the front of my little quadrant in an attempt to receive the Sacred Host my knees. Hosts were being distributed from big, shallow bowls that could have been used for punch or potato chips. People were reaching over each other's shoulders to grab the consecrated Hosts from the priests. I saw Hosts falling into the mud, where they were being trampled on. I reached down and rescued as many as I could and consumed them.

I had been going to the Tridentine Mass since the fall of 1992 and [to] the Novus Ordo on weekdays. At that moment I realized that if this kind of sacrilege could occur at a *papal Mass* because of the Novus Ordo rubrics, I could no longer be a party to the new liturgy. It was the last Novus Ordo Mass I ever attended.

Michael Matt offers testimony perhaps even more horrific:

At an outdoor papal Mass in Des Moines during the Pope's visit to that city, consecrated Hosts were being distributed from cardboard boxes that were passed through the crowd. A group of Hell's Angels helped themselves to Holy Communion. I saw them washing down the Body of Christ with cans of beer. I was only a child then, but I will never forget that awful sight as long as I live. [The practice of Communion in the hand ensures that even the papal Masses in St. Peter's Square will result in sacrilege, including the spiriting away of Hosts by Rome's many Satanists.]

Sacrileges unimaginable in 1965 are now commonplace on the Pope's endless road trips in search of the civilization of love, the new humanity and the new Advent of the Church. One must ask how any alleged spiritual good from these events can possibly outweigh the mounting insults to God that their very structure engenders. Who will make reparation for these sacrileges, heaped upon all the others made possible by the postconciliar "reforms"?

The grotesque attempt to fuse Catholicism with pop culture, to make a Woodstock of the Faith, is perhaps a last desperate struggle by the spirit of Vatican II to find a place where it can be seen to live. Everywhere in the Church the awful experiment is being tried. The Pope has allowed his personal (and suitably non-denominational) prayers to be recited on mass-marketed CDs by the likes of Britney Spears and the lead singer for Aerosmith, a Woodstock-era band still plying its trade on the concert circuit. The Pope's life has been made into a comic book, which he heartily approves. ("Karol, Karol, look out!" shouts one of Wojtyla's friends as he runs after a soccer ball with an opposing player in hot pursuit.)   There is even a Vatican-branded  VISA card — which raises an interesting question about the application of Church teaching on usury. The Woodstock of the Faith is now complete with merchandising tie-ins.

In America, as was to be expected, the fusion of Catholicism and pop culture (which Michael Matt aptly describes as "cool Catholicism") has already reached its absolute nadir. One of the most striking recent examples to come our way is a neo-Catholic magazine called *Envoy*, whose editorial policy seems to be that Catholicism must be pitched to the level of a moron in order to be attractive to young people.

*Envoy*'s website features an animated cartoon that must be seen to be believed: It begins with a 98-pound weakling, a Catholic named Joe, being confronted at the beach by a Protestant Bible-thumper, who kicks theological sand in Joe's face by quoting Scripture passages to support his attacks on the Catholic Church. Having been embarrassed in front of his bikini-clad girlfriend (who is lounging on the sand with her belly button in view), Joe goes home and bones up on *Envoy* magazine. We next see Joe in front of a mirror admiring his now-massive physique, covered only by a pair of bikini-briefs, and exclaiming: "Boy, it didn't take me long to brush up on my catechism. Now I have a deeper understanding of my Catholic faith, and a deeper faith too!" (Joe's deeper faith apparently does not include any sense of modesty.) In the next panel, Joe is back on the beach quoting Scripture to the Protestant bully, as his bikini-clad girlfriend (still lounging on the sand and displaying her belly button) exclaims, "Wow!" The strip concludes with the girlfriend rubbing up against Joe and clutching his brawny biceps as she oozes: "Oh, Joe, you make me proud to be a Catholic." In the background, another bikini-clad girl lounging on the beach says: "What a masterful grasp Joe has of the truth and beauty of the Faith." To which her boyfriend replies: "He's an *Envoy* reader."

*Envoy*'s website reports that *Envoy* cannot survive unless it obtains 50% more subscribers. That is hardly surprising. *Envoy* can be expected to fail, along with the entire postconciliar venture of debasing the Faith in a vain attempt to make it more appealing to an unbelieving world. The same lack of subscribers is what plagues the Church throughout the world today. For those who now govern the Church have renounced the divine aloofness which makes Our Lord Himself, and thus His Church, so attractive to the world-weary soul in search of the narrow road that leads away from this place to eternal beatitude. Yes, Our Lord entered the world to be a friend to His fellow man, a friend *par excellence*. But that friendship is premised on obedience to Him who is our King as well as our friend. And who would dare to slap this Friend on the back as one would some merely earthly companion!

The postconciliar program of "openness to the world" is an invitation to backslapping familiarity with the Bride of Christ: See? The Church is your friend. The Church can speak your language, after all. After so many centuries of preaching to you, the Church now wishes to *dialogue* with you and *understand* you. The Church has come to recognize your good faith, even if, in the exercise of your religious liberty, you choose not to believe. The Church no longer wishes to address you from on high or to frighten you with the prospect of God's eternal punishment. The Church now wishes, instead, to accentuate the good in all people, all cultures, and all religions. Look!—we have provided music and festivities for everyone, and even a new liturgy that will be more to your liking should you care to join us. Come, link your hands with ours in the human chain of peace, along with the members of every religion or no religion at all. Oh, and yes, we do *invite* you to consider the Gospel of Christ, which we now, at last, present to you in a non-threatening, less "ecclesiocentric" way. For the Church has discovered, after many centuries of presuming the contrary, that all or most of you are following the one path of Christ in your own way, whether you know it or not. Let us proclaim to you the good news of your salvation.

And the world replies: Since you are now open to the world, to the good in all religions, to different points of view, since you no longer threaten us with hell if we reject what you teach, since you presume that we are in good faith, why must we listen to you? And what, in the end, do we really need you for? At the very heart of the postconciliar crisis lies the inability of postconciliar churchmen to give a compelling answer to that question. And yet before the Council the answer was always promptly and clearly given: To save your soul from hell.

After some forty years of ecclesial innovations that have exceeded the worst nightmares of the great preconciliar Popes, the Roman liturgy is in ruins, the missions are practically extinct, conversions and vocations have dwindled at the same time Islam has become the fastest growing religion in former Christendom, contemporary churchmen have *de facto* embraced the errors of liberalism condemned in the *Syllabus*, and the average Catholic in the pew no longer considers himself bound to follow any teaching on faith or morals which impairs his chosen "lifestyle."

And yet there is still no admission by the Vatican that the postconciliar debacle is, in fact, a debacle. Instead, Cardinal Ratzinger opines that Catholics should get used to the "numerical reduction" of their Church, and learn to accept forms of limited participation in her life:

> The mass Church may be something lovely, but it is not necessarily the Church's only way of being. The Church of the first three centuries was small, without being, by this fact, a sectarian community.... The process of numerical reduction, which we are experiencing today, will also have to be addressed precisely by exploring *new ways of openness to the outside*, of *new ways of participation* by those who are outside

the community of believers. I have nothing against people who, though they never enter a church during the year, go to Christmas midnight Mass, or go on the occasion of some other celebration, because this is also a way of coming close to the light. Therefore, there must be different forms of involvement and participation.[426]

Nearly 2,000 years after Christ gave His Church the divine commission to make disciples of all nations, the Prefect of the Congregation for the Doctrine of the Faith seriously proposes "exploring" occasional Mass attendance as a legitimate "new way of participation" in the Church. The "mass Church" embracing all the peoples of the world is not a divine imperative but only "something lovely." It has come to this.

Like an overconfident physician who will not admit that his clinical judgment could be wrong, those who have presided over the postconciliar debacle continue to prescribe more of the same medication to a patient who is not only failing to show any sign of improvement, but has gone into a coma. Is it right that the same physicians who have induced this coma should now expect us to believe that despite all appearances the coma is a good thing, and that the patient's robust health only a short while ago was merely "something lovely" that could not be expected to last?

The most our ecclesial physicians seem willing to do is cut back a bit on the dosage, as the neo-Catholics hail the bold new treatment. According to such neo-Catholic organs as *The Wanderer*, for example, we are supposed to cheer the great recovery when the Vatican declares in *Liturgiam Authenticam* that vernacular translations of the new Mass which *the Vatican itself approved* thirty years ago are defective and must be made better. Perhaps in another thirty years the errant bishops who foisted liturgical trash on the people for an entire generation will have obeyed by improving somewhat the quality of the trash. Or perhaps not. In either case, the new liturgy will remain a

---

[426]Zenit news interview, October 1, 2001. The occasion was an interview with the Cardinal concerning his new book, *God and the World*.

disaster area—a place where even Protestants are appalled by the lack of dignity and seriousness.

Meanwhile, the Vatican does next to nothing about the doctrinal dissent and sexual scandal that riddle the Catholic hierarchy, yet is quite careful to monitor the traditional seminaries of the Priestly Fraternity of St. Peter for any signs of deviancy from postconciliar correctness. At the same time, traditionalists are herded into reservations known as "indult Mass centers," where the received and approved ancient liturgy of the Roman Rite is treated as if it were a strain of anthrax that must be contained at all costs.

In his letter to the traditionalist priests of the Priestly Fraternity, explaining why he had suspended their chapter election, imposed a new superior chosen by himself and removed the rectors of the Fraternity's wholly orthodox seminaries, Cardinal Castrillón inadvertently revealed the heart of the current ecclesial crisis. The letter claims that these heavy-handed interventions were necessary to "combat a certain spirit of rebellion against the present-day Church" among the seminarians.[427] In a later interview in *30 Days* magazine, Cardinal Castrillón stated that the "Fraternity's members must be helped in their endeavor to strike a balance between their original charism...and *the outcome of their insertion within the ecclesial reality of today.*"[428]

Not even the neo-Catholics can dispute that the priests and seminarians of the Priestly Fraternity are members of the Holy Catholic Church, and that they belong to a society of apostolic life approved by the Pope himself. Nor is there any doubt that these priests and seminarians follow the teaching of the Church on faith and morals and are loyal to the Pope who chartered their society. According to Cardinal Castrillón, that is not good enough. These faithful priests and seminarians must also cease their "rebellion against the present-day Church," and must consent to "the outcome of their insertion within the ecclesial reality of today." But if these men are already members of the

[427]Letter to General Chapter of the Priestly Fraternity of St. Peter, June 29, 2000.
[428]*30 Days*, N. 11-2000.

Catholic Church, what is meant by "the present-day Church" and "the ecclesial reality of today"? What exactly is this thing into which they are supposed to be inserted? If pressed on the matter, the Cardinal would not be able to explain with any precision what he means by "the present-day Church" and "the ecclesial reality of today," for no one has been able to do so over the past forty years. But of one thing he would no doubt be certain: traditionalists must submit to them, whatever they are.

Here, then, is our problem as Roman Catholic traditionalists at the beginning of the Church's third millennium: no matter what the evidence of its failure, the ineffable vision of Vatican II continues to dominate the thinking of postconciliar churchmen. In some way not even they can explain, the conciliar vision is at odds with Catholic tradition, such that completely orthodox priests and seminarians must be forced to adhere to it, although nothing is lacking in their Catholic faith as such. The great façade of postconciliar novelty and "renewal" must be kept standing at all costs, and we must all salute it—even as it totters and groans under the weight of priestly scandal, liturgical ruin, rampant heresy and disobedience among neo-modernist clergy and laity, and widespread loss of the integral Catholic faith among nominal Catholics in the pews, who contracept, abort their children and divorce about as readily as their non-Catholic neighbors.

"Moses and Aaron went in, and said to Pharaoh: Thus saith the Lord God of Israel: Let my people go, that they may sacrifice to me in the desert." Nearly forty years after the bronze doors closed on Vatican II, those who have simply gone on being what Catholics always were before 1965 find themselves presenting a similar petition to those who run the Vatican. No, the Pope is not a hard-hearted Pharaoh. To the contrary, there is every indication that the Pope (if only out of a certain sense of ecclesial pluralism) might well be inclined to give traditionalists practically everything they have been asking for, and thus begin the Church's restoration. But there are those around the Pope whose opposition to any "return to the pre-Vatican II spirit" would rival Pharaoh's obduracy. And so our petition to be released from the bondage of "the ecclesial reality of today" is continually denied by postconciliar pharaohs, both low and high, as we watch one plague after another descend upon the Church.

Is there any way out of the bondage in which Catholic Tradition now finds itself? Have we, in fact, gone beyond the stage of crisis, as some have suggested, to the point where the Church cannot recover what she has lost without direct divine intervention? Perhaps. But there seems to us at least one mechanism by which a return to Tradition in all its fullness might be accomplished—and not just for traditionalists, but for the Church as a whole, failing which no solution to the crisis would be adequate.

Over the past year, many traditionalists have begun to learn of a canonical structure known as an apostolic administration. Such an arrangement would make an order of priests—such as the Society of St. Pius X, to whom the idea was reportedly proposed—answerable to the Pope alone, and would allow them to operate without interference from the local bishop.

It is an extremely attractive idea, to be sure. Most obviously, it would allow the work of true reform to be carried forward, without its being sabotaged by unfriendly bishops. It would also address the difficulties traditionally associated with the so-called "indult" Mass: unsympathetic pastors, little or no parish life, weddings and funerals frequently denied, architecture unsuited to the traditional liturgy, and the like. Under an apostolic administration, traditional priests could establish entire parishes and even virtual dioceses of their own.

We stress that we do not propose that any such arrangement be accepted on condition of remaining silent about the postconciliar debacle and what traditionalists believe to be its causes. The "Church of openness and dialogue" that tolerates the likes of Hans Küng can hardly demand silence from loyal Catholics; let us not be ridiculous. Nor should traditionalists consent to any canonical arrangement that would quarantine "their spiritual and liturgical traditions" forever, like some disease, or subject completely orthodox priests and bishops to discipline and arbitrary removal from office for an alleged failure to be "inserted" into the "ecclesial reality of today." Our whole aim is to make the ecclesial reality of today *go away*, so that the Church whose traditional motto is *semper idem* — always the same — can be the same once again.

Addressing and resolving all the difficulties we have discussed in this book will not be easy.  But an apostolic administration, or perhaps even a patriarchate of the kind to which the Uniate Eastern churches belong, is an arrangement that could serve to preserve the cause of Tradition within the Church and, we hope, one day to bring about its restoration throughout the Roman Rite at large.  Now that this idea has, almost overnight, become practically mainstream — thanks to Rome's contacts and negotiations with the Society of St. Pius X — we believe that bringing about such a serious and sweeping accommodation of traditionalism is a realistic goal, and the one toward which all traditionalists should strive.

This kind of structure is not altogether without precedent. During another desperate period of Church history, a similar arrangement was granted to a small group of reformers whose accomplishments would ultimately rank among the most impressive in Church history.

The year was 910.  For the past century, Europe had been ravaged not only by the disorder and war brought on by the infighting among the heirs of Charlemagne, but also and more importantly by wave upon wave of invasions by the Vikings, the Magyars, and the Muslims.

Monastic discipline had all but collapsed throughout the West.  Simony, the sale of clerical offices, was rampant, and clerical celibacy was in many cases a distant memory.  When a poor monk named Erluin suggested that his monastery return to strict observance of the *Rule of St. Benedict*, his fellow monks ripped out his tongue and blinded him.  So much for that.

But in 910, an institution was founded whose influence would extend far beyond anyone's expectations, and that would play a historic role in reforming monastic life throughout Europe.  In that year, William the Pious, Duke of Aquitaine, established the monastery of Cluny fifteen miles northwest of Mâcon in Burgundy.  Immediately after doing so, he renounced any authority he might have enjoyed over the institution as a lay ruler.  Lay control of churches and monasteries had been the source of much mischief in those days, and, thanks to Duke William, it would not interfere with Cluny's great work.

That great work was nothing less than the restoration of religious life in Europe. Cluny would be blessed with a number of saintly abbots, who were determined to direct religious life according to the traditional Benedictine model—and then to spread their work and influence beyond the walls of their abbey. It would become a key center of Church reform, with no fewer than four reforming Popes eventually emerging from Cluniac backgrounds.

Although Cluny was not alone in promoting monastic reform, it played a role vastly disproportionate to its size. Its plan consisted both of founding new houses across western Europe and in encouraging existing monasteries that contained anything of the reform spirit to become affiliates. Here was where Cluny departed from standard Benedictine practice: while each such monastery had previously been entirely independent of all others, Cluny introduced a centralized system of administration through which it governed the houses under its charge. Thus all the Cluniac monasteries operated under the authority of the abbot of Cluny. Cluny's abbot, though he traveled a great deal, could not be everywhere at once, so the day-to-day operations of affiliated monasteries were overseen by priors—appointed not by each individual community, as had been standard in the Benedictine tradition, but by the abbot of Cluny. Every monk, in turn, was expected to spend some time at Cluny itself. Over time, Cluny would come to direct many hundreds of monasteries: 314 by the twelfth century, and 825 by the fifteenth. As many as a thousand others, while not subject to Cluniac control, would adopt its constitutions and spirit.

On a regular basis, Cluny held a general chapter at which all the priors were to be present. These meetings symbolized Cluny's great work of bringing together into one great federation so many of the previously isolated islands of reform sentiment. Thus the great Church historian Msgr. Philip Hughes writes: "In that age of general dislocation, when unity of any kind seemed but an impossible dream, and when alone the monasteries retained a semblance of stability, the importance of the new departure that bound up in one huge federation all these cells of new religious life can hardly be exaggerated."[429]

In order to allow Cluny to undertake its spiritual mission without outside interference, William of Aquitaine had declared it independent of all lay control, including his own; there remained, however, the question of ecclesiastical control. From the beginning, Cluny had worked to gain exemption from the control of local bishops, some of whom were hostile to its mission, and many of whom had attained their offices through simony. At first, this exemption took the form of Pope Gregory V's declaration in the late tenth century that "no bishop or priest should dare to enter the venerable monastery of Cluny for the ordination of priests or deacons, for the consecration of a church, or for the celebration of Mass, unless invited by the abbot." In 1016, Pope Benedict VIII declared Cluny "absolutely free from the authority of kings, bishops, and counts, being subject only to God, St. Peter, and the Pope."[430]

This was what Cluny had been seeking all along: an implicit reform mandate from Rome and, much more importantly, immunity from the bishops in carrying out that reform. Top churchmen doubtless recognized that all too many of the bishops had been appointed for the wrong reasons; recall that Cluny took hold before the outbreak of the so-called investiture controversy, in which the Church struggled to reclaim from secular authorities the right to name Church officials, including bishops. With bishops who had often been awarded their offices in exchange for a fee, or for their loyalty or other service to a secular ruler (or because they were fortunate enough to be related to some secular ruler), and with abbots of monasteries also generally appointed by kings, dukes, and counts as well, it was essential that these potential sources of corruption be bypassed entirely.

---

[429]Philip Hughes, A History of the Church, vol. 2: The Church and the World the Church Created (1935; repr., London: Sheed and Ward, 1952), p. 207.

[430]Henri Daniel-Rops, The Church in the Dark Ages, trans. Audrey Butler (London: J.M. Dent & Sons, 1959), p. 580.

This is not to say that Cluny encountered no obstacles. Some bishops were annoyed at Cluny's privileges and resented the Pope's special arrangement with this meddlesome monastery. This frustration became all too apparent when in several cases the two sides actually found themselves in violent confrontation, such as in Clermont and Mâcon. The French historian Henri Daniel-Rops records an incident at Orléans in which, after one of the bishops had seized a vineyard belonging to the abbey of Fleury (a Cluniac house), the religious "won it back by the use of a most curious instrument of warfare in the shape of two caskets full of sacred relics, before which the episcopal troops fell back in disorder!"[431]

Such incidents aside, Cluny's work proved especially fruitful. By the time of Peter the Venerable's tenure as abbot (1122-56), the *Catholic Encyclopedia* reports, it had become "second only to Rome as the chief center of the Christian world." Even in its early years, it gave the Church a small litany of saintly abbots: St. Odo, St. Maieul, St. Odilo, and St. Hugh. It had managed all this with a congregation that had begun with St. Berno, the first abbot, and twelve companions.

We should not be too hasty in drawing comparisons between the general collapse of the ninth and tenth centuries and the disastrous situation the Church faces today. The differences are clear enough. For one thing, the problem that Cluny and other Church reform movements faced, awful as it was, almost certainly constituted less of a threat to the Church's long-term health than do the problems of our day. The problems of the religious orders then were primarily matters of discipline—scandalous and lamentable to be sure, but at least susceptible of relatively straightforward remedy. Bishops and abbots guilty of simony or even of violations of celibacy may certainly have been corrupt and despicable, but they did not attempt to impose new dogmas or a supposedly updated version of Catholicism on the poor souls under their authority.

The problem today is far worse. Since Vatican II, a liberalism utterly alien to traditional Catholic thought has insinuated its

---

[431]Ibid.

way into every aspect of Catholic life, even among many people who consider themselves orthodox and exemplary. Disciplinary scandals abound now as then, but, in addition to these problems, our adversaries have attempted to remake Catholicism altogether, offering us a substitute that bears more resemblance to liberalism, Modernism, and the Enlightenment than to the traditional faith.

Having inserted this caveat, however, the example of Cluny is quite pertinent to our present impasse, for it shows how resilient the Church can be, under the worst of conditions, when even the tiniest minority of her members is passionate about genuine reform. The case of Cluny reminds us of just how much can be accomplished in the Church by a small band of rebuilders.

The success of Cluny also demonstrates the potential of the canonical structure referred to today as an apostolic administration. By allowing the Cluniac houses to bypass the authority of the bishops — who, in their day as in ours, were so often opponents of true reform — the Church gave this divinely inspired movement the room it needed to carry out its mission. Even though our situation is arguably worse than what Cluny faced, the immunity from the bishops that Cluny enjoyed would give us the ability to rebuild at least one segment of the Church. That is what Cluny did, and the rest of the Church ultimately followed.

Moreover, as Msgr. Hughes noted, this special arrangement allowed all the little cells of reform to be brought together under one umbrella, under the protection of the Holy See. That is what this structure could do today: take all the isolated (and often frustrated and demoralized) centers of Tridentine devotion around the globe, and regularize and unite them into a vibrant structure that would guarantee traditional Catholics the sacraments and spirituality that are their birthright, and that historically have borne such great fruit throughout the world. This is the message that a single tenth-century monastery, with a vision for true Catholic reform, has for us today.

In other dark periods of Church history, we find pockets of piety and reform struggling against the tide — and ultimately prevailing. The Catholic faithful who rallied to St. Athanasius during the Arian crisis come to mind. The monastery of Cluny, which we have just discussed, is yet another example. Beginning in the late fifteenth century, on the cusp of the less-than-edifying behavior of some of the Renaissance Popes, groups like the Oratory of Divine Love quietly but persistently emphasized holiness and the spiritual life.

Our time presents its own challenge: nothing less than the wholesale revival of traditional Catholicism. It is a task that will require hard work and great sacrifice on the part of traditional faithful around the world, even when Rome does grant some kind of administrative structure for traditionalists—new parishes to be opened, churches to be built, schools to be staffed, and the like. For most of us, it is a labor of love whose potential fruits transcend human calculation.

During the recent Vatican talks aimed at "regularizing" the SSPX, Bishop Bernard Fellay, the order's Superior General, reported that during a brief audience with John Paul II, the Pope, his head bent forward, looked at the Bishop out of the corner of his eye and said, "Je suis heureux"—I am happy. Entrapped by the body that has betrayed him, our poor Pope could not even turn his head to face the Bishop when he said these words.

We have no doubt that the Holy Father *would* be happy if he could effect an agreement to "regularize" the SSPX, establish the apostolic administration we propose here, and annul the "excommunication" of Archbishop Lefebvre as pronounced in *Ecclesia Dei*—the document that declared a "schism" the Vatican privately does not view as such.[432] But we also have no doubt

---

[432]Cf. Protocol N. 539/99, September 28, 1999, by Msgr. Camille Perl, Secretary of the Ecclesia Dei Commission, wherein he concedes that members of the faithful incur no penalty if they attend Sunday Mass at SSPX chapels in Arizona with the motive of "an attraction to the earlier form of the Roman rite," even though such Masses are "illicit." If the SSPX were really in a state of true and proper schism, Perl would hardly allow that the Sunday obligation could be fulfilled at its chapels. Moreover, Perl has been quoted in *The Latin Mass* as having said of SSPX adherents, "everyone knows they are Catholics."

that there are those in the Vatican apparatus who will do everything possible to prevent any papal act concerning the SSPX that would recognize that "their spiritual and liturgical traditions" have never for a moment ceased to be our traditions, and that the adherents of the SSPX have never ceased to be Catholics.

Behind the great façade of the "springtime" of Vatican II, busy eminences no doubt labor to prevent the Pope from poking a great hole through the façade so that everyone may finally see the truth. It is supremely ironic that the very Council that was supposed to have ended "rigorism" in the Church has given rise to the greatest rigorism of all, a rigorism that seeks by every means possible to suppress — or, failing that, to limit with almost laughable strictness — the Church's recovery of her own traditions.

Yet there are signs that the Holy Father, torn between the failed vision of an ill-starred Council and his own *sensus Catholicus*, is now struggling, however weakly, to make right what has gone so terribly wrong. One encouraging development occurred in early 2002: the erection of an apostolic administration for the traditionalist Society of St. John Vianney (SSJV), an order of priests in Campos, Brazil. The Pope granted to these priests the very canonical structure we here suggest, permitting them to work and to expand without (it would seem as of this writing) the consent of the local diocesan bishop. Bishop Licinio Rangel, who was ordained for the SSJV by three of the SSPX bishops in 1991, has been named Auxiliary Bishop of Zarna and the Apostolic Administrator for the SSJV.

It is highly significant for our thesis that in order to be "reconciled" with Rome and "end the schism," SSJV had merely to affirm what it never denied in the first place: that John Paul II is the Pope, that the Mass of Paul VI (when correctly celebrated according to the proper intention) is valid, that Vatican II is a Council of the Church, and that open questions are to be studied with humility and charity.[433] This was nothing more than what

---

And in Chapter 11 we noted Cardinal Cassidy's statement that the SSPX question is a matter of *internal* Church discipline.

[433]See *Statement of Administrator*, by Bishop Rangel, at unavoce.org.

Archbishop Lefebvre was willing to affirm in the aborted 1988 protocol of agreement between SSPX and the Vatican. The SSJV clergy and lay adherents abjured not one of their views and altered not one of their traditions—which are, after all, the traditions of the Roman Rite.

The ease with which this "reconciliation" was accomplished only proves that nowhere in the postconciliar program of innovation is there anything a Catholic must embrace in order to remain a Catholic. In other words, the "schism" in Campos was a legal fiction. Despite the face-saving language in SSJV's affirmation, it is the Vatican apparatus that has reconciled itself to the resistance in Campos. It is difficult to see on what ground anyone could now stand to claim that the SSPX "schism" is any less a legal fiction—especially with the Vatican assiduously avoiding any declaration of schism on the part of the pro-abortion, Communist-controlled "bishops" of the CPA "church" in Red China.

Whether SSJV's "reconciliation" proves to be an embrace or a death-grip for the traditionalists of Campos remains to be seen. There are disturbing indications that certain elements within the Vatican apparatus regard the Campos accord as nothing more than a technique to subdue one of the few pockets of resistance to the ruinous postconciliar novelties. In a very conspicuous interview within days of the accord, no less than Fr. Georges Cottier, the official theologian of the papal household, declared that "Many Lefebvrists maintain that 'our' Paul VI Mass is not valid. At least now this group [Campos] will not be able to think such a thing. *Little by little we must expect other steps as well: for example, that they also participate in concelebrations in the reformed rite.* However, we must not be in a hurry."[434] The smugness and condescension in this remark certainly justify the belief that traditionalists have little reason to trust a Vatican apparatus which—despite the postconciliar debacle it has presided over—still views a strong attachment to the Church's immemorial traditions and practices as if it were some sort of disease that needs to be cured through gradual

---

[434]Zenit, January 20, 2002.

therapy. This attitude is at the heart of the postconciliar crisis; and it is this attitude, not traditionalism, that is the real illness in the Church today. Perhaps the physician should consider healing himself.

Major questions remain to be answered, and it cannot be predicted whether the flourishing traditionalist parishes of Campos will be harassed with demands for "insertion into the ecclesial reality of today," as the Fraternity of St. Peter has been, or left in peace. While, humanly speaking, we have every reason to be pessimistic in view of the past forty years, we should not lose hope that the Holy Ghost will prevent the Campos accord from being subverted in the manner openly predicted by Cottier. If Campos does succeed as a model for the restoration of integral Catholic tradition, the suffering and sacrifices of traditional clergy and faithful these past few decades will soon bear fruit that even a few years ago we could scarcely have imagined.

A great deal remains to be done, to say the least. Very likely it will not be this Pope who finally begins the work of tearing down the great façade in earnest. Perhaps it will be the next, or the one after him. But until it happens, traditionalists will go on resisting the crisis to the limits that Catholic loyalty allows, encouraged by the example of perseverance given by the traditionalist clergy and laity of Campos, Brazil.

Meanwhile, the evidence is overwhelming that this is the great ecclesial crisis foretold in Holy Scripture and by Our Lady of Fatima and Our Lady of La Salette. It was no less than Pope St. Pius X, arguably the greatest Pope in Church history, who declared in *E Supremi* his moral certainty (only fifty-nine years before the Council) that the world had entered into the beginning of the last times foreseen in the Book of the Apocalypse.

And was it not the present Roman Pontiff himself who, in his beautiful sermon at Fatima on May 13, 2000, warned the Church to avoid the dragon described in Chapter 12 of the Apocalypse, the dragon whose tail sweeps one third of the stars, the consecrated souls, from heaven? From deep within the failing vision of a renewed Church and a perfectible world in which he has immured himself—the vision of *Gaudium et Spes*, which he helped to craft—our Pope sends out to the Church a warning, a warning that dispels the beguiling vision and reminds us that he is, after all, our father and that we must love him.

And so, in the end, our considerations lead back to where they must: to the man who governs all Catholics by the will of Christ. For in the papal office alone rests the power to cause or to cure a crisis throughout the Church. Our Pope is a man of mystery and contradiction. The same Pope who ended all further debate on women's ordination also gave us the scandal of altar girls. The Pope who has condemned the "culture of death" and fixed upon the world a phrase that rebukes it in an unforgettable way, has also legitimated Protestant preachers of the culture of death by giving them places of honor beside himself in public liturgical ceremonies, without rebuking them at all. The Pope who has presided over great liturgical destruction and called it a renewal has also given the banished traditional liturgy a precious and ever-widening foothold within the official structure of the Church. The Pope who beatified Pius IX, the fierce opponent of "the modern world," also beatified John XXIII, "the first modern Pope." The Pope who has said that Revelation does not tell us that any human souls at all will be in hell, has also preached at Fatima that many souls go to hell because they have no one to pray and make sacrifices for them. He is our Pope, our father, this man of mystery and contradiction; and like any father he needs his children, just as his children need him.

As St. Thomas teaches, sometimes children must resist their father as an act of charity. Those who condemn traditionalists so rashly have blinded themselves to the ultimate cause of the great crisis of which traditionalist resistance is but a symptom. Yet while the neo-Catholics counsel silence and submission in the face of disaster, at least some of the Pope's children cry out in protest to their wandering father in his ceaseless travels throughout an unbelieving world—a world that will not even follow his teaching on the natural law, no matter how far he travels, no matter how many crowds there are to cheer him on. Come home, Father, they cry, and put our house in order. But their brothers rebuke them for crying out, and defend the absence of the distant father.

History will render the final verdict on whether the children who cried out, or the children who remained silent, were the ones who served the father most truly.

# INDEX

and positive elements of non-Catholic religions, 338-40, 342-44
backpedaling from, 368-77
Cardinal Cassidy on, 368
compared to *Syllabus of Errors*, 334-35, 376
criticism by Protestants and Jews, 364-65
Fr. Georges Cottier on, 368-69
*filioque* and, 336
on Hell, 346
on Orthodox churches, 336, 354-56, 358-62
positive aspects of, 336, 342-43, 347, 364
Dougherty, Archbishop Dennis, 217-18
Dubost, Bishop Michael, 386
Duffy, Eamon, 184
Dulles, Avery Cardinal, 292-93
Duschak, Bishop William, 165
*E Supremi*, 113, 405
Eastern Catholic churches, 14, 397
*Ecclesia Dei*, 94-95, 175, 258, 402
Ecclesia Dei Commission, 402n.
Fraternity of St. Peter and, 124-25
Ecuador, 300
Ecumenism, ecumenical movement
1970 Directory on, 74-75
1993 Directory on, 76-78, 253
Anglican Church and, 195-96, 199
Archbishop Bruskewitz and, 147-48
as an ecclesial "virus," 65ff.
as not an article of faith, 229-30
Cardinal Ratzinger on, 202
*Dominus Iesus* and, 376ff.
Francis Cardinal George and, 121-22

interreligious prayer meetings and, 14, 45, 83-87, 140-41
John Paul II on, 67, 75, 76, 78-79, 196, 220, 253n.
Lutherans and, 198-200
Modernism and, 211-12
Orthodox churches and, 45, 46, 118, 194, 197-98
Pius XI on, 13-14, 67-68, 73, 89, 152, 194, 196, 198, 201
Pius XII (Holy Office) on, 68-69, 118, 122n., 220
preconciliar Dutch bishops on, 69
Protestant origins of, 67, 68
"reconciled diversity" and, 198-202, 352-53
results of, 30-31
traditional view on, 13-14
Vatican II on, 72-74
see also *Dominus Iesus*
Egan, Edward Cardinal, 122-23, 215
*Envoy*, 390-91
Ephesus, Council of, 327
Erluin, 397
*Essay on the Development of Christian Doctrine*, 29-30
Etchegaray, Roger Cardinal, 84, 212-13, 262-63
Eternal Word Television Network (EWTN), 21, 256, 258
selective coverage of Assisi event, 86n.
Eucharist
see Communion
Eucharistic ministers, 8, 151
*Evangeli Praecones*, 114
*Evangelium Vitae*, 241
evolution, 50, 269-71
Fatima
John Paul II's May 13, 2000 sermon at, 406
Message of, 7n., 60
Our Lady of, 118

# ABOUT THE AUTHORS

**Christopher A. Ferrara** earned his Baccalaureate and Juris Doctor degrees from Fordham University. He is President and Chief Counsel of the American Catholic Lawyers Association, Inc., a nonprofit religious organization dedicated to defending the religious liberties of Catholics in state and federal litigation, public discourse and debate. He has achieved major appellate victories in pro-life cases. Mr. Ferrara has written extensively on Catholic issues, including the postconciliar crisis in the Roman Catholic Church. His articles and commentaries have appeared frequently in *The Latin Mass*, *The Remnant*, *Christian Order*, *Catholic Family News*, and other publications. Mr. Ferrara lives in New Jersey with his wife, Wendy (a convert), and their six children.

**Thomas E. Woods, Jr.** holds a bachelor's degree in history from Harvard and his M.A., M.Phil., and Ph.D. from Columbia University. His articles have appeared in *Investor's Business Daily*, the *Christian Science Monitor*, *Modern Age*, and dozens of other periodicals. He is also a contributor to four encyclopedias, including the *Encyclopedia of the American Civil War* and the *Encyclopedia of American Studies* (Grolier). His edited volume of *The Political Writings of Rufus Choate* will be published by Regnery in late 2002. He is currently assistant professor of history at Suffolk Community College (SUNY) and associate editor of *The Latin Mass* magazine. Dr. Woods, a convert from Lutheranism, lives in New York. He is soon to be married.